CRITICAL THINKING

AN ANTHOLOGY FOR COMPOSITION

Edited by
JACK ZUCKER
Marietta College

IRA KONIGSBERG
The University of Michigan

The Macmillan Company

Second Printing, 1970

Library of Congress catalog card number: 69–12643

PRINTED IN THE UNITED STATES OF AMERICA

ACKNOWLEDGMENTS

"Sophistication" from *Winesburg, Ohio* by Sherwood Anderson. Copyright 1919 by B. W. Huebsch, Inc., 1947 by Eleanor Copenhaver Anderson. Reprinted by permission of The Viking Press, Inc.

"Billy and the Gargoyles" from *The Romantic Egoists* by Louis Auchincloss. Copyright 1954 by Louis Auchincloss. Reprinted by permission of the publisher, Houghton Mifflin Company.

"The Unknown Citizen" and "Victor, a Ballad" by W. H. Auden. Copyright 1940 by W. H. Auden. Reprinted from *Collected Shorter Poems 1927–1957,* by W. H. Auden, by permission of Random House, Inc.

"Fifth Avenue, Uptown: A Letter from Harlem," reprinted from *Nobody Knows My Name* by James Baldwin. Copyright © 1954, 1956, 1958, 1959, 1960, 1961 by James Baldwin and used by permission of the publisher, The Dial Press, Inc.

"Whither Mankind" from "Introduction" to *Whither Mankind* by Charles Beard, New York, 1928, reprinted by permission of David McKay Company, Inc.

"The Diversity of Cultures" from *Patterns of Culture* by Ruth Benedict. Copyright 1962 by Ruth Valentine. Reprinted by permission of the publisher, Houghton Mifflin Company.

Excerpt from *The Human Body,* by Logan Clendening. Copyright 1927, 1945 by Alfred A. Knopf, Inc. Reprinted by permission of the publisher.

"The Playboy" (editors' title). Reprinted with permission of The Macmillan Company from *The Secular City* by Harvey Cox. Copyright © by Harvey Cox 1965.

"There's a certain Slant of light," by Emily Dickinson. Reprinted by permission of the publishers and the Trustees of Amherst College from Thomas H. Johnson, Editor, *The Poems of Emily Dickinson,* Cambridge, Mass.: The Belknap Press of Harvard University Press, copyright, 1951, 1955, by The President and Fellows of Harvard College.

"The Dream of a Ridiculous Man." Reprinted with permission of The Macmillan Company from *An Honest Thief and Other Stories* by Fyodor Dostoevsky.

"Just as I used to say . . ." and "The pennycandystore beyond the el . . ." from *A Coney Island of the Mind* by Lawrence Ferlinghetti. Copyright © 1955, 1958 by Lawrence Ferlinghetti. Reprinted by permission of New Directions Publishing Corporation.

"The Rich Boy" (copyright 1925, 1926 Consolidated Magazines Corporation; renewal copyright 1953, 1954 Frances Scott Fitzgerald Lanahan) is reprinted with the permission of Charles Scribner's Sons from *All the Sad Young Men* by F. Scott Fitzgerald.

"What I Believe" from *Two Cheers for Democracy* by E. M. Forster, copyright, 1939, 1967, by E. M. Forster. Reprinted by permission of Harcourt, Brace & World, Inc.

"The Age of Happy Problems," reprinted from *The Age of Happy Problems* by Herbert Gold. Copyright © 1952, 1954, 1957, 1958, 1959, 1960, 1961, 1962 by Herbert Gold and used by permission of the publisher, The Dial Press, Inc.

"A Usual Case—Nothing Fancy" by Paul Goodman. Reprinted by permission of the publisher, Horizon Press, from *Compulsory Mis-Education* by Paul Goodman. Copyright 1964.

"The Invisible Land." Reprinted with permission of The Macmillan Company from *The Other America* by Michael Harrington. Copyright © by Michael Harrington 1962.

"Hurt Hawks" by Robinson Jeffers. Copyright 1928 and renewed 1956 by Robinson Jeffers. Reprinted from *Selected Poems*, by Robinson Jeffers, by permission of Random House, Inc.

"Shine, Perishing Republic" by Robinson Jeffers. Copyright 1925 and renewed 1953 by Robinson Jeffers. Reprinted from *Selected Poems*, by Robinson Jeffers, by permission of Random House, Inc.

"Limits of the New Left" by Christopher Jencks. Reprinted by permission of *The New Republic*, © 1968, Harrison-Blaine of New Jersey, Inc.

"The Horse-Dealer's Daughter" by D. H. Lawrence. From *The Complete Short Stories of D. H. Lawrence*, Volume II. Copyright 1922 by Thomas B. Seltzer, Inc., 1950 by Frieda Lawrence. Reprinted by permission of The Viking Press, Inc.

Excerpt from *The Late George Apley*, by John P. Marquand. Copyright 1936, 1937 by John P. Marquand: renewed 1964, 1965 by John P. Marquand, Jr., and Christine Welsh. Reprinted by permission of Little, Brown and Co.

"The Colonel's Lady," copyright 1946 by W. Somerset Maugham, from *Creatures of Circumstance* by W. Somerset Maugham. Reprinted by permission of Doubleday & Company, Inc.

"A Cooperative Society" from *Sex and Temperament in Three Primitive Societies*, by Margaret Mead. Reprinted by permission of William Morrow & Company, Inc. Copyright 1935, 1950, 1963 by Margaret Mead.

"I, being born a woman . . ." by Edna St. Vincent Millay. From *Collected Poems*, Harper & Row. Copyright 1923, 1951 by Edna St. Vincent Millay and Norma Millay Ellis.

"The Bored and the Violent" by Arthur Miller. Reprinted by permission of Ashley Famous Agency, Inc. Copyright © 1962 by *Harper's Magazine*.

"Utopia in Pennsylvania: The Amish" by Albert Jay Nock. Copyright © Francis Jay Nock. From *Snoring as a Fine Art and Twelve Other Essays*, by Albert Jay Nock, The Richard R. Smith, Co., 1958.

"Everything That Rises Must Converge" by Flannery O'Connor. Reprinted with the permission of Farrar, Straus & Giroux, Inc., from *Everything That Rises Must Converge* by Flannery O'Connor. Copyright © 1961 by the Estate of Mary Flannery O'Connor.

"The Coming of the Masses," reprinted from *The Revolt of the Masses* by José

Preface

Most teachers realize that significant improvement in composition occurs when the student begins to take an interest in his assignments. The student who finds himself writing on banal topics, many of them once used in his high school career, will probably not be stimulated to write good prose. Interest occurs when the teacher, without creating hostility, encourages the student to re-examine his basic values. This process should lead to the development of critical thinking and the desire for effective verbal expression.

The essays, poems, and stories in this collection are intended to aid the teacher in the task outlined above. All of the selections have been tried in class. They have led to lively discussions and often to lively papers. Students who had been dismissed as "illiterates" sometimes began to write clear and cogent prose because they found something vital to say. They had discovered that English composition was not simply a subject in which one learns mechanical rules, but a subject in which one learns to express one's thoughts.

The method suggested is partly Socratic. It makes use of intensive questioning and controversy seasoned with good will. It works well with most students who are not hostile to intellectual discourse.

The selections in this anthology deal largely with present-day American society, so that the student can use evidence gathered from his own experience. We have not, though, omitted Europe from our pages. America cannot be understood without reference to its parent culture. Nor have we ignored the past. Greater insight into the problem of conformity, for example, may be achieved when we understand that Socrates and Thoreau faced difficulties similar to those faced by nonconformists today and formulated ideas that are still controversial.

Because we have chosen our selections for the stimulation of students, we have not restricted our material to the essay form. Fiction and verse can sometimes present an issue more vividly than exposition and can inspire students to produce mature expository prose.

This book is organized thematically to aid the teacher in organizing his course. The topics are arranged so that one leads to the next—for example, a discussion of democracy might result in a consideration of America's class structure. Frequently the teacher and student will find themselves referring to literature in earlier sections.

Whenever possible we have presented different points of view, not only for fairness, but to help the student realize the complexity of the issues presented and the necessity for reasoned judgment. In all cases we have tried to present selections that will incite the student to thought and motivate him to effective self-expression.

J.Z., I.K.

Contents

SECTION 7   ALTERNATE SOCIETIES   *316*

SECTION 8   THE LIMITATIONS OF MAN   *383*

1

THE QUESTION OF DEMOCRACY

OFTEN IN AMERICA democracy is confused with goodness. Almost every action of our government is excused in the name of democracy or freedom, which are frequently taken to be one and the same. We preserve the "democratic" government of Vietnam; we are bound by treaty to Franco Spain, ostensibly part of the "free world." Yet the United States is not the only nation which misuses the term *democracy*. The Russians claim that they have created a "worker's democracy." Almost every Communist state is called a "people's democracy."

Certainly we must know what democracy means before we can participate in a meaningful political discussion. If we enquire closely, we find that it means many things to many people. To Russians democracy means low rent and free medical care. To Americans it signifies the vote and equality of opportunity. To some democracy means the absence of racial and religious prejudice.

Even the founders of our "democracy" were not certain how much democracy would be beneficial for mankind. Thomas Jefferson, the most radical of our Founding Fathers, did not advocate pure democracy. Many patriotic Americans, as well as Europeans, feared that democracy might degenerate into mob rule. Several provisions of our constitution were drawn up to ensure that some aristocratic privilege and regional autonomy would remain.

To begin our analysis, we can divide the concept *democracy* into three component parts: political democracy, social democracy, and economic democracy. Groups at different points on the political spectrum favor different aspects of democracy. Conservatives often favor economic freedom, even if it results in social inequality. Communists talk profusely about social democracy, but sneer at political democracy, which they consider a cover-up for capitalist domination. Liberals usually stress civil liberties, but sometimes fail to recognize a nation's right to preserve its stability even if such preservation may require the curtailment of individual rights.

Therefore, before anyone writes on democracy, he must first define the term. He needn't use a dictionary, nor even compose a formal definition. But he must be consistent in his use of the term. It is also helpful to know what others mean by democracy. How can one argue against Communism if one doesn't know what the Communist concept of democracy is? Though a good reference book like *The Encyclopedia of the Social Sciences* may be helpful, the most essential element is the writer's own mind, his ability to define and analyze, to call on the resources provided by his reading, to evaluate the meaning of his own experience. He must finally ask himself what democracy has meant to *him* in the context of his own life. Which actions has he considered democratic? Which undemocratic? Why?

Once the writer has firmly understood his own conception of democracy, and that of others, he is faced with an entirely new task. He may always have assumed that the United States is not only a democracy but the greatest democracy in the world. Now he must question that idea. Are all our leaders, or even most of them, the natural aristocrats Jefferson speaks of on page 4? Could it be that the institutions of France, Great Britain, and Sweden are in some ways more democratic than our own?

If he is honest, the writer will find himself hedging a little. Once he thinks in terms of reality, he is forced to speak in relative terms. He begins to see the world in shades of gray, not in black and white. He may even refuse to answer a question so simple as the following: Is the Soviet Union a democracy? He may find that he prefers to phrase the question in a different way: How much democracy is there in the Soviet Union? And even then he may have to limit himself to a specific area of Soviet life, since farmers, scientists, literary men, and Communist Party members enjoy different degrees of individual liberty, even have different degrees of political freedom.

Finally, the writer faces another problem. Is democracy really desirable? Many extreme conservatives and Marxist radicals feel that democracy isn't particularly good at all. Though this position is mainly defended by extremists, it cannot be dismissed out of hand. The true student cannot be content with name calling. To call a man a Fascist or a Communist proves little. To disprove his arguments proves a great deal. The student must himself know *why* he believes in democracy—or why he doesn't.

Thomas Jefferson

THE
NATURAL
ARISTOCRACY

Of all the Founding Fathers, Thomas Jefferson, 1743–1826, was fondest of the term democracy. Yet even Jefferson hoped to achieve not so much a pure democracy as a "natural aristocracy," not a society of equals, but a society in which all men have equal opportunity to climb to unequal rank. Jefferson explained this idea in his letter of October 28, 1813, to John Adams.

. . . I agree with you that there is a natural aristocracy among men. The grounds of this are virtue and talents. Formerly, bodily powers gave place among the aristoi. But since the invention of gunpowder has armed the weak as well as the strong with missile death, bodily strength, like beauty, good humor, politeness and other accomplishments, has become but an auxiliary ground for distinction. There is also an artificial aristocracy, founded on wealth and birth, without either virtue or talents; for with these it would belong to the first class. The natural aristocracy I consider as the most precious gift of nature, for the instruction, the trusts, and government of society. And indeed, it would have been inconsistent in creation to have formed man for the social state, and not to have provided virtue and wisdom enough to manage the concerns of the society. May we not even say, that that form of government is the best, which provides the most effectually for a pure selection of these natural aristoi into the offices of government? The artificial aristocracy is a mischievous ingredient in government, and provision should be made to prevent its ascendancy. On the question, what is the best provision, you and I differ; but we differ as rational friends, using the free exercise of our own reason, and mutually indulging its errors. You think it best to put the pseudo-aristoi into a separate chamber of legislation, where they may be hindered from doing mischief by their co-ordinate branches, and where, also, they may be a protection to wealth against the Agrarian and plundering enterprises of the majority of the people. I think that to give them power in order to prevent them from doing mischief, is arming them for it, and increasing instead of remedying the evil. For if the co-ordinate branches can arrest their action, so may they that of the co-ordinates. Mischief may be done negatively as well as positively. Of this, a cabal in the Senate of the United States has furnished many proofs. Nor do I believe them necessary to protect the wealthy; because enough of these will find their way into every branch of the legislation, to protect themselves. From fifteen to twenty legislatures of our own, in action for thirty years past, have proved that no fears of an equalization of property are to be apprehended from them. I think the best remedy is exactly that provided by all our constitutions, to leave to the citizens the free election and separation of the aristoi from the pseudo-aristoi, of the wheat from the chaff. In general they will elect the really good and wise. In some instances, wealth may corrupt, and birth blind them; but not in sufficient degree to endanger the society.

It is probable that our difference of opinion may, in some measure, be produced by a difference of character in those among whom we live. From what I have seen of Massachusetts and Connecticut myself, and still more from what I have heard, and the character given of the former by yourself, who know·them so much better, there seems to be in those two States a traditionary reverence for certain families, which has rendered the offices of the government nearly hereditary in those families. I presume that from an early period of your history, members of those families happening to possess virtue and talents, have honestly exercised them for the good of the people, and by their services have endeared their names to them. In coupling Connecticut with you, I mean it politically only, not morally. For having made the Bible the common law of their land, they seemed to have modeled their morality on the story of Jacob and Laban. But although this hereditary succession to office with you, may, in some degree, be founded in real family merit, yet in a much higher degree, it has proceeded from your strict alliance of Church and State. These families are canonized in the eyes of the people on common principles, "you tickle me, and I will tickle you." In Virginia we have nothing of this. Our clergy, before the revolution, having been secured against rivalship by fixed salaries, did not give themselves the trouble of acquiring influence over the people. Of wealth, there were great accumulations in particular families, handed down from generation to generation, under the English law of entails. But the only object of ambition for the wealthy was a seat in the King's Council. All their court then was paid to the crown and its creatures; and they Philipised in all collisions between the King and the people. Hence they were unpopular; and that unpopularity continues attached to their names. A Randolph, a Carter, or a Burwell must have great personal superiority over a common competitor to be elected by the people even at this day. At the first session of our legislature after the Declaration of Independence, we passed a law abolishing entails. And this was followed by one abolishing the privilege of primogeniture, and dividing the lands of intestates equally among all their children, or other representatives. These laws, drawn by myself, laid the ax to the foot of pseudo-aristocracy. And had another which I prepared been adopted by the legislature, our work would have been complete. It was a bill for the more general diffusion of learning. This proposed to divide every county into wards of five or six miles square, like your townships; to establish in each ward a free school for reading, writing and common arithmetic; to provide for the annual selection of the best subjects from these schools, who might receive, at the public expense, a higher degree of education at a district school; and from these district schools to select a certain number of the most promising subjects, to be completed at an University, where all the useful sciences should be taught. Worth and genius would thus have been sought out from every condition of life, and completely prepared by education for defeating the competition of wealth and birth for public trusts. My proposition had, for a further object, to impart to these wards those portions of self-government for which they are best qualified, by confiding to them the care of their poor, their roads, police, elections, the nomination of jurors, administration of justice in small cases, elementary exercises of militia; in short, to have made them little republics, with a warden at the head of each, for all those concerns which, being under their eye, they would better manage than the larger republics of the county or State. A general call of ward meetings by their wardens on the same day through the State, would at any time produce the genuine sense of the people on any required point, and would enable the State to act in mass, as your people have so often done, and with so much effect by their town meetings. The law for religious freedom, which made a part of this

system, having put down the aristocracy of the clergy, and restored to the citizen the freedom of the mind, and those of entails and descents nurturing an equality of condition among them, this on education would have raised the mass of the people to the high ground of moral respectability necessary to their own safety, and to orderly governments; and would have completed the great object of qualifying them to select the veritable aristoi, for the trusts of government, to the exclusion of the pseudalists; and the same Theognis who has furnished the epigraphs of your two letters, assures us that "Ουδεμιαν πω, Κυρν', αγαθοι πολιν ωλεσαν ανδρες." *
Although this law has not yet been acted on but in a small and inefficient degree, it is still considered as before the legislature, with other bills of the revised code, not yet taken up, and I have great hope that some patriotic spirit will, at a favorable moment, call it up, and make it the keystone of the arch of our government.

With respect to aristocracy, we should further consider, that before the establishment of the American States, nothing was known to history but the man of the old world, crowded within limits either small or overcharged, and steeped in the vices which that situation generates. A government adapted to such men would be one thing; but a very different one, that for the man of these States. Here everyone may have land to labor for himself, if he chooses; or, preferring the exercise of any other industry, may exact for it such compensation as not only to afford a comfortable subsistence, but wherewith to provide for a cessation from labor in old age. Everyone, by his property, or by his satisfactory situation, is interested in the support of law and order. And such men may safely and advantageously reserve to themselves a wholesome control over their public affairs, and a degree of freedom, which, in the hands of the *canaille* of the cities of Europe, would be instantly perverted to the demolition and destruction of everything public and private. The history of the last twenty-five years of France, and of the last forty years in America, nay of its last two hundred years, proves the truth of both parts of this observation.

But even in Europe a change has sensibly taken place in the mind of man. Science had liberated the ideas of those who read and reflect, and the American example had kindled feelings of right in the people. An insurrection has consequently begun, of science, talents, and courage,

* "Curnus, good men have never yet ruined any nation." [Ed.]

against rank and birth, which have fallen into contempt. It has failed in its first effort, because the mobs of the cities, the instrument used for its accomplishment, debased by ignorance, poverty and vice, could not be restrained to rational action. But the world will recover from the panic of this first catastrophe. Science is progressive, and talents and enterprise on the alert. Resort may be had to the people of the country, a more governable power from their principles and subordination; and rank, and birth, and tinsel-aristocracy will finally shrink into insignificance, even there. This, however, we have no right to meddle with. It suffices for us, if the moral and physical condition of our own citizens qualifies them to select the able and good for the direction of their government, with a recurrence of elections at such short periods as will enable them to displace an unfaithful servant, before the mischief he meditates may be irremediable.

I have thus stated my opinion on a point on which we differ, not with a view to controversy, for we are both too old to change opinions which are the result of a long life of inquiry and reflection; but on the suggestions of a former letter of yours, that we ought not to die before we have explained ourselves to each other. We acted in perfect harmony, through a long and perilous contest for our liberty and independence. A constitution has been acquired, which, though neither of us thinks perfect, yet both consider as competent to render our fellow citizens the happiest and the securest on whom the sun has ever shone. If we do not think exactly alike as to its imperfections, it matters little to our country, which, after devoting to it long lives of disinterested labor, we have delivered over to our successors in life, who will be able to take care of it and of themselves.

Of the pamphlet on aristocracy which has been sent to you, or who may be its author, I have heard nothing but through your letter. If the person you suspect, it may be known from the quaint, mystical, and hyperbolical ideas, involved in affected, new-fangled and pedantic terms which stamp his writings. Whatever it be, I hope your quiet is not to be affected at this day by the rudeness or intemperance of scribblers; but that you may continue in tranquillity to live and to rejoice in the prosperity of our country, until it shall be your own wish to take your seat among the aristoi who have gone before you. Ever and affectionately yours.

QUESTIONS AND TOPICS

1. Has Jefferson's dream been achieved in America today? (*Hint:* Be specific; discuss actual people, not principles cited in documents such as the Constitution and the Declaration of Independence.)
2. Let's assume that a young man wants to achieve political prominence in the United States. What qualities does he need? How would he get his foot on the first rung of the ladder?
3. Do we still have a pseudo aristocracy? If so, how does one become a member of that group? How far will his membership get him, in politics, in society, in business?
4. Write a character sketch of a pseudo aristocrat. Try to make him typical of his group.
5. Write a character sketch of a natural aristocrat. (*Hint:* Be sure to avoid exaggerated compliment, especially if the person is a member of your own family.)
6. Compare two prominent figures in American politics, one born poor, the other born rich. Does the former fit Jefferson's description of the natural aristocrat? Does the latter fit Jefferson's description of the pseudo aristocrat?
7. Does society benefit from the existence of a pseudo aristocracy?

Thomas Babington Macaulay

ON AMERICAN
INSTITUTIONS

Lord Macaulay, 1800–1859, a British essayist and historian, held an attitude toward democracy that was quite typical in Europe during the nineteenth century. The excesses of the French Revolution provided clear warning to many Europeans that popular rule might encourage violence and anarchy. Macaulay's views are made plain in a letter, dated 1857, to an American correspondent, Mr. H. S. Randall.

Sir: The four volumes of the *Colonial History of New York* reached me safely. I assure you that I shall value them highly. They contain much to interest an English as well as an American reader. Pray, accept my thanks, and convey them to the Regents of the University.

You are surprised to learn that I have not a high opinion of Mr. Jefferson, and I am surprised at your surprise. I am certain that I never wrote a line, and that I never in Parliament, in conversation or even on the hustings—a place where it is the fashion to court the populace—uttered a word indicating an opinion that the supreme authority in a State ought to be entrusted to the majority of citizens, in other words, to the poorest and most ignorant part of society. I have long been convinced that institutions purely democratic must, sooner or later, destroy liberty or civilization, or both.

In Europe, where the population is dense, the effect of such institutions would be almost instantaneous. What happened lately in France is an example. In 1848 a pure democracy was established there. During a short time there was reason to expect a general spoliation, a national bankruptcy, a new partition of the soil, a maximum of prices, a ruinous load of taxation laid on the rich for the purpose of supporting the poor in idleness. Such a system would, in twenty years, have made France as poor and barbarous as the France of the Carlovingians. Happily, the danger was averted; and now there is a despotism, a silent tribune, an enslaved press. Liberty is gone, but civilization has been saved.

I have not the smallest doubt that, if we had a purely democratic government here, the effect would be the same. Either the poor would plunder the rich and civilization would perish, or order and property would be saved by a strong military government, and liberty would perish. You may think that your country enjoys an exemption from these evils. I will frankly own to you that I am of a very different opinion. Your fate I believe to be certain, though it is deferred by a physical cause. As long as you have a boundless extent of fertile and unoccupied land, your laboring population will be far more at ease than the laboring population of the old world, and, while that is the case, the Jeffersonian polity may continue to exist without causing any fatal calamity. But the time will come when New England will be as thickly populated as Old England. Wages will be as low, and will fluctuate as much with you as with us. You will have your Manchesters and Birminghams, and in those Manchesters and Birminghams hundreds of thousands of artisans will assuredly be sometimes out of work. Then your institutions will be fairly brought to the test. Distress everywhere makes the laborer mutinous and discontented, and inclines him to listen with eagerness to agitators who tell him that it is a monstrous iniquity that one man should have a million while another cannot get a full meal.

In bad years there is plenty of grumbling here, and sometimes a little rioting. But it matters little, for here the sufferers are not the rulers. The supreme power is in the hands of a class, numerous indeed, but select; of an educated class; of a class which is, and knows itself to be, deeply interested in the security of property and maintenance of order. Accordingly, the malcontents are firmly yet gently restrained. The bad time is got over without robbing the wealthy to relieve the indigent. The springs of national prosperity soon begin to flow again; work is plentiful, wages rise, and all is tranquillity and cheerfulness. I have seen England pass three or four times through such critical seasons as I have described.

Through such seasons, the United States will have to pass in the course of the next century, if not of this. How will you pass through them? I heartily wish you a good deliverance. But my reason and my wishes are at war, and I cannot help foreboding the worst. It is quite plain that your government will never be able to restrain a distressed and discontented majority. For with you the majority is the government, and has the rich, who are always a minority, absolutely at its mercy.

The day will come when, in the State of New York, a multitude of people, none of whom has had more than half a breakfast, or expects to have more than half a dinner, will choose a Legislature. Is it possible to doubt what sort of Legislature will be chosen? On one side is a statesman preaching patience, respect for vested rights, strict observance of public faith. On the other is a demagogue ranting about the tyranny of capitalists and usurers, and asking why anybody should be permitted to drink champagne and to ride in a carriage, while thousands of honest folks are in want of necessaries. Which of the two candidates is likely to be preferred by a workingman who hears his children cry for more bread? I seriously apprehend that you will in some such season of adversity as I have described, do things which will prevent prosperity from returning; that you will act like people who should in a year of scarcity devour all the seed corn, and thus make the next year a year not of scarcity, but of absolute famine. There will be, I fear, spoliation. There is nothing to stop you. Your Constitution is all sail and no anchor.

As I said before, when a society has entered on this downward progress, either civilization or liberty must perish. Either some Caesar or Napoleon will seize the reins of government with a strong hand, or your Republic will be as fearfully plundered and laid waste by barbarians in the 20th Century as the Roman Empire was in the fifth—with this difference, that the Huns and Vandals who ravaged the Roman Empire came from without, and that your Huns and Vandals will have been engendered within your own country by your own institutions.

Thinking thus, of course, I cannot reckon Jefferson among the benefactors of mankind. I readily admit that his intentions were good and his abilities considerable. Odious stories have been circulated about his private life; but I do not know on what evidence those stories rest, and I think it probable that they are false or monstrously exaggerated. I have no doubt that I shall derive both pleasure and information from your account of him. . . .

I have the honor to be, dear sir, your faithful servant.

T. B. Macaulay
May 23, 1857

QUESTIONS AND TOPICS

1. Can you think of any instances of mob rule in our recent political history?
2. Do Macaulay's comments apply to the urban race riots or the university disturbances of the 1960's?
3. Why has American democracy not degenerated into mob rule?
4. Have you personally witnessed any instances of mob violence? What have they signified to you? Have they told you anything about democracy, or about the quality of American life?
5. Can mob rule be justified under certain circumstances?

Karl Marx
and
Friedrich Engels

from
THE
COMMUNIST
MANIFESTO

In 1848 Karl Marx, 1818–1883, and his associate Friedrich Engels, 1820–1895, wrote The Communist Manifesto. *Originally designed to be the platform of the newly formed Communist League, the* Manifesto *sets forth the cardinal doctrines of Marxism: (1) the necessity for class struggle until the advent of the Communist state; (2) the dominant influence of economics on the development of history.*

The Manifesto *not only attacks capitalism but also postulates that Western democracy and its legal structures are merely devices to perpetuate the supremacy of the bourgeoisie. Yet Marx did not oppose democracy per se; rather he denied that capitalist democracy was true democracy. True democracy, Marx thought, would be achieved under Communism, when all men earned equal incomes.*

Though the student may disagree with Marx, he must particularly avoid identifying Marx's theories

with the practices of the Soviet gov-
ernment, unless he can prove that
the Soviet government is a true em-
bodiment of Marxist ideas.

The history of all hitherto existing society is the history of class struggles.

Freeman and slave, patrician and plebeian, lord and serf, guild-master and journeyman, in a word, oppressor and oppressed, stood in constant opposition to one another, carried on an uninterrupted, now hidden, now open fight, a fight that each time ended, either in a revolutionary reconstitution of society at large, or in the common ruin of the contending classes.

In the earlier epochs of history, we find almost everywhere a complicated arrangement of society into various orders, a manifold gradation of social rank. In ancient Rome we have patricians, knights, plebeians, slaves; in the Middle Ages, feudal lords, vassals, guild-masters, journeymen, apprentices, serfs; in almost all of these classes, again, subordinate gradations.

The modern bourgeois society that has sprouted from the ruins of feudal society, has not done away with class antagonisms. It has but established new classes, new conditions of oppression, new forms of struggle in place of the old ones.

Our epoch, the epoch of the bourgeoisie, possesses, however, this distinctive feature: It has simplified the class antagonisms. Society as a whole is more and more splitting up into two great hostile camps, into two great classes directly facing each other—bourgeoisie and proletariat.

From the serfs of the Middle Ages sprang the chartered burghers of the earliest towns. From these burgesses the first elements of the bourgeoisie were developed. . . .

The feudal system of industry, in which industrial production was monopolised by closed guilds, now no longer sufficed for the growing wants of the new markets. The manufacturing system took its place. The guild-masters were pushed aside by the manufacturing middle class; division of labour between the different corporate guilds vanished in the face of division of labour in each single workshop.

Meantime the markets kept ever growing, the demand ever rising. Even manufacture no longer sufficed. Thereupon, steam and machinery revolutionised industrial production. The place of manufacture was taken by the giant, modern industry, the place of the industrial middle class, by industrial millionaires—the leaders of whole industrial armies, the modern bourgeois.

Modern industry has established the world market, for which the discovery of America paved the way. This market has given an immense development to commerce, to navigation, to communication by land. This development has, in its turn, reacted on the extension of industry; and in proportion as industry, commerce, navigation, railways extended, in the same proportion the bourgeoisie developed, increased its capital, and pushed into the background every class handed down from the Middle Ages.

We see, therefore, how the modern bourgeosie is itself the product of a long course of development, of a series of revolutions in the modes of production and of exchange.

Each step in the development of the bourgeoisie was accompanied by a corresponding political advance of that class. An oppressed class under the sway of the feudal nobility, it became an armed and self-governing association in the medieval commune; here independent urban republic (as in Italy and Germany), there taxable "third estate" of the monarchy (as in France); afterwards, in the period of manufacture proper, serving either the semi-feudal or the absolute monarchy as a counterpoise against the nobility, and, in fact, corner-stone of the great monarchies in general —the bourgeoisie has at last, since the establishment of modern industry and of the world market, conquered for itself, in the modern representative state, exclusive political sway. The executive of the modern state is but a committee for managing the common affairs of the whole bourgeoisie.

The bourgeoisie has played a most revolutionary role in history.

The bourgeoisie, wherever it has got the upper hand, has put an end to all feudal, patriarchal, idyllic relations. It has pitilessly torn asunder the motley feudal ties that bound man to his "natural superiors," and has left no other bond between man and man than naked self-interest, than callous "cash payment." It has drowned the most heavenly ecstasies of religious fervour, of chivalrous enthusiasm, of philistine sentimentalism, in the icy water of egotistical calculation. It has resolved personal worth into exchange value, and in place of the numberless indefeasible chartered freedoms, has set up that single, unconscionable freedom—Free Trade. In one word, for exploitation, veiled by religious and political illusions, it has substituted naked, shameless, direct, brutal exploitation.

The bourgeoisie has stripped of its halo every occupation hitherto honoured and looked up to with reverent awe. It has converted the physician, the lawyer, the priest, the poet, the man of science, into its paid wage-labourers.

The bourgeoisie has torn away from the family its sentimental veil, and has reduced the family relation to a mere money relation.

The bourgeoisie has disclosed how it came to pass that the brutal display of vigour in the Middle Ages, which reactionaries so much admire, found its fitting complement in the most slothful indolence. It has been the first to show what man's activity can bring about. It has accomplished wonders far surpassing Egyptian pyramids, Roman aqueducts, and Gothic cathedrals; it has conducted expeditions that put in the shade all former migrations of nations and crusades.

The bourgeoisie cannot exist without constantly revolutionising the instruments of production, and thereby the relations of production, and with them the whole relations of society. Conservation of the old modes of production in unaltered form, was, on the contrary, the first condition of existence for all earlier industrial classes. Constant revolutionising of production, uninterrupted disturbance of all social conditions, everlasting uncertainty and agitation distinguished the bourgeois epoch from all earlier ones. All fixed, fast-frozen relations, with their train of ancient and venerable prejudices and opinions, are swept away, all new-formed ones become antiquated before they can ossify. All that is solid melts into air, all that is holy is profaned, and man is at last compelled to face with sober senses his real conditions of life and his relations with his kind.

The need of a constantly expanding market for its products chases the bourgeoisie over the whole surface of the globe. It must nestle everywhere, settle everywhere, establish connections everywhere.

The bourgeoisie has through its exploitation of the world market given a cosmopolitan character to production and consumption in every country. To the great chagrin of reactionaries, it has drawn from under the feet of industry the national ground on which it stood. All old-established national industries have been destroyed or are daily being destroyed. They are dislodged by new industries, whose introduction becomes a life and death question for all civilised nations, by industries that no longer work up indigenous raw material, but raw material drawn from the remotest zones; industries whose products are consumed, not only at home, but in every quarter of the globe. In place of the old wants, satisfied by the production of the country, we find new wants, requiring for their satisfaction the products of distant lands and climes. In place of the old local and national seclusion and self-sufficiency, we have intercourse in every direction, universal inter-dependence of nations. And as in material, so also in intellectual production. The intellectual creations of individual nations become common property. National one-sidedness and narrow-mindedness become more and more impossible, and from the numerous national and local literatures there arises a world literature.

The bourgeoisie, by the rapid improvement of all instruments of production, by the immensely facilitated means of communication, draws all nations, even the most barbarian, into civilisation. The cheap prices of its commodities are the heavy artillery with which it batters down all Chinese walls, with which it forces the barbarians' intensely obstinate hatred of foreigners to capitulate. It compels all nations, on pain of extinction, to adopt the bourgeois mode of production; it compels them to introduce what it calls civilisation into their midst, *i.e.,* to become bourgeois themselves. In a word, it creates a world after its own image.

The bourgeoisie has subjected the country to the rule of the towns. It has created enormous cities, has greatly increased the urban population as compared with the rural, and has thus rescued a considerable part of the population from the idiocy of rural life. Just as it has made the country dependent on the towns, so it has made barbarian and semi-barbarian countries dependent on the civilised ones, nations of peasants on nations of bourgeois, the East on the West.

More and more the bourgeoisie keeps doing away with the scattered state of the population, of the means of production, and of property. It has agglomerated population, centralised means of production, and has concentrated property in a few hands. The necessary consequence of this was political centralisation. Independent, or but loosely connected provinces, with separate interests, laws, governments, and systems of taxation, became lumped together into one nation, with one government, one code of laws, one national class interest, one frontier and one customs tariff.

The bourgeoisie, during its rule of scarce one hundred years, has created more massive and more colossal productive forces than have all preceding generations together. Subjection of nature's forces to man, machinery, application of chemistry to industry and agriculture, steam-navigation, railways, electric telegraphs, clearing of whole continents for cultivation, canalisation of rivers, whole populations conjured out of the ground—

what earlier century had even a presentiment that such productive forces slumbered in the lap of social labour?

We see then that the means of production and of exchange, which served as the foundation for the growth of the bourgeoisie, were generated in feudal organisation of agriculture and manufacturing industry, in a word, the feudal relations of property became no longer compatible with the already developed productive forces; they became so many fetters. They had to be burst asunder; they were burst asunder.

Into their place stepped free competition, accompanied by a social and political constitution adapted to it, and by the economic and political sway of the bourgeois class.

A similar movement is going on before our own eyes. Modern bourgeois society with its relations of production, of exchange and of property, a society that has conjured up such gigantic means of production and exchange, is like the sorcerer who is no longer able to control the powers of the nether world whom he has called up by his spells. For many a decade past the history of industry and commerce is but the history of the revolt of modern productive forces against modern conditions of production, against the property relations that are the conditions for the existence of the bourgeoisie and of its rule. It is enough to mention the commercial crises that by their periodical return put the existence of the entire bourgeois society on trial, each time more threateningly. In these crises a great part not only of the existing products, but also of the previously created productive forces, are periodically destroyed. In these crises there breaks out an epidemic that, in all earlier epochs, would have seemed an absurdity—the epidemic of over-production. Society suddenly finds itself put back into a state of momentary barbarism; it appears as if a famine, a universal war of devastation had cut off the supply of every means of subsistence; industry and commerce seem to be destroyed. And why? Because there is too much civilisation, too much means of subsistence, too much industry, too much commerce. . . .

The weapons with which the bourgeoisie felled feudalism to the ground are now turned against the bourgeoisie itself.

But not only has the bourgeoisie forged the weapons that bring death to itself; it has also called into existence the men who are to wield those weapons—the modern working class—the proletarians.

In proportion as the bourgeoisie, *i.e.*, capital, is developed, in the same proportion is the proletariat, the modern working class, developed—a class of labourers, who live only so long as they find work, and who find work only so long as their labour increases capital. These labourers, who must sell themselves piecemeal, are a commodity, like every other article of commerce, and are consequently exposed to all the vicissitudes of competition, to all the fluctuations of the market.

Owing to the extensive use of machinery and to division of labour, the work of the proletarians has lost all individual character, and consequently, all charm for the workman. He becomes an appendage of the machine, and it is only the most simple, most monotonous, and most easily acquired knack, that is required of him. Hence, the cost of production of a workman is restricted, almost entirely, to the means of subsistence that he requires for his maintenance, and for the propagation of his race. But the price of a commodity, and therefore also of labour, is equal to its cost of production. In proportion, therefore, as the repulsiveness of the work increases, the wage decreases. Nay more, in proportion as the use of machinery and division of labour increases, in the same proportion the burden of toil also increases, whether by prolongation of the working hours, by increase of the work exacted in a given time, or by increased speed of the machinery, etc.

Modern industry has converted the little workshop of the patriarchal master into the great factory of the industrial capitalist. Masses of labourers, crowded into the factory, are organised like soldiers. As privates of the industrial army they are placed under the command of a perfect hierarchy of officers and sergeants. Not only are they slaves of the bourgeois class, and of the bourgeois state; they are daily and hourly enslaved by the machine, by the over-looker, and, above all, by the individual bourgeois manufacturer himself. The more openly this despotism proclaims gain to be its end and aim, the more petty, the more hateful and the more embittering it is. . . .

No sooner has the labourer received his wages in cash, for the moment escaping exploitation by the manufacturer, than he is set upon by the other portions of the bourgeoisie, the landlord, the shopkeeper, the pawnbroker, etc.

The lower strata of the middle class—the small tradespeople, shopkeepers, and retired tradesmen generally, the handicraftsmen and peasants—all these sink gradually into the proletariat, partly because their diminutive capital does not suffice for the scale on which modern industry is carried on, and is swamped in the competition with the large capitalists, partly because their specialised skill is rendered worthless by new methods of production. Thus the proletariat is recruited from all classes of the population.

The proletariat goes through various stages of development. With its birth begins its struggle with the bourgeoisie. At first the contest is carried on by individual labourers, then by the work people of a factory, then by the operatives of one trade, in one locality, against the individual bourgeois who directly exploits them. They direct their attacks not against the instruments of production themselves; they destroy imported wares that compete with their labour, they smash machinery to pieces, they set factories ablaze, they seek to restore by force the vanished status of the workman of the Middle Ages. . . .

Now and then the workers are victorious, but only for a time. The real fruit of their battles lies, not in the immediate result, but in the ever expanding union of the workers. This union is furthered by the improved means of communication which are created by modern industry, and which place the workers of different localities in contact with one another. It was just this contact that was needed to centralise the numerous local struggles, all of the same character, into one national struggle between classes. But every class struggle is a political struggle. And that union, to attain which the burghers of the Middle Ages, with their miserable highways, required centuries, the modern proletarians, thanks to railways, achieve in a few years.

This organisation of the proletarians into a class, and consequently into a political party, is continually being upset again by the competition between the workers themselves. But it ever rises up again, stronger, firmer, mightier. It compels legislative recognition of particular interests of the workers, by taking advantage of the divisions among the bourgeoisie itself. Thus the ten-hour bill in England was carried.

Altogether, collisions between the classes of the old society further the course of development of the proletariat in many ways. The bourgeoisie finds itself involved in a constant battle. At first with the aristocracy; later on, with those portions of the bourgeoisie itself whose interests have become antagonistic to the progress of industry; at all times with the bourgeoisie of foreign countries. In all these battles it sees itself compelled to appeal to the proletariat, to ask for its help, and thus, to drag it into the political arena. The bourgeoisie itself, therefore, supplies the proletariat with its own elements of political and general education, in other words, it furnishes the proletariat with weapons for fighting the bourgeoisie.

Further, as we have already seen, entire sections of the ruling classes are, by the advance of industry, precipitated into the proletariat, or are at least threatened in their conditions of existence. These also supply the proletariat with fresh elements of enlightenment and progress.

Finally, in times when the class struggle nears the decisive hour, the process of dissolution going on within the ruling class, in fact within the whole range of old society, assumes such a violent, glaring character, that a small section of the ruling class cuts itself adrift, and joins the revolutionary class, the class that holds the future in its hands. Just as, therefore, at an earlier period, a section of the nobility went over to the bourgeoisie, so now a portion of the bourgeoisie goes over to the proletariat, and in particular, a portion of the bourgeois ideologists, who have raised themselves to the level of comprehending theoretically the historical movement as a whole.

Of all the classes that stand face to face with the bourgeoisie today, the proletariat alone is a really revolutionary class. The other classes decay and finally disappear in the face of modern industry; the proletariat is its special and essential product.

The lower middle class, the small manufacturer, the shopkeeper, the artisan, the peasant, all these fight against the bourgeoisie, to save from extinction their existence as fractions of the middle class. They are therefore not revolutionary, but conservative. Nay more, they are reactionary, for they try to roll back the wheel of history. If by chance they are revolutionary, they are so only in view of their impending transfer into the proletariat; they thus defend not their present, but their future interests; they desert their own standpoint to adopt that of the proletariat.

The "dangerous class," the social scum (*Lumpenproletariat*), that passively rotting mass thrown off by the lowest layers of old society, may, here and there, be swept into the movement by a proletarian revolution; its conditions of life, however, prepare it far more for the part of a bribed tool of reactionary intrigue.

The social conditions of the old society no longer exist for the proletariat. The proletarian is without property; his relation to his wife and children has no longer anything in common with bourgeois family relations; modern industrial labour, modern subjection to capital, the same in England as in France, as in America as in Germany, has stripped him of every trace of national character. Law, morality, religion, are to him so many bourgeois prejudices, behind which lurk in ambush just as many bourgeois interests.

All the preceding classes that got the upper hand, sought to fortify their already acquired status by subjecting society at large to their conditions of appropriation. The proletarians cannot become masters of the productive forces of society, except by abolishing their own previous mode of appropriation. They have nothing of their own to secure and to fortify; their mission is to destroy all previous securities for, and insurances of, individual property.

All previous historical movements were movements of minorities, or in the interest of minorities. The proletarian movement is the self-conscious, independent movement of the immense majority, in the interest of the immense majority. The proletariat, the lowest stratum of our present society, cannot stir, cannot raise itself up, without the whole superincumbent strata of official society being sprung into the air. . . .

We Communists have been reproached with the desire of abolishing the right of personally acquiring property as the fruit of a man's own labour, which property is alleged to be the groundwork of all personal freedom, activity and independence.

Hard-won, self-acquired, self-earned property! Do you mean the property of the petty artisan and of the small peasant, a form of property that preceded the bourgeois form? There is no need to abolish that; the development of industry has to a great extent already destroyed it, and is still destroying it daily.

Or do you mean modern bourgeois private property?

But does wage-labour create any property for the labourer? Not a bit. It creates capital, *i.e.,* that kind of property which exploits wage-labour, and which cannot increase except upon condition of begetting a new supply of wage-labour for fresh exploitation. Property, in its present form, is based on the antagonism of capital and wage-labour. . . .

And the abolition of this state of things is called by the bourgeois, abolition of individuality and freedom! And rightly so. The abolition of bourgeois individuality, bourgeois independence, and bourgeois freedom is undoubtedly aimed at.

By freedom is meant, under the present bourgeois conditions of production, free trade, free selling and buying.

But if selling and buying disappears, free selling and buying disappears also. This talk about free selling and buying, and all the other "brave words" of our bourgeoisie about freedom in general, have a meaning, if any, only in contrast with restricted selling and buying, with the fettered traders of the Middle Ages, but have no meaning, when opposed to the Communist abolition of buying and selling, of the bourgeois conditions of production, and of the bourgeoisie itself.

You are horrified at our intending to do away with private property. But in your existing society, private property is already done away with for nine-tenths of the population; its existence for the few is solely due to its non-existence in the hands of those nine-tenths. You reproach us, therefore, with intending to do away with a form of property, the necessary condition for whose existence is the non-existence of any property for the immense majority of society.

In a word, you reproach us with intending to do away with your property. Precisely so; that is just what we intend.

From the moment when labour can no longer be converted into capital, money, or rent, into a social power capable of being monopolised, *i.e.,* from the moment when individual property can no longer be transformed into bourgeois property, into capital, from that moment, you say, individuality vanishes.

You must, therefore, confess that by "individual" you mean no other person than the bourgeois, than the middle class owner of property. This person must, indeed, be swept out of the way, and made impossible.

Communism deprives no man of the power to appropriate the products of society; all that it does is to deprive him of the power to subjugate the labour of others by means of such appropriation.

It has been objected, that upon the abolition of private property all work will cease, and universal laziness will overtake us.

According to this, bourgeois society ought long ago to have gone to the dogs through sheer idleness; for those of its members who work, acquire nothing, and those who acquire anything, do not work. The whole of this objection is but another expression of the tautology: There can no longer be any wage-labour when there is no longer any capital.

All objections urged against the Communist mode of producing and appropriating material products, have, in the same way, been urged against the Communist modes of producing and appropriating intellectual products. Just as, to the bourgeois, the disappearance of class property is the disappearance of production itself, so the disappearance of class culture is to him identical with the disappearance of all culture.

That culture, the loss of which he laments, is, for the enormous majority, a mere training to act as a machine.

But don't wrangle with us so long as you apply, to our intended abolition of bourgeois property, the standard of your bourgeois notions of freedom, culture, law, etc. Your very ideas are but the outgrowth of the conditions of your bourgeois production and bourgeois property, just as your jurisprudence is but the will of your class made into a law for all, a will whose essential character and direction are determined by the economic conditions of existence of your class.

The selfish misconception that induces you to transform into eternal laws of nature and of reason, the social forms springing from your present mode of production and form of property—historical relations that rise and disappear in the progress of production—this misconception you share with every ruling class that has preceded you. What you see clearly in the case of ancient property, what you admit in the case of feudal property, you are of course forbidden to admit in the case of your own bourgeois form of property. . . .

The Communists are further reproached with desiring to abolish countries and nationality.

The workingmen have no country. We cannot take from them what they have not got. Since the proletariat must first of all acquire political supremacy, must rise to be the leading class of the nation, must constitute itself *the* nation, it is, so far, itself national, though not in the bourgeois sense of the word.

National differences and antagonisms between peoples are vanishing gradually from day to day, owing to the development of the bourgeoisie, to freedom of commerce, to the world market, to uniformity in the mode of production and in the conditions of life corresponding thereto.

The supremacy of the proletariat will cause them to vanish still faster. United action, of the leading civilised countries at least, is one of the first conditions for the emancipation of the proletariat.

In proportion as the exploitation of one individual by another is put an end to, the exploitation of one nation by another will also be put an end to. In proportion as the antagonism between classes within the nation vanishes, the hostility of one nation to another will come to an end.

The charges against Communism made from a religious, a philosophical, and, generally, from an ideological standpoint, are not deserving of serious examination.

Does it require deep intuition to comprehend that man's ideas, views, and conceptions, in one word, man's consciousness, changes with every change in the conditions of his material existence, in his social relations and in his social life?

What else does the history of ideas prove, than that intellectual production changes its character in proportion as material production is changed? The ruling ideas of each age have ever been the ideas of its ruling class.

When people speak of ideas that revolutionise society, they do but express the fact that within the old society the elements of a new one have been created, and that the dissolution of the old ideas keeps even pace with the dissolution of the old conditions of existence.

When the ancient world was in its last throes, the ancient religions were overcome by Christianity. When Christian ideas succumbed in the 18th century to rationalist ideas, feudal society fought its death-battle with the then revolutionary bourgeoisie. The ideas of religious liberty and freedom of conscience, merely gave expression to the sway of free competition within the domain of knowledge.

"Undoubtedly," it will be said, "religion, moral, philosophical and juridical ideas have been modified in the course of historical development. But religion, morality, philosophy, political science, and law, constantly survived this change."

"There are, besides, eternal truths, such as Freedom, Justice, etc., that are common to all states of society. But Communism abolishes eternal truths, it abolishes all religion, and all morality, instead of constituting them on a new basis; it therefore acts in contradiction to all past historical experience."

What does this accusation reduce itself to? The history of all past society has consisted in the development of class antagonisms, antagonisms that assumed different forms at different epochs.

But whatever form they may have taken, one fact is common to all past ages, *viz.,* the exploitation of one part of society by the other. No wonder, then, that the social consciousness of past ages, despite all the multiplicity and variety it displays, moves within certain common forms, or general ideas, which cannot completely vanish except with the total disappearance of class antagonisms.

The Communist revolution is the most radical rupture with traditional property relations; no wonder that its development involves the most radical rupture with traditional ideas.

But let us have done with the bourgeois objections to Communism.

We have seen above, that the first step in the revolution by the working class, is to raise the proletariat to the position of ruling class, to establish democracy.

The proletariat will use its political supremacy to wrest, by degrees, all capital from the bourgeoisie, to centralise all instruments of production in the hands of the state, *i.e.*, of the proletariat organised as the ruling class; and to increase the total of productive forces as rapidly as possible.

Of course, in the beginning, this cannot be effected except by means of despotic inroads on the rights of property, and on the conditions of bourgeois production; by means of measures, therefore, which appear economically insufficient and untenable, but which, in the course of the movement, outstrip themselves, necessitate further inroads upon the old social order, and are unavoidable as a means of entirely revolutionising the mode of production.

These measures will of course be different in different countries.

Nevertheless in the most advanced countries, the following will be pretty generally applicable.

1. Abolition of property in land and application of all rents of land to public purposes.

2. A heavy progressive or graduated income tax.

3. Abolition of all right of inheritance.

4. Confiscation of the property of all emigrants and rebels.

5. Centralisation of credit in the hands of the state, by means of a national bank with state capital and an exclusive monopoly.

6. Centralisation of the means of communication and transport in the hands of the state.

7. Extension of factories and instruments of production owned by the state; the bringing into cultivation of waste lands, and the improvement of the soil generally in accordance with a common plan.

8. Equal obligation of all to work. Establishment of industrial armies, especially for agriculture.

9. Combination of agriculture with manufacturing industries; gradual abolition of the distinction between town and country, by a more equable distribution of the population over the country.

10. Free education for all children in public schools. Abolition of child factory labour in its present form. Combination of education with industrial production, etc.

When, in the course of development, class distinctions have disappeared, and all production has been concentrated in the hands of a vast association of the whole nation, the public power will lose its political character. Political power, properly so called, is merely the organised power of one class for oppressing another. If the proletariat during its contest with the bourgeoisie is compelled, by the force of circumstances, to organise itself as a class; if, by means of a revolution, it makes itself the ruling class, and, as such, sweeps away by force the old conditions of production, then, it will, along with these conditions, have swept away the conditions for the existence of class antagonisms, and of classes generally, and will thereby have abolished its own supremacy as a class.

In place of the old bourgeois society, with its classes and class antagonisms, we shall have an association, in which the free development of each is the condition for the free development of all. . . .

In short, the Communists everywhere support every revolutionary movement against the existing social and political order of things.

In all these movements they bring to the front, as the leading question in each case, the property question, no matter what its degree of development at the time.

Finally, they labour everywhere for the union and agreement of the democratic parties of all countries.

The Communists disdain to conceal their views and aims. They openly declare that their ends can be attained only by the forcible overthrow of all existing social conditions. Let the ruling classes tremble at a Communist revolution. The proletarians have nothing to lose but their chains. They have a world to win.

Workingmen of all countries, unite!

QUESTIONS AND TOPICS

1. To what degree is the following statement true: "The executive of the modern state is but a committee for managing the common affairs of the whole bourgeoisie"?

2. Would a socialist system, democratically administered, be better for the large mass of people? Is the achievement of such a system worth the violence and bloodshed Marx envisioned?
3. Marx predicted that the workingman in capitalist states would grow poorer and poorer, yet that has not been true of the American workingman. Does the American workingman fit Marx's definition of a proletarian?
4. Is bourgeois culture "for the enormous majority, a mere training to act as a machine"?
5. Quite interestingly, Marx, like many extreme conservatives, felt that industrial society was inferior to feudal society because it "substituted naked, shameless, direct, brutal exploitation" for exploitation "veiled by religious and political illusions." Do you agree?
6. Marx felt that capitalism would doom itself by the constant recurrence of "commercial crises," acute inflation and depression. Why hasn't that happened yet? Can it happen in the future?
7. Note that Marx did not feel sympathetic to the class he called the *Lumpenproletariat*, "the 'dangerous class,' the social scum." Does any class in American society fit that description?

Walt Whitman

ON
DEMOCRACY

Walt Whitman, 1819–1892, often considered one of our greatest poets, was a proud advocate of democracy, which he saw as a new creed, almost a new religion.

FOR YOU, O DEMOCRACY

Come, I will make the continent indissoluble,
I will make the most splendid race the sun ever shone upon,
I will make divine magnetic lands,
    With the love of comrades,
        With the life-long love of comrades.

I will plant companionship thick as trees along the rivers of America,
    and along the shores of the great lakes, and all over the prairies,
I will make inseparable cities with their arms about each other's necks,
    By the love of comrades,
        By the manly love of comrades.

For you these from me, O Democracy, to serve you, *ma femme!*
For you, for you, I am trilling these songs.

From SONG OF MYSELF

    12
The butcher-boy puts off his killing-clothes, or sharpens his knife at the
    stall in the market,
I loiter enjoying his repartee and his shuffle and breakdown.

Blacksmiths with grimed and hairy chests environ the anvil,
Each has his main-sledge, they are all out, there is a great heat in the fire.

From the cinder-strew'd threshold I follow their movements,
The lithe sheer of their waists plays even with their massive arms,
Overhand the hammers swing, overhand so slow, overhand so sure,
They do not hasten, each man hits in his place.

14
. . . I am enamour'd of growing out-doors,
Of men that live among cattle or taste of the ocean or woods,
Of the builders and steerers of ships and the wielders of axes and mauls,
    and the drivers of horses,
I can eat and sleep with them week in and week out.

What is commonest, cheapest, nearest, easiest, is Me,
Me going in for my chances, spending for vast returns,
Adorning myself to bestow myself on the first that will take me,
Not asking the sky to come down to my good will,
Scattering it freely forever.

24
Walt Whitman, a kosmos, of Manhattan the son,
Turbulent, fleshy, sensual, eating, drinking, and breeding,
No sentimentalist, no stander above men and women or apart from them,
No more modest than immodest.

Unscrew the locks from the doors!
Unscrew the doors themselves from their jambs!

Whoever degrades another degrades me,
And whatever is done or said returns at last to me.

Through me the afflatus surging and surging, through me the current
    and index.

I speak the pass-word primeval, I give the sign of democracy,
By God! I will accept nothing which all cannot have their counterpart of
    on the same terms.

Through me many long dumb voices,
Voices of the interminable generations of prisoners and slaves,
Voices of the diseas'd and despairing and of thieves and dwarfs,
Voices of cycles of preparation and accretion,
And of the threads that connect the stars, and of wombs and of the
    father-stuff,
And of the rights of them the others are down upon,
Of the deform'd, trivial, flat, foolish, despised,
Fog in the air, beetles rolling balls of dung.

Through me forbidden voices,
Voices of sexes and lusts, voices veil'd and I remove the veil,
Voices indecent by me clarified and transfigur'd.

I do not press my fingers across my mouth,
I keep as delicate around the bowels as around the head and heart,
Copulation is no more rank to me than death is.

I believe in the flesh and the appetites,
Seeing, hearing, feeling, are miracles, and each part and tag of me is a
    miracle.

Divine am I inside and out, and I make holy whatever I touch or am
    touch'd from,
The scent of these arm-pits aroma finer than prayer,
This head more than churches, bibles, and all the creeds. . . .

QUESTIONS AND TOPICS

1. In the verses from "Song of Myself," does Whitman intend his "I" character to represent merely himself or something more?
2. How do Whitman's ideas differ from Jefferson's? Which do you prefer?
3. Why does Whitman seem to find sex relevant in stanza 24 from "Song of
   Myself"? What relationship can you find between sex and democracy?
4. In his essays, particularly in "Democratic Vistas," 1870, Whitman speaks of
   "democratic manners." Using these poems, can you explain Whitman's definition of "democratic manners"? Would you like to live where "democratic
   manners" are practiced?
5. Does Whitman's diction and verse form reinforce his ideas?

Peter Viereck

INDEFENSIBLE
AND
UNINHABITABLE

Peter Viereck, 1916–, is a contemporary poet and essayist who is associated with the conservative movement. Unlike Whitman, he has very little faith in immediate progress or in the common man. Unlike Marx, he does not believe that man can consciously manipulate his social environment.

So long as people believe in the perfectibility of man, they will continue to use those freedom-destroying "bad means" (totalitarianism) that promise the quickest shortcut to this "good end." According to the perceptive Polish poet and anti-communist, Czeslaw Milosz, "A gradual disappearance of the faith in the earthly paradise which justifies all crimes, is an essential preliminary to the destruction of totalitarianism." By rejecting the possibility of an earthly paradise, conservatism rejects all brands of Rousseauistic perfectibility of man, rejecting the *a priori* utopias not only of Jacobinism and of socialism but also of doctrinaire *laissez faire* capitalism.

The most blood-curdling crimes are done not by criminals but by perfectionists. Criminals normally stop killing when they attain their modest goal: loot. Perfectionists never stop killing because their goal is never attainable: the ideal society.

The guillotine of a Robespierre comes from ideals too abstractly perfect for man, not from the imperfect, the organically evolved. The guillotine occurs in an enlightened geometric France, not in a ramshackle unsymmetric Hapsburg Empire. Tom Paine proved the French Revolution simply had to be good, peaceful, free. Deductively, his proof was irrefutable. Concretely, the French Revolution became the terror Burke had predicted and for the reason he had predicted: namely, that the well-built, infallible bed of Procrustes * did not fit the fallible, concrete flesh. When Paine was jailed by the same French Revolution he had defended, that ingratitude was profoundly just. The man who sacrificed concrete flesh to Procrustes's abstract bed became fittingly, like later the Old Bolsheviks, its own victim.

Earth is one of the uninhabitable planets. Unlike the habitable ones ` earth is a planet with a built-in cellar of error, death, decay. If frail children scrawl blueprints of progress on the ceiling, how will that conjure away the reality of the cellar?—does not everything in the house including the ceiling itself, rest on the foundation of that cellar of error, death, decay? Just as our planet is uninhabitable, so our society is indefensible. Every conceivable society of man will always be indefensible, innately unjust, world without end. Yet somehow we must live within the unbearable but inescapable framework of this uninhabitable planet, this indefensible social order. To act as if there were no such things as error, death, decay, will not abolish but redouble their unbearableness.

Then is any human betterment possible at all? Sustained betterment never; fluctuating betterment often. Gradual, limited reform can indeed be accomplished, always working within a rooted framework, moving always from particular to particular. Such humane reforms can be achieved and urgently ought to be, despite the resistance of reactionaries (a resistance as doctrinaire as progressivism). We must build what society we can out of what clay we have: the clay of decay, the clay of frailty and constant unpredictable blunder. But the good builder builds with the clay at hand; never does he pile up utopias from some ideal airy clay that does not exist on his particular planet.

It is not a question of being inhumanely blind to the monstrous faults of the old order, of all old orders. It is simply a matter of learning inductively the impossibility of any new program too sweeping, any progress long sustained. Only dead chemicals can be sweepingly reorganized, sustainedly perfected; everything alive is indefensible because infinitely precarious. Humanity is wilful, wanton, unpredictable. It is not there to be organized for its own good by coercive righteous busybodies. Man is a ceaseless anti-managerial revolution.

---

* Procrustes was a Greek bandit who captured wayfarers in the vicinity of Eleusis and fastened them to an iron bed. If his victims were too tall for the bed, he would chop off their feet. If they were too short, he would stretch them to size [Ed.]

Whenever enlightened reformers expect the crowd to choose Christ, it cheers for Barabbas. Whenever some Weimar Republic gets rid of some old monarchy, the liberated crowd turns its republic over to some Hitler. Then what consolation remains for the brute fact that sustained progress is impossible? Sheer self-deception is the hope of overcoming man's doom by founding a more exact social science. How can there ever be an exact science dealing with man? Science is exact when dealing with predictable chemicals; only art can deal with flesh. There are indeed consolations for man's precariousness, but they consist not of trying to end it but of learning to find in it not only the lowest but the highest reaches of the spirit, not only cruel social wrongs but the holy welding-flame of the lyric imagination, transfiguring frailty into beauty. This is the Baudelairean truth that the best roses grow from manure.

During a recent discussion of these points, an able social scientist rejoined: "Yes, you are partly right. But only about the past. A truly scientific planner has nothing but contempt for communists and Jacobins; they planned things wrong. Men did not know enough in those backward days. But next time we shall have learnt so much more about improving human nature. *Next time we shall plan everything better.*"

When that day comes, when human reactions can be predicted like test tubes and adjusted into bliss, this writer will take to the hills. Meanwhile, whether you blame it on original sin or on the id, the clay remains refractory; and this fact is not only bitter but exalting. The ultimate unadjustedness of the putty of humanity is the source of all the beauty as well as misery of life on earth.

QUESTIONS AND TOPICS

1. Is Viereck right to reject the contention of his friend, the "able social scientist," that a planned society can work?
2. What is "progress" anyway? Is it totally dependent on science and industry? Can it be measured in terms of dollars and cents?
3. Viereck writes: "Every conceivable society of man will always be indefensible, innately unjust, world without end." Can this judgment be applied to present-day America?
4. Read B. F. Skinner's novel, *Walden Two,* or that section of the work in-

cluded in this anthology. Contrast Skinner's ideas with Viereck's. State your own position.

5. Do you agree with Viereck's implication that only naive men strive for immediate implementation of social justice?

E. M. Forster

WHAT
I BELIEVE

*E. M. Forster, 1879–, is the re-
nowned author of* Passage to India
and Howards End. *In this essay,
published in 1951, he presents his
creed, an agnostic liberalism which
supports democracy without making
extravagant claims for it.*

I do not believe in belief. But this is an age of faith, in which one is
surrounded by so many militant creeds that, in self-defense, one has to
formulate a creed of one's own. Tolerance, good temper, and sympathy are
no longer enough in a world which is rent by religious and racial persecution, in a world where ignorance rules, and science, which ought to have
ruled, plays the subservient pimp. Tolerance, good temper, and sympathy
—well, they are what matter really, and if the human race is not to collapse
they must come to the front before long. But for the moment they don't
seem enough; their action is no stronger than a flower battered beneath a
military jack-boot. They want stiffening, even if the process coarsens them.
Faith, to my mind, is a stiffening process, a sort of mental starch, which
ought to be applied as sparingly as possible. I dislike the stuff. I do not
believe in it, for its own sake, at all. My lawgivers are Erasmus and
Montaigne, not Moses and St. Paul. My temple stands not upon Mount
Moriah but in that Elysian Field where even the immoral are admitted.

I have, however, to live in an Age of Faith—the sort of thing I used to
hear praised and recommended when I was a boy. It is damned unpleasant,
really. It is bloody in every sense of the word. And I have to keep my
end up in it. Where do I start?

With personal relationships. Here is something comparatively solid in a
world full of violence and cruelty. Not absolutely solid, for psychology has
split and shattered the idea of a "person" and has shown that there is
something incalculable in each of us, which may at any moment rise to

the surface and destroy our normal balance. We don't know what we're like. We can't know what we're like. We can't know what other people are like. How then can we put any trust in personal relationships, or cling to them in the gathering political storm? In theory we can't. But in practice we can and do. For the purpose of living one has to assume that the personality is solid, and the "self" is an entity, and to ignore all contrary evidence. And since to ignore evidence is one of the characteristics of faith, I certainly can proclaim that I believe in personal relationships.

Starting from them, I get a little order into the contemporary chaos. One must be fond of people and trust them if one isn't to make a mess of life, and it is therefore essential that they shouldn't let one down. They often do. The moral of which is that I must, myself, be as reliable as possible, and this I try to be. But reliability isn't a matter of contract. It is a matter for the heart, which signs no documents. In other words, reliability is impossible unless there is a natural warmth. Most men possess this warmth, though they often have bad luck and get chilled. Personal relationships are despised today. They are regarded as bourgeois luxuries, as products of a time of fair weather which has now passed, and we are urged to get rid of them, and to dedicate ourselves to some movement or cause instead. I hate the idea of dying for a cause, and if I had to choose between betraying my country and betraying my friend, I hope I should have the guts to betray my country. Such a choice may scandalize the modern reader, and he may stretch out his patriotic hand to the telephone at once, and ring up the police. It wouldn't have shocked Dante, though. Dante placed Brutus and Cassius in the lowest circle of Hell because they had chosen to betray their friend Julius Caesar, rather than their country, Rome.

This brings me along to democracy, "even Love, the Beloved Republic, which feeds upon Freedom and lives." Democracy isn't a beloved republic really, and never will be. But it is less hateful than other contemporary forms of government, and to that extent it deserves our support. It does start from the assumption that the individual is important, and that all types are needed to make a civilization. It doesn't divide its citizens into the bossers and the bossed, as an efficiency-regime tends to do. The people I admire most are those who are sensitive and want to create something or discover something, and don't see life in terms of power, and such people get more of a chance under a democracy than elsewhere. They found religions, great or small, or they produce literature and art, or they do disinterested scientific research, or they may be what are called "ordinary people," who are creative in their private lives, bring up their children decently, for instance, or help their neighbors. All these people need to express themselves, they can't do so unless society allows them liberty to do so, and the society which allows them most liberty is a democracy.

Democracy has another merit. It allows criticism, and if there isn't public criticism there are bound to be hushed-up scandals. That is why I believe in the press, despite all its lies and vulgarity, and why I believe in Parliament. The British Parliament is often sneered at because it's a talking-shop. Well, I believe in it *because* it is a talking-shop. I believe in the Private Member who makes himself a nuisance. He gets snubbed and is told that he is cranky or ill-informed, but he exposes abuses which would otherwise never have been mentioned, and very often an abuse gets put right just by being mentioned. Occasionally, too, in my country, a well-meaning public official loses his head in the cause of efficiency, and thinks himself God Almighty. Such officials are particularly frequent in the Home Office. Well, there will be questions about them in Parliament sooner or later, and then they'll have to mend their ways. Whether Parliament is either a representative body or an efficient one is very doubtful, but I value it because it criticizes and talks, and because its chatter gets widely reported.

So two cheers for democracy: one because it admits variety and one because it permits criticism. Two cheers are quite enough: there is no occasion to give three. Only Love, the Beloved Republic, deserves that.

What about force, though? While we are trying to be sensitive and advanced and affectionate and tolerant, an unpleasant question pops up; doesn't all society rest upon force? If a government can't count upon the police and the army how can it hope to rule? And if an individual gets knocked on the head or sent to a labor camp, of what significance are his opinions?

This dilemma doesn't worry me as much as it does some. I realize that all society rests upon force. But all the great creative actions, all the decent human relations, occur during the intervals when force has not managed to come to the front. These intervals are what matter. I want them to be as frequent and as lengthy as possible and I call them "civilization." Some people idealize force and pull it into the foreground and worship it, instead of keeping it in the background as long as possible. I think they make a mistake, and I think that their opposites, the mystics, err even more when they declare that force doesn't exist. I believe that it does exist, and that one of our jobs is to prevent it from getting out of its box. It gets out sooner or later, and then it destroys us and all the lovely things which we have made. But it isn't out all the time, for the fortunate reason that the strong are so stupid. Consider their conduct for a moment in the Niebelung's Ring. The giants there have the gold, or in other words the guns; but they do nothing with it, they do not realize that they are all-powerful, with the result that the catastrophe is delayed and the castle of Valhalla, insecure but glorious, fronts the storms for generations. Fafnir, coiled round his hoard, grumbles and grunts; we can hear him under Europe today; the leaves of the wood already tremble, and the Bird calls its warnings uselessly. Fafnir will destroy us, but by a blessed dispensation he is stupid and slow, and creation goes on just outside the poisonous blast of his breath. The Nietzschean would hurry the monster up, the mystic would say he didn't exist, but Wotan, wiser than either, hastens to create warriors before doom declares itself. The Valkyries are symbols not only of courage but of intelligence; they represent the human spirit snatching its opportunity while the going is good, and one of them even finds time to love. Brunhilde's last song hymns the recurrence of love, and since it is the privilege of art to exaggerate, she goes even further and proclaims the love which is eternally triumphant and feeds upon Freedom, and lives.

So that is what I feel about force and violence. I look the other way until fate strikes me. Whether this is due to courage or to cowardice in my own case I cannot be sure. But I know that if men hadn't looked the other way in the past nothing of any value would survive. The people I respect most behave as if they were immortal and as if society were eternal. Both assumptions are false: both of them must be accepted as true if we are to go on eating and working and loving, and are to keep open a few breathing holes for the human spirit. No millennium seems likely to descend upon humanity; no better and stronger League of Nations will be instituted; no form of Christianity and no alternative to Christianity will bring peace to the world or integrity to the individual; no "change of heart" will occur. And yet we needn't despair, indeed we cannot despair; the evidence of history shows us that men have always insisted on behaving creatively under the shadow of the sword, and that we had better follow their example under the shadow of the airplanes.

There is of course hero worship, fervently recommended as a panacea in some quarters. But here we shall get no help. Hero worship is a dangerous vice, and one of the minor merits of a democracy is that it does not encourage it, or produce that unmanageable type of citizen known as the

Great Man. It produces instead different kinds of small men, and that's a much finer achievement. But people who can't get interested in the variety of life and can't make up their own minds get discontented over this, and they long for a hero to bow down before and to follow blindly. It's significant that a hero is an integral part of the authoritarian stock-in-trade today. An efficiency-regime can't be run without a few heroes stuck about to carry off the dullness—much as plums have to be put into a bad pudding to make it palatable. One hero at the top and a smaller one each side of him is a favorite arrangement, and the timid and the bored are comforted by such a trinity and, bowing down, feel exalted by it.

No, I distrust Great Men. They produce a desert of uniformity around them and often a pool of blood, too, and I always feel a little man's pleasure when they come a cropper. I believe in aristocracy though—if that's the right word, and if a democrat may use it. Not an aristocracy of power, based upon rank and influence, but an aristocracy of the sensitive, the considerate, and the plucky. Its members are to be found in all nations and classes, and all through the ages, and there is a secret understanding between them when they meet. They represent the true human tradition, the one permanent victory of our queer race over cruelty and chaos. Thousands of them perish in obscurity; a few are great names. They are sensitive for others as well as for themselves, they are considerate without being fussy, their pluck is not swankiness but the power to endure, and they can take a joke. I give no examples—it is risky to do that—but the reader may as well consider whether this is the type of person he would like to meet and to be, and whether (going further with me) he would prefer that the type should *not* be an ascetic one. I'm against asceticism myself. I'm with the old Scotchman who wanted less chastity and more delicacy. I don't feel that my aristocrats are a real aristocracy if they thwart their bodies, since bodies are the instruments through which we register and enjoy the world. Still, I don't insist here. This isn't a major point. It's clearly possible to be sensitive, considerate, and plucky and yet be an ascetic too, and if anyone possesses the first three qualities, I'll let him in! On they go—an invincible army, yet not a victorious one. The aristocrats, the elect, the chosen, the best people—all the words that describe them are false, and all attempts to organize them fail. Again and again authority, seeing their value, has tried to net them and to utilize them as the Egyptian priesthood or the Christian church or the Chinese civil service or the Group Movement, or some other worthy stunt. But they slip through the net and are gone; when the door is shut they are no longer in the room;

their temple, as one of them remarked, is the holiness of the heart's imagination, and their kingdom, though they never possess it, is the wide-open
world.

With this type of person knocking about, and constantly crossing one's
path if one has eyes to see or hands to feel, the experiment of earthly life
cannot be dismissed as a failure. But it may well be hailed as a tragedy,
the tragedy being that no device has been found by which these private
decencies can be transferred to public affairs. As soon as people have power
they go crooked and sometimes dotty, too, because the possession of power
lifts them into a region where normal honesty never pays. For instance,
the man who is selling newspapers outside the House of Parliament can
safely leave his papers to go for a drink, and his cap beside them: anyone
who takes a paper is sure to drop a copper into the cap. But the men who
are inside the houses of Parliament—they can't trust one another like that;
still less can the government they compose trust other governments. No
caps upon the pavement here, but suspicion, treachery, and armaments.
The more highly public life is organized the lower does its morality sink;
the nations of today behave to each other worse than they ever did in the
past; they cheat, rob, bully, and bluff, make war without notice, and kill
as many women and children as possible; whereas primitive tribes were at
all events restrained by taboos.

The Savior of the future—if ever he comes—will not preach a new
gospel. He will merely utilize my aristocracy; he will make effective the
good will and the good temper which are already existing. In other words
he will introduce a new technique. In economics, we are told that if there
was a new technique of distribution, there need be no poverty, and people
would not starve in one place while crops were dug under in another. A
similar change is needed in the sphere of morals and politics. The desire
for it is by no means new; it was expressed, for example, in theological
terms by Jacopone da Todi over six hundred years ago. "Ordina questo
amore, O tu che mi ami," he said. ("O thou who lovest me, set this love
in order.") His prayer was not granted and I do not myself believe that
it ever will be, but here, and not through a change of heart, is our probable
route. Not by becoming better, but by ordering and distributing his native
goodness, will man shut up force into its box, and so gain time to explore
the universe and to set his mark upon it worthily.

Such a change, claim the orthodox, can only be made by Christianity,
and will be made by it in God's good time: man always has failed and al-

ways will fail to organize his own goodness, and it is presumptuous of him to try. This claim leaves me cold. I cannot believe that Christianity will ever cope with the present worldwide mess, and I think that such influence as it retains in modern society is due to its financial backing rather than to its spiritual appeal. It was a spiritual force once, but the indwelling spirit will have to be restated if it is to calm the waters again, and probably in a non-Christian form.

These are the reflections of an individualist and a liberal who has found his liberalism crumbling beneath him and at first felt ashamed. Then, looking around, he decided there was no special reason for shame, since other people, whatever they felt, were equally insecure. And as for individualism—there seems no way out of this, even if one wants to find one. The dictator-hero can grind down his citizens till they are all alike, but he can't melt them into a single man. He can order them to merge, he can incite them to mass-antics, but they are obliged to be born separately and to die separately and, owing to these unavoidable termini, will always be running off the totalitarian rails. The memory of birth and the expectation of death always lurk within the human being, making him separate from his fellows and consequently capable of intercourse with them. Naked I came into the world, naked I shall go out of it! And a very good thing, too, for it reminds me that I am naked under my shirt. Until psychologists and biologists have done much more tinkering than seems likely, the individual remains firm and each of us must consent to be one, and to make the best of the difficult job.

QUESTIONS AND TOPICS

1. Compare Forster's reasons for supporting democracy with those of Whitman and Jefferson.
2. Why does Forster give only "two cheers" for democracy?
3. Could another kind of political structure also allow for variety and individual liberty? Monarchy? Socialism?
4. Do you agree that democracy does not produce the Great Man? Do you regard that as a virtue or a fault? (*Hint:* Be sure to define what you mean by a great man.)
5. Compare Forster's concept of aristocracy with Jefferson's.

Robinson Jeffers

HURT HAWKS
and
SHINE, PERISHING REPUBLIC

Robinson Jeffers, 1887–1962, was a modern poet who spoke out strongly against democracy, which he equated with mediocrity and communal living. In the first poem his hawk stands for the fiercely independent qualities Jeffers valued, qualities not possessed by the common man.

HURT HAWKS

I

The broken pillar of the wing jags from the clotted shoulder,
The wing trails like a banner in defeat,
No more to use the sky forever but live with famine
And pain a few days: cat nor coyote
Will shorten the week of waiting for death, there is game without talons.
He stands under the oak-bush and waits
The lame feet of salvation; at night he remembers freedom
And flies in a dream, the dawns ruin it.
He is strong and pain is worse to the strong, incapacity is worse.
The curs of the day come and torment him
At distance, no one but death the redeemer will humble that head,
The intrepid readiness, the terrible eyes.
The wild God of the world is sometimes merciful to those
That ask mercy, not often to the arrogant.
You do not know him, you communal people, or you have forgotten him;

Intemperate and savage, the hawk remembers him;
Beautiful and wild, the hawks, and men that are dying, remember him.

II

I'd sooner, except the penalties, kill a man than a hawk; but the great
    redtail
Had nothing left but unable misery
From the bone too shattered for mending, the wing that trailed under his
    talons when he moved.
We had fed him six weeks, I gave him freedom,
He wandered over the foreland hill and returned in the evening, asking
    for death,
Not like a beggar, still eyed with the old
Implacable arrogance. I gave him the lead gift in the twilight. What fell
    was relaxed,
Owl-downy, soft feminine feathers; but what
Soared: the fierce rush: the night-herons by the flooded river cried fear at
    its rising
Before it was quite unsheathed from reality.

SHINE, PERISHING REPUBLIC

While this America settles in the mould of its vulgarity, heavily thickening
    to empire,
And protest, only a bubble in the molten mass, pops and sighs out, and the
    mass hardens,

I sadly smiling remember that the flower fades to make fruit, the fruit rots
    to make earth.
Out of the mother; and through the spring exultances, ripeness and deca-
    dence; and home to the mother.

You making haste haste on decay: not blameworthy; life is good, be it
    stubbornly long or suddenly
A mortal splendor: meteors are not needed less than mountains: shine,
    perishing republic.

But for my children, I would have them keep their distance from the thickening center; corruption
Never has been compulsory, when the cities lie at the monster's feet there
are left the mountains.

And boys, be in nothing so moderate as in love of man, a clever servant,
insufferable master.
There is the trap that catches noblest spirits, that caught—they say—God,
when he walked on earth.

QUESTIONS AND TOPICS

---

1. What qualities are embodied in Jeffers' hawk? Do you agree with him that
   a "communal people," such as the mass of Americans, does not possess these
   qualities?
2. Are hawk-like individuals necessary for society's survival? Are they desirable
   for other reasons?
3. Judging from both poems, why did Jeffers find America corrupt and
   decadent?
4. In "Shine, Perishing Republic" Jeffers wishes his sons to remain aloof from
   the corruption of modern America. Can such independence be achieved?

2

CLASS STRUCTURE

MOST PEOPLE tend to classify the rest of humanity according to race, religion, wealth, social background, educational background, profession, or intelligence. The student is probably aware of his own tendency to classify his fellow students as well as his teachers. Classification is sometimes very useful. It can help give one the sense of an ordered world; it can also help to explain the behavior of many people.

But the classification of humanity can also be troublesome. It can force us to think in stereotypes and ignore individual differences. Flannery O'Connor's characters in "Everything That Rises Must Converge" are trapped by the social attitudes they have inherited or acquired; they tend to see others not as individuals but as members of a social group, and the result is a total failure of understanding and the breakdown of human relations.

Such classifications can also force people to assume expected roles. At the end of Mark Twain's *Huckleberry Finn,* the Negro Jim, for example, seems to play the role of the stupid, selfish, frightened Southern "nigger" because, under the circumstances, it seems the best thing for him to do.

Though the United States is a country founded on democratic principles, certain groups have more difficulty rising on the social ladder than others, possibly because of their racial background or the poor education they are afforded. Such groups have always existed, but today their presence is a more unpleasant reality because the remainder of our country has achieved so much affluence. Their cause has been dramatically described by writers like Michael Harrington and James Baldwin.

Another problem in discussing America's class structure lies in the fact that so much of it is taken up by the middle class. Because of our country's wealth and because there has been great opportunity for advancement, a large part of our population has been able to rise to that level. But the student will find many distinctions in the middle class—distinctions in income, styles of living, values, and beliefs that make the term "middle class" almost meaningless in any careful analysis. We can say that America is largely a middle-class country, but this only means that most Americans live comfortably, have opportunity for education, and pay taxes.

Misunderstandings are also prevalent in popular conceptions of the wealthy. The rich have often been glamorized because they have the money and power to lead lives that most people desire. For this reason they have also been envied and maligned. Some Americans admire the rich, because many have satisfied our country's ideals of individualism and advancement through hard work. On the other hand, writers like Ezra Pound have attacked them for living useless and wasteful lives. But the student will probably realize that some wealthy people have devoted themselves to public service.

The student, then, should approach the problem of class structure in America with a fear of simplification and a willingness to put aside his own prejudices. He should realize the complexities in discussing class in a country which advocates equality but encourages individuals to compete for power and status.

Michael Harrington

THE
INVISIBLE
LAND

The Other America, by Michael Harrington, 1928–, examines factually and realistically the invisible world of America's lower depths. The following selection from Chapter 1 of that book sets forth in general terms the hidden but destructive nature of poverty in our affluent society.

There is a familiar America. It is celebrated in speeches and advertised on television and in the magazines. It has the highest mass standard of living the world has ever known.

In the 1950's this America worried about itself, yet even its anxieties were products of abundance. The title of a brilliant book was widely misinterpreted, and the familiar America began to call itself "the affluent society." There was introspection about Madison Avenue and tail fins; there was discussion of the emotional suffering taking place in the suburbs. In all this, there was an implicit assumption that the basic grinding economic problems had been solved in the United States. In this theory the nation's problems were no longer a matter of basic human needs, of food, shelter, and clothing. Now they were seen as qualitative, a question of learning to live decently amid luxury.

While this discussion was carried on, there existed another America. In it dwelt somewhere between 40,000,000 and 50,000,000 citizens of this land. They were poor. They still are.

To be sure, the other America is not impoverished in the same sense as those poor nations where millions cling to hunger as a defense against starvation. This country has escaped such extremes. That does not change the fact that tens of millions of Americans are, at this very moment, maimed in body and spirit, existing at levels beneath those necessary for human decency. If these people are not starving, they are hungry, and sometimes fat with hunger, for that is what cheap foods do. They are without adequate housing and education and medical care.

The Government has documented what this means to the bodies of the poor, and the figures will be cited throughout this book. But even more basic, this poverty twists and deforms the spirit. The American poor are pessimistic and defeated, and they are victimized by mental suffering to a degree unknown in Suburbia. . . .

I

The millions who are poor in the United States tend to become increasingly invisible. Here is a great mass of people, yet it takes an effort of the intellect and will even to see them.

I discovered this personally in a curious way. After I wrote my first article on poverty in America, I had all the statistics down on paper. I had proved to my satisfaction that there were around 50,000,000 poor in this country. Yet, I realized I did not believe my own figures. The poor existed in the Government reports; they were percentages and numbers in long, close columns, but they were not part of my experience. I could prove that the other America existed, but I had never been there.

My response was not accidental. It was typical of what is happening to an entire society, and it reflects profound social changes in this nation. The other America, the America of poverty, is hidden today in a way that it never was before. Its millions are socially invisible to the rest of us. No wonder that so many misinterpreted Galbraith's title and assumed that "the affluent society" meant that everyone had a decent standard of life. The misinterpretation was true as far as the actual day-to-day lives of two-thirds of the nation were concerned. Thus, one must begin a description of the other America by understanding why we do not see it.

There are perennial reasons that make the other America an invisible land.

Poverty is often off the beaten track. It always has been. The ordinary tourist never left the main highway, and today he rides interstate turnpikes. He does not go into the valleys of Pennsylvania where the towns look like movie sets of Wales in the thirties. He does not see the company houses in rows, the rutted roads (the poor always have bad roads whether they live in the city, in towns, or on farms), and everything is black and dirty. And even if he were to pass through such a place by accident, the tourist would not meet the unemployed men in the bar or the women coming home from a runaway sweatshop.

Then, too, beauty and myths are perennial masks of poverty. The traveler comes to the Appalachians in the lovely season. He sees the hills, the streams, the foliage—but not the poor. Or perhaps he looks at a run-down mountain house and, remembering Rousseau rather than seeing with his eyes, decides that "those people" are truly fortunate to be living the way they are and that they are lucky to be exempt from the strains and tensions of the middle class. The only problem is that "those people," the quaint inhabitants of those hills, are undereducated, underprivileged, lack medical care, and are in the process of being forced from the land into a life in the cities, where they are misfits.

These are normal and obvious causes of the invisibility of the poor. They operated a generation ago; they will be functioning a generation hence. It is more important to understand that the very development of American society is creating a new kind of blindness about poverty. The poor are increasingly slipping out of the very experience and consciousness of the nation.

If the middle class never did like ugliness and poverty, it was at least aware of them. "Across the tracks" was not a very long way to go. There were forays into the slums at Christmas time; there were charitable organizations that brought contact with the poor. Occasionally, almost everyone passed through the Negro ghetto or the blocks of tenements, if only to get downtown to work or to entertainment.

Now the American city has been transformed. The poor still inhabit the miserable housing in the central area, but they are increasingly isolated from contact with, or sight of, anybody else. Middle-class women coming in from Suburbia on a rare trip may catch the merest glimpse of the other America on the way to an evening at the theater, but their children are segregated in suburban schools. The business or professional man may drive along the fringes of slums in a car or bus, but it is not an important experience to him. The failures, the unskilled, the disabled, the aged, and the minorities are right there, across the tracks, where they have always been. But hardly anyone else is.

In short, the very development of the American city has removed poverty from the living, emotional experience of millions upon millions of middle-class Americans. Living out in the suburbs, it is easy to assume that ours is, indeed, an affluent society.

This new segregation of poverty is compounded by a well-meaning ignorance. A good many concerned and sympathetic Americans are aware that there is much discussion of urban renewal. Suddenly, driving through the city, they notice that a familiar slum has been torn down and that there are towering, modern buildings where once there had been tenements or hovels. There is a warm feeling of satisfaction, of pride in the way things are working out: the poor, it is obvious, are being taken care of.

The irony in this . . . is that the truth is nearly the exact opposite to the impression. The total impact of the various housing programs in post-war America has been to squeeze more and more people into existing slums. More often than not, the modern apartment in a towering building rents at $40 a room or more. For, during the past decade and a half, there has been more subsidization of middle- and upper-income housing than there has been of housing for the poor.

Clothes make the poor invisible too: America has the best-dressed poverty the world has ever known. For a variety of reasons, the benefits of mass production have been spread much more evenly in this area than in many others. It is much easier in the United States to be decently dressed than it is to be decently housed, fed, or doctored. Even people with terribly depressed incomes can look prosperous.

This is an extremely important factor in defining our emotional and existential ignorance of poverty. In Detroit the existence of social classes became much more difficult to discern the day the companies put lockers in the plants. From that moment on, one did not see men in work clothes on the way to the factory, but citizens in slacks and white shirts. This process has been magnified with the poor throughout the country. There are tens of thousands of Americans in the big cities who are wearing shoes, perhaps even a stylishly cut suit or dress, and yet are hungry. It is not a matter of planning, though it almost seems as if the affluent society had given out costumes to the poor so that they would not offend the rest of society with the sight of rags.

Then, many of the poor are the wrong age to be seen. A good number of them (over 8,000,000) are sixty-five years of age or better; an even larger number are under eighteen. The aged members of the other America are often sick, and they cannot move. Another group of them live out their lives in loneliness and frustration: they sit in rented rooms, or else they stay close to a house in a neighborhood that has completely changed from the old days. Indeed, one of the worst aspects of poverty among the aged is that these people are out of sight and out of mind, and alone.

The young are somewhat more visible, yet they too stay close to their neighborhoods. Sometimes they advertise their poverty through a lurid tabloid story about a gang killing. But generally they do not disturb the quiet streets of the middle class.

And finally, the poor are politically invisible. It is one of the cruelest ironies of social life in advanced countries that the dispossessed at the bottom of society are unable to speak for themselves. The people of the other America do not, by far and large, belong to unions, to fraternal organizations, or to political parties. They are without lobbies of their own; they put forward no legislative program. As a group, they are atomized. They have no face; they have no voice.

Thus, there is not even a cynical political motive for caring about the poor, as in the old days. Because the slums are no longer centers of powerful political organizations, the politicians need not really care about their inhabitants. The slums are no longer visible to the middle class, so much of the idealistic urge to fight for those who need help is gone. Only the social agencies have a really direct involvement with the other America, and they are without any great political power.

To the extent that the poor have a spokesman in American life, that role is played by the labor movement. The unions have their own particular idealism, an ideology of concern. More than that, they realize that the existence of a reservoir of cheap, unorganized labor is a menace to wages and working conditions throughout the entire economy. Thus, many union legislative proposals—to extend the coverage of minimum wage and social security, to organize migrant farm laborers—articulate the needs of the poor.

That the poor are invisible is one of the most important things about them. They are not simply neglected and forgotten as in the old rhetoric of reform; what is much worse, they are not seen. . . .

Forty to 50,000,000 people are becoming increasingly invisible. That is a shocking fact. But there is a second basic irony of poverty that is equally important: if one is to make the mistake of being born poor, he should choose a time when the majority of the people are miserable too.

J. K. Galbraith develops this idea in *The Affluent Society,* and in doing so defines the "newness" of the kind of poverty in contemporary America. The old poverty, Galbraith notes, was general. It was the condition of life of an entire society, or at least of that huge majority who were without special skills or the luck of birth. When the entire economy advanced, a good many of these people gained higher standards of living. Unlike the poor today, the majority poor of a generation ago were an immediate (if cynical) concern of political leaders. The old slums of the immigrants had the votes; they provided the basis for labor organizations; their very numbers could be a powerful force in political conflict. At the same time the new technology required higher skills, more education, and stimulated an upward movement for millions.

Perhaps the most dramatic case of the power of the majority poor took place in the 1930's. The Congress of Industrial Organizations literally organized millions in a matter of years. A labor movement that had been declining and confined to a thin stratum of the highly skilled suddenly embraced masses of men and women in basic industry. At the same time this acted as a pressure upon the Government, and the New Deal codified some of the social gains in laws like the Wagner Act. The result was not a basic transformation of the American system, but it did transform the lives of an entire section of the population.

In the thirties one of the reasons for these advances was that misery was general. There was no need then to write books about unemployment and poverty. That was the decisive social experience of the entire society, and the apple sellers even invaded Wall Street. There was political sympathy from middle-class reformers; there were an élan and spirit that grew out of a deep crisis.

Some of those who advanced in the thirties did so because they had unique and individual personal talents. But for the great mass, it was a question of being at the right point in the economy at the right time in history, and utilizing that position for common struggle. Some of those who failed did so because they did not have the will to take advantage of new opportunities. But for the most part the poor who were left behind had been at the wrong place in the economy at the wrong moment in history.

These were the people in the unorganizable jobs, in the South, in the minority groups, in the fly-by-night factories that were low on capital and high on labor. When some of them did break into the economic mainstream—when, for instance, the CIO opened up the way for some Negroes to find good industrial jobs—they proved to be as resourceful as anyone else. As a group, the other Americans who stayed behind were not originally composed primarily of individual failures. Rather, they were victims of an impersonal process that selected some for progress and discriminated against others.

Out of the thirties came the welfare state. Its creation had been stimulated by mass impoverishment and misery, yet it helped the poor least of all. Laws like unemployment compensation, the Wagner Act, the various farm programs, all these were designed for the middle third in the cities, for the organized workers, and for the upper third in the country, for the big market farmers. If a man works in an extremely low-paying job, he may not even be covered by social security or other welfare programs. If he receives unemployment compensation, the payment is scaled down according to his low earnings.

One of the major laws that was designed to cover everyone, rich and poor, was social security. But even here the other Americans suffered discrimination. Over the years social security payments have not even provided a subsistence level of life. The middle third have been able to supplement the Federal pension through private plans negotiated by unions, through joining medical insurance schemes like Blue Cross, and so on. The poor have not been able to do so. They lead a bitter life, and then have to pay for that fact in old age.

Indeed, the paradox that the welfare state benefits those least who need help most is but a single instance of a persistent irony in the other America. Even when the money finally trickles down, even when a school is built in a poor neighborhood, for instance, the poor are still deprived. Their entire environment, their life, their values, do not prepare them to take advantage of the new opportunity. The parents are anxious for the children to go to work; the pupils are pent up, waiting for the moment when their education has complied with the law.

Today's poor, in short, missed the political and social gains of the thirties. They are, as Galbraith rightly points out, the first minority poor in history, the first poor not to be seen, the first poor whom the politicians could leave alone.

The first step toward the new poverty was taken when millions of people proved immune to progress. When that happened, the failure was not individual and personal, but a social product. But once the historic accident takes place, it begins to become a personal fate.

The new poor of the other America saw the rest of society move ahead. They went on living in depressed areas, and often they tended to become depressed human beings. In some of the West Virginia towns, for instance, an entire community will become shabby and defeated. The young and the adventurous go to the city, leaving behind those who cannot move and those who lack the will to do so. The entire area becomes permeated with failure, and that is one more reason the big corporations shy away.

Indeed, one of the most important things about the new poverty is that it cannot be defined in simple, statistical terms. Throughout this book a crucial term is used: aspiration. If a group has internal vitality, a will— if it has aspiration—it may live in dilapidated housing, it may eat an inadequate diet, and it may suffer poverty, but it is not impoverished. So it was in those ethnic slums of the immigrants that played such a dramatic role in the unfolding of the American dream. The people found themselves in slums, but they were not slum dwellers.

But the new poverty is constructed so as to destroy aspiration; it is a system designed to be impervious to hope. The other America does not contain the adventurous seeking a new life and land. It is populated by the failures, by those driven from the land and bewildered by the city, by old people suddenly confronted with the torments of loneliness and poverty, and by minorities facing a wall of prejudice.

In the past, when poverty was general in the unskilled and semi-skilled work force, the poor were all mixed together. The bright and the dull, those who were going to escape into the great society and those who were to stay behind, all of them lived on the same street. When the middle third rose, this community was destroyed. And the entire invisible land of the other Americans became a ghetto, a modern poor farm for the rejects of society and of the economy.

It is a blow to reform and the political hopes of the poor that the middle class no longer understands that poverty exists. But, perhaps more important, the poor are losing their links with the great world. If statistics and sociology can measure a feeling as delicate as loneliness (and some of the attempts to do so will be cited later on), the other America is becoming increasingly populated by those who do not belong to anybody or anything. They are no longer participants in an ethnic culture from the old country; they are less and less religious; they do not belong to unions or clubs. They are not seen, and because of that they themselves cannot see. Their horizon has become more and more restricted; they see one another, and that means they see little reason to hope. . . .

Finally, one might summarize the newness of contemporary poverty by saying: These are the people who are immune to progress. But then the facts are even more cruel. The other Americans are the victims of the very inventions and machines that have provided a higher living standard for the rest of the society. They are upside-down in the economy, and for them greater productivity often means worse jobs; agricultural advance becomes hunger.

In the optimistic theory, technology is an undisguised blessing. A general increase in productivity, the argument goes, generates a higher standard of living for the whole people. And indeed, this has been true for the middle and upper thirds of American society, the people who made such striking gains in the last two decades. It tends to overstate the automatic character of the process, to omit the role of human struggle. (The CIO was organized by men in conflict, not by economic trends.) Yet it states a certain truth—for those who are lucky enough to participate in it.

But the poor, if they were given to theory, might argue the exact opposite. They might say: Progress is misery.

As the society became more technological, more skilled, those who learn to work the machines, who get the expanding education, move up. Those who miss out at the very start find themselves at a new disadvantage. A generation ago in American life, the majority of the working people did not have high-school educations. But at that time industry was organized on a lower level of skill and competence. And there was a sort of continuum in the shop: the youth who left school at sixteen could begin as a laborer, and gradually pick up skill as he went along.

Today the situation is quite different. The good jobs require much more academic preparation, much more skill from the very outset. Those who lack a high-school education tend to be condemned to the economic underworld—to low-paying service industries, to backward factories, to sweeping and janitorial duties. If the fathers and mothers of the contemporary poor were penalized a generation ago for their lack of schooling, their children will suffer all the more. The very rise in productivity that created more money and better working conditions for the rest of the society can be a menace to the poor.

But then this technological revolution might have an even more disastrous consequence: it could increase the ranks of the poor as well as intensify the disabilities of poverty. At this point it is too early to make any final judgment, yet there are obvious danger signals. There are millions of Americans who live just the other side of poverty. When a recession comes, they are pushed onto the relief rolls. (Welfare payments in New York respond almost immediately to any economic decline.) If automation continues to inflict more and more penalties on the unskilled and the semiskilled, it could have the impact of permanently increasing the population of the other America.

Even more explosive is the possibility that people who participated in the gains of the thirties and the forties will be pulled back down into poverty. Today the mass-production industries where unionization made such a difference are contracting. Jobs are being destroyed. In the process, workers who had achieved a certain level of wages, who had won working conditions in the shop, are suddenly confronted with impoverishment. This is particularly true for anyone over forty years of age and for members of minority groups. Once their job is abolished, their chances of ever getting similar work are very slim.

It is too early to say whether or not this phenomenon is temporary, or whether it represents a massive retrogression that will swell the numbers of the poor. To a large extent, the answer to this question will be determined by the political response of the United States in the sixties. If serious and massive action is not undertaken, it may be necessary for statisticians to add some old-fashioned, pre-welfare-state poverty to the misery of the other America.

Poverty in the 1960's is invisible and it is new, and both these factors make it more tenacious. It is more isolated and politically powerless than ever before. It is laced with ironies, not the least of which is that many of the poor view progress upside-down, as a menace and a threat to their lives. And if the nation does not measure up to the challenge of automation, poverty in the 1960's might be on the increase.

II

There are mighty historical and economic forces that keep the poor down; and there are human beings who help out in this grim business, many of them unwittingly. There are sociological and political reasons why poverty is not seen; and there are misconceptions and prejudices that literally blind the eyes. The latter must be understood if anyone is to make the necessary act of intellect and will so that the poor can be noticed.

Here is the most familiar version of social blindness: "The poor are that way because they are afraid of work. And anyway they all have big cars. If they were like me (or my father or my grandfather), they could pay their own way. But they prefer to live on the dole and cheat the tax-payers."

This theory, usually thought of as a virtuous and moral statement, is one of the means of making it impossible for the poor ever to pay their way. There are, one must assume, citizens of the other America who choose impoverishment out of fear of work (though, writing it down, I really do not believe it). But the real explanation of why the poor are where they are is that they made the mistake of being born to the wrong parents, in the wrong section of the country, in the wrong industry, or in the wrong racial or ethnic group. Once that mistake has been made, they could have been paragons of will and morality, but most of them would never even have had a chance to get out of the other America.

There are two important ways of saying this: The poor are caught in a vicious circle; or, The poor live in a culture of poverty.

In a sense, one might define the contemporary poor in the United States as those who, for reasons beyond their control, cannot help themselves. All the most decisive factors making for opportunity and advance are against them. They are born going downward, and most of them stay down. They are victims whose lives are endlessly blown round and round the other America.

Here is one of the most familiar forms of the vicious circle of poverty. The poor get sick more than anyone else in the society. That is because they live in slums, jammed together under unhygienic conditions; they have inadequate diets, and cannot get decent medical care. When they become sick, they are sick longer than any other group in the society. Because they are sick more often and longer than anyone else, they lose wages and work, and find it difficult to hold a steady job. And because of this, they cannot pay for good housing, for a nutritious diet, for doctors. At any given point in the circle, particularly when there is a major illness, their prospect is to move to an even lower level and to begin the cycle, round and round, toward even more suffering.

This is only one example of the vicious circle. Each group in the other America has its own particular version of the experience, and these will be detailed throughout this book. But the pattern, whatever its variations, is basic to the other America.

The individual cannot usually break out of this vicious circle. Neither can the group, for it lacks the social energy and political strength to turn its misery into a cause. Only the larger society, with its help and resources, can really make it possible for these people to help themselves. Yet those who could make the difference too often refuse to act because of their ignorant, smug moralisms. They view the effects of poverty—above all, the warping of the will and spirit that is a consequence of being poor— as choices. Understanding the vicious circle is an important step in breaking down this prejudice.

There is an even richer way of describing this same, general idea: Poverty in the United States is a culture, an institution, a way of life.

There is a famous anecdote about Ernest Hemingway and F. Scott Fitzgerald. Fitzgerald is reported to have remarked to Hemingway, "The rich are different." And Hemingway replied, "Yes, they have money." Fitzgerald had much the better of the exchange. He understood that being rich was not a simple fact, like a large bank account, but a way of looking at reality, a series of attitudes, a special type of life. If this is true of the rich, it is ten times truer of the poor. Everything about them, from the condition of their teeth to the way in which they love, is suffused and permeated by the fact of their poverty. And this is sometimes a hard idea for a Hemingway-like middle-class America to comprehend.

The family structure of the poor, for instance, is different from that of the rest of the society. There are more homes without a father, there is less marriage, more early pregnancy and, if Kinsey's statistical findings can be used, markedly different attitudes toward sex. As a result of this, to take but one consequence of the fact, hundreds of thousands, and perhaps millions, of children in the other America never know stability and "normal" affection.

Or perhaps the policeman is an even better example. For the middle class, the police protect property, give directions, and help old ladies. For the urban poor, the police are those who arrest you. In almost any slum there is a vast conspiracy against the forces of law and order. If someone approaches asking for a person, no one there will have heard of him, even if he lives next door. The outsider is "cop," bill collector, investigator (and, in the Negro ghetto, most dramatically, he is "the Man").

While writing this book, I was arrested for participation in a civil-rights demonstration. A brief experience of a night in a cell made an abstraction personal and immediate: the city jail is one of the basic institutions of the other America. Almost everyone whom I encountered in the "tank" was poor: skid-row whites, Negroes, Puerto Ricans. Their poverty was an incitement to arrest in the first place. (A policeman will be much more careful with a well-dressed, obviously educated man who might have political connections than he will with someone who is poor.) They did not have money for bail or for lawyers. And, perhaps most important, they waited their arraignment with stolidity, in a mood of passive acceptance. They expected the worst, and they probably got it.

There is, in short, a language of the poor, a psychology of the poor, a world view of the poor. To be impoverished is to be an internal alien, to grow up in a culture that is radically different from the one that dominates the society. The poor can be described statistically; they can be analyzed as a group. But they need a novelist as well as a sociologist if we are to see them. They need an American Dickens to record the smell and texture and quality of their lives. The cycles and trends, the massive forces, must be seen as affecting persons who talk and think differently.

I am not that novelist. Yet in this book I have attempted to describe the faces behind the statistics, to tell a little of the "thickness" of personal life in the other America.

QUESTIONS AND TOPICS

1. Do you agree with Harrington that the poor are invisible in America?
2. Do you feel that we should be less concerned, since the percentage of poor people is diminishing so rapidly? Is Harrington right to think that a "minority poor" is far more hopeless and demoralized than a "majority poor"?
3. Harrington believes that poor people are culturally different from others. He speaks of a "culture of poverty" which needs a novelist to describe it. Do you agree with Harrington? Or do you think that poor people are like other people, except poorer?
4. One of Harrington's main points is that poor people as a group are caught in a vicious circle, that most are victims of circumstance rather than lazy people in search of welfare payments. What is your view on this controversial and complex question?

James Baldwin

FIFTH AVENUE, UPTOWN: A LETTER FROM HARLEM

Before one can understand the causes of America's most tragic dilemma, racial inequality, he must first acquaint himself with the realities of the black ghetto. James Baldwin, 1924–, one of America's most eloquent spokesmen for the black man, may possibly be the writer Harrington wished for, the artist who compels us to live for a while in the culture of poverty. Though Baldwin's essays are sometimes overstrained and angry, the experience he projects has the ring of truth.

There is a housing project standing now where the house in which we grew up once stood, and one of those stunted city trees is snarling where our doorway used to be. This is on the rehabilitated side of the avenue. The other side of the avenue—for progress takes time—has not been rehabilitated yet and it looks exactly as it looked in the days when we sat with our noses pressed against the windowpane, longing to be allowed to go "across the street." The grocery store which gave us credit is still there, and there can be no doubt that it is still giving credit. The people in the project certainly need it—far more, indeed, than they ever needed the project. The last time I passed by, the Jewish proprietor was still standing among his shelves, looking sadder and heavier but scarcely any older. Farther down the block stands the shoe-repair store in which our shoes were repaired until reparation became impossible and in which, then, we bought all our "new" ones. The Negro proprietor is still in the window, head down, working at the leather.

These two, I imagine, could tell a long tale if they would (perhaps they would be glad to if they could), having watched so many, for so long, struggling in the fishhooks, the barbed wire, of this avenue.

The avenue is elsewhere the renowned and elegant Fifth. The area I am describing, which, in today's gang parlance, would be called "the turf," is bounded by Lenox Avenue on the west, the Harlem River on the east, 135th Street on the north, and 130th Street on the south. We never lived beyond these boundaries; this is where we grew up. Walking along 145th Street—for example—familiar as it is, and similar, does not have the same impact because I do not know any of the people on the block. But when I turn east on 131st Street and Lenox Avenue, there is first a soda-pop joint, then a shoeshine "parlor," then a grocery store, then a dry cleaners', then the houses. All along the street there are people who watched me grow up, people who grew up with me, people I watched grow up along with my brothers and sisters; and, sometimes in my arms, sometimes underfoot, sometimes at my shoulder—or on it—their children, a riot, a forest of children, who include my nieces and nephews.

When we reach the end of this long block, we find ourselves on wide, filthy, hostile Fifth Avenue, facing that project which hangs over the avenue like a monument to the folly, and the cowardice, of good intentions. All along the block, for anyone who knows it, are immense human gaps, like craters. These gaps are not created merely by those who have moved away, inevitably into some other ghetto; or by those who have risen, almost always into a greater capacity for self-loathing and self-delusion; or yet by those who, by whatever means—World War II, the Korean war, a policeman's gun or billy, a gang war, a brawl, madness, an overdose of heroin, or, simply, unnatural exhaustion—are dead. I am talking about those who are left, and I am talking principally about the young. What are they doing? Well, some, a minority, are fanatical churchgoers, members of the more extreme of the Holy Roller sects. Many, many more are "moslems," by affiliation or sympathy, that is to say that they are united by nothing more—and nothing less—than a hatred of the white world and all its works. The are present, for example, at every Buy Black street-corner meeting—meetings in which the speaker urges his hearers to cease trading with white men and establish a separate economy. Neither the speaker nor his hearers can possibly do this, of course, since Negroes do not own General Motors or RCA or the A & P, nor, indeed, do they own more than a wholly insufficient fraction of anything else in Harlem (those who *do* own anything are more interested in their profits than in their fellows). But these meetings nevertheless keep alive in the participators a certain pride of bitterness without which, however futile this bitterness may be, they could scarcely remain alive at all. Many have given up. They stay home and watch the TV screen, living on the earnings of their parents, cousins, brothers, or uncles, and only leave the house to go to the movies or to the nearest bar. "How're you making it?" one may ask, running into them along the block, or in the bar. "Oh, I'm TV-ing it"; with the saddest, sweetest, most shamefaced of smiles, and from a great distance. This distance one is compelled to respect; anyone who has traveled so far will not easily be dragged again into the world. There are further retreats, of course, than the TV screen or the bar. There are those who are simply sitting on their stoops, "stoned," animated for a moment only, and hideously, by the approach of someone who may lend them the money for a "fix." Or by the approach of someone from whom they can purchase it, one of the shrewd ones, on the way to prison or just coming out.

And the others, who have avoided all of these deaths, get up in the morning and go downtown to meet "the man." They work in the white man's world all day and come home in the evening to this fetid block. They struggle to instill in their children some private sense of honor or dignity which will help the child to survive. This means, of course, that they must struggle, stolidly, incessantly, to keep this sense alive in themselves, in spite of the insults, the indifference, and the cruelty they are certain to encounter in their working day. They patiently browbeat the landlord into fixing the heat, the plaster, the plumbing; this demands prodigious patience; nor is patience usually enough. In trying to make their hovels habitable, they are perpetually throwing good money after bad. Such frustration, so long endured, is driving many strong, admirable men and women whose only crime is color to the very gates of paranoia.

One remembers them from another time—playing handball in the playground, going to church, wondering if they were going to be promoted at school. One remembers them going off to war—gladly, to escape this block. One remembers their return. Perhaps one remembers their wedding day. And one sees where the girl is now—vainly looking for salvation from some other embittered, trussed, and struggling boy—and sees the all-but-abandoned children in the streets.

Now I am perfectly aware that there are other slums in which white men are fighting for their lives, and mainly losing. I know that blood is also flowing through those streets and that the human damage there is incalculable. People are continually pointing out to me the wretchedness of white people in order to console me for the wretchedness of blacks. But an itemized account of the American failure does not console me and it should not console anyone else. That hundreds of thousands of white people are living, in effect, no better than the "niggers" is not a fact to be regarded with complacency. The social and moral bankruptcy suggested by this fact is of the bitterest, most terrifying kind.

The people, however, who believe that this democratic anguish has some consoling value are always pointing out that So-and-So, white, and So-and-So, black, rose from the slums into the big time. The existence—the public existence—of, say, Frank Sinatra and Sammy Davis, Jr., proves to them that America is still the land of opportunity and that inequalities vanish before the determined will. It proves nothing of the sort. The determined will is rare—at the moment, in this country, it is unspeakably rare—and the inequalities suffered by the many are in no way justified by the rise of a few. A few have always risen—in every country, every era, and in the teeth of regimes which can by no stretch of the imagination be thought of as free. Not all of these people, it is worth remembering, left the world better than they found it. The determined will is rare, but it is not invariably benevolent. Furthermore, the American equation of success with the big time reveals an awful disrespect for human life and human achievement. This equation has placed our cities among the most dangerous in the world and has placed our youth among the most empty and most bewildered. The situation of our youth is not mysterious. Children have never been very good at listening to their elders, but they have never failed to imitate them. They must, they have no other models. That is exactly what our children are doing. They are imitating our immorality, our disrespect for the pain of others.

All other slum dwellers, when the bank account permits it, can move out of the slum and vanish altogether from the eye of persecution. No Negro in this country has ever made that much money and it will be a long time before any Negro does. The Negroes in Harlem, who have no money, spend what they have on such gimcracks as they are sold. These include "wider" TV screens, more "faithful" hi-fi sets, more "powerful" cars, all of which, of course, are obsolete long before they are paid for. Anyone who has ever struggled with poverty knows how extremely expensive it is to be poor; and if one is a member of a captive population, economically speaking, one's feet have simply been placed on the treadmill forever. One is victimized, economically, in a thousand ways—rent, for example, or car insurance. Go shopping one day in Harlem—for anything—and compare Harlem prices and quality with those downtown.

The people who have managed to get off this block have only got as far as a more respectable ghetto. This respectable ghetto does not even have the advantages of the disreputable one—friends, neighbors, a familiar church, and friendly tradesmen; and it is not, moreover, in the nature of any ghetto to remain respectable long. Every Sunday, people who have left the block take the lonely ride back, dragging their increasingly discontented children with them. They spend the day talking, not always with words, about the trouble they've seen and the trouble—one must watch their eyes as they watch their children—they are only too likely to see. For children do not like ghettos. It takes them nearly no time to discover exactly why they are there.

The projects in Harlem are hated. They are hated almost as much as policemen, and this is saying a great deal. And they are hated for the same reason: both reveal, unbearably, the real attitude of the white world, no matter how many liberal speeches are made, no matter how many lofty editorials are written, no matter how many civil-rights commissions are set up.

The projects are hideous, of course, there being a law, apparently respected throughout the world, that popular housing shall be as cheerless as a prison. They are lumped all over Harlem, colorless, bleak, high, and revolting. The wide windows look out on Harlem's invincible and indescribable squalor: the Park Avenue railroad tracks, around which, about forty years ago, the present dark community began; the unrehabilitated houses, bowed down, it would seem, under the great weight of frustration and bitterness they contain; the dark, the ominous schoolhouses from which the child may emerge maimed, blinded, hooked, or enraged for life; and the churches, churches, block upon block of churches, niched in the walls like cannon in the walls of a fortress. Even if the administration of the projects were not so insanely humiliating (for example: one must report raises in salary to the management, which will then eat up the profit by raising one's rent; the management has the right to know who is staying in your apartment; the management can ask you to leave, at their discretion), the projects would still be hated because they are an insult to the meanest intelligence.

Harlem got its first private project, Riverton *—which is now, naturally, a slum—about twelve years ago because at that time Negroes were not allowed to live in Stuyvesant Town. Harlem watched Riverton go up, therefore, in the most violent bitterness of spirit, and hated it long before the builders arrived. They began hating it at about the time people began moving out of their condemned houses to make room for this additional proof of how thoroughly the white world despised them. And they had scarcely moved in, naturally, before they began smashing windows, defacing walls, urinating in the elevators, and fornicating in the playgrounds. Liberals, both white and black, were appalled at the spectacle. I was appalled by the liberal innocence—or cynicism, which comes out in practice as much the same thing. Other people were delighted to be able to point to proof positive that nothing could be done to better the lot of the colored people. They were, and are, right in one respect: that nothing can be done as long as they are treated like colored people. The people in Harlem know they are living there because white people do not think they are good enough to live anywhere else. No amount of "improvement" can sweeten this fact. Whatever money is now being earmarked to improve this, or any other ghetto, might as well be burnt. A ghetto can be improved in one way only: out of existence.

Similarly, the only way to police a ghetto is to be oppressive. None of the Police Commissioner's men, even with the best will in the world, have any way of understanding the lives led by the people they swagger about in twos and threes controlling. Their very presence is an insult, and it would be, even if they spent their entire day feeding gumdrops to children. They represent the force of the white world, and that world's real inten-

---

* The inhabitants of Riverton were much embittered by this description; they have, apparently, forgotten how their project came into being; and have repeatedly informed me that I cannot possibly be referring to Riverton, but to another housing project which is directly across the street. It is quite clear, I think, that I have no interest in accusing any individuals or families of the depredations herein described: but neither can I deny the evidence of my own eyes. Nor do I blame anyone in Harlem for making the best of a dreadful bargain. But anyone who lives in Harlem and imagines that he has not struck this bargain, or that what he takes to be his status (in whose eyes?) protects him against the common pain, demoralization, and danger, is simply self-deluded.

tions are, simply, for that world's criminal profit and ease, to keep the black man corraled up here, in his place. The badge, the gun in the holster, and the swinging club make vivid what will happen should his rebellion become overt. Rare, indeed, is the Harlem citizen, from the most circumspect church member to the most shiftless adolescent, who does not have a long tale to tell of police incompetence, injustice, or brutality. I myself have witnessed and endured it more than once. The businessmen and racketeers also have a story. And so do the prostitutes. (And this is not, perhaps, the place to discuss Harlem's very complex attitude toward black policemen, nor the reasons, according to Harlem, that they are nearly all downtown.)

It is hard, on the other hand, to blame the policeman, blank, good-natured, thoughtless, and insuperably innocent, for being such a perfect representative of the people he serves. He, too, believes in good intentions and is astounded and offended when they are not taken for the deed. He has never, himself, done anything for which to be hated—which of us has? —and yet he is facing, daily and nightly, people who would gladly see him dead, and he knows it. There is no way for him not to know it: there are few things under heaven more unnerving than the silent, accumulating contempt and hatred of a people. He moves through Harlem, therefore, like an occupying soldier in a bitterly hostile country; which is precisely what, and where, he is, and is the reason he walks in twos and threes. And he is not the only one who knows why he is always in company: the people who are watching him know why, too. Any street meeting, sacred or secular, which he and his colleagues uneasily cover has as its explicit or implicit burden the cruelty and injustice of the white domination. And these days, of course, in terms increasingly vivid and jubilant, it speaks of the end of that domination. The white policeman standing on a Harlem street corner finds himself at the very center of the revolution now occurring in the world. He is not prepared for it—naturally, nobody is—and, what is possibly much more to the point, he is exposed, as few white people are, to the anguish of the black people around him. Even if he is gifted with the merest mustard grain of imagination, something must seep in. He cannot avoid observing that some of the children, in spite of their color, remind him of children he has known and loved, perhaps even of his own children. He knows that he certainly does not want *his* children living this way. He can retreat from his uneasiness in only one direction: into a callousness which very shortly becomes second nature. He becomes more callous, the population becomes more hostile, the situation grows more tense, and the police force is increased. One day, to everyone's astonishment, someone drops a match in the powder keg and everything blows up. Before the dust has settled or the blood congealed, editorials, speeches, and civil-rights commissions are loud in the land, demanding to know what happened. What happened is that Negroes want to be treated like men.

Negroes want to be treated like men: a perfectly straightforward statement, containing only seven words. People who have mastered Kant, Hegel, Shakespeare, Marx, Freud, and the Bible find this statement utterly impenetrable. The idea seems to threaten profound, barely conscious assumptions. A kind of panic paralyzes their features, as though they found themselves trapped on the edge of a steep place. I once tried to describe to a very well-known American intellectual the conditions among Negroes in the South. My recital disturbed him and made him indignant; and he asked me in perfect innocence, "Why don't all the Negroes in the South move North?" I tried to explain what *has* happened, unfailingly, whenever a significant body of Negroes move North. They do not escape Jim Crow: they merely encounter another, not-less-deadly variety. They do not move to Chicago, they move to the South Side; they do not move to New York, they move to Harlem. The pressure within the ghetto causes the ghetto walls to expand, and this expansion is always violent. White people hold the line as long as they can, and in as many ways as they can, from verbal intimidation to physical violence. But inevitably the border which has divided the ghetto from the rest of the world falls into the hands of the ghetto. The white people fall back bitterly before the black horde; the landlords make a tidy profit by raising the rent, chopping up the rooms, and all but dispensing with the upkeep; and what has once been a neighborhood turns into a "turf." This is precisely what happened when the Puerto Ricans arrived in their thousands—and the bitterness thus caused is, as I write, being fought out all up and down those streets.

Northerners indulge in an extremely dangerous luxury. They seem to feel that because they fought on the right side during the Civil War, and won, they have earned the right merely to deplore what is going on in the South, without taking any responsibility for it; and that they can ignore what is happening in Northern cities because what is happening in Little Rock or Birmingham is worse. Well, in the first place, it is not possible for anyone who has not endured both to know which is "worse." I know Negroes who prefer the South and white Southerners, because "At least there, you haven't got to play any guessing games!" The guessing games referred to have driven more than one Negro into the narcotics ward, the madhouse, or the river. I know another Negro, a man very dear to me, who says, with conviction and with truth, "The spirit of the South is the spirit of America." He was born in the North and did his military training in the South. He did not, as far as I can gather, find the South "worse"; he found it, if anything, all too familiar. In the second place, though, even if Birmingham *is* worse, no doubt Johannesburg, South Africa, beats it by several miles, and Buchenwald was one of the worst things that ever happened in the entire history of the world. The world has never lacked for horrifying examples; but I do not believe that these examples are meant to be used as justification for our own crimes. This perpetual justification empties the heart of all human feeling. The emptier our hearts become, the greater will be our crimes. Thirdly, the South is not merely an embarrassingly backward region, but a part of this country, and what happens there concerns every one of us.

As far as the color problem is concerned, there is but one great difference between the Southern white and the Northerner: the Southerner remembers, historically and in his own psyche, a kind of Eden in which he loved black people and they loved him. Historically, the flaming sword laid across this Eden is the Civil War. Personally, it is the Southerner's sexual coming of age, when, without any warning, unbreakable taboos are set up between himself and his past. Everything, thereafter, is permitted him except the love he remembers and has never ceased to need. The resulting, indescribable torment affects every Southern mind and is the basis of the Southern hysteria.

None of this is true for the Northerner. Negroes represent nothing to him personally, except, perhaps, the dangers of carnality. He never sees Negroes. Southerners see them all the time. Northerners never think about them whereas Southerners are never really thinking of anything else. Negroes are, therefore, ignored in the North and are under surveillance in the South, and suffer hideously in both places. Neither the Southerner nor the Northerner is able to look on the Negro simply as a man. It seems to be indispensable to the national self-esteem that the Negro be considered either as a kind of ward (in which case we are told how many Negroes, comparatively, bought Cadillacs last year and how few, comparatively, were lynched), or as a victim (in which case we are promised that he will never vote in our assemblies or go to school with our kids). They are two sides of the same coin and the South will not change—*cannot* change—

until the North changes. The country will not change until it reexamines itself and discovers what it really means by freedom. In the meantime, generations keep being born, bitterness is increased by incompetence, pride, and folly, and the world shrinks around us.

It is a terrible, an inexorable, law that one cannot deny the humanity of another without diminishing one's own: in the face of one's victim, one sees oneself. Walk through the streets of Harlem and see what we, this nation, have become.

QUESTIONS AND TOPICS

1. Baldwin seems to feel sympathetic to the young people on his block who give way to despair. Why?
2. Try to imagine yourself living on upper Fifth Avenue. In what ways would you be a different person?
3. Baldwin considers the black man's dilemma to be racial in origin—a denial of love by white people. Others consider it to be a class problem. What do you think is the major cause?
4. Do black people, as Baldwin tells us, suffer more than other poor people from "the insults, the indifference, and the cruelty they are certain to encounter in their working day"?
5. "Whatever money is now being earmarked to improve this, or any other ghetto, might as well be burnt. A ghetto can be improved in one way only: out of existence." Do you agree? Do you feel that the Negro has any justification for defacing public housing?
6. Do you think the black man ought to understand that "the world has never lacked for horrifying examples" and therefore be patient?
7. Baldwin feels that American treatment of the black is a public crime. He cites Buchenwald (a Nazi concentration camp) and Johannesburg, South Africa, as relevant parallels to the Harlem ghetto. Do you agree?

Flannery O'Connor

EVERYTHING
THAT RISES
MUST CONVERGE

*In this story Flannery O'Connor,
1925–1964, has created a moving
tale of the dilemma of the present-
day South. Though the story is
about a mother and her son, it is
also about Southern traditionalism,
which involves definite ideas about
the place of the black man in the
social structure. But this is a story
which does not allow for simple
moral judgments.*

Her doctor had told Julian's mother that she must lose twenty pounds
on account of her blood pressure, so on Wednesday nights Julian had to
take her downtown on the bus for a reducing class at the Y. The reducing
class was designed for working girls over fifty, who weighed from 165 to
200 pounds. His mother was one of the slimmer ones, but she said ladies
did not tell their age or weight. She would not ride the buses by herself at
night since they had been integrated, and because the reducing class was
one of her few pleasures, necessary for her health, and *free,* she said Julian
could at least put himself out to take her, considering all she did for him.
Julian did not like to consider all she did for him, but every Wednesday
night he braced himself and took her.

She was almost ready to go, standing before the hall mirror, putting
on her hat, while he, his hands behind him, appeared pinned to the door
frame, waiting like Saint Sebastian for the arrows to begin piercing him.
The hat was new and had cost her seven dollars and a half. She kept
saying, "Maybe I shouldn't have paid that for it. No, I shouldn't have.
I'll take it off and return it tomorrow. I shouldn't have bought it."

Julian raised his eyes to heaven. "Yes, you should have bought it," he said. "Put it on and let's go." It was a hideous hat. A purple velvet flap came down on one side of it and stood up on the other; the rest of it was green and looked like a cushion with the stuffing out. He decided it was less comical than jaunty and pathetic. Everything that gave her pleasure was small and depressed him.

She lifted the hat one more time and set it down slowly on top of her head. Two wings of gray hair protruded on either side of her florid face, but her eyes, sky-blue, were as innocent and untouched by experience as they must have been when she was ten. Were it not that she was a widow who had struggled fiercely to feed and clothe and put him through school and who was supporting him still, "until he got on his feet," she might have been a little girl that he had to take to town.

"It's all right, it's all right," he said. "Let's go." He opened the door himself and started down the walk to get her going. The sky was a dying violet and the houses stood out darkly against it, bulbous liver-colored monstrosities of a uniform ugliness though no two were alike. Since this had been a fashionable neighborhood forty years ago, his mother persisted in thinking they did well to have an apartment in it. Each house had a narrow collar of dirt around it in which sat, usually, a grubby child. Julian walked with his hands in his pockets, his head down and thrust forward and his eyes glazed with the determination to make himself completely numb during the time he would be sacrificed to her pleasure.

The door closed and he turned to find the dumpy figure, surmounted by the atrocious hat, coming toward him. "Well," she said, "you only live once and paying a little more for it, I at least won't meet myself coming and going."

"Some day I'll start making money," Julian said gloomily—he knew he never would—"and you can have one of those jokes whenever you take the fit." But first they would move. He visualized a place where the nearest neighbors would be three miles away on either side.

"I think you're doing fine," she said, drawing on her gloves. "You've only been out of school a year. Rome wasn't built in a day."

She was one of the few members of the Y reducing class who arrived in hat and gloves and who had a son who had been to college. "It takes time," she said, "and the world is in such a mess. This hat looked better on me than any of the others, though when she brought it out I said, 'Take that thing back. I wouldn't have it on my head,' and she said, 'Now wait till you see it on,' and when she put it on me, I said, 'We-ull,' and she said, 'If you ask me, that hat does something for you and you do something for the hat, and besides,' she said, 'with that hat, you won't meet yourself coming and going.'"

Julian thought he could have stood his lot better if she had been selfish, if she had been an old hag who drank and screamed at him. He walked along, saturated in depression, as if in the midst of his martyrdom he had lost his faith. Catching sight of his long, hopeless, irritated face, she stopped suddenly with a grief-stricken look, and pulled back on his arm. "Wait on me," she said. "I'm going back to the house and take this thing off and tomorrow I'm going to return it. I was out of my head. I can pay the gas bill with that seven-fifty."

He caught her arm in a vicious grip. "You are not going to take it back," he said. "I like it."

"Well," she said, "I don't think I ought . . ."

"Shut up and enjoy it," he muttered, more depressed than ever.

"With the world in the mess it's in," she said, "it's a wonder we can enjoy anything. I tell you, the bottom rail is on the top."

Julian sighed.

"Of course," she said, "if you know who you are, you can go anywhere." She said this every time he took her to the reducing class. "Most of them in it are not our kind of people," she said, "but I can be gracious to anybody. I know who I am."

"They don't give a damn for your graciousness," Julian said savagely. "Knowing who you are is good for one generation only. You haven't the foggiest idea where you stand now or who you are."

She stopped and allowed her eyes to flash at him. "I most certainly do know who I am," she said, "and if you don't know who you are, I'm ashamed of you."

"Oh hell," Julian said.

"Your great-grandfather was a former governor of this state," she said. "Your grandfather was a prosperous landowner. Your grandmother was a Godhigh."

"Will you look around you," he said tensely, "and see where you are now?" and he swept his arm jerkily out to indicate the neighborhood, which the growing darkness at least made less dingy.

"You remain what you are," she said. "Your great-grandfather had a plantation and two hundred slaves."

"There are no more slaves," he said irritably.

"They were better off when they were," she said. He groaned to see that she was off on that topic. She rolled onto it every few days like a train on an open track. He knew every stop, every junction, every swamp along the way, and knew the exact point at which her conclusion would roll majestically into the station: "It's ridiculous. It's simply not realistic. They should rise, yes, but on their own side of the fence."

"Let's skip it," Julian said.

"The ones I feel sorry for," she said, "are the ones that are half white. They're tragic."

"Will you skip it?"

"Suppose we were half white. We would certainly have mixed feelings."

"I have mixed feelings now," he groaned.

"Well let's talk about something pleasant," she said. "I remember going to Grandpa's when I was a little girl. Then the house had double stairways that went up to what was really the second floor—all the cooking was done on the first. I used to like to stay down in the kitchen on account of the way the walls smelled. I would sit with my nose pressed against the plaster and take deep breaths. Actually the place belonged to the Godhighs but your grandfather Chestny paid the mortgage and saved it for them. They were in reduced circumstances," she said, "but reduced or not, they never forgot who they were."

"Doubtless that decayed mansion reminded them," Julian muttered. He never spoke of it without contempt or thought of it without longing. He had seen it once when he was a child before it had been sold. The double stairways had rotted and been torn down. Negroes were living in it. But it remained in his mind as his mother had known it. It appeared in his dreams regularly. He would stand on the wide porch, listening to the rustle of oak leaves, then wander through the high-ceilinged hall into the parlor that opened onto it and gaze at the worn rugs and faded draperies. It occurred to him that it was he, not she, who could have appreciated it. He preferred its threadbare elegance to anything he could name and it was because of it that all the neighborhoods they had lived in had been a torment to him—whereas she had hardly known the difference. She called her insensitivity "being adjustable."

"And I remember the old darky who was my nurse, Caroline. There was no better person in the world. I've always had a great respect for my colored friends," she said. "I'd do anything in the world for them and they'd . . ."

"Will you for God's sake get off that subject?" Julian said. When he got on a bus by himself, he made it a point to sit down beside a Negro, in reparation as it were for his mother's sins.

"You're mighty touchy tonight," she said. "Do you feel all right?"

"Yes I feel all right," he said. "Now lay off."

She pursed her lips. "Well, you certainly are in a vile humor," she observed. "I just won't speak to you at all."

They had reached the bus stop. There was no bus in sight and Julian, his hands still jammed in his pockets and his head thrust forward, scowled down the empty street. The frustration of having to wait on the bus as well as ride on it began to creep up his neck like a hot hand. The presence of his mother was borne in upon him as she gave a pained sigh. He looked at her bleakly. She was holding herself very erect under the preposterous hat, wearing it like a banner of her imaginary dignity. There was in him an evil urge to break her spirit. He suddenly unloosened his tie and pulled it off and put it in his pocket.

She stiffened. "Why must you look like *that* when you take me to town?" she said. "Why must you deliberately embarrass me?"

"If you'll never learn where you are," he said, "you can at least learn where I am."

"You look like a—thug," she said.

"Then I must be one," he murmured.

"I'll just go home," she said. "I will not bother you. If you can't do a little thing like that for me . . ."

Rolling his eyes upward, he put his tie back on. "Restored to my class," he muttered. He thrust his face toward her and hissed, "True culture is in the mind, the *mind*," he said, and tapped his head, "the mind."

"It's in the heart," she said, "and in how you do things and how you do things is because of who you *are*."

"Nobody in the damn bus cares who you are."

"I care who I am," she said icily.

The lighted bus appeared on top of the next hill and as it approached, they moved out into the street to meet it. He put his hand under her elbow and hoisted her up on the creaking step. She entered with a little smile, as if she were going into a drawing room where everyone had been waiting for her. While he put in the tokens, she sat down on one of the broad front seats for three which faced the aisle. A thin woman with protruding teeth and long yellow hair was sitting on the end of it. His mother moved up beside her and left room for Julian beside herself. He sat down and looked at the floor across the aisle where a pair of thin feet in red and white canvas sandals were planted.

His mother immediately began a general conversation meant to attract anyone who felt like talking. "Can it get any hotter?" she said and removed from her purse a folding·fan, black with a Japanese scene on it, which she began to flutter before her.

"I reckon it might could," the woman with the protruding teeth said, "but I know for a fact my apartment couldn't get no hotter."

"It must get the afternoon sun," his mother said. She sat forward and looked up and down the bus. It was half filled. Everybody was white. "I see we have the bus to ourselves," she said. Julian cringed.

"For a change," said the woman across the aisle, the owner of the red and white canvas sandals. "I come on one the other day and they were thick as fleas—up front and all through."

"The world is in a mess everywhere," his mother said. "I don't know how we've let it get in this fix."

"What gets my goat is all those boys from good families stealing automobile tires," the woman with the protruding teeth said. "I told my boy, I said you may not be rich but you been raised right and if I ever catch you in any such mess, they can send you on to the reformatory. Be exactly where you belong."

"Training tells," his mother said. "Is your boy in high school?"

"Ninth grade," the woman said.

"My son just finished college last year. He wants to write but he's selling typewriters until he gets started," his mother said.

The woman leaned forward and peered at Julian. He threw her such a malevolent look that she subsided against the seat. On the floor across the aisle there was an abandoned newspaper. He got up and got it and opened it out in front of him. His mother discreetly continued the conversation in a lower tone but the woman across the aisle said in a loud voice, "Well that's nice. Selling typewriters is close to writing. He can go right from one to the other."

"I tell him," his mother said, "that Rome wasn't built in a day."

Behind the newspaper Julian was withdrawing into the inner compartment of his mind where he spent most of his time. This was a kind of mental bubble in which he established himself when he could not bear to be a part of what was going on around him. From it he could see out and judge but in it he was safe from any kind of penetration from without. It was the only place where he felt free of the general idiocy of his fellows. His mother had never entered it but from it he could see her with absolute clarity.

The old lady was clever enough and he thought that if she had started from any of the right premises, more might have been expected of her. She lived according to the laws of her own fantasy world, outside of which he had never seen her set foot. The law of it was to sacrifice herself for him after she had first created the necessity to do so by making a mess of things. If he had permitted her sacrifices, it was only because her lack of foresight had made them necessary. All of her life had been a struggle to act like a Chestny without the Chestny goods, and to give him everything she thought a Chestny ought to have; but since, said she, it was fun to struggle, why complain? And when you had won, as she had won, what fun to look back on the hard times! He could not forgive her that she had enjoyed the struggle and that she thought *she* had won.

What she meant when she said she had won was that she had brought him up successfully and had sent him to college and that he had turned out so well—good looking (her teeth had gone unfilled so that his could be straightened), intelligent (he realized he was too intelligent to be a success), and with a future ahead of him (there was of course no future ahead of him). She excused his gloominess on the grounds that he was still growing up and his radical ideas on his lack of practical experience. She said he didn't yet know a thing about "life," that he hadn't even entered the real world—when already he was as disenchanted with it as a man of fifty.

The further irony of all this was that in spite of her, he had turned out so well. In spite of going to only a third-rate college, he had, on his own initiative, come out with a first-rate education; in spite of growing up dominated by a small mind, he had ended up with a large one; in spite of all her foolish views, he was free of prejudice and unafraid to face facts. Most miraculous of all, instead of being blinded by love for her as she was for him, he had cut himself emotionally free of her and could see her with complete objectivity. He was not dominated by his mother.

The bus stopped with a sudden jerk and shook him from his meditation. A woman from the back lurched forward with little steps and barely escaped falling in his newspaper as she righted herself. She got off and a large Negro got on. Julian kept his paper lowered to watch. It gave him a certain satisfaction to see injustice in daily operation. It confirmed his view that with a few exceptions there was no one worth knowing within a radius of three hundred miles. The Negro was well dressed and carried a briefcase. He looked around and then sat down on the other end of the seat where the woman with the red and white canvas sandals was sitting. He immediately unfolded a newspaper and obscured himself behind it. Julian's mother's elbow at once prodded insistently into his ribs. "Now you see why I won't ride on these buses by myself," she whispered.

The woman with the red and white canvas sandals had risen at the same time the Negro sat down and had gone further back in the bus and taken the seat of the woman who had got off. His mother leaned forward and cast her an approving look.

Julian rose, crossed the aisle, and sat down in the place of the woman with the canvas sandals. From this position, he looked serenely across at his mother. Her face had turned an angry red. He stared at her, making his eyes the eyes of a stranger. He felt his tension suddenly lift as if he had openly declared war on her.

He would have liked to get in conversation with the Negro and to talk with him about art or politics or any subject that would be above the comprehension of those around them, but the man remained entrenched behind his paper. He was either ignoring the change of seating or had never noticed it. There was no way for Julian to convey his sympathy.

His mother kept her eyes fixed reproachfully on his face. The woman with the protruding teeth was looking at him avidly as if he were a type of monster new to her.

"Do you have a light?" he asked the Negro.

Without looking away from his paper, the man reached in his pocket and handed him a packet of matches.

"Thanks," Julian said. For a moment he held the matches foolishly. A NO SMOKING sign looked down upon him from over the door. This alone would not have deterred him; he had no cigarettes. He had quit smoking some months before because he could not afford it. "Sorry," he muttered and handed back the matches. The Negro lowered the paper and gave him an annoyed look. He took the matches and raised the paper again.

His mother continued to gaze at him but she did not take advantage of his momentary discomfort. Her eyes retained their battered look. Her face seemed to be unnaturally red, as if her blood pressure had risen. Julian allowed no glimmer of sympathy to show on his face. Having got the advantage, he wanted desperately to keep it and carry it through. He would have liked to teach her a lesson that would last her a while, but there seemed no way to continue the point. The Negro refused to come out from behind his paper.

Julian folded his arms and looked stolidly before him, facing her but as if he did not see her, as if he had ceased to recognize her existence. He visualized a scene in which, the bus having reached their stop, he would remain in his seat and when she said, "Aren't you going to get off?" he would look at her as at a stranger who had rashly addressed him. The corner they got off on was usually deserted, but it was well lighted and it would not hurt her to walk by herself the four blocks to the Y. He decided to wait until the time came and then decide whether or not he would let her get off by herself. He would have to be at the Y at ten to bring her back, but he could leave her wondering if he was going to show up. There was no reason for her to think she could always depend on him.

He retired again into the high-ceilinged room sparsely settled with large pieces of antique furniture. His soul expanded momentarily but then he became aware of his mother across from him and the vision shriveled. He studied her coldly. Her feet in little pumps dangled like a child's and did not quite reach the floor. She was training on him an exaggerated look of reproach. He felt completely detached from her. At that moment he could with pleasure have slapped her as he would have slapped a particularly obnoxious child in his charge.

He began to imagine various unlikely ways by which he could teach her a lesson. He might make friends with some distinguished Negro professor or lawyer and bring him home to spend the evening. He would be entirely justified but her blood pressure would rise to 300. He could not push her to the extent of making her have a stroke, and moreover, he had never been successful at making any Negro friends. He had tried to strike up an acquaintance on the bus with some of the better types, with ones that looked like professors or ministers or lawyers. One morning he had sat down next to a distinguished-looking dark brown man who had answered his questions with a sonorous solemnity but who had turned out to be an undertaker. Another day he had sat down beside a cigar-smoking Negro with a diamond ring on his finger, but after a few stilted pleasantries, the Negro had rung the buzzer and risen, slipping two lottery tickets into Julian's hand as he climbed over him to leave.

He imagined his mother lying desperately ill and his being able to secure only a Negro doctor for her. He toyed with that idea for a few minutes and then dropped it for a momentary vision of himself participating as a sympathizer in a sit-in demonstration. This was possible but he did not linger with it. Instead, he approached the ultimate horror. He brought home a beautiful suspiciously Negroid woman. Prepare yourself, he said. There is nothing you can do about it. This is the woman I've chosen. She's intelligent, dignified, even good, and she's suffered and she hasn't thought it *fun*. Now persecute us, go ahead and persecute us. Drive her out of here, but remember, you're driving me too. His eyes were narrowed and through the indignation he had generated, he saw his mother across the aisle, purple-faced, shrunken to the dwarf-like proportions of her moral nature, sitting like a mummy beneath the ridiculous banner of her hat.

He was tilted out of his fantasy again as the bus stopped. The door opened with a sucking hiss and out of the dark a large, gaily dressed, sullen-looking colored woman got on with a little boy. The child, who might have been four, had on a short plaid suit and a Tyrolean hat with a blue feather in it. Julian hoped that he would sit down beside him and that the woman would push in beside his mother. He could think of no better arrangement.

As she waited for her tokens, the woman was surveying the seating possibilities—he hoped with the idea of sitting where she was least wanted. There was something familiar-looking about her but Julian could not place what it was. She was a giant of a woman. Her face was set not only to meet opposition but to seek it out. The downward tilt of her large lower lip was like a warning sign: DON'T TAMPER WITH ME. Her bulging figure was encased in a green crepe dress and her feet overflowed in red shoes. She had on a hideous hat. A purple velvet flap came down on one side of it and stood up on the other; the rest of it was green and looked like a cushion with the stuffing out. She carried a mammoth red pocketbook that bulged throughout as if it were stuffed with rocks.

To Julian's disappointment, the little boy climbed up on the empty seat beside his mother. His mother lumped all children, black and white, into the common category, "cute," and she thought little Negroes were on the whole cuter than little white children. She smiled at the little boy as he climbed on the seat.

Meanwhile the woman was bearing down upon the empty seat beside Julian. To his annoyance, she squeezed herself into it. He saw his mother's face change as the woman settled herself next to him and he realized with satisfaction that this was more objectionable to her than it was to him. Her face seemed almost gray and there was a look of dull recognition in her eyes, as if suddenly she had sickened at some awful confrontation. Julian saw that it was because she and the woman had, in a sense, swapped sons. Though his mother would not realize the symbolic significance of this, she would feel it. His amusement showed plainly on his face.

The woman next to him muttered something unintelligible to herself. He was conscious of a kind of bristling next to him, a muted growling like that of an angry cat. He could not see anything but the red pocketbook upright on the bulging green thighs. He visualized the woman as she had stood waiting for her tokens—the ponderous figure, rising from the red shoes upward over the solid hips, the mammoth bosom, the haughty face, to the green and purple hat.

His eyes widened.

The vision of the two hats, identical, broke upon him with the radiance of a brilliant sunrise. His face was suddenly lit with joy. He could not believe that Fate had thrust upon his mother such a lesson. He gave a loud chuckle so that she would look at him and see that he saw. She turned her eyes on him slowly. The blue in them seemed to have turned a bruised purple. For a moment he had an uncomfortable sense of her innocence, but it lasted only a second before principle rescued him. Justice entitled him to laugh. His grin hardened until it said to her as plainly as if he were saying aloud: Your punishment exactly fits your pettiness. This should teach you a permanent lesson.

Her eyes shifted to the woman. She seemed unable to bear looking at him and to find the woman preferable. He became conscious again of the bristling presence at his side. The woman was rumbling like a volcano about to become active. His mother's mouth began to twitch slightly at one corner. With a sinking heart, he saw incipient signs of recovery on her face and realized that this was going to strike her suddenly as funny and was going to be no lesson at all. She kept her eyes on the woman and an amused smile came over her face as if the woman were a monkey that had stolen her hat. The little Negro was looking up at her with large fascinated eyes. He had been trying to attract her attention for some time.

"Carver!" the woman said suddenly. "Come heah!"

When he saw that the spotlight was on him at last, Carver drew his feet up and turned himself toward Julian's mother and giggled.

"Carver!" the woman said. "You heah me? Come heah!"

Carver slid down from the seat but remained squatting with his back against the base of it, his head turned slyly around toward Julian's mother, who was smiling at him. The woman reached a hand across the aisle and snatched him to her. He righted himself and hung backwards on her knees, grinning at Julian's mother. "Isn't he cute?" Julian's mother said to the woman with the protruding teeth.

"I reckon he is," the woman said without conviction.

The Negress yanked him upright but he eased out of her grip and shot across the aisle and scrambled, giggling wildly, onto the seat beside his love.

"I think he likes me," Julian's mother said, and smiled at the woman. It was the smile she used when she was being particularly gracious to an inferior. Julian saw everything lost. The lesson had rolled off her like rain on a roof.

The woman stood up and yanked the little boy off the seat as if she were snatching him from contagion. Julian could feel the rage in her at having no weapon like his mother's smile. She gave the child a sharp slap across his leg. He howled once and then thrust his head into her stomach and kicked his feet against her shins. "Be-have," she said vehemently.

The bus stopped and the Negro who had been reading the newspaper got off. The woman moved over and set the little boy down with a thump between herself and Julian. She held him firmly by the knee. In a moment he put his hands in front of his face and peeped at Julian's mother through his fingers.

"I see yoooooooo!" she said and put her hand in front of her face and peeped at him.

The woman slapped his hand down. "Quit yo' foolishness," she said, "before I knock the living Jesus out of you!"

Julian was thankful that the next stop was theirs. He reached up and pulled the cord. The woman reached up and pulled it at the same time. Oh my God, he thought. He had the terrible intuition that when they got off the bus together, his mother would open her purse and give the little boy a nickel. The gesture would be as natural to her as breathing. The bus stopped and the woman got up and lunged to the front, dragging the child, who wished to stay on, after her. Julian and his mother got up and followed. As they neared the door, Julian tried to relieve her of her pocketbook.

"No," she murmured, "I want to give the little boy a nickel."

"No!" Julian hissed. "No!"

She smiled down at the child and opened her bag. The bus door opened and the woman picked him up by the arm and descended with him, hanging at her hip. Once in the street she set him down and shook him.

Julian's mother had to close her purse while she got down the bus step but as soon as her feet were on the ground, she opened it again and began to rummage inside. "I can't find but a penny," she whispered, "but it looks like a new one."

"Don't do it!" Julian said fiercely between his teeth. There was a street-light on the corner and she hurried to get under it so that she could better see into her pocketbook. The woman was heading off rapidly down the street with the child still hanging backward on her hand.

"Oh little boy!" Julian's mother called and took a few quick steps and caught up with them just beyond the lamppost. "Here's a bright new penny for you," and she held out the coin, which shone bronze in the dim light.

The huge woman turned and for a moment stood, her shoulders lifted and her face frozen with frustrated rage, and stared at Julian's mother. Then all at once she seemed to explode like a piece of machinery that had been given one ounce of pressure too much. Julian saw the black fist swing out with the red pocketbook. He shut his eyes and cringed as he heard the woman shout, "He don't take nobody's pennies!" When he opened his eyes, the woman was disappearing down the street with the little boy staring wide-eyed over her shoulder. Julian's mother was sitting on the sidewalk.

"I told you not to do that," Julian said angrily. "I told you not to do that!"

He stood over her for a minute, gritting his teeth. Her legs were stretched out in front of her and her hat was on her lap. He squatted down and looked her in the face. It was totally expressionless. "You got exactly what you deserved," he said. "Now get up."

He picked up her pocketbook and put what had fallen out back in it. He picked the hat up off her lap. The penny caught his eye on the side-walk and he picked that up and let it drop before her eyes into the purse. Then he stood up and leaned over and held his hands out to pull her up. She remained immobile. He sighed. Rising above them on either side were black apartment buildings, marked with irregular rectangles of light.

At the end of the block a man came out of a door and walked off in the opposite direction. "All right," he said, "suppose somebody happens by and wants to know why you're sitting on the sidewalk?"

She took the hand and, breathing hard, pulled heavily up on it and then stood for a moment, swaying slightly as if the spots of light in the darkness were circling around her. Her eyes, shadowed and confused, finally settled on his face. He did not try to conceal his irritation. "I hope this teaches you a lesson," he said. She leaned forward and her eyes raked his face. She seemed trying to determine his identity. Then, as if she found nothing familiar about him, she started off with a headlong movement in the wrong direction.

"Aren't you going on to the Y?" he asked.

"Home," she muttered.

"Well, are we walking?"

For answer she kept going. Julian followed along, his hands behind him. He saw no reason to let the lesson she had had go without backing it up with an explanation of its meaning. She might as well be made to understand what had happened to her. "Don't think that was just an uppity Negro woman," he said. "That was the whole colored race which will no longer take your condescending pennies. That was your black double. She can wear the same hat as you, and to be sure," he added gratuitously (because he thought it was funny), "it looked better on her than it did on you. What all this means," he said, "is that the old world is gone. The old manners are obsolete and your graciousness is not worth a damn." He thought bitterly of the house that had been lost for him. "You aren't who you think you are," he said.

She continued to plow ahead, paying no attention to him. Her hair had come undone on one side. She dropped her pocketbook and took no notice. He stooped and picked it up and handed it to her but she did not take it.

"You needn't act as if the world had come to an end," he said, "because it hasn't. From now on you've got to live in a new world and face a few realities for a change. Buck up," he said, "it won't kill you."

She was breathing fast.

"Let's wait on the bus," he said.

"Home," she said thickly.

"I hate to see you behave like this," he said. "Just like a child. I should be able to expect more of you." He decided to stop where he was and make her stop and wait for a bus. "I'm not going any farther," he said, stopping. "We're going on the bus."

She continued to go on as if she had not heard him. He took a few steps and caught her arm and stopped her. He looked into her face and caught his breath. He was looking into a face he had never seen before. "Tell Grandpa to come get me," she said.

He stared, stricken.

"Tell Caroline to come get me," she said.

Stunned, he let her go and she lurched forward again, walking as if one leg were shorter than the other. A tide of darkness seemed to be sweeping her from him. "Mother!" he cried. "Darling, sweetheart, wait!" Crumpling, she fell to the pavement. He dashed forward and fell at her side, crying, "Mamma, Mamma!" He turned her over. Her face was fiercely distorted. One eye, large and staring, moved slightly to the left as if it had become unmoored. The other remained fixed on him, raked his face again, found nothing and closed.

"Wait here, wait here!" he cried and jumped up and began to run for help toward a cluster of lights he saw in the distance ahead of him. "Help, help!" he shouted, but his voice was thin, scarcely a thread of sound. The lights drifted farther away the faster he ran and his feet moved numbly as if they carried him nowhere. The tide of darkness seemed to sweep him back to her, postponing from moment to moment his entry into the world of guilt and sorrow.

QUESTIONS AND TOPICS

1. Write character sketches of Julian and his mother. Tell about each character's attitude toward Southern traditionalism.
2. What is the significance of the gift of the penny?
3. Which character, if any, does Flannery O'Connor favor?
4. Does the story have a definite theme? Is Flannery O'Connor saying something about the entire situation of the South today?
5. Compare Flannery O'Connor's view of the Negro to James Baldwin's. What influence, if any, do you think their different upbringings and allegiances had in forming their views?

Herbert Gold

THE AGE
OF HAPPY
PROBLEMS

Herbert Gold, 1924–, is a contem-
porary novelist and short story
writer who is particularly concerned
with the daily life of today's upper-
middle class. In this essay he ana-
lyzes the hopes and frustrations of
young professionals who have be-
gun to establish homes and careers.

Recently I have had occasion to live again near my old college campus.
I went into a hole-in-the-wall bakery where the proprietor recognized me
after ten years. "You haven't changed a bit, son," he said, "but can you
still digest my pumpernickel? The stomach gets older, no? Maybe you
want something softer now—a nice little loaf I got here."

He had worn slightly. But for me the change was from twenty-two to
thirty-two, and it is this ten-year time that I want to think about—the
generation which came back from the war to finish college on the GI Bill
and is now deep into its career. We are the generation which knew the
Depression only through the exhilaration of the burgeoning New Deal
and the stunned passion of war. I remember the bank crash because my
mother wept and I said, "If we're poor now, can I wear corduroy
pants?" For the most part, we were taken care of and never hopelessly
hunted jobs. Now some of us say we are cool, say we are beat; but most
of us are allrightniks—doing okay. We are successful. In the late forties
and the fifties, it was hard to know economic struggle and want—and for
the most part we didn't experience these traditional elements of youth—
and it was hard for the skilled and the trained not to know success. We
did not doubt overmuch. We have done well. How well?

"Money money money," as Theodore Roethke says.

I have married my hands to perpetual agitation,
I run, I run to the whistle of money.

Money money money
Water water water

I should like to take a look at some of the college idealists. The lawyer, fascinated by "the philosophy of law," now uses his study to put a smooth surface on his cleverness. Cardozo and Holmes? Very interesting, but let's find that loophole. The doctor who sent flowers to the first mother whose baby he delivered now specializes in "real-estate medicine"—his practice gives him capital for buying apartment houses. The architect who sat up all night haranguing his friends about Lewis Mumford and Frank Lloyd Wright now works for a mass builder who uses bulldozers to level trees and slopes, then puts up tri-level, semi-detached, twenty-year mortgaged, fundamentally identical dormitories for commuters. He admits that his designs make no decent sense, but they do have that trivial, all-important meaning: "It's what the market wants, man. You'd rather I taught city planning for six thousand a year?"

The actor becomes a disk jockey, the composer an arranger, the painter a designer; the writer does TV scripts in that new classic formula, "happy stories about happy people with happy problems." How hard it is to be used at our best! One of the moral issues of every age has been that of finding a way for men and women to test, reach, and overreach their best energies. Society has always worked to level us. Socrates has always made it hot for the citizens in the market place. But there was usually room for the heroic—hemlock not a serious deterrent—and perhaps rarely so much room on all levels as in the frontier turbulence of the nineteenth and early twentieth century in America. Hands reached out like the squirming, grasping, struggling railroad networks; the open society existed; freedom had a desperate allure for the strongly ambitious, and men stepped up to take their chances—Abraham Lincoln and William James, Mark Twain and Melville, Edison and Rockefeller and Bet-a-Million Gates.

Allowing for a glitter of nostalgia on what we imagine about the past, still something has happened to change the old, movemented, free, open American society to something persuasive, plausible, comfortable, and much less open. We are prosperous, we get what we think we want, we have a relatively stable economy without totalitarian rule. "I'm not selling out," my friend the architect says, "I'm buying in." Without attempting a simple explanation of the causes of this age of happy problems, let us look at its consequences for the new post-war young people who should be in full action toward their ambitions and the surest, sturdiest signs of a civilization's health.

What are these personal symptoms? How is the vital individual human creature doing in his staff meetings, at his family's table, over the baby's bassinet, and with that distant secret self that he may sometimes meet at the water cooler? Well, for this man it is very hard to be exceptional. Talent apart, he has too much to do, too much on his mind, to give himself over to his best energies. Think, for example, of the writers in the advertising agencies, on TV, or in the colleges. They all wanted to write great books; they tend now to prefer "competence" as an ideal to greatness. Some of them are trying, but they risk the situation of the girl in the short-story writing class: "I can't be a creative writer, I can't, because I'm still a stupid virgin." She will take up going steady, she will take up marriage; she will be mildly disappointed; she will remain as she was, but aging—"adjusted," "integrated," virgin to danger, struggle, and the main chance of love and work.

In composite, in our thirties, we of this prosperous and successful generation are still in good health and rather fast at tennis (but practicing place shots which will eliminate the need to rush the net); hair receding but still attractive to college girls, or at least recent graduates; a slight heaviness at the middle which makes us fit our jackets with especial care (sullen jowls beginning, too) or, if not that, a skinniness of anxiety (etching around the mouth, dryness of lips). We go to an athletic club. We play handball in heavy shirts "to sweat it off."

The girls we marry are beautiful in wondrous ways. Savant make-up is no longer sufficient. Blemishes are scraped until the skin is pink and new; scars are grown away by cortisone injections—what reason to be marked in this world?; noses are remade, the same for mother and daughter, just like heredity. Money is spent much more gracefully than in those fantastic times when silver coins were put in ears and jewels in navels.

The old truth—"we must all come from someplace"—is amended in 1956. We can create ourselves in our own image. And what is our own image? The buttery face in the Pond's advertisement, the epicene face in the Marlboro publicity.

The matters that we are told to worry about—and perhaps we think we worry about them—do not really trouble us. The prospect of war is like a vague headache, no worse. The memory of war is even dimmer. A depression is something which will reduce the value of our shares in the mutual fund, make us keep the old car another year. Radioactive fallout and the slow destruction of the human species through cancerous mutation—well, what is so much bother to imagine cannot really come to pass. Who lets the newspaper interfere with a good meal?

II

Still, we are not blithe spirits; birds we are not. This generation is particularly distinguished by its worry about making its wives happy, about doing right by its kids (title of a hugely popular paper-bound book: *How to Play with Your Child*), about acquiring enough leisure and symbols of leisure, which it hopes to cash in for moral comfort. *Fortune* reports a method used by salesmen to get the second room air conditioner to the couple which already has one in its bedroom. "The machine operates as expected? Fine! You sleep better with it? So do I, that's just dandy. But, friends, let me tell you how I sleep so much better now that I know my kiddies are cool and comfy, too."

This capitalizes on the child-oriented anxiety which the class known commercially as Young Marrieds has been taught to feel by modern psychiatry. Advertisements for *McCall's*, "The Magazine of Togetherness," demonstrate Togetherness in a brilliant summer scene. The man, wearing a white shirtlike apron and a proud simper, is bending to serve a steak to his wife (summer frock, spike heels), who will season it for them and for their happy gamboling children. The little boy and girl are peeking and smiling. The wife is lying in a garden chair. Togetherness consists in the husband's delighting his wife and kids by doing the cooking.

Actually, of course, most American women don't want to go this far. They are already equal with men. Women are usually too wise to define "equal" as "better than." It is not momism or any such simple psychological gimmick that tells this sad tale. The consumer culture—in which leisure is a menace to be met by anxious continual consuming—devours both the masculinity of men and the femininity of women. The life of consuming requires a neuter anxiety, and the pressure to conform, to watch for our cues, to consume, makes us all the same—we are customers—only with slightly different gadgets. Women have long bought men's shirts; men are buying colognes with "that exciting musky masculine tang."

Togetherness represents a curious effort by a woman's magazine to bring men back into the American family. Togetherness does not restore to the man a part of his old-time independence. It does not even indicate that he may be the provider with an independent role defined partly by ambitions outside his family. Instead, it suggests the joys of being a helpmate, a part of the woman's full life, and battens greedily on the contemporary male's anxiety about pleasing his wife. The Togetherness theme has been a great commercial success. A full-page advertisement by that canny old American institution, the New York Stock Exchange, shows a photograph of a harried young man pleading with a young woman on a parlor couch. She remains unconvinced, pouting, hands gloved and folded together, as brutal as the shocked beauties in the classical halitosis or B.O. tragedies. The capition reads: "Is the girl you want to marry reluctant to say Yes? Do you need to build character with your wife? Then just use the magic words: *I'll start a monthly investment plan.*"

It used to be thought that answering economic needs was the main purpose of man's economic efforts. Now, however, an appeal to emotional insecurity about money—without crass financial trouble—can do good work for an advertiser. "Do you need to build character with your wife?" This is whimsey with a whammy in it. Money works symbolically to stimulate, then assuage male doubts.

SHE. What can the stock do for our marriage?

HE. It can help keep it sweet and jolly because when we own stock we are part-owners of the company.

In the image projected by this advertisement, the wife is prosecutor, judge, and jury. She may fall into a less exalted role, however, while her husband is downtown making the money which will go for food, clothing, shelter, and sound common stocks. That she too frets about keeping her marriage sweet and jolly is obvious. The popular media again point to trouble while pitching a new solution to her problems. One of the former radio soap operas is now sponsored by Sleepeze. Apparently almost everyone uses soap these days, but not everyone has caught on to the virtues of non-habit-forming sedatives. Want your husband to love you? This pill will help or your money back. "Ladies! Fall asleep without that unsightly twisting and turning."

It's time to mention Barbara. A tough wise creature of a girl, Barbara comes to this observation out of her marriage and love life: "Men worry too much about making the girl happy. We seem to scare them out of themselves. Let them really be pleased—that's what we want most of all—and then we'll be happy. Delighted. But really."

In other words, long live primary narcissism! And secondary. And tertiary. But let us call it by an older, better name—respect for the possibilities of the self. This includes the possibility of meaningful relationships with meaningful others.

Our wounds as a people in this time and place are not unique in kind, but the quality of difference makes this a marvelously disturbing period. The economic problem, no longer rooted in hunger for essential goods, food, housing, clothing, is an illustration of the difference. Sure, we are still busy over food—but packaged foods, luxury foods, goodies in small cans; housing—but the right house in the right neighborhood with the right furnishings and the right mortgage; clothing—but the cap with the strap in the back, Ivy League pants, charcoal gray last year and narrow lapels this year, and male fashions changing as fast as female.

It used to be thought that, given money, relative job security, and the short work week, culture would then bloom like the gardens in the suburbs and the individual spirit would roar with the driving power of a Thunderbird getting away after a red light.

Who could have predicted that we would have to keep pace with a cultural assembly line in the leisure-time sweatshop? At least in the older sweatshop, you sighed, packed, and left the plant at last. Now we are forever harassed to give more, more, more. We no longer have to keep up with the Joneses; we must keep up with Clifton Fadiman. He is watching *you.* The steady pressure to consume, absorb, participate, receive, by eye, ear, mouth, and mail, involves a cruelty to intestines, blood pressure, and psyche unparalleled in history. The frontiersmen could build a stockade against the Indians, but what home is safe from Gilbert Highet? We are being killed with kindness. We are being stifled with cultural and material joys. Our wardrobes are full. What we really need is a new fabric that we don't have to wrinkle, spot, wash, iron, or wear. At a beautiful moment in *Walden,* Thoreau tells how he saw a beggar walking along with all his belongings in a single sack on his back. He wanted to weep for the poor man—because he still had that sack to carry.

The old-style sweatshop crippled mainly the working people. Now there are no workers left in America; we are almost all middle class as to income and expectations. Even the cultural elite labors among the latest in hi-fi equipment, trips to Acapulco and Paris, the right books in the sewn paper editions (Elizabeth Bowen, Arnold Toynbee, Jacques Barzun —these are the cultivated ones, remember), *Fortune* and the *Reporter,* art movies and the barbecue pit and the Salzburg music festival. It is too easy to keep up with the Joneses about cars and houses, but the Robert Shaw Chorale is a *challenge.* In the meantime, the man in the sweatshop is divorced or psychoanalyzed (these are perhaps remedies in a few cases); he raises adjusted children, or kills them trying; he practices Togetherness in a home with a wife who is frantic to be a woman and a non-woman at the same time; he broods about a job which does not ask the best that he can give. But it does give security; it is a good job. (In college this same man learned about the extreme, tragic instances of desire. Great men, great books. Now he reads Evelyn Waugh.)

In his later, philosophical transmogrification, David Riesman consoles the radar-flaunting other-directeds by holding out the reward of someday being "autonomous" if they are very, very good. Same thing, brother, same thing. When he describes the autonomous personality's "intelligent" distinctions among consumer products, exercising his creative imagination by figuring out why "High Noon" is a better western than a Gene Autry, well, then, in the words of Elvis Presley:—

> Ah feel so lonely,
> Ah feel so lo-oh-oh-lonely.

We're in Heartbreak Hotel where, as another singer, Yeats, put it:—

> The ceremony of innocence is drowned;
> The best lack all conviction, while the worst
> Are full of passionate intensity.

Refusal to share to the fullest degree in the close amity of the leisure-time sweatshop is—for Mr. Riesman—a kind of ethical bohemianism. His autonomous consumer, sociable, trained, and in the know, is a critic of the distinctions between the Book-of-the-Month Club and the Reader's Subscription, Inc., marks the really good shows in his TV guide, buys educational comic books for his children, tastes the difference in fine after-dinner coffee, knows that the novel is a dead form and why. Bumper to bumper in the traffic home from work, or jammed into the commuter train, he has plenty of time to think. And he does think (thinking means worrying) while the radio blares "The House with the Stained Glass

Window" or "The Magic of Believing," a little rock-and-roll philosophical number.

Does he have a moral problem, let's say, about leaving a changing neighborhood "for the sake of the children"? He is a liberal, of course, but after all, the Negroes who are moving in come from a different world and he should not inflict his principles on his children. Still, there is a certain discomfort. He discusses it with his analyst. *Why* does he suffer from this moral qualm? Does it have some link with the ever ambiguous relationship with parents? *What* moral problem? They are all psychological. Anxiety can be consumed like any product. And from his new, split-level, sapling-planted housing development he speeds into the city now ten miles further out.

We are a disappointed generation. We are a discontented people. Our manner of life says it aloud even if discreetly our public faces smile. The age of happy problems has brought us confusion and anxiety amid the greatest material comfort the world has ever seen. Culture has become a consolation for the sense of individual powerlessness in politics, work, and love. With gigantic organizations determining our movements, manipulating the dominion over self which alone makes meaningful communion with others possible, we ask leisure, culture, and recreation to return to us a sense of ease and authority. But work, love, and culture need to be connected. Otherwise we carry our powerlessness with us onto the aluminum garden furniture in the back yard. Power lawn mowers we can buy, of course.

The solution in our age of happy problems is not to install (on time) a central air-conditioning system and a color TV this year because the room air conditioner and the black-and-white TV last year did not change our lives in any important respect. The solution is not in stylish religious conversions or a new political party. The answer is not even that Panglossian fantasy about "the autonomous personality" which will naturally emerge out of the fatal meeting of the other-directed consumer with a subscription to the *Saturday Review*.

The ache of unfulfilled experience throbs within us. Our eyes hurt. Vicarious pleasures buzz in our heads. Isn't there something more, something more?

There is still awareness; there is still effort. "It should be every man's ambition to be his own doctor." This doesn't mean that he should not see a dentist when his tooth hurts, perhaps a psychoanalyst when his psyche hurts; but he must hold in mind the ideal maximum of humanity—the exercise of intelligence and desire within a context of active health. The Stoic philosophers had a great although impossible idea for these crowding times: cultivate your own garden. We cannot retreat from the world any more—we never really could—but we can look for our best gardens within the world's trouble. There we must give ourselves silence and space; we can see what the will wants; we can make decisions. Only then —having come to terms with our own particularities—can we give the world more than a graceless prefabricated commodity.

Hope? Some sweet Barbara is hope. And a work we love. And the strength, O Lord, not to accept the easy pleasures (easy anxieties) which have pleased us (made us anxious) so far. And the strength, O Lord, you who reign undefined above the psychoanalysts and the sociologists, the market researchers and the advertising agencies, the vice presidents and the book clubs, to refuse the easy solutions which have becalmed us so far.

Then with good belly luck we will be able to digest strong, irregular, yeasty, black bread.

QUESTIONS AND TOPICS

1. Are professional people as concerned about the purchasing of objects as Gold makes them out to be? Is such "materialism" necessarily bad? Is it time-wasting? Is it spiritually destructive? Does it have its virtues?
2. Does Gold accurately reflect the life of educated, middle-class people, or does he indulge in caricature?
3. Does Gold overestimate the effect of advertising on people's lives? Do college-educated people really get anxieties or "happy problems" from TV? Do other people?
4. Are most young marrieds worried about "togetherness"? Is such worry destructive, as Gold contends? Or does it contribute to a solid marriage?
5. Why does Gold satirize those who turn to the consumption of culture once their material needs are fulfilled? Does the rich man who sleeps in his box at the opera constitute a social evil?
6. Is psychiatry, as Gold implies, another form of conspicuous consumption? Is it a substitute for purpose? Or does Gold merely add to popular misconceptions about psychiatry?
7. Does Gold offer specific solutions for "happy problems"? Do you have your own solutions? Are "happy problems" worthy of serious consideration?

John Updike

A & P

Though "A & P," by John Updike, 1932–, is about the development of a young man's sexual maturity and his rejection of provincial values, it is also about class. Everyone in the story belongs to the large American middle class, yet two groups are distinguishable, that represented by Lengel, the manager of the A & P, and that represented by the summer people.

In walks these three girls in nothing but bathing suits. I'm in the third checkout slot, with my back to the door, so I don't see them until they're over by the bread. The one that caught my eye first was the one in the plaid green two-piece. She was a chunky kid, with a good tan and a sweet broad soft-looking can with those two crescents of white just under it, where the sun never seems to hit, at the top of the backs of her legs. I stood there with my hand on a box of HiHo crackers trying to remember if I rang it up or not. I ring it up again and the customer starts giving me hell. She's one of these cash-register-watchers, a witch about fifty with rouge on her cheekbones and no eyebrows, and I know it made her day to trip me up. She'd been watching cash registers for fifty years and probably never seen a mistake before.

By the time I got her feathers smoothed and her goodies into a bag—she gives me a little snort in passing, if she'd been born at the right time they would have burned her over in Salem—by the time I get her on her way the girls had circled around the bread and were coming back, without a pushcart, back my way along the counters, in the aisle between the checkouts and the Special bins. They didn't even have shoes on. There was this chunky one, with the two-piece—it was bright green and the seams on the bra were still sharp and her belly was still pretty pale so I guessed she just got it (the suit)—there was this one, with one of those chubby berry-faces, the lips all bunched together under her nose, this one, and a tall one, with black hair that hadn't quite frizzed right, and one of these sunburns right across under the eyes, and a chin that was too long —you know, the kind of girl other girls think is very "striking" and "attractive" but never quite makes it, as they very well know, which is why they like her so much—and then the third one, that wasn't quite so tall. She was the queen. She kind of led them, the other two peeking around and making their shoulders round. She didn't look around, not this queen, she just walked straight on slowly, on these long white prima-donna legs. She came down a little hard on her heels, as if she didn't walk in her bare feet that much, putting down her heels and then letting the weight move along to her toes as if she was testing the floor with every step, putting a little deliberate extra action into it. You never know for sure how girls' minds work (do you really think it's a mind in there or just a little buzz like a bee in a glass jar?) but you got the idea she had talked the other two into coming in here with her, and now she was showing them how to do it, walk slow and hold yourself straight.

She had on a kind of dirty-pink—beige maybe, I don't know—bathing suit with a little nubble all over it and, what got me, the straps were down. They were off her shoulders looped loose around the cool tops of her arms, and I guess as a result the suit had slipped a little on her, so all around the top of the cloth there was this shining rim. If it hadn't been there you wouldn't have known there could have been anything whiter than those shoulders. With the straps pushed off, there was nothing between the top of the suit and the top of her head except just *her,* this clean bare plane of the top of her chest down from the shoulder bones like a dented sheet of metal tilted in the light. I mean, it was more than pretty.

She had sort of oaky hair that the sun and salt had bleached, done up in a bun that was unravelling, and a kind of prim face. Walking into the A & P with your straps down, I suppose it's the only kind of face you *can* have. She held her head so high her neck, coming up out of those white shoulders, looked kind of stretched, but I didn't mind. The longer her neck was, the more of her there was.

She must have felt in the corner of her eye me and over my shoulder Stokesie in the second slot watching, but she didn't tip. Not this queen. She kept her eyes moving across the racks, and stopped, and turned so slow it made my stomach rub the inside of my apron, and buzzed to the other two, who kind of huddled against her for relief, and then they all three of them went up the cat-and-dog-food-breakfast-cereal-macaroni-rice-raisins-seasonings-spreads-spaghetti-soft-drinks-crackers-and-cookies aisle. From the third slot I look straight up this aisle to the meat counter, and I watched them all the way. The fat one with the tan sort of fumbled with the cookies, but on second thought she put the package back. The sheep pushing their carts down the aisle—the girls were walking against the usual traffic (not that we have one-way signs or anything)—were pretty hilarious. You could see them, when Queenie's white shoulders dawned on them, kind of jerk, or hop, or hiccup, but their eyes snapped back to their own baskets and on they pushed. I bet you could set off dynamite in an A & P and the people would by and large keep reaching and checking oatmeal off their lists and muttering "Let me see, there was a third thing, began with A, asparagus, no, ah, yes, applesauce!" or whatever it is they do mutter. But there was no doubt, this jiggled them. A few houseslaves in pin curlers even looked around after pushing their carts past to make sure what they had seen was correct.

You know, it's one thing to have a girl in a bathing suit down on the beach, where what with the glare nobody can look at each other much anyway, and another thing in the cool of the A & P, under the fluorescent lights, against all those stacked packages, with her feet paddling along naked over our checkerboard green-and-cream rubber-tile floor.

"Oh Daddy," Stokesie said beside me. "I feel so faint."

"Darling," I said. "Hold me tight." Stokesie's married, with two babies chalked up on his fuselage already, but as far as I can tell that's the only difference. He's twenty-two, and I was nineteen this April.

"Is it done?" he asks, the responsible married man finding his voice. I forgot to say he thinks he's going to be manager some sunny day, maybe in 1990 when it's called the Great Alexandrov and Petrooshki Tea Company or something.

What he meant was, our town is five miles from a beach, with a big summer colony out on the Point, but we're right in the middle of town, and the women generally put on a shirt or shorts or something before they get out of the car into the street. And anyway these are usually women with six children and varicose veins mapping their legs and nobody, including them, could care less. As I say, we're right in the middle of town, and if you stand at our front doors you can see two banks and the Congregational church and the newspaper store and three real-estate offices and about twenty-seven old freeloaders tearing up Central Street because the sewer broke again. It's not as if we're on the Cape; we're north of Boston and there's people in this town haven't seen the ocean for twenty years.

The girls had reached the meat counter and were asking McMahon something. He pointed, they pointed, and they shuffled out of sight behind a pyramid of Diet Delight peaches. All that was left for us to see was old McMahon patting his mouth and looking after them sizing up their joints. Poor kids, I began to feel sorry for them, they couldn't help it.

· · ·

Now here comes the sad part of the story, at least my family says it's sad, but I don't think it's so sad myself. The store's pretty empty, it being Thursday afternoon, so there was nothing much to do except lean on the register and wait for the girls to show up again. The whole store was like a pinball machine and I didn't know which tunnel they'd come out of. After a while they come around out of the far aisle, around the light bulbs, records at discount of the Caribbean Six or Tony Martin Sings or some such gunk you wonder they waste the wax on, sixpacks of candy bars, and plastic toys done up in cellophane that fall apart when a kid looks at them anyway. Around they come, Queenie still leading the way, and holding a little gray jar in her hand. Slots Three through Seven are unmanned and I could see her wondering between Stokes and me, but Stokesie with his usual luck draws an old party in baggy gray pants who stumbles up with four giant cans of pineapple juice (what do these bums *do* with all that pineapple juice? I've often asked myself) so the girls come to me. Queenie puts down the jar and I take it into my fingers icy cold. Kingfish Fancy Herring Snacks in Pure Sour Cream: 49¢. Now her hands are empty, not a ring or a bracelet, bare as God made them, and I wonder where the money's coming from. Still with that prim look she lifts a folded dollar bill out of the hollow at the center of her nubbled pink top. The jar went heavy in my hand. Really, I thought that was so cute.

Then everybody's luck begins to run out. Lengel comes in from haggling with a truck full of cabbages on the lot and is about to scuttle into that door marked MANAGER behind which he hides all day when the girls touch his eye. Lengel's pretty dreary, teaches Sunday school and the rest, but he doesn't miss that much. He comes over and says, "Girls, this isn't the beach."

Queenie blushes, though maybe it's just a brush of sunburn I was noticing for the first time, now that she was so close. "My mother asked me to pick up a jar of herring snacks." Her voice kind of startled me, the way voices do when you see the people first, coming out so flat and dumb yet kind of tony, too, the way it ticked over "pick up" and "snacks." All of a sudden I slid right down her voice into her living room. Her father and the other men were standing around in ice-cream coats and bow ties and the women were in sandals picking up herring snacks on toothpicks off a big glass plate and they were all holding drinks the color of water with olives and sprigs of mint in them. When my parents have somebody over they get lemonade and if it's a real racy affair Schlitz in tall glasses with "They'll Do It Every Time" cartoons stencilled on.

"That's all right," Lengel said. "But this isn't the beach." His repeating this struck me as funny, as if it had just occurred to him, and he had been thinking all these years the A & P was a great big dune and he was the head lifeguard. He didn't like my smiling—as I say he doesn't miss much—but he concentrates on giving the girls that sad Sunday-school-superintendent stare.

Queenie's blush is no sunburn now, and the plump one in plaid, that I liked better from the back—a really sweet can—pipes up, "We weren't doing any shopping. We just came in for the one thing."

"That makes no difference," Lengel tells her, and I could see from the way his eyes went that he hadn't noticed she was wearing a two-piece before. "We want you decently dressed when you come in here."

"We *are* decent," Queenie says suddenly, her lower lip pushing, getting sore now that she remembers her place, a place from which the crowd that runs the A & P must look pretty crummy. Fancy Herring Snacks flashed in her very blue eyes.

"Girls, I don't want to argue with you. After this come in here with your shoulders covered. It's our policy." He turns his back. That's policy for you. Policy is what the kingpins want. What the others want is juvenile delinquency.

All this while, the customers had been showing up with their carts but, you know, sheep, seeing a scene, they had all bunched up on Stokesie, who shook open a paper bag as gently as peeling a peach, not wanting to miss a word. I could feel in the silence everybody getting nervous, most of all Lengel, who asks me, "Sammy, have you rung up their purchase?"

I thought and said "No" but it wasn't about that I was thinking. I go through the punches, 4, 9, GROC, TOT—it's more complicated than you think, and after you do it often enough, it begins to make a little song, that you hear words to, in my case "Hello (*bing*) there, you (*gung*) hap-py *pee*-pul (*splat*)!"—the *splat* being the drawer flying out. I uncrease the bill, tenderly as you may imagine, it just having come from between the two smoothest scoops of vanilla I had ever known were there, and pass a half and a penny into her narrow pink palm, and nestle the herrings in a bag and twist its neck and hand it over, all the time thinking.

The girls, and who'd blame them, are in a hurry to get out, so I say "I quit" to Lengel quick enough for them to hear, hoping they'll stop and watch me, their unsuspected hero. They keep right on going, into the electric eye; the door flies open and they flicker across the lot to their car, Queenie and Plaid and Big Tall Goony-Goony (not that as raw material she was so bad), leaving me with Lengel and a kink in his eyebrow.

"Did you say something, Sammy?"

"I said I quit."

"I thought you did."

"You didn't have to embarrass them."

"It was they who were embarrassing us."

I started to say something that came out "Fiddle-de-doo." It's a saying of my grandmother's, and I know she would have been pleased.

"I don't think you know what you're saying," Lengel said.

"I know you don't," I said. "But I do." I pull the bow at the back of my apron and start shrugging it off my shoulders. A couple customers that had been heading for my slot begin to knock against each other, like scared pigs in a chute.

Lengel sighs and begins to look very patient and old and gray. He's been a friend of my parents for years. "Sammy, you don't want to do this to your Mom and Dad," he tells me. It's true, I don't. But it seems to me that once you begin a gesture it's fatal not to go through with it. I fold the apron, "Sammy" stitched in red on the pocket, and put it on the counter, and drop the bow tie on top of it. The bow tie is theirs, if you've ever wondered. "You'll feel this for the rest of your life," Lengel says, and I know that's true, too, but remembering how he made that pretty girl blush makes me so scrunchy inside I punch the No Sale tab and the machine whirs "pee-pul" and the drawer splats out. One advantage to this scene taking place in summer, I can follow this up with a clean exit, there's no fumbling around getting your coat and galoshes, I just saunter into the electric eye in my white shirt that my mother ironed the night before, and the door heaves itself open, and outside the sunshine is skating around on the asphalt.

I look around for my girls, but they're gone, of course. There wasn't anybody but some young married screaming with her children about some candy they didn't get by the door of a powder-blue Falcon station wagon. Looking back in the big windows, over the bags of peat moss and aluminum lawn furniture stacked on the pavement, I could see Lengel in my place in the slot, checking the sheep through. His face was dark gray and his back stiff, as if he'd just had an injection of iron, and my stomach kind of fell as I felt how hard the world was going to be to me hereafter.

QUESTIONS AND TOPICS

1. People often speak of middle-class attitudes or middle-class morality, yet in this story we see two groups of the middle class. Can you give each group a name? Can you describe the differences in their customs and attitudes?
2. Why does the young man quit his job? Why does he think the world will be hard on him thereafter?
3. Can you think of any distinct groups among the middle classes other than those described? Can you analyze their behavior?
4. Is it valid to talk of middle-class morality in America today when we have such diversity among the middle classes? Do these different groups have anything in common?

JOHN P. MARQUAND

from
THE LATE
GEORGE APLEY

John P. Marquand, 1893–1960, wrote a group of novels which gently satirize the upper class. His best-known work, The Late George Apley, 1937, consists largely of the correspondence of George Apley, a wealthy man of integrity and honesty, who is caught in the net of his social environment. According to Marquand, in his introduction to the novel, Apley's approach to life "is in no sense confined to such a limited sphere as Boston. . . . It is an attitude bred of security, the familiar viewpoint of generations of the rentier class." *

The imminence of war which was largely averted by the time that John Apley and his companions were leaving Framingham for the Border was succeeded for George Apley by a crisis of a somewhat different nature, occasioned by the death and burial of Mrs. Henry Apley, a somewhat distant family connection. Her sons, entirely within their right, buried their mother in the Apley lot of the Mt. Auburn Cemetery—that gracious, well-endowed, and beautifully attended piece of ground where so many have found their final resting place and where others hope to, including the present writer. It was Apley's invariable custom to attend every funeral of the family, but on this occasion, being much pressed for time, he was not among those present at the grave, nor did he attend to the

---

* A *rentier* is one deriving a fixed income from sources such as land, stocks, or bonds. [Ed.]

grave's location, although he was one of the trustees of the Apley lot. Instead, he entrusted these details to his second cousin, Roger Apley, greatly to his subsequent regret. His letters, however, are self-explanatory:—

Dear Roger:—

Yesterday, happening to be motoring with Catharine toward Concord, we stopped at Mt. Auburn Cemetery as is our habit whenever we pass by it. I was particularly anxious to see how the young arbor vitae which we decided, after so much debate, to plant on the southern border, were surviving the early summer heat. I was pleased to see that they were doing very well indeed and, in fact, was about to leave when I noticed that Cousin Hattie had been placed in that part of the lot which I had always understood, and which I believe everyone in the family has understood, was reserved for my particular branch. I refer to the part of ground around the oak tree which my father had ordered planted. This was a favourite place of his and has a peculiarly sentimental significance to me and to my children. As you know, these matters grow more important with the growing years. I cannot conceive what prompted you to allow Cousin Hattie to occupy this spot. Not only do I think she should not be there, but also her pink granite headstone with the recumbent figure on top of it, which I suppose represents an angel, makes a garish contrast to our own plain, white marble stones.

I admit that the Henry Apleys are connections of the family, though so distant that they might almost not be considered as such. I might also call to your attention that the Henry Apleys, due to their straitened circumstances, did not and have never contributed to the purchase and maintenance fund of our ground. Except for Thanksgiving dinner, I do not recall ever having seen Cousin Hattie except twice when she had difficulty in meeting her grandson's tuition bills. Under these circumstances it seems to me somewhat pushing and presumptuous, although I like neither of the words, of the Henry Apleys to preëmpt the place they did without at least consulting me. I may tell you confidentially that I was very much disturbed by the reaction of Adam, our chauffeur, who came with us, carrying some potted geraniums, slips from some which my mother had planted. It was clear to both Catharine and me that Adam was very much shocked, from his manner, if not from any words.

It is no use to embroider any further upon this, but I cannot forget that I left these arrangements to you, as a member of the trustees' committee.

I feel very sure you did not realize how your decision would have affected me, and how it would affect my Uncle William who is planning to rest near that spot, I am afraid in the very near future. Uncle William, as you know, has a series of violent dislikes and among them was Cousin Hattie. I hesitate to tell him that she is there, and yet I am afraid I must do so because he has asked me to go with him next week to Mt. Auburn so that he may pick out the exact spot he desires. I dread the repercussions of his discovery so much that I think it is up to you to make representations to the Henry Apley branch and to arrange that Cousin Hattie be exhumed and placed near the arbor vitae trees on the other slope. This section of the lot is not occupied at present. Will you please let me know what you can do about this. . . .

Dear Roger:—

I am very much gratified that you realize the seriousness of this situation. I agree with you it requires delicacy in handling, but I do not agree with you that it is too late to do anything about it. When the subway was built under Boston Common a great many bodies were exhumed from the old graveyard there and again buried. I note that you feel that you cannot see the Henry Apleys yourself, therefore you had better refer them to me. I shall write to Henry Apley to-day as you suggest. . . .

Dear Henry:—

Through a piece of mismanagement which I cannot believe is any fault of yours, your mother's remains have been placed in a spot in our family ground which I have always felt was tacitly at the disposal of our branch. I am afraid I must come to the point at once and ask that your mother be removed near the arbor vitae hedges on the opposite slope. I hope very much that you will agree with me when you consider the various implications involved, and believe me, I realize that my request may be trying to you in this period of your grief. I cannot avoid the feeling also that this accident has occurred because of my own preoccupation in other matters, therefore I want you to realize that I, of course, shall defray all expenses. Please let me know at once about this as the matter is important. . . .

Dear Henry:—

I can ascribe much of your letter to the natural agitation which you must feel at such a time, but I see no reason for your final decision. The plot is family property until it is fully occupied. My one objection was regarding location. I do not feel that I have the slightest right in suggesting that your mother's remains be removed from the Apley plot, and I beg you to remember that I never did suggest it.

If, however, you feel that this removal is the most satisfactory solution of this difficulty and will relieve your own feelings, I shall not urge you not to do it. I repeat again that I stand ready to defray all expenses.

Such a contretemps, it will be recognized, bears no great novelty; rather it is a difficulty which has been faced by so many that nearly any reader may feel a sympathy for Apley's point of view and may comprehend as well the importance of such a negotiation. The consequence obviously foreshadowed a rift within the family and explains the reason for many breaches which are yet unhealed. At the time Apley was considerably surprised and not a little hurt by the unsympathetic, if not actually hostile, reactions of his own blood relations. He became aware for the first time that in spite of his most generous efforts certain of his own kin harbored for him a tacit resentment that bordered dangerously on dislike. It may only be added that he faced it with his usual composure in the belief that he had conscientiously done what was right.

Even his own uncle, Horatio Brent, who was suffering severely at the time from gout and from heart complications, saw fit in spite of his devotion to George Apley to remonstrate with his nephew's point of view. His letter, which is quoted here, is additionally useful in showing the impression that George Apley was making upon a certain segment of his own group. If this impression is neither a true nor a welcome one to those who admired him most, it serves merely as another proof that no man of definite character can help but create opposition.

Dear George:—

Here I am at Pachogue Neck. I am sitting on the old piazza where you have been so often, with my foot swathed in bandages. Your aunt, who sends you her love, will not allow me to take stimulants and is arranging to have an elevator installed to pull me upstairs to bed. Old Bess, my pointer bitch, who you remember took first prize in the Dedham Field Trial six years back, is sitting here beside me creaky in her joints and I am afraid the vet will have to put her out of the way by autumn. Frankly, I wish we had vets instead of doctors, because I believe I should be put out of the way too quite as much as Bess.

It seems funny to see the whole world look as young as ever, to smell the salt air and to see the water sparkling on the bay, and to be so old myself. Frankly, George, it is damnably unpleasant. I think of all the good times we had together. I think of when your aunt and I took you to Paris with Henrietta to get you over that abortive romance. You can laugh at it now, I guess. I think of lots of things, because there is nothing else to do, and I hope you won't mind your uncle writing a few words to you because he is fond of you.

Of course I have heard about the Mt. Auburn Cemetery row. Everybody at Pachogue Neck has been talking about it for the past two weeks. I don't mind where Hattie is buried. I don't mind much where anyone is buried except that I do not like the idea of throwing around ashes, but I wonder if you see yourself the way other people see you. I don't like people outside of the family to be laughing at you, George. I don't like to have them say that you are exhibiting a sense of your own pompousness and your own importance, because I know that you are not. I know what the trouble is with you: it is the *galère* * in which we have all had to live. We have all been told from the nursery that we are important and that we must do the right thing. Believe me you don't feel important when you have the gout. I want to tell you something that it won't hurt to remember. I know that I have forgotten it often enough myself, but here it is. Most people in the world don't know who the Apleys are and they don't give a damn. I don't intend this as rudeness but as a sort of comfort. I know it has been a comfort to me sometimes when talking with your aunt. Just remember that most people don't give a damn. When you remember it, you won't feel the necessity of taking the Apleys so seriously. I hope you know the way I mean it. . . .

QUESTIONS AND TOPICS

1. Write a character sketch of George Apley based on this selection. You might read the entire novel and compare your impressions.
2. According to Marquand, Apley is typical of the long-established rich. Do you agree? Others of George Apley's class, in particular his Uncle Horatio, seem to have different attitudes. Are they less typical of their class? Can one dis-

* The galleys, imprisonment with hard labor, drudgery. [Ed.]

tinguish which characteristics of George Apley are determined by his class and which are individually determined.

3. What are George's real motives for taking offense at the Henry Apley branch of the family?

4. The letter from Henry informing George Apley that Cousin Hattie will be removed from the Apley plot is not included in the text. Write the letter yourself.

5. The Narrator writes that George "became aware for the first time that . . . certain of his own kind harbored for him a tacit resentment that bordered dangerously on dislike." George is, of course, the richest in his family. Does such resentment often occur in families containing rich and poor branches? Why? Analyze such a relationship in your own family.

Ezra Pound

SALUTATION
and
THE GARDEN

Though Ezra Pound, 1885–, is more widely known for his difficult Cantos, his earlier work, Personae, 1909, 1926, from which these selections are taken, contains many excellent poems, some dealing directly with Pound's views on the class structure.

SALUTATION

O generation of the thoroughly smug
  and thoroughly uncomfortable,
I have seen fishermen picnicking in the sun,
I have seen them with untidy families,
I have seen their smiles full of teeth
  and heard ungainly laughter.
And I am happier than you are,
And they were happier than I am;
And the fish swim in the lake
  and do not even own clothing.

QUESTIONS AND TOPICS

1. Which class does Pound call the "generation of the thoroughly smug/and thoroughly uncomfortable"?
2. Why does Pound prefer the fishermen to the generation of the smug and uncomfortable? What is the significance of the last two lines?

3. Do you think Pound romanticizes the life of the fishermen? What might Harrington reply to Pound?

THE GARDEN

En robe de parade.

Samain

Like a skein of loose silk blown against a wall
She walks by the railing of a path in Kensington Gardens,
And she is dying piece-meal
     of a sort of emotional anæmia.

And round about there is a rabble
Of the filthy, sturdy, unkillable infants of the very poor.
They shall inherit the earth.

In her is the end of breeding.
Her boredom is exquisite and excessive.
She would like some one to speak to her,
And is almost afraid that I
     will commit that indiscretion.

QUESTIONS AND TOPICS

1. Characterize the woman Pound describes in this poem. What relation is there between the woman and the "sturdy, unkillable infants of the very poor"?
2. What is Pound's attitude toward the woman's class? Is he justified? The woman obviously is English. Are the American rich different? Are there sub-groups within the American or English rich?
3. Can you perceive the character of the poet? What is the significance of the final two lines?

3

CONFORMITY
TO
LAW AND CUSTOM

THE QUESTION OF CONFORMITY often leads to muddled thinking on both sides of the political fence. Some assume that any principled opposition to custom and even to law is justified, while others assume that all nonconformity is sinful. The thoughtful student, however, understands that some kinds of conformity are necessary, some harmless, and some disturbing. He avoids such general considerations as whether conformity or nonconformity is preferable at all times, and makes discriminations of degree and kind. How much conformity is necessary to keep a society stable? What kinds of conformity are desirable (or undesirable)?

Students who write poorly on the question of conformity usually do so for any of several reasons.

The first reason is lack of knowledge. Such students generally know few leftists, beats, or hippies, but are only too ready to give a detailed account of their beliefs, morals, and lives. What frequently emerges is a superficial account based upon television and newspaper coverage and the skimpiest personal experience.

Another reason for poor writing on the subject is emotionalism. One student rages at nonconformists, imagining that in some undefined way they threaten his life-pattern, while another glorifies the nonconformist life for its glamour and freedom. Research and solid substantiation will aid both students in writing more controlled compositions.

Less confused, but still inaccurate, is the student who has had enough experience with nonconformist groups to notice that their members either embrace a common dogma or wear a kind of uniform. He concludes that nonconformity does not exist, since everyone conforms to some kind of standard. His problem is oversimplification. Nonconformity exists in opposition to widely accepted patterns. There *is* a difference between the person who follows the doctrines of the majority and the person who follows the doctrines of an isolated minority. Except in unusual situations, the second choice is more difficult. The nonconformist who is serious may find himself unable to live in most parts of the country, unable to gain employment in the major areas of our economy, or unable to pursue certain careers, because his beliefs or life pattern differ from those of most Americans.

Finally, we have the student who writes poorly on the nonconformists because he is one. He might be sincere in his beliefs, but his enthusiasm and lack of self-criticism lead to a wholesale and sometimes blind acceptance of a creed or way of life. On the other hand, he might have joined a fringe group because it is currently "in." Such a person is likely to leave the group when it has lost its glamour and novelty. His papers will probably reflect his lack of knowledge of the real issues involved, and, more important, his lack of self-knowledge.

Alexis de Tocqueville

TYRANNY
OF THE
MAJORITY

De Tocqueville, 1805–1859, was a Frenchman who visited the United States during the early nineteenth century. Afterward he wrote a book, Democracy in America, 1835, *now considered a classic of social observation. In the following extract, he seeks to prove that the guiding principle of American democracy, particularly in relation to state government, is unity, not diversity. He criticizes the strength of majority opinion, which governs invisibly at the expense of dissent.*

I hold it to be an impious and detestable maxim that, politically speaking, the people have a right to do anything; and yet I have asserted that all authority originates in the will of the majority. Am I, then, in contradiction with myself?

A general law, which bears the name of justice, has been made and sanctioned, not only by a majority of this or that people, but by a majority of mankind. The rights of every people are therefore confined within the limits of what is just. A nation may be considered as a jury which is empowered to represent society at large and to apply justice, which is its law. Ought such a jury, which represents society, to have more power than the society itself whose laws it executes?

When I refuse to obey an unjust law, I do not contest the right of the majority to command, but I simply appeal from the sovereignty of the people to the sovereignty of mankind. Some have not feared to assert that a people can never outstep the boundaries of justice and reason in those affairs which are peculiarly its own; and that consequently full power may be given to the majority by which it is represented. But this is the language of a slave.

A majority taken collectively is only an individual, whose opinions, and frequently whose interests, are opposed to those of another individual, who is styled a minority. If it be admitted that a man possessing absolute power may misuse that power by wronging his adversaries, why should not a majority be liable to the same reproach? Men do not change their characters by uniting with one another; nor does their patience in the presence of obstacles increase with their strength. For my own part, I cannot believe it; the power to do everything, which I should refuse to one of my equals, I will never grant to any number of them.

I do not think that, for the sake of preserving liberty, it is possible to combine several principles in the same government so as really to oppose them to one another. The form of government that is usually termed *mixed* has always appeared to me a mere chimera. Accurately speaking, there is no such thing as a *mixed government,* in the sense usually given to that word, because in all communities some one principle of action may be discovered which preponderates over the others. England in the last century—which has been especially cited as an example of this sort of government—was essentially an aristocratic state, although it comprised some great elements of democracy; for the laws and customs of the country were such that the aristocracy could not but preponderate in the long run and direct public affairs according to its own will. The error arose from seeing the interests of the nobles perpetually contending with those of the people, without considering the issue of the contest, which was really the important point. When a community actually has a mixed government—that is to say, when it is equally divided between adverse principles—it must either experience a revolution, or fall into anarchy.

I am therefore of the opinion, that social power superior to all others must always be placed somewhere; but I think that liberty is endangered when this power finds no obstacle which can retard its course and give it time to moderate its own vehemence.

Unlimited power is in itself a bad and dangerous thing. Human beings are not competent to exercise it with discretion. God alone can be omnipotent, because his wisdom and his justice are always equal to his power. There is no power on earth so worthy of honor in itself or clothed with rights so sacred that I would admit its uncontrolled and all-predominant authority. When I see that the right and the means of absolute command are conferred on any power whatever, be it called a people or a king, an aristocracy or a democracy, a monarchy or a republic, I say there is the germ of tyranny, and I seek to live elsewhere, under other laws.

In my opinion, the main evil of the present democratic institutions of the United States does not arise, as is often asserted in Europe, from their weakness, but from their irresistible strength. I am not so much alarmed at the excessive liberty which reigns in that country as at the inadequate securities which one finds there against tyranny.

When an individual or a party is wronged in the United States, to whom can he apply for redress? If to public opinion, public opinion constitutes the majority; if to the legislature, it represents the majority and implicitly obeys it; if to the executive power, it is appointed by the majority and serves as a passive tool in its hands. The public force consists of the majority under arms; the jury is the majority invested with the right of hearing judicial cases; and in certain states even the judges are elected by the majority. However iniquitous or abused the measure of which you complain, you must submit to it as well as you can.*

* A striking instance of the excesses that may be occasioned by the despotism of the majority occurred at Baltimore during the War of 1812. At that time the war was very popular in Baltimore. A newspaper that had taken the other side excited, by its opposition, the indignation of the inhabitants. The mob assembled, broke the printing-presses, and attacked the house of the editors. The militia was called out, but did not obey the call; and the only means of saving the wretches who were threatened by the frenzy of the mob was to throw them into prison as common malefactors. But even this precaution was ineffectual; the mob collected again during the night; the magistrates again made a vain attempt to call out the militia; the prison was forced, one of the newspaper editors was killed upon the spot, and others were left for dead. The guilty parties, when they were brought to trial, were acquitted by the jury.

I said one day to an inhabitant of Pennsylvania: "Be so good as to explain to me how it happens that in a state founded by Quakers, and celebrated for its toleration, free blacks are not allowed to exercise civil rights. They pay taxes; is it not fair that they shoud vote?"

"You insult us," replied my informant, "if you imagine that our legislators could have committed so gross an act of injustice and intolerance."

"Then the blacks possess the right of voting in this country?"

"Without doubt."

"How comes it, then, that at the polling-booth this morning I did not perceive a single Negro?"

If on the other hand, a legislative power could be so constituted as to represent the majority without necessarily being the slave of its passions, an executive so as to retain a proper share of authority, and a judiciary so as to remain independent of the other two powers, a government would be formed which would still be democratic while incurring scarcely any risk of tyranny.

I do not say that there is a frequent use of tyranny in America at the present day; but I maintain that there is no sure barrier against it, and that the causes which mitigate the government there are to be found in the circumstances and the manners of the country more than in its laws.

It is in the examination of the exercise of thought in the United States that we clearly perceive how far the power of the majority surpasses all the powers with which we are acquainted in Europe. Thought is an invisible and subtle power that mocks all the efforts of tyranny. At the present time the most absolute monarchs in Europe cannot prevent certain opinions hostile to their authority from circulating in secret through their dominions and even in their courts. It is not so in America; as long as the majority is still undecided, discussion is carried on; but as soon as its decision is irrevocably pronounced, everyone is silent, and the friends as well as the opponents of the measure unite in assenting to its propriety. The reason for this is perfectly clear: no monarch is so absolute as to combine all the powers of society in his own hands and to conquer all opposition, as a majority is able to do, which has the right both of making and of executing the laws.

The authority of a king is physical and controls the actions of men without subduing their will. But the majority possesses a power that is physical and moral at the same time, which acts upon the will as much

---

"That is not the fault of the law. The Negroes have an undisputed right of voting, but they voluntarily abstain from making their appearance."

"A very pretty piece of modesty on their part!" rejoined I.

"Why, the truth is that they are not disinclined to vote, but they are afraid of being maltreated; in this country the law is sometimes unable to maintain its authority without the support of the majority. But in this case the majority entertains very strong prejudices against the blacks, and the magistrates are unable to protect them in the exercise of their legal rights."

"Then the majority claims the right not only of making the laws, but of breaking the laws it has made?"

as upon the actions and represses not only all contest, but all controversy.

I know of no country in which there is so little independence of mind and real freedom of discussion as in America. In any constitutional state in Europe every sort of religious and political theory may be freely preached and disseminated; for there is no country in Europe so subdued by any single authority as not to protect the man who raises his voice in the cause of truth from the consequences of his hardihood. If he is unfortunate enough to live under an absolute government, the people are often on his side; if he inhabits a free country, he can, if necessary, find a shelter behind the throne. The aristocratic part of society supports him in some countries, and the democracy in others. But in a nation where democratic institutions exist, organized like those of the United States, there is but one authority, one element of strength and success, with nothing beyond it.

In America the majority raises formidable barriers around the liberty of opinion; within these barriers an author may write what he pleases, but woe to him if he goes beyond them. Not that he is in danger of an *auto-da-fé*, but he is exposed to continued obloquy and persecution. His political career is closed forever, since he has offended the only authority that is able to open it. Every sort of compensation, even that of celebrity, is refused to him. Before making public his opinions he thought he had sympathizers; now it seems to him that he has none any more since he has revealed himself to everyone; then those who blame him criticize loudly and those who think as he does keep quiet and move away without courage. He yields at length, overcome by the daily effort which he has to make, and subsides into silence, as if he felt remorse for having spoken the truth.

Fetters and headsmen were the coarse instruments that tyranny formerly employed; but the civilization of our age has perfected despotism itself, though it seemed to have nothing to learn. Monarchs had, so to speak, materialized oppression; the democratic republics of the present day have rendered it as entirely an affair of the mind as the will which it is intended to coerce. Under the absolute sway of one man the body was attacked in order to subdue the soul; but the soul escaped the blows which were directed against it and rose proudly superior. Such is not the course adopted by tyranny in democratic republics; there the body is left free, and the soul is enslaved. The master no longer says: "You shall think as I do or you shall die"; but he says: "You are free to think differently from me and to retain your life, your property, and all that you possess; but you are henceforth a stranger among your people. You may retain your civil rights, but they will be useless to you, for you will never be chosen by your fellow citizens if you solicit their votes; and they will affect to scorn you if you ask for their esteem. You will remain among men, but you will be deprived of the rights of mankind. Your fellow creatures will shun you like an impure being; and even those who believe in your innocence will abandon you, lest they should be shunned in their turn. Go in peace! I have given you your life, but it is an existence worse than death."

Absolute monarchies had dishonored despotism; let us beware lest democratic republics should reinstate it and render it less odious and degrading in the eyes of the many by making it still more onerous to the few.

Works have been published in the proudest nations of the Old World, expressly intended to censure the vices and the follies of the times: Labruyère inhabited the palace of Louis XIV when he composed his chapter upon the Great, and Molière criticized the courtiers in the plays that were acted before the court. But the ruling power in the United States is not to be made game of. The smallest reproach irritates its sensibility, and the slightest joke that has any foundation in truth renders it indignant; from the forms of its language up to the solid virtues of its character, everything must be made the subject of encomium. No writer, whatever be his eminence, can escape paying this tribute of adulation to his fellow citizens. The majority lives in the perpetual utterance of self-applause, and there are certain truths which the Americans can learn only from strangers or from experience.

If America has not as yet had any great writers, the reason is given in these facts; there can be no literary genius without freedom of opinion, and freedom of opinion does not exist in America. The Inquisition has never been able to prevent a vast number of anti-religious books from circulating in Spain. The empire of the majority succeeds much better in the United States, since it actually removes any wish to publish them. Unbelievers are to be met with in America, but there is no public organ of infidelity. Attempts have been made by some governments to protect morality by prohibiting licentious books. In the United States no one is punished for this sort of books, but no one is induced to write them; not because all the citizens are immaculate in conduct, but because the majority of the community is decent and orderly.

In this case the use of power is unquestionably good; and I am discussing the nature of the power itself. This irresistible authority is a constant fact, and its judicious exercise is only an accident.

The tendencies that I have just mentioned are as yet but slightly perceptible in political society, but they already exercise an unfavorable influence upon the national character of the Americans. I attribute the small number of distinguished men in political life to the ever increasing despotism of the majority in the United States.

When the American Revolution broke out, they arose in great numbers; for public opinion then served, not to tyrannize over, but to direct the exertions of individuals. Those celebrated men, sharing the agitation of mind common at that period, had a grandeur peculiar to themselves, which was reflected back upon the nation, but was by no means borrowed from it.

In absolute governments the great nobles who are nearest to the throne flatter the passions of the sovereign and voluntarily truckle to his caprices. But the mass of the nation does not degrade itself by servitude; it often submits from weakness, from habit, or from ignorance, and sometimes from loyalty. Some nations have been known to sacrifice their own desires to those of the sovereign with pleasure and pride, thus exhibiting a sort of independence of mind in the very act of submission. These nations are miserable, but they are not degraded. There is a great difference between doing what one does not approve, and feigning to approve what one does; the one is the weakness of a feeble person, the other befits the temper of a lackey.

In free countries, where everyone is more or less called upon to give his opinion on affairs of state, in democratic republics, where public life is incessantly mingled with domestic affairs, where the sovereign authority is accessible on every side, and where its attention can always be attracted by vociferation, more persons are to be met with who speculate upon its weaknesses and live upon ministering to its passions than in absolute monarchies. Not because men are naturally worse in these states than elsewhere, but the temptation is stronger and at the same time of easier access. The result is a more extensive debasement of character.

Democratic republics extend the practice of currying favor with the many and introduce it into all classes at once; this is the most serious reproach that can be addressed to them. This is especially true in demo-

cratic states organized like the American republics, where the power of
the majority is so absolute and irresistible that one must give up one's
rights as a citizen, and almost abjure one's qualities as a man, if one in-
tends to stray from the track which it prescribes.

In that immense crowd which throngs the avenues to power in the
United States, I found very few men who displayed that manly candor
and masculine independence of opinion which frequently distinguished
the Americans in former times, and which constitutes the leading feature
in distinguished characters wherever they may be found. It seems at first
sight as if all the minds of the Americans were formed upon one model,
so accurately do they follow the same route. A stranger does, indeed, sometimes meet with Americans who dissent from the rigor of these formulas,
with men who deplore the defects of the laws, the mutability and the
ignorance of democracy, who even go so far as to observe the evil tendencies that impair the national character, and to point out such remedies
as it might be possible to apply; but no one is there to hear them except
yourself, and you, to whom these secret reflections are confided, are a
stranger and a bird of passage. They are very ready to communicate truths
which are useless to you, but they hold a different language in public.

If these lines are ever read in America, I am well assured of two things
—in the first place, that all who peruse them will raise their voices to
condemn me; and, in the second place, that many of them will acquit me
at the bottom of their conscience.

I have heard of patriotism in the United States, and I have found true
patriotism among the people, but never among the leaders of the people.
This may be explained by analogy: despotism debases the oppressed much
more than the oppressor: in absolute monarchies the king often has great
virtues, but the courtiers are invariably servile. It is true that American
courtiers do not say "Sire," or "Your Majesty,"—a distinction without a
difference. They are forever talking of the natural intelligence of the people whom they serve; they do not debate the question which of the virtues
of their master is pre-eminently worthy of admiration, for they assure him
that he possesses all the virtues without having acquired them, or without
caring to acquire them; they do not give him their daughters and their
wives to be raised at his pleasure to the rank of his concubines; but by
sacrificing their opinions they prostitute themselves. Moralists and philosophers in America are not obliged to conceal their opinions under the
veil of allegory; but before they venture upon a harsh truth, they say: "We

are aware that the people whom we are addressing are too superior to the weaknesses of human nature to lose the command of their temper for an instant. We should not hold this language if we were not speaking to men whom their virtues and their intelligence render more worthy of freedom than all the rest of the world." The sycophants of Louis XIV could not flatter more dexterously.

For my part, I am persuaded that in all governments, whatever their nature may be, servility will cower to force, and adulation will follow power. The only means of preventing men from degrading themselves is to invest no one with that unlimited authority which is the sure method of debasing them.

Governments usually perish from impotence or from tyranny. In the former case, their power escapes from them; it is wrested from their grasp in the latter. Many observers who have witnessed the anarchy of democratic states have imagined that the government of those states was naturally weak and impotent. The truth is that when war is once begun between parties, the government loses its control over society. But I do not think that a democratic power is naturally without force or resources; say, rather, that it is almost always by the abuse of its force and the misemployment of its resources that it becomes a failure. Anarchy is almost always produced by its tyranny or its mistakes, but not by its want of strength.

It is important not to confuse stability with force, or the greatness of a thing with its duration. In democratic republics the power that directs * society is not stable, for it often changes hands and assumes a new direction. But whichever way it turns, its force is almost irresistible. The governments of the American republics appear to me to be as much centralized as those of the absolute monarchies of Europe, and more energetic than they are. I do not, therefore, imagine that they will perish from weakness.†

* This power may be centralized in an assembly, in which case it will be strong without being stable; or it may be centralized in an individual, in which case it will be less strong, but more stable.

† I presume that it is scarcely necessary to remind the reader here, as well as throughout this chapter, that I am speaking, not of the Federal government, but of the governments of the individual states, which the majority controls at its pleasure.

If ever the free institutions of America are destroyed, that event may be attributed to the omnipotence of the majority, which may at some future time urge the minorities to desperation and oblige them to have recourse to physical force. Anarchy will then be the result, but it will have been brought about by despotism.

Mr. Madison expresses the same opinion in *The Federalist*, No. 51. "It is of great importance in a republic, not only to guard the society against the oppression of its rulers, but to guard one part of the society against the injustice of the other part. Justice is the end of government. It is the end of civil society. It ever has been, and ever will be, pursued until it be obtained, or until liberty be lost in the pursuit. In a society, under the forms of which the stronger faction can readily unite and oppress the weaker, anarchy may as truly be said to reign as in a state of nature, where the weaker individual is not secured against the violence of the stronger: and as, in the latter state, even the stronger individuals are prompted by the uncertainty of their condition to submit to a government which may protect the weak as well as themselves, so, in the former state, will the more powerful factions be gradually induced by a like motive to wish for a government which will protect all parties, the weaker as well as the more powerful. It can be little doubted, that, if the State of Rhode Island was separated from the Confederacy and left to itself, the insecurity of right under the popular form of government within such narrow limits would be displayed by such reiterated oppressions of the factious majorities, that some power altogether independent of the people would soon be called for by the voice of the very factions whose misrule had proved the necessity of it."

Jefferson also said: "The executive power in our government is not the only, perhaps not even the principal, object of my solicitude. The tyranny of the legislature is really the danger most to be feared, and will continue to be so for many years to come. The tyranny of the executive power will come in its turn, but at a more distant period."

I am glad to cite the opinion of Jefferson upon this subject rather than that of any other, because I consider him the most powerful advocate democracy has ever had.

QUESTIONS AND TOPICS

1. How applicable are de Tocqueville's remarks to your home town? Your high school? (*Hint:* Be sure to distinguish between an actual and an apparent minority. The Republican Party is *not* a minority, even if it loses an election. The Communist Party and the John Birch Society are minorities. So are atheist, nudist, and prohibitionist groups.)
2. Which groups, if any, suffer most from the tyranny of the majority?
3. In which states would one be likely to find the most tyranny of the majority? The least? In which industries and professions?
4. Universities are regarded as havens of free thought and enquiry. Do you find that your professors have more freedom than your high-school teachers? What kinds of public statements can a professor make without losing his job? Can he put forth opinions in his publications that he cannot advocate in his classroom?
5. Does the modern university foster too much free thought?
6. Is too much free thought an evil? Can excessive freedom of publication become an evil?
7. Since the time of de Tocqueville, a great deal of social change has taken place in the United States. Are any of his illustrations dated? What is your opinion about the growing freedom in regard to sex and religion?

Henry David Thoreau

from
ON THE DUTY
OF CIVIL
DISOBEDIENCE

Shortly after his graduation from Harvard, Henry David Thoreau, 1817–1862, decided to leave the common path and live, for a time, a life of economic and social freedom. Walden *is the story of that life. Thoreau's independence also showed itself in his opposition to slavery and the Mexican War. His essay* On the Duty of Civil Disobedience, *1848, explains why Thoreau was willing to go to jail rather than pay his poll tax.*

I heartily accept the motto,—"That government is best which governs least"; and I should like to see it acted up to more rapidly and systematically. Carried out, it finally amounts to this, which also I believe,—"That government is best which governs not at all"; and when men are prepared for it, that will be the kind of government they will have. Government is at best but an expedient; but most governments are usually, and all governments are sometimes, inexpedient. . . .

But, to speak practically and as a citizen, unlike those who call themselves no-government men, I ask for, not at once no government, but *at once* a better government. Let every man make known what kind of government would command his respect, and that will be one step toward obtaining it.

After all, the practical reason why, when the power is once in the hands of the people, a majority are permitted, and for a long period continue, to rule is not because they are most likely to be in the right, nor because this seems fairest to the minority, but because they are physically the strongest. But a government in which the majority rule in all cases cannot be based on justice, even as far as men understand it. Can there not be a government in which majorities do not virtually decide right and wrong, but conscience?—in which majorities decide only those questions to which the rule of expediency is applicable? Must the citizen ever for a moment, or in the least degree, resign his conscience to the legislator? Why has every man a conscience, then? I think that we should be men first, and subjects afterward. It is not desirable to cultivate a respect for the law, so much as for the right. The only obligation which I have a right to assume is to do at any time what I think right. It is truly enough said, that a corporation has no conscience; but a corporation of conscientious men is a corporation *with* a conscience. Law never made men a whit more just; and, by means of their respect for it, even the well-disposed are daily made the agents of injustice. A common and natural result of an undue respect for law is, that you may see a file of soldiers, colonel, captain, corporal, privates, powder-monkeys, and all, marching in admirable order over hill and dale to the wars, against their wills, ay, against their common sense and consciences, which makes it very steep marching indeed, and produces a palpitation of the heart. They have no doubt that it is a damnable business in which they are concerned; they are all peaceable inclined. Now, what are they? Men at all? or small movable forts and magazines, at the service of some unscrupulous man in power? Visit the Navy-Yard, and behold a marine, such a man as an American government can make, or such as it can make a man with its black arts,—a mere shadow and reminiscence of humanity, a man laid out alive and standing, and already, as one may say, buried under arms with funeral accompaniments, though it may be,—

> Not a drum was heard, not a funeral note,
>   As his corse to the rampart we hurried;
> Not a soldier discharged his farewell shot
>   O'er the grave where our hero we buried.

The mass of men serve the state thus, not as men mainly, but as machines, with their bodies. They are the standing army, and the militia, jailers, constables, *posse comitatus,* etc. In most cases there is no free exercise whatever of the judgment or of the moral sense; but they put themselves on a level with wood and earth and stones; and wooden men can perhaps be manufactured that will serve the purpose as well. Such command no more respect than men of straw or a lump of dirt. They have the same sort of worth only as horses and dogs. Yet such as these even are commonly esteemed good citizens. Others—as most legislators, politicians, lawyers, ministers, and office-holders—serve the state chiefly with their heads; and, as they rarely make any moral distinctions, they are as likely to serve the Devil, without *intending* it, as God. A very few, as heroes, patriots, martyrs, reformers in the great sense, and *men,* serve the state with their consciences also, and so necessarily resist it for the most part; and they are commonly treated as enemies by it. . . .

How does it become a man to behave toward this American government to-day? I answer, that he cannot without disgrace be associated with it. I cannot for an instant recognize that political organization as *my* government which is the *slave's* government also.

All men recognize the right of revolution; that is, the right to refuse allegiance to, and to resist, the government, when its tyranny or its inefficiency are great and unendurable. But almost all say that such is not the case now. But such was the case, they think, in the Revolution of '75. If one were to tell me that this was a bad government because it taxed certain foreign commodities brought to its ports, it is most probable that I should not make an ado about it, for I can do without them. All machines have their friction; and possibly this does enough good to counterbalance the evil. At any rate, it is a great evil to make a stir about it. But when the friction comes to have its machine, and oppression and robbery are organized, I say, let us not have such a machine any longer. In other words, when a sixth of the population of a nation which has undertaken to be the refuge of liberty are slaves, and a whole country is unjustly overrun and conquered by a foreign army, and subjected to military law, I think that it is not too soon for honest men to rebel and revolutionize. What makes this duty the more urgent is the fact that the country so overrun is not our own, but ours is the invading army.

Paley, a common authority with many on moral questions, in his chapter on the "Duty of Submission to Civil Government," resolves all civil obligation into expediency; and he proceeds to say, "that so long as the interest of the whole society requires it, that is, so long as the established government cannot be resisted or changed without public inconveniency, it is the will of God that the established government be obeyed, and no longer. . . . This principle being admitted, the justice of every particular case of resistance is reduced to a computation of the quantity of the danger and grievance on the one side, and of the probability and expense of redressing it on the other." Of this, he says, every man shall judge for himself. But Paley appears never to have contemplated those cases to which the rule of expediency does not apply, in which a people, as well as an individual, must do justice, cost what it may. If I have unjustly wrested a plank from a drowning man, I must restore it to him though I drown myself. This, according to Paley, would be inconvenient. But he that would save his life, in such a case, shall lose it. This people must cease to hold slaves, and to make war on Mexico, though it cost them their existence as a people.

In their practice, nations agree with Paley; but does any one think that Massachusetts does exactly what is right at the present crisis?

> A drab of state, a cloth-o'-silver slut,
>   To have her train borne up, and her soul trail in the dirt.

Practically speaking, the opponents to a reform in Massachusetts are not a hundred thousand politicians at the South, but a hundred thousand merchants and farmers here, who are more interested in commerce and agriculture than they are in humanity, and are not prepared to do justice to the slave and to Mexico, *cost what it may.* I quarrel not with far-off foes, but with those who, near at home, cooperate with, and do the bidding of, those far away, and without whom the latter would be harmless. . . . There are thousands who are *in opinion* opposed to slavery and to the war, who yet in effect do nothing to put an end to them; who, esteeming themselves children of Washington and Franklin, sit down with their hands in their pockets, and say that they know not what to do, and do nothing; who even postpone the question of freedom to the question of free-trade, and quietly read the prices-current along with the latest advice from Mexico, after dinner, and, it may be, fall asleep over them both. What is the price-current of an honest man and patriot today? They hesitate, and they regret, and sometimes they petition; but they do nothing in earnest and with effect. They will wait, well disposed, for others to remedy the evil, that they may no longer have it to regret. At most, they give only a cheap vote, and a feeble countenance and God-speed, to the right, as it goes by them. There are nine hundred and ninety-nine patrons of virtue to one virtuous man. But it is easier to deal with the real possessor of a thing than with the temporary guardian of it. . . .

How many *men* are there to a square thousand miles in this country? Hardly one. Does not America offer any inducement for men to settle here? The American has dwindled into an Odd Fellow,—one who may be known by the development of his organ of gregariousness, and a manifest lack of intellect and cheerful self-reliance. . . .

It is not a man's duty, as a matter of course, to devote himself to the eradication of any, even the most enormous wrong; he may still properly have other concerns to engage him; but it is his duty, at least, to wash his hands of it, and, if he gives it no thought longer, not to give it practically his support. If I devote myself to other pursuits and contemplations, I must first see, at least, that I do not pursue them sitting upon another man's shoulders. I must get off him first, that he may pursue his contemplations too. See what gross inconsistency is tolerated. I have heard some of my townsmen say, "I should like to have them order me out to help put down an insurrection of the slaves, or to march to Mexico; —see if I would go;" and yet these men have each, directly by their allegiance, and so indirectly, at least, by their money, furnished a substitute.* The soldier is applauded who refuses to serve in an unjust war by those who do not refuse to sustain the unjust government which makes the war; is applauded by those whose own act and authority he disregards and sets at naught; as if the state were penitent to that degree that it hired one to scourge it while it sinned, but not to that degree that it left off sinning for a moment. Thus, under the name of Order and Civil Government, we are all made at last to pay homage to and support our own meanness. After the first blush of sin comes its indifference; and from immoral it becomes, as it were, *un*moral, and not quite unnecessary to that life which we have made. . . .

. . . Those who, while they disapprove of the character and measures of a government, yield to it their allegiance and support are undoubtedly its most conscientious supporters, and so frequently the most serious obstacles to reform. Some are petitioning the state to dissolve the Union, to disregard the requisitions of the President. Why do they not dissolve it themselves,—the union between themselves and the state,—and refuse to pay their quota into its treasury? Do not they stand in the same relation to the state that the state does to the Union? And have not the same

---

* During Thoreau's time a man could avoid military service by paying for a substitute. [Ed.]

reasons prevented the state from resisting the Union which have prevented them from resisting the state?

How can a man be satisfied to entertain an opinion merely, and enjoy *it*? Is there any enjoyment in it, if his opinion is that he is aggrieved? If you are cheated out of a single dollar by your neighbor, you do not rest satisfied with knowing that you are cheated, or with saying that you are cheated, or even with petitioning him to pay you your due; but you take effectual steps at once to obtain the full amount, and see that you are never cheated again. Action from principle, the perception and the performance of right, changes things and relations; it is essentially revolutionary, and does not consist wholly with anything which was. It not only divides states and churches, it divides families; ay, it divides the *individual,* separating the diabolical in him from the divine.

Unjust laws exist: shall we be content to obey them, or shall we endeavor to amend them, and obey them until we have succeeded, or shall we transgress them at once? Men generally, under such a government as this, think that they ought to wait until they have persuaded the majority to alter them. They think that, if they should resist, the remedy would be worse than the evil. But it is the fault of the government itself that the remedy is worse than the evil. *It* makes it worse. Why is it not more apt to anticipate and provide for reform? Why does it not cherish its wise minority? Why does it cry and resist before it is hurt? Why does it not encourage its citizens to be on the alert to point out its faults, and *do* better than it would have them? Why does it always crucify Christ, and excommunicate Copernicus and Luther, and pronounce Washington and Franklin rebels? . . .

If the injustice is part of the necessary friction of the machine of government, let it go, let it go: perchance it will wear smooth,—certainly the machine will wear out. If the injustice has a spring, or a pulley, or a rope, or a crank, exclusively for itself, then perhaps you may consider whether the remedy will not be worse than the evil; but if it is of such a nature that it requires you to be the agent of injustice to another, then, I say, break the law. Let your life be a counter friction to stop the machine. What I have to do is to see, at any rate, that I do not lend myself to the wrong which I condemn.

As for adopting the ways which the state has provided for remedying the evil, I know not of such ways. They take too much time, and a man's life will be gone. I have other affairs to attend to. I came into this world, not chiefly to make this a good place to live in, but to live in it, be it good or bad. A man has not everything to do, but something; and because he cannot do *everything*, it is not necessary that he should do *something* wrong. It is not my business to be petitioning the Governor or the Legislature any more than it is theirs to petition me; and if they should not hear my petition, what should I do then? But in this case the state has provided no way: its very Constitution is the evil. This may seem to be harsh and stubborn and unconciliatory; but it is to treat with the utmost kindness and consideration the only spirit that can appreciate or deserves it. So is all change for the better, like birth and death, which convulse the body.

I do not hesitate to say, that those who call themselves Abolitionists should at once effectually withdraw their support, both in person and property, from the government of Massachusetts and not wait till they constitute a majority of one, before they suffer the right to prevail through them. I think that it is enough if they have God on their side, without waiting for that other one. Moreover, any man more right than his neighbors constitutes a majority of one already.

I meet this American government, or its representative, the state government, directly, and face to face, once a year—no more—in the person of its tax-gatherer; this is the only mode in which a man situated as I am necessarily meets it; and it then says distinctly, Recognize me; and the simplest, most effectual, and, in the present posture of affairs, the indispensablest mode of treating with it on this head, of expressing your little satisfaction with and love for it, is to deny it then. My civil neighbor, the tax-gatherer, is the very man I have to deal with,—for it is, after all, with men and not with parchment that I quarrel,—and he has voluntarily chosen to be an agent of the government. . . . I know this well, that if one thousand, if one hundred, if ten men whom I could name,—if ten *honest* men only,—ay, if *one* HONEST man, in this State of Massachusetts, *ceasing to hold slaves,* were actually to withdraw from this copartnership, and be locked up in the county jail therefor, it would be the abolition of slavery in America. For it matters not how small the beginning may seem to be: what is once well done is done forever. But we love better to talk about it: that we say is our mission. . . .

Under a government which imprisons any unjustly, the true place for a just man is also a prison. The proper place today, the only place which Massachusetts has provided for her free and less desponding spirits, is in her prisons, to be put out and locked out of the State by her own act, as they have already put themselves out by their principles. It is there that the fugitive slave, and the Mexican prisoner on parole, and the Indian come to plead the wrongs of his race should find them; on that separate, but more free and honorable ground, where the State places those who are not *with* her, but *against* her,—the only house in a slave State in which a free man can abide with honor. If any think that their influence would be lost there, and their voices no longer afflict the ear of the State, that they would not be as an enemy within its walls, they do not know by how much truth is stronger than error, nor how much more eloquently and effectively he can combat injustice who has experienced a little in his own person. Cast your whole vote, not a strip of paper merely, but your whole influence. A minority is powerless while it conforms to the majority; it is not even a minority then; but it is irresistible when it clogs by its whole weight. If the alternative is to keep all just men in prison, or give up war and slavery, the State will not hesitate which to choose. If a thousand men were not to pay their tax-bills this year, that would not be a violent and bloody measure, as it would be to pay them, and enable the State to commit violence and shed innocent blood. This is, in fact, the definition of a peaceable revolution, if any such is possible. If the tax-gatherer, or any other public officer, asks me, as one has done, "But what shall I do?" my answer is, "If you really wish to do anything, resign your office." When the subject has refused allegiance, and the officer has resigned his office, then the revolution is accomplished. But even suppose blood should flow. Is there not a sort of blood shed when the conscience is wounded? Through this wound a man's real manhood and immortality flow out, and he bleeds to an everlasting death. I see this blood flowing now.

I have contemplated the imprisonment of the offender, rather than the seizure of his goods,—though both will serve the same purpose,—because they who assert the purest right, and consequently are most dangerous to a corrupt State, commonly have not spent much time in accumulating property. To such the State renders comparatively small service, and a slight tax is wont to appear exorbitant, particularly if they are obliged to earn it by special labor with their hands. If there were one who lived wholly without the use of money, the State itself would hesitate to demand it of him. But the rich man—not to make any invidious comparison —is always sold to the institution which makes him rich. Absolutely speaking, the more money, the less virtue; for money comes between a man and his objects, and obtains them for him; and it was certainly no great virtue to obtain it. It puts to rest many questions which he would otherwise be taxed to answer; while the only new question which it puts is the hard but superfluous one, how to spend it. Thus his moral ground is taken from under his feet. The opportunities of living are diminished in proportion as what are called the "means" are increased. The best thing a man can do for his culture when he is rich is to endeavor to carry out those schemes which he entertained when he was poor. Christ answered the Herodians according to their condition. "Show me the tribute-money," said he;—and one took a penny out of his pocket;—if you use money which has the image of Caesar on it and which he has made current and valuable, that is, *if you are men of the State,* and gladly enjoy the advantages of Caesar's government, then pay him back some of his own when he demands it. "Render therefore to Caesar that which is Caesar's, and to God those things which are God's,"—leaving them no wiser than before as to which; for they did not wish to know.

When I converse with the freest of my neighbors, I perceive that, whatever they may say about the magnitude and seriousness of the question, and their regard for the public tranquillity, the long and the short of the matter is, that they cannot spare the protection of the existing government, and they dread the consequences to their property and families of disobedience to it. For my own part, I should not like to think that I ever rely on the protection of the State. But, if I deny the authority of the State when it presents its tax-bill, it will soon take and waste all my property, and so harass me and my children without end. This is hard. This makes it impossible for a man to live honestly, and at the same time comfortably, in outward respects. It will not be worth the while to accumulate property; that would be sure to go again. You must hire or squat somewhere, and raise but a small crop, and eat that soon. You must live within yourself, and depend upon yourself always tucked up and ready for a start, and not have many affairs. A man may grow rich in Turkey even, if he will be in all respects a good subject of the Turkish government. Confucius said: "If a state is governed by the principles of reason, poverty and misery are subjects of shame; if a state is not governed by the principles of reason, riches and honors are the subjects of shame." . . .

I have paid no poll-tax for six years. I was put into a jail once on this account, for one night; and, as I stood considering the walls of solid stone, two or three feet thick, the door of wood and iron, a foot thick, and the iron grating which strained the light, I could not help being struck with the foolishness of that institution which treated me as if I were mere flesh and blood and bones, to be locked up. I wondered that it should have concluded at length that this was the best use it could put me to, and had never thought to avail itself of my services in some way. I saw that, if there was a wall of stone between me and my townsmen, there was a still more difficult one to climb or break through before they could get to be as free as I was. I did not for a moment feel confined, and the walls seemed a great waste of stone and mortar. I felt as if I alone of all my townsmen had paid my tax. They plainly did not know how to treat me, but behaved like persons who are underbred. In every threat and in every compliment there was a blunder; for they thought that my chief desire was to stand the other side of that stone wall. I could not but smile to see how industriously they locked the door on my meditations, which followed them out again without let or hindrance, and *they* were really all that was dangerous. As they could not reach me, they had resolved to punish my body; just as boys, if they cannot come at some person against whom they have a spite, will abuse his dog. I saw that the State was half-witted, that it was timid as a lone woman with her silver spoons, and that it did not know its friends from its foes, and I lost all my remaining respect for it, and pitied it.

Thus the State never intentionally confronts a man's sense, intellectual or moral, but only his body, his senses. It is not armed with superior wit or honesty, but with superior physical strength. I was not born to be forced. I will breathe after my own fashion. Let us see who is the strongest. What force has a multitude? They only can force me who obey a higher law than I. They force me to become like themselves. I do not hear of *men* being *forced* to live this way or that by masses of men. What sort of life were that to live? When I meet a government which says to me, "Your money or your life," why should I be in haste to give it my money? It may be in a great strait, and not know what to do: I cannot help that. It must help itself; do as I do. It is not worth the while to snivel about it. I am not responsible for the successful working of the machinery of society. I am not the son of the engineer. I perceive that, when an acorn and a chestnut fall side by side, the one does not remain inert to make way for the other, but both obey their own laws, and spring and grow and flourish as best they can, till one, perchance, overshadows and destroys the other. If a plant cannot live according to its nature, it dies; and so a man.

The night in prison was novel and interesting enough. The prisoners in their shirt-sleeves were enjoying a chat and the evening air in the door-way, when I entered. But the jailer said, "Come, boys, it is time to lock up;" and so they dispersed, and I heard the sound of their steps returning into the hollow apartments. My room-mate was introduced to me by the jailer as "a first-rate fellow and a clever man." When the door was locked, he showed me where to hang my hat, and how he managed matters there. The rooms were white-washed once a month; and this one, at least, was the whitest, most simply furnished, and probably the neatest apartment in the town. He naturally wanted to know where I came from, and what brought me there; and, when I had told him, I asked him in my turn how he came there, presuming him to be an honest man, of course; and, as the world goes, I believe he was. "Why," said he, "they accuse me of burn-ing a barn; but I never did it." As near as I could discover, he had prob-ably gone to bed in a barn when drunk, and smoked his pipe there; and so a barn was burnt. He had the reputation of being a clever man, had been there some three months waiting for his trial to come on, and would have to wait as much longer; but he was quite domesticated and con-tented, since he got his board for nothing, and thought that he was well treated.

He occupied one window, and I the other; and I saw that if one stayed there long, his principal business would be to look out the window. I had soon read all the tracts that were left there, and examined where former prisoners had broken out, and where a grate had been sawed off, and heard the history of the various occupants of that room; for I found that even here there was a history and a gossip which never circulated beyond the walls of the jail. Probably this is the only house in the town where verses are composed, which are afterward printed in a circular form, but not published. I was shown quite a long list of verses which were com-posed by some young men who had been detected in an attempt to escape, who avenged themselves by singing them.

I pumped my fellow-prisoner as dry as I could, for fear I should never see him again; but at length he showed me which was my bed, and left me to blow out the lamp.

It was like travelling into a far country, such as I had never expected to behold, to lie there for one night. It seemed to me that I never had heard the town-clock before, nor the evening sounds of the village; for we slept with the windows open, which were inside the grating. It was to see my native village in the light of the Middle Ages, and our Concord was turned into a Rhine stream, and visions of knights and castles passed before me. They were the voices of old burghers that I heard in the streets. I was an involuntary spectator and auditor of whatever was done and said in the kitchen of the adjacent village-inn,—a wholly new and rare experience to me. It was a closer view of my native town. I was fairly inside of it. I never had seen its institutions before. This is one of its peculiar institutions; for it is a shire town. I began to comprehend what its inhabitants were about.

In the morning, our breakfasts were put through the hole in the door, in small oblong-square tin pans, made to fit, and holding a pint of chocolate, with brown bread, and an iron spoon. When they called for the vessels again, I was green enough to return what bread I had left; but my comrade seized it, and said that I should lay that up for lunch or dinner. Soon after he was let out to work at haying in a neighboring field, whither he went every day, and would not be back till noon; so he bade me goodday, saying that he doubted if he should see me again.

When I came out of prison,—for some one interfered, and paid that tax,—I did not perceive that great changes had taken place on the common, such as he observed who went in a youth and emerged a tottering and gray-headed man; and yet a change had to my eyes come over the scene,—the town, and State, and country,—greater than any that mere time could effect. I saw yet more distinctly the State in which I lived. I saw to what extent the people among whom I lived could be trusted as good neighbors and friends; that their friendship was for summer weather only; that they did not greatly propose to do right; that they were a distinct race from me by their prejudices and superstitions, as the Chinamen and Malays are; that in their sacrifices to humanity they ran no risks, not even to their property; that after all they were not so noble but they treated the thief as he had treated them, and hoped, by a certain outward observance and a few prayers, and by walking in a particular straight though useless path from time to time, to save their souls. This may be to judge my neighbors harshly; for I believe that many of them are not aware that they have such an institution as the jail in their village. . . .

. . . I sometimes say to myself, When many millions of men, without heat, without ill will, without personal feeling of any kind, demand of you a few shillings only, without the possibility, such is their constitution, of retracting or altering their present demand, and without the possibility, on your side, of appeal to any other millions, why expose yourself to this overwhelming brute force? You do not resist cold and hunger, the winds and the waves, thus obstinately; you quietly submit to a thousand similar necessities. You do not put your head into the fire. But just in proportion as I regard this as not wholly a brute force, but partly a human force, and consider that I have relations to those millions as to so many millions of men, and not of mere brute or inanimate things, I see that appeal is possible, first and instantaneously, from them to the Maker of them, and, secondly, from them to themselves. But if I put my head deliberately into the fire, there is no appeal to fire or to the Maker of fire, and I have only myself to blame. If I could convince myself that I have any right to be satisfied with men as they are, and to treat them accordingly, and not according, in some respects, to my requisitions and expectations of what they and I ought to be, then, like a good Mussulman and fatalist, I should endeavor to be satisfied with things as they are, and say it is the will of God. And, above all, there is this difference between resisting this and a purely brute or natural force, that I can resist this with some effect; but I cannot expect, like Orpheus, to change the nature of the rocks and trees and beasts. . . .

The authority of government, even such as I am willing to submit to,— for I will cheerfully obey those who know and can do better than I, and in many things even those who neither know nor can do so well,—is still an impure one: to be strictly just, it must have the sanction and consent of the governed. It can have no pure right over my person and property but what I concede to it. The progress from an absolute to a limited monarchy, from a limited monarchy to a democracy, is a progress toward a true respect for the individual. Even the Chinese philosopher was wise enough to regard the individual as the basis of the empire. Is a democracy, such as we know it, the last improvement possible in government? Is it not possible to take a step further towards recognizing and organizing the rights of man? There will never be a really free and enlightened State until the State comes to recognize the individual as a higher and independent power, from which all its own power and authority are derived, and treats him accordingly. I please myself with imagining a State at last which can afford to be just to all men, and to treat the individual with respect as a neighbor; which even would not think it inconsistent with its own repose if a few were to live aloof from it, not meddling with it, nor embraced by it, who fulfilled all the duties of neighbors and fellow-men. A State which bore this kind of fruit, and suffered it to drop off as fast as it ripened, would prepare the way for a still more perfect and glorious State, which also I have imagined, but not yet anywhere seen.

QUESTIONS AND TOPICS

1. Would you agree with Thoreau that "government is at best but an expedient"? Do you regard any form of government as permanent and sacred?
2. Do you agree with Thoreau that the masses of men, those who obey the government without question, "have the same sort of worth only as horses and dogs"?
3. Thoreau cites two issues of his time which he thinks worthy of civil disobedience: the Mexican War and the slavery question. Do you think any issue today justifies civil disobedience?
4. Can a family man take Thoreau's attitude toward civil disobedience? Does he owe more to his principles or to his wife and family?
5. Is Thoreau's scorn for those who applaud dissent, but do not risk their own skins, deserved?
6. Are there certain laws existing which a man may break for reasons of conscience? Or are all laws equally sacred?

Plato

CRITO

Plato, 428–347 B.C., wrote several dialogues dealing with the trial and execution of his beloved master, Socrates. Crito is one of them. Socrates has been convicted of corrupting the youth of Athens and has been sentenced to death. Awaiting execution, he is visited by a well-meaning friend who offers to help him escape. Socrates' defense of the right of Athens to imprison and execute him, even on false and unjust charges, and his refusal to evade his execution, contrast strongly with Thoreau's rejection of the sacredness of institutions.

SCENE:—The Prison of Socrates.

Socrates. Why have you come at this hour, Crito? it must be quite early?

Crito. Yes, certainly.

Socrates. What is the exact time?

Crito. The dawn is breaking.

Socrates. I wonder that the keeper of the prison would let you in.

Crito. He knows me, because I often come, Socrates; moreover, I have done him a kindness.

Socrates. And are you only just arrived?

Crito. No, I came some time ago.

Socrates. Then why did you sit and say nothing, instead of at once awakening me?

Crito. By the Gods, Socrates, I would rather not myself have all this sleeplessness and sorrow. And I have been wondering at your peaceful

Note: Dialogue translated by B. Jowett (The Clarendon Press: Oxford, 1867).

slumbers, which was the reason why I did not awaken you, because I wanted you to be out of pain. I have always thought you of a happy disposition; but never did I see anything like the easy, tranquil manner in which you bear this calamity.

Socrates. Why, Crito, when a man has reached my age he ought not to be repining at the prospect of death.

Crito. And yet other old men find themselves in similar misfortunes, and age does not prevent them from repining.

Socrates. That may be. But you have not told me why you come at this early hour.

Crito. I come to bring you a message which is sad and painful; not, as I believe, to yourself, but to all of us who are your friends, and saddest of all to me.

Socrates. What? Has the ship come from Delos, on the arrival of which I am to die?

Crito. No, the ship has not actually arrived, but she will probably be here to-day, as persons who have come from Sunium tell me that they left her there; and therefore to-morrow, Socrates, will be the last day of your life.

Socrates. Very well, Crito; if such is the will of God, I am willing; but my belief is that there will be a delay of a day.

Crito. Why do you think so?

Socrates. I will tell you. I am to die on the day after the arrival of the ship.

Crito. Yes; that is what the authorities say.

Socrates. But I do not think that the ship will be here until to-morrow; this I infer from a vision which I had last night, or rather only just now, when you fortunately allowed me to sleep.

Crito. And what was the nature of the vision?

Socrates. There came to me the likeness of a woman, fair and comely, clothed in white raiment, who called to me and said: O Socrates,

'The third day hence to Phthia shalt thou go.' *

Crito. What a singular dream, Socrates!

Socrates. There can be no doubt about the meaning, Crito, I think.

Crito. Yes; the meaning is only too clear. But, Oh! my beloved Socrates,

---

* Homer, *Iliad,* Book ix. [Ed.]

let me entreat you once more to take my advice and escape. For if you die I shall not only lose a friend who can never be replaced, but there is another evil: people who do not know you and me will believe that I might have saved you if I had been willing to give money, but that I did not care. Now, can there be a worse disgrace than this—that I should be thought to value money more than the life of a friend? For the many will not be persuaded that I wanted you to escape, and that you refused.

Socrates. But why, my dear Crito, should we care about the opinion of the many? Good men, and they are the only persons who are worth considering, will think of these things truly as they occurred.

Crito. But you see, Socrates, that the opinion of the many must be regarded, for what is now happening shows that they can do the greatest evil to any one who has lost their good opinion.

Socrates. I only wish, Crito, that they could; for then they could also do the greatest good, and that would be well. But in reality they can do neither; for they cannot either make a man wise or make him foolish; and whatever they do is the result of chance.

Crito. Well, I will not dispute with you; but please to tell me, Socrates, whether you are not acting out of regard to me and your other friends: are you not afraid that if you escape from prison we may get into trouble with the informers for having stolen you away, and lose either the whole or a great part of our property; or that even a worse evil may happen to us? Now, if this is your fear, be at ease; for in order to save you, we ought surely to run this, or even a greater risk; be persuaded, then, and do as I say.

Socrates. Yes, Crito, that is one fear which you mention, but by no means the only one.

Crito. Fear not. There are persons who at no great cost are willing to save you and bring you out of prison; and as for the informers, they are far from being exorbitant in their demands; you may observe that a little money will satisfy them. My means, which are certainly ample, are at your service, and if you have a scruple about spending all mine, here are strangers who will give you the use of theirs; and one of them, Simmias the Theban, has brought a sum of money for this very purpose; and Cebes and many others are willing to spend their money too. I say therefore, do not on that account hesitate about making your escape, and do not say, as you did in the court, that you will have a difficulty in knowing what to do with yourself if you escape. For men will love you in other places to which you may go, and not in Athens only; there are friends of mine in Thessaly,* if you like to go to them, who will value and protect you, and no Thessalian will give you any trouble. Nor can I think that you are justified, Socrates, in betraying your own life when you might be saved; this is playing into the hands of your enemies and destroyers; and further I should say that you were deserting your own children; for you might bring them up and educate them; instead of which you go away and leave them, and they will have to take their chance; and if they do not meet with the usual fate of orphans, there will be small thanks to you. No man should bring children into the world who is unwilling to persevere to the end in their nurture and education. But you appear to be choosing the easier part, not the better and manlier, which would rather have become one who professes to care for virtue in all his actions, like yourself. And indeed, I am ashamed not only of you, but of us who are your friends, when I reflect that this affair of yours will be attributed entirely to our want of courage. The trial need never have come on, or might have been managed differently; and this last act, or crowning folly, will seem to have occurred through our negligence and cowardice, who might have saved you, if we had been good for anything, as you might have saved yourself, for there was no difficulty at all. See now, Socrates, how sad and dishonourable are the consequences, both to us and you. Make up your mind then, or rather have your mind already made up, for the time of deliberation is over, and there is only one thing to be done, which must be done this very night, and if we delay at all will be no longer practicable or possible; I beseech you therefore, Socrates, be persuaded by me, and do as I say.

Socrates. Dear Crito, your zeal is invaluable, if a right one; but if wrong, the greater the zeal the greater the danger; and therefore we ought to consider whether I shall or shall not do as you say. For I am and always have been one of those natures who must be guided by reason, whatever the reason may be which upon reflection appears to me to be the best; and now that this fortune has come upon me, I cannot put away the conclusion at which I had arrived: the principles which I have hitherto honoured and revered I still honour, and unless we can at once find other and better principles, I am certain not to agree with you; no, not even if the power of the multitude could inflict many more imprisonments, con-

---

* City in northern Greece. [Ed.]

fiscations, deaths, frightening us like children with hobgoblin terrors. But what will be the fairest way of considering the question? Shall I return to your old argument about the opinions of men? some of which are to be regarded, and others, as we were saying, are not to be regarded. Now were we right in maintaining this before I was condemned? And has the argument which was once good now proved to be talk for the sake of talking;—in fact an amusement only, and altogether vanity? That is what I want to consider with your help, Crito:—whether, under my present circumstances, the argument appears to be in any way different or not; and is to be allowed by me or disallowed. That argument, which, as I believe, is maintained by many who assume to be authorities, was to the effect, as I was saying, that the opinions of some men are to be regarded, and of other men not to be regarded. Now you, Crito, are a disinterested person who are not going to die to-morrow—at least, there is no human probability of this, and you are therefore not liable to be deceived by the circumstances in which you are placed. Tell me then, whether I am right in saying that some opinions, and the opinions of some men only, are to be valued, and that other opinions, and the opinions of other men, are not to be valued. I ask you whether I was right in maintaining this?

Crito. Certainly.

Socrates. The good are to be regarded, and not the bad?

Crito. Yes.

Socrates. And the opinions of the wise are good, and the opinions of the unwise are evil?

Crito. Certainly.

Socrates. And what was said about another matter? Was the disciple in gymnastics supposed to attend to the praise and blame and opinion of every man, or of one man only—his physician or trainer, whoever that was?

Crito. Of one man only.

Socrates. And he ought to fear the censure and welcome the praise of that one only, and not of the many?

Crito. That is clear.

Socrates. And he ought to act and train, and eat and drink in the way which seems good to his single master who has understanding, rather than according to the opinion of all other men put together?

Crito. True.

Socrates. And if he disobeys and disregards the opinion and approval of the one, and regards the opinion of the many who have no understanding, will he not suffer evil?

Crito. Certainly he will.

Socrates. And what will the evil be, whither tending and what affecting, in the disobedient person?

Crito. Clearly, affecting the body; that is what is destroyed by the evil.

Socrates. Very good; and is not this true, Crito, of other things which we need not separately enumerate? In questions of just and unjust, fair and foul, good and evil, which are the subjects of our present consultation, ought we to follow the opinion of the many and to fear them; or the opinion of the one man who has understanding? ought we not to fear and reverence him more than all the rest of the world: and if we desert him shall we not destroy and injure that principle in us which may be assumed to be improved by justice and deteriorated by injustice;—there is such a principle?

Crito. Certainly there is, Socrates.

Socrates. Take a parallel instance:—if, acting under the advice of men who have no understanding, we destroy that which is improved by health and is deteriorated by disease, would life be worth having? And that which has been destroyed is—the body?

Crito. Yes.

Socrates. Could we live, having an evil and corrupted body?

Crito. Certainly not.

Socrates. And will life be worth having, if that higher part of man be destroyed, which is improved by justice and deteriorated by injustice? Do we suppose that principle, whatever it may be in man, which has to do with justice and injustice, to be inferior to the body?

Crito. Certainly not.

Socrates. More honoured, then?

Crito. Far more honoured.

Socrates. Then, my friend, we must not regard what the many say of us: but what he, the one man who has understanding of just and unjust, will say, and what the truth will say. And therefore you begin in error when you advise that we should regard the opinion of the many about just and unjust, good and evil, honourable and dishonourable.—'Well,' some one will say, 'but the many can kill us.'

Crito. Yes, Socrates; that will clearly be the answer.

Socrates. That is true: but still I find with surprise that the old argument is, as I conceive, unshaken as ever. And I should like to know whether I may say the same of another proposition—that not life, but a good life, is to be chiefly valued?

Crito. Yes, that also remains.

Socrates. And a good life is equivalent to a just and honourable one—that holds also?

Crito. Yes, that holds.

Socrates. From these premises I proceed to argue the question whether I ought or ought not to try and escape without the consent of the Athenians: and if I am clearly right in escaping, then I will make the attempt; but if not, I will abstain. The other considerations which you mention, of money and loss of character and the duty of educating one's children, are, I fear, only the doctrines of the multitude, who would be as ready to call people to life, if they were able, as they are to put them to death—and with as little reason. But now, since the argument has thus far prevailed, the only question which remains to be considered is, whether we shall do rightly either in escaping or in suffering others to aid in our escape and paying them in money and thanks, or whether we shall not do rightly; and if the latter, then death or any other calamity which may ensue on my remaining here must not be allowed to enter into the calculation.

Crito. I think that you are right, Socrates; how then shall we proceed?

Socrates. Let us consider the matter together, and do you either refute me if you can, and I will be convinced; or else cease, my dear friend, from repeating to me that I ought to escape against the wishes of the Athenians: for I am extremely desirous to be persuaded by you, but not against my own better judgment. And now please to consider my first position, and try how you can best answer me.

Crito. I will.

Socrates. Are we to say that we are never intentionally to do wrong, or that in one way we ought and in another way we ought not to do wrong, or is doing wrong always evil and dishonourable, as I was just now saying, and as has been already acknowledged by us? Are all our former admissions which were made within a few days to be thrown away? And have we, at our age, been earnestly discoursing with one another all our life long only to discover that we are no better than children? Or, in spite of the opinion of the many, and in spite of consequences whether better or worse, shall we insist on the truth of what was then said, that injustice is always an evil and dishonour to him who acts unjustly? Shall we say so or not?

Crito. Yes.

Socrates. Then we must do no wrong?

Crito. Certainly not.

Socrates. Nor when injured injure in return, as the many imagine; for we must injure no one at all?

Crito. Clearly not.

Socrates. Again, Crito, may we do evil?

Crito. Surely not, Socrates.

Socrates. And what of doing evil in return for evil, which is the morality of the many—is that just or not?

Crito. Not just.

Socrates. For doing evil to another is the same as injuring him?

Crito. Very true.

Socrates. Then we ought not to retaliate or render evil for evil to any one, whatever evil we may have suffered from him. But I would have you consider, Crito, whether you really mean what you are saying. For this opinion has never been held, and never will be held, by any considerable number of persons; and those who are agreed and those who are not agreed upon this point have no common ground, and can only despise one another when they see how widely they differ. Tell me, then, whether you agree with and assent to my first principle, that neither injury nor retaliation nor warding off evil by evil is ever right. And shall that be the premiss of our argument? Or do you decline and dissent from this? For thus I have ever thought, and still think; but, if you are of another opinion, let me hear what you have to say. If, however, you remain of the same mind as formerly, I will proceed to the next step.

Crito. You may proceed, for I have not changed my mind.

Socrates. Then I will proceed to the next step, which may be put in the form of a question:—Ought a man to do what he admits to be right, or ought he to betray the right?

Crito. He ought to do what he thinks right.

Socrates. But if this is true, what is the application? In leaving the prison against the will of the Athenians, do I wrong any? or rather do I not wrong those whom I ought least to wrong? Do I not desert the principles which were acknowledged by us to be just—what do you say?

Crito. I cannot tell, Socrates; for I do not know.

Socrates. Then consider the matter in this way:—Imagine that I am about to play truant (you may call the proceeding by any name which you like), and the laws and the government come and interrogate me: 'Tell us, Socrates,' they say; 'what are you about? are you going by an act of yours to overturn us—the laws, and the whole state, as far as in you lies? Do you imagine that a state can subsist and not be overthrown, in which the decisions of law have no power, but are set aside and overthrown by individuals?' What will be our answer, Crito, to these and the like words? Any one, and especially a rhetorician, will have a good deal to say on behalf of the law which requires a sentence to be carried out;—he will argue that this law should not be set aside; and we might reply, 'Yes; but the state has injured us and given an unjust sentence.' Suppose I say that?

Crito. Very good, Socrates.

Socrates. 'And was that our agreement with you?' the law would reply; 'or were you to abide by the sentence of the state?' And if I were to express my astonishment at their words, the law would probably add: 'Answer, Socrates, instead of opening your eyes: you are in the habit of asking and answering questions. Tell us what complaint you have to make against us which justifies you in attempting to destroy us and the state? In the first place did we not bring you into existence? Your father married your mother by our aid and begat you. Say whether you have any objection to urge against those of us who regulate marriage?' None, I should reply. 'Or against those of us who after birth regulate the nurture and education of children, in which you also were trained? Were not the laws, which have the charge of education, right in commanding your father to train you in music and gymnastic?' Right, I should reply. 'Well then, since you were brought into the world and nurtured and educated by us, can you deny in the first place that you are our child and slave, as your fathers were before you? And if this is true you are not on equal terms with us; nor can you think that you have a right to do to us what we are doing to you. Would you have any right to strike or revile or do any other evil to your father or your master, if you had one, because you have been struck or reviled by him, or received some other evil at his hands?—you would not say this? And because we think right to destroy you, do you think that you have any right to destroy us in return, and your country as far as in you lies? Will you, O professor of true virtue, pretend that you are justified in this? Has a philosopher like you failed to discover that our country is more to be valued and higher and holier far than mother or father or any ancestor, and more to be regarded in the eyes of the gods and of men of understanding? also to be soothed, and gently and reverently entreated when angry, even more than a father, and if not persuaded, obeyed? And when we are punished by her, whether with imprisonment or stripes, the punishment is to be endured in silence; and if she lead us to wounds or death in battle, thither we follow as is right; neither may any one yield or retreat or leave his rank, but whether in battle or in a court of law, or in any other place, he must do what his city and his country order him; or he must change their view of what is just: and if he may do no violence to his father or mother, much less may he do violence to his country.' What answer shall we make to this, Crito? Do the laws speak truly, or do they not?

Crito. I think that they do.

Socrates. Then the laws will say: 'Consider, Socrates, if we are speaking truly that in your present attempt you are going to do us an injury. For, after having brought you into the world, and nurtured and educated you, and given you and every other citizen a share in every good which we had to give, we further proclaim to every Athenian, that if he does not like us when he has come of age and has seen the ways of the city, and made our acquaintance, he may go where he pleases and take his goods with him; and none of us laws will forbid him or interfere with him. Any of you who does not like us and the city, and who wants to emigrate to a colony or to any other city, may go where he likes, and take his goods with him. But he who has experience of the manner in which we order justice and administer the state, and still remains, has entered into an implied contract that he will do as we command him. And he who disobeys us is, as we maintain, thrice wrong; first, because in disobeying us he is disobeying his parents; secondly, because we are the authors of his education; thirdly, because he has made an agreement with us that he will duly obey our commands; and he neither obeys them nor convinces us that our commands are unjust; and we do not rudely impose them, but give him the alternative of obeying or convincing us;—that is what we offer, and he does neither. These are the sort of accusations to which, as we were saying, you, Socrates, will be exposed if you accomplish your intentions; you, above all other Athenians.' Suppose I ask, why is this? they will justly retort upon me that I above all other men have acknowledged the agreement. 'There is clear proof,' they will say, 'Socrates, that we and the city were not displeasing to you. Of all Athenians you have been the most constant resident in the city, which, as you never leave, you may be supposed to love. For you never went out of the city either to see the games, except once when you went to the Isthmus, or to any other place unless when you were on military service; nor did you travel as other men do. Nor had you any curiosity to know other states or their laws: your affections did not go beyond us and our state; we were your special favourites, and you acquiesced in our government of you; and here in this city you begat your children, which is a proof of your satisfaction. Moreover, you might, if you had liked, have fixed the penalty at banishment in the course of the trial—the state which refuses to let you go now would have let you go then. But you pretended that you preferred death to exile, and that you were not grieved at death. And now you have forgotten these fine sentiments, and pay no respect to us the laws, of whom you are the destroyer; and are doing what only a miserable slave would do, running away and turning your back upon the compacts and agreements which you made as a citizen. And first of all answer this very question: Are we right in saying that you agreed to be governed according to us in deed, and not in word only? Is that true or not?' How shall we answer, Crito? Must we not assent?

Crito. There is no help, Socrates.

Socrates. Then will they not say: 'You, Socrates, are breaking the covenants and agreements which you made with us at your leisure, not in any haste or under any compulsion or deception, but having had seventy years to think of them, during which time you were at liberty to leave the city, if we were not to your mind, or if our covenants appeared to you to be unfair. You had your choice, and might have gone either to Lacedaemon * or Crete,† which you often praise for their good government, or to some other Hellenic or foreign state. Whereas you, above all other Athenians, seemed to be so fond of the state, or, in other words, of us her laws (for who would like a state that has no laws), that you never stirred out of her; the halt, the blind, the maimed were not more stationary in her than you were. And now you run away and forsake your agreements. Not so, Socrates, if you will take our advice; do not make yourself ridiculous by escaping out of the city.

'For just consider, if you transgress and err in this sort of way, what good will you do either to yourself or to your friends? That your friends will be driven into exile and deprived of citizenship, or will lose their property, is tolerably certain; and you yourself, if you fly to one of the neighbouring cities, as, for example, Thebes or Megara, both of which are

---

* Sparta. [Ed.]
† Large island south of Greece. [Ed.]

well-governed cities, will come to them as an enemy, Socrates, and their government will be against you, and all patriotic citizens will cast an evil eye upon you as a subverter of the laws, and you will confirm in the minds of the judges the justice of their own condemnation of you. For he who is a corruptor of the laws is more than likely to be a corruptor of the young and foolish portion 'of mankind. Will you then flee from well-ordered cities and virtuous men? and is existence worth having on these terms? Or will you go to them without shame, and talk to them, Socrates? And what will you say to them? What you say here about virtue and justice and institutions and laws being the best things among men? Would that be decent of you? Surely not. But if you go away from well-governed states to Crito's friends in Thessaly, where there is great disorder and licence, they will be charmed to have the tale of your escape from prison, set off with ludicrous particulars of the manner in which you were wrapped in a goatskin or some other disguise, and metamorphosed as the fashion of runaways is—that is very likely; but will there be no one to remind you that in your old age you were not ashamed to violate the most sacred laws from a miserable desire of a little more life? Perhaps not, if you keep them in a good temper; but if they are out of temper you will hear many degrading things; you will live, but how?—as the flatterer of all men, and the servant of all men; and doing what?—eating and drinking in Thessaly, having gone abroad in order that you may get a dinner. And where will be your fine sentiments about justice and virtue then? Say that you wish to live for the sake of your children, that you may bring them up and educate them—will you take them into Thessaly and deprive them of Athenian citizenship? Is that the benefit which you would confer upon them? Or are you under the impression that they will be better cared for and educated here if you are still alive, although absent from them; for that your friends will take care of them? Do you fancy that if you are an inhabitant of Thessaly they will take care of them, and if you are an inhabitant of the other world that they will not take care of them? Nay; but if they who call themselves friends are good for anything, they surely will.

'Listen, then, Socrates, to us who have brought you up. Think not of life and children first, and of justice afterwards, but of justice first, that you may be justified before the princes of the world below. For neither will you nor any that belong to you be happier or holier or juster in this life, or happier in another, if you do as Crito bids. Now you depart in innocence, a sufferer and not a doer of evil; a victim, not of the laws but of men. But if you go forth, returning evil for evil, and injury for injury, breaking the covenants and agreements which you have made with us, and wronging those whom you ought least to wrong, that is to say, yourself, your friends, your country, and us, we shall be angry with you while you live, and our brethren, the laws in the world below, will receive you as an enemy; for they will know that you have done your best to destroy us. Listen, then, to us and not to Crito.'

This is the voice which I seem to hear murmuring in my ears, like the sound of the flute in the ears of the mystic; that voice, I say, is humming in my ears and prevents me from hearing any other. And I know that anything more which you may say will be vain. Yet speak, if you have anything to say.

Crito. I have nothing to say, Socrates.

Socrates. Leave me then to follow whithersoever God leads.

QUESTIONS AND TOPICS

1. What conception of Socrates' character have you gained from this brief dialogue? Do you think him a madman, a saint, or neither?
2. Do you feel, with Socrates, that an individual owes more to his country, assuming that he has consented to live there, than he owes to his mother and father? Do you think that a man unjustly convicted of a crime should accept his punishment because it has been decided by the country he loves?
3. Do you think any principle is worth dying for?
4. Can an individual's civil disobedience weaken his country?
5. Assume that we apply Socrates' principles to a war, rather than to a civil trial. Is the state justified in demanding absolute obedience of the individual, whether he considers the war just or unjust?
6. In *Crito* Socrates likens the state, with its laws, to a kind of supreme parent. Is this comparison valid?

Louis Auchincloss

BILLY
AND THE
GARGOYLES

Louis Auchincloss, 1917–, is a contemporary novelist who writes about the manners and problems of the very rich. "Billy and the Gargoyles," one of his best short stories, analyzes the conflict between a young nonconformist and the traditions of an established preparatory school, which might represent society at large.

Shirley school in appearance was gloomy enough to look at, but it was only when we returned there in later years that it seemed so to us. As boys, we took its looks for granted. The buildings were grouped in orderly lines around a square campus; they were of gray stone and had tall, Gothic windows. The ceilings inside were high, making large wall spaces which were covered with faded lithographs of Renaissance paintings. There was a chapel, a gymnasium, a schoolhouse, several dormitories and, scattered about at a little distance from the campus, the cottages of the married masters. No fence separated the school from the surrounding New England countryside, but none was needed. Shirley was a community unto itself; its very atmosphere prohibited escape or intrusion. The runaway boy would know that he was only running from his own future, and a trespasser would immediately feel that he was intruding on futures never intended for him. For Shirley, even through the shabby stone of its lamentable architecture, exuded the atmosphere of a hundred years of accumulated idealism. You were made as a boy to feel that great things would be expected of you after graduation; you would rise in steady ascent on the escalator of success as inevitably as you rose from one form to another in the school. Life was a pyramid, except that there was more room at the top, and anyone who had been through the dark years of hazing and athletic competitions, who had prayed and washed and conformed at Shirley, should and would get there. It was good to be ambitious because, being educated and God-fearing, you would raise the general level as you yourself rose to power, to riches, to a bishopric or to the presidency of a large university. At the end there was death, it was true, but with it even greater rewards, and old age, unlike Macbeth's, would be sweetened by a respectful lull broken only by the rattle of applause at testimonial dinners. I find that I can still look at life and feel that it ought to be this way, that I can still vaguely wonder why one year has not put me farther ahead than its predecessor. There were no such doubts at Shirley, unless they were felt by Billy Prentiss.

Billy was my cousin and the only other boy at school whom I knew when I went there first at the age of thirteen. The contrast between us, however, was not one to make me presume on the relationship. Billy came of a large and prosperous family, and I was an only child whose mother gave bridge lessons at summer hotels to help with my Shirley tuition. Billy, though thin and far from strong, was tall and fair and had an easy-going, outgiving personality; I was short, dark and of a truculent disposition. But these contrasts were as nothing before the overriding distinction between the "old kid" and the "new kid." Billy and I may have been in the same form, but he had completed a year at the school before my arrival, which gave him great social prerogatives. By Shirley's rigid code there should have been only the most formal relations between us.

Billy, however, did not recognize the code. That is what I mean when I say that he had doubts at Shirley. He greeted me from the first in a friendly manner that was entirely improper, as if we had been at home and not at school. He helped me to unpack and showed me my gymnasium locker and supplied me with white stiff collars for Sunday wear. He talked in an easy, chatty manner about how my mother had taught him bridge and what he had seen during the summer with his family in Europe, as if he believed that such things could be balanced against the things that were happening at Shirley, the real things. He was certainly an odd figure for an old kid; I think of him now as he looked during my first months at school, stalking through the corridors of the Lower Forms Building on his way to or from the library, running the long fingers of his left hand through his blond hair and whistl'ng "Mean To Me." He lived in a world of his own, and, with all my gratitude, I was sufficiently conservative to wonder if it wasn't Utopian. It embarrassed me, for example, when he was openly nice to me in the presence of other old kids.

"How are you getting on, Peter?" he asked me one morning after chapel as we walked to the schoolhouse. Nobody else called me by my Christian name. "Have you got everything you need? Can I lend you any books or clothes?"

"No, I'm fine, thank you."

"You're a cousin, you know," he said, looking at me seriously. "Cousins ought to help each other out. Even second cousins."

I didn't really believe that anyone could help me. Homesickness was like cutting teeth or having one's tonsils out. I nodded, but said nothing.

"If you have any trouble with the old kids, let me know," he continued. "I could speak to them. It might help."

"Oh, no please!" I explained. Nothing could have more impressed me with his otherworldliness than a suggestion so unorthodox. "You mustn't do that! It wouldn't be the thing at all!"

We were interrupted by voices from behind us, loud, sneering voices. It was what I had been afraid of.

"Is that Prentiss I see talking to a new kid? Can he so demean himself?"

"Do you pal around with new kids, Billy?"

"What's come over you, Prentiss?"

The last voice was stern; it was George Neale's.

"Peter Westcott happens to be my cousin," Billy answered with dignity, turning around to face them. "And there's nothing in the world wrong with him. Is there a law that I may not talk to my own cousin?"

He turned again to me, but I hurried ahead to join a group of new kids. I'm afraid I was shocked that he should speak in this fashion to a boy like George Neale. George, after all, was one of the undisputed leaders of the form. He was a small, fat, clumsy boy who commanded by the sheer deadliness of his tongue and the intensity of his animosities. He also enjoyed an immunity from physical retaliation through the reputation of a bad heart, the after-effect, it was generally said, of a childhood attack of rheumatic fever. He had chosen for his mission in school the persecution of those who failed to meet exactly the rigid standards of social behavior that our formmates, represented by himself, laid down. I sometimes wonder, in trying to recollect how George first appeared to me, if he derived the fierce satisfaction from his activities that I believed at the time. It seems more probable, as I bring back the straight, rather rigid features of

his round face and his tone of dry impatience, that he looked at nonconformists as Spanish Inquisitors looked at heretics who were brought before
them, as part of the day's work, something that had to be done, boring and
arduous though it might be. Why George should have been chosen as
the avenging agent of the gods it was not for him to ask; what mattered
only was that they required, for dim but cogent reasons of their own, a
division of the world into the oppressed and their oppressors. He and his
victims were the instruments of these gods, caught in the ruthless pattern
of what was and what was not "Shirley," a pattern more fundamental
and significant in the lives of all of us than the weak and distant humanitarianism of the faculty, who brooded above us, benevolent but powerless
to help, like the twentieth-century protestant God whom we worshiped in
the Gothic chapel.

George was in charge of the program of hazing the new kids, and
Billy's ill-considered kindness only resulted in bringing me prematurely to
his attention. Custom required that each new kid be singled out for a
particular ordeal, and I was soon made aware, from the conversation of
the old kids who raised their voices as I passed, that mine had been
decided on. Apparently I was to have my head shaved. I lived from this
point on in such an agony of apprehension that it was almost a relief to
discover one Sunday morning, from the atmosphere of huddles and whis-
pers around me, that George had chosen his moment. I retreated instinctively to the library to stay there until chapel, but the first time I looked
up from the book I was pretending to read, it was to find George and the
others gathered before me.

"Won't you come outside, Westcott?" George asked me in a mild, dry
tone. "We'd like to have a little talk with you."

"It won't take a minute, Westcott," another added with a leer.

No violence was allowed in the library; it was sanctuary. I could have
waited until the bell for chapel and departed in safety. George knew this,
but he knew too, as I knew, and he knew that I knew it, that the fruition
of his scheme was like the fall of Hamlet's sparrow: if it was not now, it
would be still to come. I got up without a word and walked out of the
library, down the corridor and out to the back lawn. There I turned around
and faced them.

There was a moment of hesitation, and then someone pushed me. I
went sprawling over on the grass, for George, unnoticed, had knelt behind
me. They all jumped on me, and I struggled violently, too violently,

destroying whatever sympathy might have been latent in them by giving one boy, whose heart was not really in it, a vicious kick in the stomach. In another moment I was overwhelmed and held firmly down while George produced the razor. I closed my eyes and felt giddy with hatred.

Then the miracle occurred. I distinctly heard a window open and a voice cry:

"Cheese it, fellows! Mr. O'Neil!"

And in a second twenty hands had released me, and I heard the thump of retreating feet in the earth under my head. I sat up dazedly and looked around. Nobody was there but Billy; he was standing inside the building looking out at me through an open window. He smiled and climbed over the low sill. He was actually helping me to my feet.

"Where did they go?" I demanded.

"They beat it."

"But why?"

He laughed.

"Didn't you hear me?"

I stared at him in perplexity.

"Then where's Mr. O'Neil?" I asked.

He laughed again.

"How should I know?"

I rubbed my head.

"Why did you do it, Billy?" I asked.

He helped me brush the grass off my blue suit.

"Because you're my cousin," he said cheerfully. "And because they're down on you. Isn't that enough?"

I felt for the first time since I had come to Shirley that I might be going to cry.

"They'll be back," I pointed out, "when they find out."

"Then let's clear out."

"You go," I said. "They're not after you."

Incredibly, he laughed again.

"They will be now."

Again we heard the stamping of feet, this time from within the building. The door burst open, and they surrounded us.

"What's the idea, Prentiss?" George snarled, stepping out of the circle toward him. "Where's Mr. O'Neil?"

Billy shrugged his shoulders and put his hands in his pockets.

"Didn't you see him? He and his wife were coming over by the hedge on their way to chapel."

He flung this off coolly, as if to him it was a matter of the utmost indifference whether or not he was believed. Then he gave his attitude a further emphasis by turning to me, quite casually, and smiling.

"We saw them, didn't we, Peter?" he said.

"Well, *we* didn't!" George cried.

"I can't be bothered with what you see and don't see," Billy retorted. "If you didn't, you didn't."

"Are you siding with Westcott, Prentiss?" George demanded. "Are you on the side of the new kids? Is that where you stand, Prentiss?"

He glanced from side to side at the others as he said this.

"What about it, Billy?"

"Are you with the new kids, Billy?"

"Let's *get* Prentiss!"

But just then the bell for assembly, at long last, jangled sharply from within the building, and the crowd burst apart and rushed up the steps to the door. I can still remember the fierce joy with which, as George Neale leaned down to pick up the comb that had slipped from his pocket, I stamped on it and broke it in two. He didn't even bother to look at me, but turned and hurried after his friends.

George was not a boy to let an assembly bell stand between him and his victim, and I lived for days in dread of a renewed effort to execute the head-shaving plan. I soon found out, however, that I had nothing personally to be afraid of. George, it was rumored, had put the new kids quite out of his mind; he was concentrating his energies on a project against the person whose basic challenge of authority he had so immediately recognized. One Sunday after chapel, when Billy was waylaid by the gang and pelted with the icy snowballs of the season's first snow, his books flung in the mud and the lining ripped from his hat, we knew that George's campaign had begun in earnest.

"I don't know if I'm quite as popular as I supposed," Billy told me, with a sort of desperate gaiety, as he and I engaged in the sorry task of collecting his books and rubbing them off. "I would suggest that I might be a good person to stay away from for a while."

"Cousins should help each other," I said tersely. "You told me that."

Every persecution has a pattern, and George soon revealed the nature of his. It was to establish that Billy was really not a boy at all, not even an effeminate boy, but a girl. This was carried out with the special vindictiveness which old kids reserved for other old kids who had been disloyal. George devised not one but several nicknames for his victim; Billy became known as "Bella," then as "Angela" and finally, with a venomous simplicity, as "Woman." George trained his boys to carry through the identification with a completeness that would have done credit to a secret police. He knew at an early age that the way to break a human being is never to relax, to follow him through the day and into the night until he lets down his guard for just a moment, a private moment, alone in his cubicle, in the lavatory, in his seat at chapel, and then to strike hardest. If George and the others found Billy taking a shower in the morning when they came into the lavatory, they would act like men who have stumbled into a ladies' room. "Eek!" they would shriek. "It's Angela! Excuse me." And they would leave the lavatory and insist on waiting outside even when the prefect on duty came by and ordered them in to take their showers, shouting in voices clearly audible to poor Billy: "But we can't go in! There's a naked woman in there," until the bewildered prefect would go in and find Billy and order them in, but not without a leer to show that he sided with the conspirators, grinning at their joke and looking the other way when, upon entering, they pelted Billy with pieces of soap, crying, "Cover her up! For the sake of decency cover her up!" George was careful to carry the use of the female pronoun into every department of life at school; if commenting on a translation of Billy's in Latin class he would say, even if reprimanded, "She left off the adjective in line ten, sir," or filing into the schoolroom for prayers he would always step aside, pushing the others with him, on Billy's arrival and cry, "Ladies first!" Even in chapel, the sacred chapel, where the headmaster, lost in illusion, believed that freedom of worship existed, I have seen Billy, intensely religious as one can only be at thirteen, interrupted from his devotions by having a hat jammed on his head by George, crouching in the pew ahead, and hearing him hiss: "Ladies always wear hats in church. Didn't Saint Paul say so?"

Billy's reaction to all of this seemed designed to bring out the worst in George. He simply appeared to ignore the whole thing. He would stare blankly, at times even pityingly at the crowd that baited him and then turn on his heel, carefully smoothing back the hair which they would inevitably have rumpled. He never seemed to lose his temper or strike back except when he was physically overwhelmed and pinned to the ground and then in a sudden galvanization of wheeling arms and legs, with closed eyes, he would try to fight himself free with an ineffective frenzy that only aroused laughter. But such moments were rare. For the most part he was remote and disdainful, like a marquise in a tumbrel looking over the heads of the mob.

The very fact that I think of a marquise and not a marquis shows the effectiveness of George's propaganda. I saw it all, for I stayed close to Billy throughout this period. The fact that he was in trouble on my account overcame, I am glad to say, my instinctive, if rather sullen, deference to the majority. And then, too, I should add, there was a certain masochistic pleasure in sacrificing myself on the altar of Billy's unpopularity. My real difficulty came less in sharing his distress than in sharing his attitude of superiority to it, for I believed, superstitiously, in all the things that he sneered at. I believed, as George believed, in the system, the hazing, in the whole grim division of the school world into those who "belonged" and those who didn't. The fact that I was one of the latter, partly at my own election, was not important; I was still a part of the system. It bothered me that Billy, on our Sunday walks in the country, insisted on discussing faraway, unreal things—home and his mother and her friends and what they did and talked about. He would never talk about George Neale, for example. One afternoon I made a point of this.

"Do you suppose there will always be people like Neale in life?" I asked him as we walked down the wooded path to the river. "Will we always have to be watching out for them?"

"George?" Billy queried, as if not quite sure to whom I had referred. He paused. "Why, people like George simply don't exist in my parents' world." He shrugged his shoulders. "After all, you can't spend your time throwing snowballs at people and expect to be invited out much. You don't make friends by going up to your host at a party and calling him by a woman's name."

"But he might learn to do other things, mightn't he?" I persisted. "Spread lies and things like that?"

"My dear Peter," Billy said with an amiable condescension, "George will be utterly helpless without his gang. And his gang, you see, will have grown up."

But he couldn't quite dispel my idea that some of the ugliness that was George might survive the grim barriers of our school days. Billy's faith in the future was a touching faith in a warm and sunny world where people moved to and fro without striking each other and conversed without insults, a world where the idea was appreciated, the mannerism ignored. I could feel the attraction of this future, so different from the Shirley future of struggle and success; I could even yearn for it, but try as I would, I could never quite bring myself to believe in it. As the sky grew darker and we turned back to the school and saw ahead over the trees the Gothic tower of the chapel, my heart contracted with a sense of guilt that I had been avoiding, even for an afternoon, the sober duty of facing Shirley facts.

"I don't know if the world will be so terribly different from school," I said gloomily. "I bet it's very much the same."

Even Billy's face clouded at this. It was as if I had voiced a doubt that he was desperately repressing, a doubt that if admitted would have made his troubles at school too much to bear. He gazed up at the tower, anticipating perhaps all that we were returning to, the changing of shirts and collars, the evening meal, the long study period amid the sniggering, the note-passing, the sly kick from the desk behind.

"It should have gargoyles, like cathedrals in Europe," he said suddenly. "Grinning little gargoyles like George Neale."

Even George could not keep a thing going forever, and the persecution of Billy at length became a bore to his gang. We had been through the long New England winter, and in the spring of second-form year we were beginning to emerge as individuals from the gray anonymity of childhood. We were even forming friendships based on something besides mutual insecurity and joint hostility to others, friendships more intense than any relationships that we were to know for many years. It was a time in our lives that the headmaster viewed with suspicion, conducive, as he believed it to be, to a state of mind which he darkly described as "sentimental," but it was nonetheless exciting to us to be aware of ourselves for the first time as something other than boys at Shirley. We were beginning to discover, in spite of everything, that there were not only blacks and whites, but reds and yellows in the world around us and that life itself could be something more than a struggle.

It seems clear to me now that George must have resented our maturing and the breakup of the old hard line between the accepted and the unaccepted. He tried to maintain his waning control over his group by reminding boys of their ungainliness and ineptitudes of a few months before, by reviving old issues and screaming the battle cries that used to range the group against the individual. He sought new victims, new scapegoats, but public opinion was increasingly unmanageable. George represented the past, or at most the passing; he was like an angry Indian medicine man who finds his tribe turning away to the attractions of a broader civilization. Though he could beat his drum and dance his dance, though he could even still manage to burn a few victims, essentially his day was over. But if George had been left behind, so, oddly enough, had Billy. Instead of stepping forward to take his place among the boys who would now have received him, he preferred to remain alone and aloof. He seemed tired, now that the ordeal was over, discouraged, just when there was hope. It was as if, in the struggle, he had received a small, deep wound that was only now beginning to fester. George, deprived of other victims, seemed to sense this, for he pressed the attack against Billy all alone, with a desperate vindictiveness, as if to deliver the last and fatal blow of which his declining power was capable. Their conflict had come to be an individual thing, almost a curiosity to the rest of us. They stood apart, fighting their own fight, quaint if rather grim reminders of a standard of values that had passed.

Toward the middle of spring Billy developed the habit of reporting sick to the infirmary. He would go there for two or three days at a time, using the old trick of touching his thermometer to a lamp bulb when the nurse was out of the room. The infirmary had its pleasant side; like the library it was sanctuary, an insulated white box where one could stay in bed and read the thick, rebound volumes of Dickens and Baroness Orczy. It so happened that we were both there, I with a sinus infection and he with the pretense of one, on the day of the game with Pollock School, the great event of the baseball season. I hated to miss the game, for it involved a half holiday, a trip to Pollock and a celebration afterward if we won. Billy, less regretful, was sharing a room with me on the empty second floor.

Late in the afternoon of the game, as we were working on a picture puzzle, Mrs. Jones, the matron's assistant, hurried in, greatly excited. One of the masters had just telephoned from Pollock to report that we had won the game. I gave a little yell of enthusiasm, partly sincere, partly perfunctory. Billy looked at me bleakly.

"Now we'll have that damn celebration," he said curtly. "Drums and cheers, drums and cheers, all night. God! And for what?"

He lost all interest in what we were doing and refused to discuss it with me. He lay back in bed and simply stared at the ceiling while I turned back to the unfinished puzzle.

It was late in the afternoon, about six o'clock, when the buses which had taken the school to Pollock began to return. We could hear the crunch of their wheels on the drive on the other side of the building and the excited yells of the disembarking boys. From across the campus came the muffled roll of the drums. Already the celebration was starting. The entire school and all the masters would now assemble before the steps of the headmaster's house. He would come out in a straw hat and a red blazer and be raised to the shoulders of the school prefect on a chair strapped to two poles. Waving his megaphone he would be borne away at the head of a procession to a martial tune of the fife and drum corps on a circuit of all the school buildings. Before each of these the crowd would stop and in response to the headmaster's deep "What have we here?" would shout the name of the building followed by the school cheer. As the slow procession wended its way around the campus it would become noisier and the cheers more numerous; wives of popular masters would be thunderously applauded and would have to appear at the windows of their houses to acknowledge the ovation; statues, gates, memorial fountains would be cheered until the procession wound up by the athletic field, where a bonfire would be built and the members of the triumphant team tossed aloft by multitudinous arms and cheered in the flickering light of the flames. And all the while the "outside," the big bell over the gymnasium which sounded the hours for rising, for going to chapel, for attending meals, a knell that brought daily to the countryside the austere routine of Shirley School, would toll and toll, symbolizing in its shocking unrestraint the extraordinary liberty of the day.

The atmosphere pervaded even the infirmary. Mrs. Gardner, the matron, and her assistant watched from the dispensary window. The infirmary cook gave Billy and me an extra helping of ice cream. I moved my bed over to the window and listened to the distant throb of the band. When it stopped we would know that the headmaster was speaking and a moment later would come the roar of the school cheer. Glancing at Billy, after one of these roars, I noticed that he looked pale and tense.

"Listen to that damn bell," he complained, when he saw me looking at him. "It gets on my nerves. It's like Saint Bartholomew's Day, with everyone coming after the Huguenots."

I said nothing to this, but there was something contagious about his tensity. As the shouts grew louder and more distinct, as we finally made out the stamp of feet, I got out of my bed and pushed it away from the window.

"What are you doing?" Billy asked me sharply. "Are you ashamed of being in the infirmary?"

He sat up suddenly and got out of bed. He walked to the open window and stood before it, his hands on his hips. From behind him, looking into the courtyard below, I could see the first boys arriving, waving school banners and blowing horns.

"Billy, get back," I begged him. "They'll see you! Please, Billy!"

Then I spotted the headmaster's chair coming around the corner of the adjacent building and ducked out of sight. Billy ignored me completely. From below, through the open windows, almost unbelievably close now, came the din of the assembling school. The drums kept beating, and laughter and jokes, often from recognizable voices, came to our ears. It seemed to me, as I shrank against the wall near the window, pressing my spinal cord against its white coldness, as though every shout and drumbeat, every retort, detaching itself from the general roar and suddenly coherent, every laugh and cheer, each sound of feet on gravel, was part of some huge reptilian figure surrounding the infirmary and our very room with the cold, muscular coils of its body. Fear pounded in me, sharp and irrational.

"Billy!" I called again at him. "Billy!"

There was a sudden silence outside, and we heard the rich, assured tones of the headmaster's voice, starting his classic interrogatory to the crowd.

"What is this building that I see before me?"

"The infirmary!" thundered the school.

"And who is the good lady who runs the infirmary?"

"Mrs. Gardner!"

"And does Mrs. Gardner have an assistant?"

"Mrs. Jones," roared the crowd.

This would have been followed immediately, in normal procedure, by the headmaster's request for cheers for the infirmary and for the good women who ran it. Instead there was an unexpected pause, a silence, and then, as my blood froze I heard the headmaster's other voice, his disciplinary voice, directed up and into the very window at which Billy was standing.

"Who is that boy in the window? Go away from that window, boy, and get to bed." It then added, with a chuckle for the benefit of the crowd: "Good gracious me, anyone might think he wasn't sick." There was a roar of laughter.

Billy, however, continued to stand there as if he hadn't heard, and the momentary hush that followed was broken by the sharp, clear tones of George Neale.

"Go back to bed, Angela! Can't you hear? Take the wax out of your ears!"

Once again there was a startled quiet. The amazement must have been as much at George's impudence as at Billy's immobility; it was unheard of for a boy to second the headmaster's order. The old struggle between George and Billy hung like a lantern in the darkening air before the upturned eyes of three hundred boys. It may have been the use of his nickname, the bold, casual, unconventional use of it before the boys and the faculty, before Mrs. Gardner and Mrs. Jones watching from the window of the dispensary, before the townspeople from Shirley who had come to watch the celebration, that broke Billy down. It was as if he had been stamped "Angela" unredeemably and for the ages. The future, in spite of all his protest, would be a Shirley future. He suddenly waved his arms in a frenzied, circular fashion at the mob.

"Three cheers for Pollock!" he screamed in a harsh voice that did not sound like him at all. "Three cheers for Pollock School!" he screamed. "I wish they'd licked us! I wish they had!"

What I remember feeling at this unbelievable outburst, as I pressed my back harder against the wall, was its inadequacy to express the outrage with which Billy was throbbing. It was too hopelessly disloyal, too hurt, too puerile to do more than dismay or shock. Yet he had said it. He had actually said it! Then the door opened and Mrs. Gardner came in, followed by Mr. O'Neil. I was moved at once to another room, and Billy at last was left alone.

He was taken out of school for good a few days later. His parents drove up from New York and had a long conference with the headmaster. Immediately afterward his things were packed. I was out of the infirmary by then and went to see his mother at the parents' house. She wept a good deal and talked to me as though I were grown up, which flattered me. She said that Billy had had a little "nervous trouble" and would be going home. She added that he was tired and would not be able to see anyone before he left. Then she kissed me and tucked a five-dollar bill in my pocket. I'm afraid that I rather enjoyed my sadness over the whole catastrophe.

At school, after Billy had gone, I did much better. In the ensuing years I rose to be manager of the school press, head librarian and even achieved the dignified status of rober to the headmaster in chapel. Billy diminished in retrospect to a thin, shrill figure lost in the past darkness of lower-school years. But it was only a part of me that felt this way. There was another part that was always uneasy about my disloyalty to the desperate logic of his isolation. It was as though I owed the warmth and friendliness that I later found at Shirley to a compromise that he had not been able to make. Whether or not I was justified in any such reservation can only be determined for himself by each individual who has passed as a boy through that semi-eternity which begins with homesickness and hazing and snowballs and ends, such seeming ages afterwards, with the white flannels and blue coats of commencement in the full glory of a New England spring.

QUESTIONS AND TOPICS

1. Write a character sketch of Billy. To what extent is he a victim of the system? To what extent does he doom himself?
2. Write a character sketch of George Neale. Why does he persecute Billy? Why do most of the boys follow him?
3. Is the system at Shirley School like that at other kinds of institutions? Do such systems exist in college? In adult life?
4. Write about an experience of your own that involves the persecution of a nonconformist. Be sure to analyze your reactions.
5. At the end of the story the narrator, Peter, feels that he "owed the warmth and friendliness that [he] later found at Shirley to a compromise that [Billy] had not been able to make." Do you think that one ought to compromise with the system in order to be accepted?

W. H. Auden

THE
UNKNOWN
CITIZEN

W. H. Auden, 1907–, has had a long and influential career as a poet. Born in England, he later became an American citizen, but he has maintained his reputation on both sides of the ocean. He has published consistently, commenting keenly and effectively on contemporary society.

(TO JS/07/M/378
This Marble Monument
Is Erected by the State)

He was found by the Bureau of Statistics to be
One against whom there was no official complaint,
And all the reports on his conduct agree
That in the modern sense of an old-fashioned word, he was a saint,
For in everything he did he served the Greater Community.
Except for the War till the day he retired
He worked in a factory and never got fired,
But satisfied his employers, Fudge Motors Inc.
Yet he wasn't a scab or odd in his views,
For his Union reports that he paid his dues,
(Our report on his Union shows it was sound)
And our Social Psychology workers found
That he was popular with his mates and liked a drink.
The Press are convinced that he bought a paper every day
And that his reactions to advertisements were normal in every way.
Policies taken out in his name prove that he was fully insured,
And his Health-card shows he was once in hospital but left it cured.

Both Producers Research and High-Grade Living declare
He was fully sensible to the advantages of the Instalment Plan
And had everything necessary to the Modern Man,
A phonograph, a radio, a car and a frigidaire.
Our researchers into Public Opinion are content
That he held the proper opinions for the time of year;
When there was peace, he was for peace; when there was war, he went.
He was married and added five children to the population,
Which our Eugenist says was the right number for a parent of his
    generation,
And our teachers report that he never interfered with their education.
Was he free? Was he happy? The question is absurd:
Had anything been wrong, we should certainly have heard.

QUESTIONS AND TOPICS

1. Is the unknown citizen a believable person, or is he merely a caricature?
   Which type of characterization would help Auden make his point most
   effectively?
2. Auden implies that the machine and machine civilization, which number
   everything and everybody, are destructive of human values. Do you agree?
   Does a social security number make a person more anonymous?
3. Auden seems worried that future society may contain even more unknown
   citizens. Do you think that further automation and mechanization will
   increase the type of conformity the unknown citizen represents?

4

THE QUALITY OF MODERN CIVILIZATION

DURING THE NINETEENTH CENTURY and early twentieth century, many social critics were concerned not only with the social structure of what seemed to be a newly emerging world order, but also with the quality of life within it. Was this new civilization worth the discomfort and dislocation that had accompanied its creation? Did it make life better for the poor, for the middle classes, for the highly educated?

Many nineteenth-century writers visited the United States to observe the new, democratic ideology in action. They felt, with some justification, that America constituted the future, but once they were there they felt uncomfortable. Like de Tocqueville and Arnold, many found America to be a nation whose culture was determined not by the aristocrat or the intellectual but by the masses.

The Industrial Revolution in Europe also brought consternation to many of the same social critics. Men like Ruskin and Arnold noted with distaste the smoking factories of Birmingham and Manchester and the working-class villages sprawling beside them. To Arnold the new ugliness was embodied in the awkward place names being created both in England and America.

The Industrial Revolution brought about changes of other kinds: it fostered the growth of science; it allowed common men to improve their lot; it shifted the class structure so radically that, by the twentieth century, in many Western nations the middle class predominated not only in numbers but in doctrine.

In 1930 Ortega y Gasset published *The Revolt of The Masses,* a book which linked the advance of equality and prosperity with the declining quality of modern civilization. Modern society worked, Ortega thought, so that the elite, distinguished by birth or by talent, were no longer a controlling force. The masses were now in control. Yet they could be distinguished not by inferior rank or birth, but by mediocrity and slavishness of taste.

Many twentieth-century authors seem to have sided with Oretga. According to Nathanael West, even the large middle class created by the Industrial Revolution became part of Ortega's masses. This class had inherited the earth, but for what reason, to what purpose? All it had earned by the middle of the twentieth century, West tells us, was a pension check and vague dreams—the right to retire to Florida or California and feel even more lost.

According to one of our most eminent literary critics, West's type of disillusionment is not exceptional in modern writing. "Any historian of the literature of the modern age," Lionel Trilling writes, "will take virtually for granted the adversary intention, the actually subversive intention, that characterizes modern writing—he will perceive its clear purpose of detaching the reader from the habits of thought and feeling that the larger culture imposes." *

Yet others, like Charles Beard, felt modern society to be not only inevitable but, on the whole, beneficial. How long, they argued, could mankind remain trapped in rigid class structures? How can any society last which depends on a mass of poor and unskilled workers? According to Beard, only science and industry can satisfy the desire of ordinary people for a healthy and prosperous life.

* Lionel Trilling, "Preface" to *Beyond Culture* (New York: The Viking Press, 1965), p. xii.

Matthew Arnold

from
CIVILISATION
IN THE
UNITED STATES

Matthew Arnold, 1822–1888, a great nineteenth-century British essayist and poet, wished to resurrect the quality of life that he believed had existed during classical times. Civilized values were more important to him than all the accomplishments of industrialization, and such values, he felt, were sadly deficient in America.

Perhaps it is not likely that any one will now remember what I said three years ago here about the success of the Americans in solving the political and social problem. I will sum it up in the briefest possible manner. I said that the United States had constituted themselves in a modern age; that their institutions complied well with the form and pressure of those circumstances and conditions which a modern age presents. Quite apart from all question how much of the merit for this may be due to the wisdom and virtue of the American people, and how much to their good fortune, it is undeniable that their institutions do work well and happily. The play of their institutions suggests, I said, the image of a man in a suit of clothes which fits him to perfection, leaving all his movements unimpeded and easy; a suit of clothes loose where it ought to be loose, and sitting close where its sitting close is an advantage; a suit of clothes able, moreover, to adapt itself naturally to the wearer's growth, and to admit of all enlargements as they successively arise.

So much as to the solution, by the United States, of the political problem. As to the social problem, I observed that the people of the United States were a community singularly free from the distinction of classes, singularly homogeneous; that the division between rich and poor was consequently less profound there than in countries where the distinction of classes accentuates that division. I added that I believed there was exaggeration in the reports of their administrative and judicial corruption; and altogether, I concluded, the United States, politically and socially, are a country living prosperously in a natural modern condition, and conscious of living prosperously in such a condition. And being in this healthy case, and having this healthy consciousness, the community there uses its understanding with the soundness of health; it in general, as to its own political and social concerns, sees clear and thinks straight. Comparing the United States with ourselves, I said that while they are in this natural and healthy condition, we on the contrary are so little homogeneous, we are living with a system of classes so intense, with institutions and a society so little modern, so unnaturally complicated, that the whole action of our minds is hampered and falsened by it; we are in consequence wanting in lucidity, we do not see clear or think straight, and the Americans have here much the advantage of us.

Yet we find an acute and experienced Englishman saying that there is no country, calling itself civilised, where one would not rather live than in the United States, except Russia! The civilisation of the United States must somehow, if an able man can think thus, have shortcomings, in spite of the country's success and prosperity. What is civilisation? It is the humanisation of man in society, the satisfaction for him, in society, of the true law of human nature. Man's study, says Plato, is to discover the right answer to the question *how to live?* our aim, he says, is very and true life. We are more or less civilised as we come more or less near to this aim, in that social state which the pursuit of our aim essentially demands. But several elements or powers, as I have often insisted, go to build up a complete human life. There is the power of conduct, the power of intellect and knowledge, the power of beauty, the power of social life and manners; we have instincts responding to them all, requiring them all. And we are perfectly civilised only when all these instincts in our nature, all these elements in our civilisation, have been adequately recognised and satisfied. But of course this adequate recognition and satisfaction of all the elements in question is impossible; some of them are recognised more than others, some of them more in one community, some in another; and the satisfactions found are more or less worthy.

And meanwhile, people use the term *civilisation* in the loosest possible way, for the most part attaching to it, however, in their own mind some meaning connected with their own preferences and experiences. The most common meaning thus attached to it is perhaps that of a satisfaction, not of all the main demands of human nature, but of the demand for the comforts and conveniences of life, and of this demand as made by the sort of person who uses the term.

Now we should always attend to the common and prevalent use of an important term. Probably Sir Lepel Griffin had this notion of the comforts and conveniences of life much in his thoughts when he reproached American civilisation with its shortcomings. For men of his kind, and for all that large number of men, so prominent in this country and who make their voice so much heard, men who have been at the public schools and universities, men of the professional and official class, men who do the most part of our literature and our journalism, America is not a comfortable place of abode. A man of this sort has in England everything in his favour; society appears organised expressly for his advantage. A Rothschild or a Vanderbilt can buy his way anywhere, and can have what comforts and luxuries he likes whether in America or in England. But it is in England that an income of from three or four to fourteen or fifteen hundred a year does so much for its possessor, enables him to live with so many of the conveniences of far richer people. For his benefit, his benefit above all, clubs are organised and hansom cabs ply; service is abundant, porters stand waiting at the railway stations. In America all luxuries are dear except oysters and ice; service is in general scarce and bad; a club is a most expensive luxury; the cab-rates are prohibitive—more than half of the people who in England would use cabs must in America use the horse-cars, the tram. The charges of tailors and mercers are about a third higher than they are with us. I mention only a few striking points as to which there can be no dispute, and in which a man of Sir Lepel Griffin's class would feel the great difference between America and England in the conveniences at his command. There are a hundred other points one might mention, where he would feel the same thing. When a man is passing judgment on a country's civilisation, points of this kind crowd to his memory, and determine his sentence.

On the other hand, for that immense class of people, the great bulk of the community, the class of people whose income is less than three or four hundred a year, things in America are favourable. It is easier for them there than in the Old World to rise and to make their fortune; but I am not now speaking of that. Even without making their fortune, even with their income below three or four hundred a year, things are favourable to them in America, society seems organised there for their benefit. To begin with, the humbler kind of work is better paid in America than with us, the higher kind worse. The official, for instance, gets less, his office-keeper gets more. The public ways are abominably cut up by rails and blocked with horse-cars; but the inconvenience is for those who use private carriages and cabs, the convenience is for the bulk of the community who but for the horse-cars would have to walk. The ordinary railway cars are not delightful, but they are cheap, and they are better furnished and in winter are warmer than third-class carriages in England. Luxuries are, as I have said, very dear —above all, European luxuries; but a working man's clothing is nearly as cheap as in England, and plain food is on the whole cheaper. Even luxuries of a certain kind are within a labouring man's easy reach. I have mentioned ice, I will mention fruit also. The abundance and cheapness of fruit is a great boon to people of small incomes in America. Do not believe the Americans when they extol their peaches as equal to any in the world, or better than any in the world; they are not to be compared to peaches grown under glass. Do not believe that the American Newtown pippins appear in the New York and Boston fruit-shops as they appear in those of London and Liverpool; or that the Americans have any pear to give you like the Marie Louise. But what labourer, or artisan, or small clerk, ever gets hot-house peaches, or Newtown pippins, or Marie Louise pears? Not such good pears, apples, and peaches as those, but pears, apples, and peaches by no means to be despised, such people and their families do in America get in plenty.

Well, now, what would a philosopher or a philanthropist say in this case? Which would he say was the more civilised condition—that of the country where the balance of advantage, as to the comforts and conveniences of life, is greatly in favour of the people with incomes below three hundred a year, or that of the country where it is greatly in favour of those with incomes above that sum?

Many people will be ready to give an answer to that question without the smallest hesitation. They will say that they are, and that all of us ought to be, for the greatest happiness of the greatest number. However, the question is not one which I feel bound now to discuss and answer. Of course, if happiness and civilisation consist in being plentifully supplied with the comforts and conveniences of life, the question presents little difficulty. But I believe neither that happiness consists, merely or mainly, in being plentifully supplied with the comforts and conveniences of life, nor that civilisation consists in being so supplied; therefore I leave the question unanswered.

I prefer to seek for some other and better tests by which to try the civilisation of the United States. I have often insisted on the need of more equality in our own country, and on the mischiefs caused by inequality over here. In the United States there is not our intense division of classes, our inequality; there is great equality. Let me mention two points in the system of social life and manners over there in which this equality seems to me to have done good. The first is a mere point of form, but it has its significance. Every one knows it is the established habit with us in England, if we write to people supposed to belong to the class of gentlemen, of addressing them by the title of *Esquire,* while we keep *Mr.* for people not supposed to belong to that class. If we think of it, could one easily find a habit more ridiculous, more offensive? . . .

The other point goes deeper. Much may be said against the voices and intonation of American women. But almost every one acknowledges that there is a charm in American women—a charm which you find in almost all of them, wherever you go. It is the charm of a natural manner, a manner not self-conscious, artificial, and constrained. It may not be a beautiful manner always, but it is almost always a natural manner, a free and happy manner; and this gives pleasure. Here we have, undoubtedly, a note of civilisation, and an evidence, at the same time, of the good effect of equality upon social life and manners. I have often heard it observed that a perfectly natural manner is as rare among Englishwomen of the middle classes as it is general among American women of like condition with them. And so far as the observation is true, the reason of its truth no doubt is, that the Englishwoman is living in presence of an upper class, as it is called—in presence, that is, of a class of women recognised as being the right thing in style and manner, and whom she imagines criticising *her* style and manner, finding this or that to be amiss with it, this or that to be vulgar. Hence self-consciousness and constraint in her. The American woman lives in presence of no such class; there may be circles trying to pass themselves off as such a class, giving themselves airs as such, but they command no recognition, no authority. The American woman in general, is perfectly unconcerned about their opinion, is herself, enjoys her existence, and has consequently a manner happy and natural. It is her great charm; and it is moreover, as I have said, a real note of civilisation, and one which has to be reckoned to the credit of American life, and of its equality.

But we must get nearer still to the heart of the question raised as to the character and worth of American civilisation. I have said how much the word civilisation really means—the humanisation of man in society; his making progress there towards his true and full humanity. Partial and material achievement is always being put forward as civilisation. We hear a nation called highly civilised by reason of its industry, commerce, and wealth, or by reason of its liberty or equality, or by reason of its numerous churches, schools, libraries, and newspapers. But there is something in human nature, some instinct of growth, some law of perfection, which rebels against this narrow account of the matter. And perhaps what human nature demands in civilisation, over and above all those obvious things which first occur to our thoughts—what human nature, I say, demands in civilisation, if it is to stand as a high and satisfying civilisation, is best described by the word *interesting*. Here is the extraordinary charm of the old Greek civilisation—that it is so *interesting*. Do not tell me only, says human nature, of the magnitude of your industry and commerce; of the beneficence of your institutions, your freedom, your equality; of the great and growing number of your churches and schools, libraries and newspapers; tell me also if your civilisation—which is the grand name you give to all this development—tell me if your civilisation is *interesting*. . . .

Amiel, that contemplative Swiss whose journals the world has been reading lately, tells us that "the human heart is, as it were, haunted by confused reminiscences of an age of gold; or rather, by aspirations towards a harmony of things which everyday reality denies to us." He says that the splendour and refinement of high life is an attempt by the rich and cultivated classes to realise this ideal, and is "a form of poetry." And the interest which this attempt awakens in the classes which are not rich or cultivated, their indestructible interest in the pageant and fairy tale, as to them it appears, of the life in castles and palaces, the life of the great, bears witness to a like imaginative strain in them also, a strain tending after the elevated and the beautiful. In short, what Goethe describes as "was uns alle bändigt, *das Gemeine*—that which holds us all in bondage, the common and ignoble," is, notwithstanding its admitted prevalence, contrary to a deep-seated instinct of human nature and repelled by it. Of civilisation, which is to humanise us in society, we demand, before we will consent to be satisfied with it—we demand, however much else it may give us, that it shall give us, too, the *interesting*.

Now, the great sources of the *interesting* are distinction and beauty: that which is elevated, and that which is beautiful. Let us take the beautiful first, and consider how far it is present in American civilisation. Evidently this is that civilisation's weak side. There is little to nourish and delight the sense of beauty there. In the long-settled States east of the Alleghanies the landscape in general is not interesting, the climate harsh and in extremes. The Americans are restless, eager to better themselves and to make fortunes; the inhabitant does not strike his roots lovingly down into the soil, as in rural England. In the valley of the Connecticut you will find farm after farm which the Yankee settler has abandoned in order to go West, leaving the farm to some new Irish immigrant. The charm of beauty which comes from ancientness and permanence of rural life the country could not yet have in a high degree, but it has it in an even less degree than might be expected. Then the Americans come originally, for the most part, from that great class in English society amongst whom the sense for conduct and business is much more strongly developed than the sense for beauty. If we in England were without the cathedrals, parish churches, and castles of the catholic and feudal age, and without the houses of the Elizabethan age, but had only the towns and buildings which the rise of our middle class has created in the modern age, we should be in much the same case as the Americans. We should be living with much the same absence of training for the sense of beauty through the eye, from the aspect of outward things. The American cities have hardly anything to please a trained or a natural sense for beauty. They have buildings which cost a great deal of money and produce a certain effect—buildings, shall I say, such as our Midland Station at St. Pancras; but nothing such as Somerset House or Whitehall. One architect of genius they had—Richardson. I had the pleasure to know him; he is dead, alas! Much of his work was injured by the conditions under which he was obliged to execute it; I can recall but one building, and that of no great importance, where he seems to have had his own way, to be fully himself; but that is indeed excellent. In general, where the Americans succeed best in their architecture—in that art so indicative and educative of a people's sense for beauty —is in the fashion of their villa-cottages in wood. These are often original and at the same time very pleasing, but they are pretty and coquettish, not beautiful. Of the really beautiful in the other arts, and in literature, very little has been produced there as yet. I asked a German portrait painter, whom I found painting and prospering in America, how he liked the country? "How *can* an artist like it?" was his answer. The American artists live chiefly in Europe; all Americans of cultivation and wealth visit Europe more and more constantly. The mere nomenclature of the country acts upon a cultivated person like the incessant pricking of pins. What people in whom the sense for beauty and fitness was quick could have invented, or could tolerate, the hideous names ending in *ville,* the Briggsvilles, Higginsvilles, Jacksonvilles, rife from Maine to Florida; the jumble of unnatural and inappropriate names everywhere? On the line from Albany to Buffalo you have, in one part, half the names in the classical dictionary to designate the stations; it is said that the folly is due to a surveyor who, when the country was laid out, happened to possess a classical dictionary, but a people with any artist-sense would have put down that surveyor. The Americans meekly retain his names; and indeed his strange Marcellus or Syracuse is perhaps not much worse than their congenital Briggsville.

So much as to beauty, and as to the provision, in the United States, for the sense of beauty. As to distinction, and the interest which human nature seeks from enjoying the effect made upon it by what is elevated, the case is much the same. There is very little to create such an effect, very much to thwart it. Goethe says somewhere that "the thrill of awe is the best thing humanity has":

Das Schaudern ist der Menschheit bestes Theil.

But, if there be a discipline in which the Americans are wanting, it is the discipline of awe and respect. An austere and intense religion imposed on their Puritan founders the discipline of respect, and so provided for them the thrill of awe; but this religion is dying out. The Americans have produced plenty of men strong, shrewd, upright, able, effective; very few who are highly distinguished. Alexander Hamilton is indeed a man of rare distinction; Washington, though he has not the high mental distinction of Pericles or Caesar, has true distinction of style and character. But these men belong to the pre-American age. Lincoln's recent American biographers declare that Washington is but an Englishman, an English officer; the typical American, they say, is Abraham Lincoln. Now Lincoln is shrewd, sagacious, humorous, honest, courageous, firm; he is a man with qualities deserving the most sincere esteem and praise, but he has not distinction.

In truth everything is against distinction in America, and against the sense of elevation to be gained through admiring and respecting it. The glorification of "the average man," who is quite a religion with statesmen and publicists there, is against it. The addiction to "the funny man," who is a national misfortune there, is against it. Above all, the newspapers are against it.

It is often said that every nation has the government it deserves. What is much more certain is that every nation has the newspapers it deserves. The newspaper is the direct product of the want felt; the supply answers closely and inevitably to the demand. I suppose no one knows what the American newspapers are, who has not been obliged, for some length of time, to read either those newspapers or none at all. Powerful and valuable contributions occur scattered about in them. But on the whole, and taking the total impression and effect made by them, I should say that if one were searching for the best means to efface and kill in a whole nation the discipline of respect, the feeling for what is elevated, one could not do better than take the American newspapers. The absence of truth and soberness in them, the poverty in serious interest, the personality and sensation-mongering, are beyond belief. There are a few newspapers which are in whole, or in part, exceptions. The *New York Nation,* a weekly paper, may be paralleled with the *Saturday Review* as it was in its old and good days; but the *New York Nation* is conducted by a foreigner, and has an extremely small sale. In general, the daily papers are such that when one returns home one is moved to admiration and thankfulness not only at the great London papers, like the *Times* or the *Standard,* but quite as much at the great provincial newspapers too—papers like the *Leeds Mercury* and the *Yorkshire Post* in the north of England, like the *Scotsman* and the *Glasgow Herald* in Scotland.

The Americans used to say to me that what they valued was news, and that this their newspapers gave them. I at last made the reply: "Yes, news for the servants' hall!" I remember that a New York newspaper, one of the first I saw after landing in the country, had a long account, with the prominence we should give to the illness of the German Emperor or the arrest of the Lord Mayor of Dublin, of a young woman who had married a man who was a bag of bones, as we say, and who used to exhibit himself as a skeleton; of her growing horror in living with this man, and finally of her death. All this in the most minute detail, and described with all the writer's powers of rhetoric. This has always remained by me as a specimen of what the Americans call news. . . .

I once declared that in England the born lover of ideas and of light could not but feel that the sky over his head is of brass and iron. And so I say that, in America, he who craves for the *interesting* in civilisation, he who requires from what surrounds him satisfaction for his sense of beauty, his sense for elevation, will feel the sky over his head to be of brass and iron. The human problem, then, is as yet solved in the United States most imperfectly; a great void exists in the civilisation over there: a want of what is elevated and beautiful, of what is interesting.

The want is grave; it was probably, though he does not exactly bring it out, influencing Sir Lepel Griffin's feelings when he said that America is one of the last countries in which one would like to live. The want is such as to make any educated man feel that many countries, much less free and prosperous than the United States, are yet more truly civilised; have more which is interesting, have more to say to the soul; are countries, therefore, in which one would rather live.

The want is graver because it is so little recognised by the mass of Americans; nay, so loudly denied by them. If the community over there perceived the want and regretted it, sought for the right ways of remedying it, and resolved that remedied it should be; if they said, or even if a number of leading spirits amongst them said: "Yes, we see what is wanting to our civilisation, we see that the average man is a danger, we see that our newspapers are a scandal, that bondage to the common and ignoble is our snare; but under the circumstances our civilisation could not well have been expected to begin differently. What you see are *beginnings,* they are crude, they are too predominantly material, they omit much, leave much to be desired—but they could not have been otherwise, they have been inevitable, and we will rise above them"; if the Americans frankly said this, one would have not a word to bring against it. One would *then* insist on no shortcoming, one would accept their admission that the human problem is at present quite insufficiently solved by them, and would press the matter no further. One would congratulate them on having solved the political problem and the social problem so successfully, and only remark, as I have said already, that in seeing clear and thinking straight on *our* political and social questions, we have great need to follow the example they set us on theirs.

But now the Americans seem, in certain matters, to have agreed, as a people, to deceive themselves, to persuade themselves that they have what they have not, to cover the defects in their civilisation by boasting, to fancy that they well and truly solve, not only the political and social problem, but the human problem too. One would say that they do really hope to find in tall talk and inflated sentiment a substitute for that real sense of elevation which human nature, as I have said, instinctively craves—and a substitute which may do as well as the genuine article. The thrill of awe, which Goethe pronounces to be the best thing humanity has, they would fain create by proclaiming themselves at the top of their voices to be "the greatest nation upon earth," by assuring one another, in the language of their national historian, that "American democracy proceeds in its ascent as uniformly and majestically as the laws of being, and is as certain as the decrees of eternity."

Or, again, far from admitting that their newspapers are a scandal, they assure one another that their newspaper press is one of their most signal distinctions. Far from admitting that in literature they have as yet produced little that is important, they play at treating American literature as if it were a great independent power; they reform the spelling of the English language by the insight of their average man. For every English writer they have an American writer to match. And him good Americans read; the Western States are at this moment being nourished and formed, we hear, on the novels of a native author called Roe, instead of those of Scott and Dickens. Far from admitting that their average man is a danger, and that his predominance has brought about a plentiful lack of refinement, distinction, and beauty, they declare in the words of my friend Colonel Higginson, a prominent critic at Boston, that "Nature said, some years since: 'Thus far the English is my best race, but we have had Englishmen enough; put in one drop more of nervous fluid and make the American.' And with that drop a new range of promise opened on the human race, and a lighter, finer, more highly organised type of mankind was born." . . .

The worst of it is that all this tall talk and self-glorification meets with hardly any rebuke from sane criticism over there. I will mention, in regard to this, a thing which struck me a good deal. A Scotchman who has made a great fortune at Pittsburg, a kind friend of mine, one of the most hospitable and generous of men, Mr. Andrew Carnegie, published a year or two ago a book called *Triumphant Democracy,* a most splendid picture of American progress. The book is full of valuable information, but religious people thought that it insisted too much on mere material progress, and did not enough set forth America's deficiencies and dangers. And a friendly clergyman in Massachusetts, telling me how he regretted this, and how apt the Americans are to shut their eyes to their own dangers, put into

my hands a volume written by a leading minister among the Congrega-
tionalists, a very prominent man, which he said supplied a good antidote
to my friend Mr. Carnegie's book. The volume is entitled *Our Country*.
I read it through. The author finds in evangelical Protestantism, as the
orthodox Protestant sects present it, the grand remedy for the deficiencies
and dangers of America. On this I offer no criticism; what struck me, and
that on which I wish to lay stress, is, the writer's entire failure to perceive
that such self-glorification and self-deception as I have been mentioning is
one of America's dangers, or even that it *is* self-deception at all. He himself
shares in all the self-deception of the average man among his countrymen,
he flatters it. In the very points where a serious critic would find the
Americans most wanting he finds them superior; only they require to have
a good dose of evangelical Protestantism still added. "Ours is the elect
nation," preaches this reformer of American faults—"ours is the elect
nation for the age to come. We are the chosen people." Already, says he,
we are taller and heavier than other men, longer lived than other men,
richer and more energetic than other men, above all, "of finer nervous
organisation" than other men. Yes, this people, who endure to have the
American newspaper for their daily reading, and to have their habitation
in Briggsville, Jacksonville, and Marcellus—this people is of finer, more
delicate nervous organisation than other nations! . . .

The new West promises to beat in the game of brag even the stout
champions I have been quoting. Those belong to the old Eastern States;
and the other day there was sent to me a Californian newspaper which
calls all the Easterners "the unhappy denizens of a forbidding clime," and
adds: "The time will surely come when all roads will lead to California.
Here will be the home of art, science, literature, and profound knowledge."

Common-sense criticism, I repeat, of all this hollow stuff there is in
America next to none. There are plenty of cultivated, judicious, delightful
individuals there. They are our hope and America's hope; it is through
their means that improvement must come. They know perfectly well how
false and hollow the boastful stuff talked is; but they let the storm of self-
laudation rage, and say nothing. For political opponents and their doings
there are in America hard words to be heard in abundance; for the real
faults in American civilisation, and for the foolish boasting which prolongs
them, there is hardly a word of regret or blame, at least in public. Even in
private, many of the most cultivated Americans shrink from the subject, are

irritable and thin-skinned when it is canvassed. Public treatment of it, in a cool and sane spirit of criticism, there is none. In vain I might plead that I had set a good example of frankness, in confessing over here, that, so far from solving our problems successfully, we in England find ourselves with an upper class materialised, a middle class vulgarised, and a lower class brutalised. But it seems that nothing will embolden an American critic to say firmly and aloud to his countrymen and to his newspapers, that in America they do not solve the human problem successfully, and that with their present methods they never can. Consequently the masses of the American people do really come to believe all they hear about their finer nervous organisation, and the rightness of the American accent, and the importance of American literature; that is to say, they see things not as they are, but as they would like them to be; they deceive themselves totally. And by such self-deception they shut against themselves the door to improvement, and do their best to make the reign of *das Gemeine* eternal. In what concerns the solving of the political and social problem they see clear and think straight; in what concerns the higher civilisation they live in a fool's paradise. This it is which makes a famous French critic speak of "the hard unintelligence of the people of the United States"—*la dure inintelligence des Américains du Nord*—of the very people who in general pass for being specially intelligent—and so, within certain limits, they are. But they have been so plied with nonsense and boasting that outside those limits, and where it is a question of things in which their civilisation is weak, they seem, very many of them, as if in such things they had no power of perception whatever, no idea of a proper scale, no sense of the difference between good and bad. And at this rate they can never, after solving the political and social problem with success, go on to solve happily the human problem too, and thus at last to make their civilisation full and interesting.

QUESTIONS AND TOPICS

1. Does Arnold present adequate evidence to substantiate his assertion that civilization in the United States is lacking in quality?
2. Do you agree with Arnold that the naming of towns or cities in some way defines the quality of a civilization?

3. Are American newspapers still sensational and lacking in quality? (Use specific examples.)
4. Do Americans still brag excessively? Is our national tendency to self-applause a virtue or a fault?
5. How does Arnold compare Great Britain with the United States? (For further information on this subject see Arnold's *Culture and Anarchy*.)

Matthew Arnold

DOVER
BEACH

*"Dover Beach" reveals another facet
of Arnold's dissatisfaction with modern civilization. He feels profoundly
sad because the "Sea of Faith" is
now "Retreating, to the breath/Of
the night-wind, down the vast edges
drear/And naked shingles * of the
world." Arnold's solution for this
dilemma is a very modern one,
which some have termed privatism.*

The sea is calm tonight,
The tide is full, the moon lies fair
Upon the straits—on the French coast the light
Gleams and is gone; the cliffs of England stand,
Glimmering and vast, out on the tranquil bay.
Come to the window; sweet is the night-air!
Only, from the long line of spray
Where the sea meets the moon-blanched land,
Listen! you hear the grating roar
Of pebbles which the waves draw back, and fling,
At their return, up the high strand,
Begin, and cease, and then again begin,
With tremulous cadence slow, and bring
The eternal note of sadness in.

Sophocles long ago
Heard it on the Aegean, and it brought
Into his mind the turbid ebb and flow

* Shingles: small, round stones on the seashore.

Of human misery; we
Find also in the sound a thought,
Hearing it by this distant northern sea.

The Sea of Faith
Was once, too, at the full, and round earth's shore
Lay like the folds of a bright girdle furled;
But now I only hear
Its melancholy, long, withdrawing roar,
Retreating, to the breath
Of the night-wind, down the vast edges drear
And naked shingles of the world.
Ah, love, let us be true
To one another! for the world, which seems
To lie before us like a land of dreams,
So various, so beautiful, so new,
Hath really neither joy, nor love, nor light,
Nor certitude, nor peace, nor help for pain;
And we are here as on a darkling plain
Swept with confused alarms of struggle and flight,
Where ignorant armies clash by night.

QUESTIONS AND TOPICS

1. Do you agree with Arnold that the "Sea of Faith" is now retreating? If so, do you think its retreat is a matter of grave concern?
2. The last lines of "Dover Beach" reveal Arnold's solution to his dilemma, withdrawal from a world which "Hath really neither joy, nor love, nor light," and movement toward individual relationships. Do you think that personal relations are an adequate substitute for belief?
3. Do you agree with Arnold that the modern world is a place "Where ignorant armies clash by night"? What "armies" does Arnold refer to?

José Ortega y Gasset

from
THE COMING
OF THE MASSES

> *José Ortega y Gasset, 1883–1955,*
> *was a Spanish philosopher whose*
> *most famous book is* The Revolt of
> the Masses, *1930. In the excerpt*
> *following, he examines one of the*
> *most startling changes brought*
> *about by the Industrial Revolution.*
> *Everywhere Ortega looked the ex-*
> *clusive society he had known as a*
> *child had vanished, and in its place*
> *he found the "masses."*

There is one fact which, whether for good or ill, is of utmost importance in the public life of Europe at the present moment. This fact is
the accession of the masses to complete social power. As the masses, by
definition, neither should nor can direct their own personal existence, and
still less rule society in general, this fact means that actually Europe is
suffering from the greatest crisis that can afflict peoples, nations, and
civilisation. Such a crisis has occurred more than once in history. Its characteristics and its consequences are well known. So also is its name. It is
called the rebellion of the masses. In order to understand this formidable
fact, it is important from the start to avoid giving to the words "rebellion,"
"masses," and "social power" a meaning exclusively or primarily political.
Public life is not solely political, but equally, and even primarily, intellectual, moral, economic, religious; it comprises all our collective habits, including our fashions both of dress and of amusement.

Perhaps the best line of approach to this historical phenomenon may
be found by turning our attention to a visual experience, stressing one
aspect of our epoch which is plain to our very eyes. This fact is quite
simple to enunciate, though not so to analyse. I shall call it the fact of

agglomeration, of "plenitude." Towns are full of people, houses full of tenants, hotels full of guests, trains full of travellers, cafés full of customers, parks full of promenaders, consulting-rooms of famous doctors full of patients, theatres full of spectators, and beaches full of bathers. What previously was, in general, no problem, now begins to be an everyday one, namely, to find room.

That is all. Can there be any fact simpler, more patent, more constant in actual life? Let us now pierce the plain surface of this observation and we shall be surprised to see how there wells forth an unexpected spring in which the white light of day, of our actual day, is broken up into its rich chromatic content. What is it that we see, and the sight of which causes us so much surprise? We see the multitude, as such, in possession of the places and the instruments created by civilisation. The slightest reflection will then make us surprised at our own surprise. What about it? Is this not the ideal state of things? The theatre has seats to be occupied— in other words, so that the house may be full—and now they are over-flowing; people anxious to use them are left standing outside. Though the fact be quite logical and natural, we cannot but recognise that this did not happen before and that now it does; consequently, there has been a change, an innovation, which justifies, at least for the first moment, our surprise.

To be surprised, to wonder, is to begin to understand. This is the sport, the luxury, special to the intellectual man. The gesture characteristic of his tribe consists in looking at the world with eyes wide open in wonder. Everything in the world is strange and marvellous to well-open eyes. This faculty of wonder is the delight refused to your football "fan," and, on the other hand, is the one which leads the intellectual man through life in the perpetual ecstasy of the visionary. His special attribute is the wonder of the eyes. Hence it was that the ancients gave Minerva her owl, the bird with ever-dazzled eyes.

Agglomeration, fullness, was not frequent before. Why then is it now? The components of the multitudes around us have not sprung from noth-ing. Approximately the same number of people existed fifteen years ago. Indeed, after the war it might seem natural that their number should be less. Nevertheless, it is here we come up against the first important point. The individuals who made up these multitudes existed, but not *qua* multi-tude. Scattered about the world in small groups, or solitary, they lived a life, to all appearances, divergent, dissociate, apart. Each individual or small group occupied a place, its own, in country, village, town, or quarter of the great city. Now, suddenly, they appear as an agglomeration, and looking in any direction our eyes meet with the multitudes. Not only in any direction, but precisely in the best places, the relatively refined creation of human culture, previously reserved to lesser groups, in a word, to minorities. The multitude has suddenly become visible, installing itself in the preferential positions in society. Before, if it existed, it passed unnoticed, occupying the background of the social stage; now it has advanced to the footlights and is the principal character. There are no longer protagonists; there is only the chorus.

The concept of the multitude is quantitative and visual. Without changing its nature, let us translate it into terms of sociology. We then meet with the notion of the "social mass." Society is always a dynamic unity of two component factors: minorities and masses. The minorities are individuals or groups of individuals which are specially qualified. The mass is the assemblage of persons not specially qualified. By masses, then, is not to be understood, solely or mainly, "the working masses." The mass is the average man. In this way what was mere quantity—the multitude— is converted into a qualitative determination: it becomes the common social quality, man as undifferentiated from other men, but as repeating in himself a generic type. What have we gained by this conversion of quantity into quality? Simply this: by means of the latter we understand the genesis of the former. It is evident to the verge of platitude that the normal formation of a multitude implies the coincidence of desires, ideas, ways of life, in the individuals who constitute it. It will be objected that this is just what happens with every social group, however select it may strive to be. This is true; but there is an essential difference. In those groups which are characterised by not being multitude and mass, the effective coincidence of its members is based on some desire, idea, or ideal, which of itself excludes the great number. To form a minority, of whatever kind, it is necessary beforehand that each member separate himself from the multitude for *special*, relatively personal, reasons. Their coincidence with the others who form the minority is, then, secondary, posterior to their having each adopted an attitude of singularity, and is consequently, to a large extent, a coincidence in not coinciding. There are cases in which this singularising character of the group appears in the light of day: those English groups, which style themselves "nonconformists," where we have the grouping together of those who agree only in their disagreement in regard to the limitless multitude. This coming together of the minority precisely in order to separate themselves from the majority is a necessary ingredient in the formation of every minority. Speaking of the limited public which listened to a musician of refinement, Mallarmé wittily says that this public by its presence in small numbers stressed the absence of the multitude.

Strictly speaking, the mass, as a psychological fact, can be defined without waiting for individuals to appear in mass formation. In the presence of one individual we can decide whether he is "mass" or not. The mass is all that which sets no value on itself—good or ill—based on specific grounds, but which feels itself "just like everybody," and nevertheless is not concerned about it; is, in fact, quite happy to feel itself as one with everybody else. Imagine a humble-minded man who, having tried to estimate his own worth on specific grounds—asking himself if he has any talent for this or that, if he excels in any direction—realises that he possesses no quality of excellence. Such a man will feel that he is mediocre and commonplace, ill-gifted, but will not feel himself "mass."

When one speaks of "select minorities" it is usual for the evil-minded to twist the sense of this expression, pretending to be unaware that the select man is not the petulant person who thinks himself superior to the rest, but the man who demands more of himself than the rest, even though he may not fulfill in his person those higher exigencies. For there is no doubt that the most radical division that it is possible to make of humanity is that which splits it into two classes of creatures: those who make great demands on themselves, piling up difficulties and duties; and those who demand nothing special of themselves, but for whom to live is to be every moment what they already are, without imposing on themselves any effort towards perfection; mere buoys that float on the waves. This reminds me that orthodox Buddhism is composed of two distinct religions: one, more rigorous and difficult, the other easier and more trivial: the Mahayana—"great vehicle" or "great path"—and the Hinayana—"lesser vehicle" or "lesser path." The decisive matter is whether we attach our life to one or the other vehicle, to a maximum or a minimum of demands upon ourselves.

The division of society into masses and select minorities is, then, not a division into social classes, but into classes of men, and cannot coincide with the hierarchic separation of "upper" and "lower" classes. It is, of course, plain that in these "upper" classes, when and as long as they really are so, there is much more likelihood of finding men who adopt the "great vehicle," whereas the "lower" classes normally comprise individuals of minus quality. But, strictly speaking, within both these social classes, there are to be found mass and genuine minority. As we shall see, a characteristic of our times is the predominance, even in groups traditionally selective, of the mass and the vulgar. Thus, in the intellectual life, which of its essence requires and presupposes qualification, one can note the progressive triumph of the pseudo-intellectual, unqualified, unqualifiable, and, by their very mental texture, disqualified. Similarly, in the surviving groups of the "nobility," male and female. On the other hand, it is not rare to find to-day amongst working men, who before might be taken as the best example of what we are calling "mass," nobly disciplined minds.

There exist, then, in society, operations, activities, and functions of the most diverse order, which are of their very nature special, and which consequently cannot be properly carried out without special gifts. For example: certain pleasures of an artistic and refined character, or again the functions of government and of political judgment in public affairs. Previously these special activities were exercised by qualified minorities, or at least by those who claimed such qualification. The mass asserted no right to intervene in them; they realised that if they wished to intervene they would necessarily have to acquire those special qualities and cease being mere mass. They recognised their place in a healthy dynamic social system.

If we now revert to the facts indicated at the start, they will appear clearly as the heralds of a changed attitude in the mass. They all indicate that the mass has decided to advance to the foreground of social life, to occupy the places, to use the instruments and to enjoy the pleasures hitherto reserved to the few. It is evident, for example, that the places were never intended for the multitude, for their dimensions are too limited, and the crowd is continuously overflowing; thus manifesting to our eyes and in the clearest manner the new phenomenon: the mass, without ceasing to be mass, is supplanting the minorities.

No one, I believe, will regret that people are to-day enjoying themselves in greater measure and numbers than before, since they have now both the desire and the means of satisfying it. The evil lies in the fact that this decision taken by the masses to assume the activities proper to the minorities is not, and cannot be, manifested solely in the domain of pleasure, but that it is a general feature of our time. Thus—to anticipate what we shall see later—I believe that the political innovations of recent times signify nothing less than the political domination of the masses. The old democracy was tempered by a generous dose of liberalism and of enthusiasm for law. By serving these principles the individual bound himself to maintain a severe discipline over himself. Under the shelter of liberal principles and the rule of law, minorities could live and act. Democracy and law—life in common under the law—were synonymous. To-day we are witnessing the triumphs of a hyperdemocracy in which the mass acts directly, outside the law, imposing its aspirations and its desires by means of material pressure. It is a false interpretation of the new situation to say that the mass has grown tired of politics and handed over the exercise of it to specialised persons. Quite the contrary. That was what happened previously; that was democracy. The mass took it for granted that after all, in spite of their defects and weaknesses, the minorities understood a little more of public problems than it did itself. Now, on the other hand, the mass believes that it has the right to impose and to give force of law to notions born in the café. I doubt whether there have been other periods of history in which the multitude has come to govern more directly than in our own. That is why I speak of hyperdemocracy.

The same thing is happening in other orders, particularly in the intellectual. I may be mistaken, but the present-day writer, when he takes his pen in hand to treat a subject which he has studied deeply, has to bear in mind that the average reader, who has never concerned himself with this subject, if he reads does so with the view, not of learning something from the writer, but rather, of pronouncing judgment on him when he is not in agreement with the commonplaces that the said reader carries in his head. If the individuals who make up the mass believed themselves specially qualified, it would be a case merely of personal error, not a sociological subversion. *The characteristic of the hour is that the commonplace mind, knowing itself to be commonplace, has the assurance to proclaim the rights of the commonplace and to impose them wherever it will.* As they say in the United States: "to be different is to be indecent." The mass crushes beneath it everything that is different, everything that is excellent, individual, qualified and select. Anybody who is not like everybody, who does not think like everybody, runs the risk of being eliminated. And it is clear, of course, that this "everybody" is not "everybody." "Everybody" was normally the complex unity of the mass and the divergent, specialised minorities. Nowadays, "everybody" is the mass alone. Here we have the formidable fact of our times, described without any concealment of the brutality of its features.

QUESTIONS AND TOPICS

1. What is Ortega's definition of "mass-man"? Does Ortega identify "mass-man" with a particular social group?
2. Is Ortega's distinction between the masses and special-interest groups valid?
3. Do you agree that certain areas of society, government, education, and the arts are best left in the hands of the educated minorities?
4. Is the United States government an expert minority or a group which represents the "political domination of the masses"?
5. Can people be easily divided, as Ortega implies, into those who choose the great or the lesser path? Does his distinction suggest a certain amount of snobbery? Can you define Ortega's snobbery and differentiate it from the usual class snobbery?
6. Ortega suggests that mass man may eventually predominate and crush the elect. What is your own view?

Charles Beard

WHITHER
MANKIND

In this essay published in 1928, Charles Beard, 1874–1948, an eminent American historian, tries to defend modern civilization from the charges of critics such as Matthew Arnold and José Ortega y Gasset. Beard identifies modern civilization with the machine and mass production.

What is called Western or modern civilization by way of contrast with the civilization of the Orient or mediæval times is at bottom a civilization that rests upon machinery and science as distinguished from one founded on agriculture or handicraft commerce. It is in reality a technological civilization. It is only about two hundred years old, and, far from shrinking in its influence, is steadily extending its area into agriculture as well as handicrafts. If the records of patent offices, the statistics of production, and the reports of laboratories furnish evidence worthy of credence, technological civilization, instead of showing signs of contraction, threatens to overcome and transform the whole globe.

Considered with respect to its intrinsic nature, technological civilization presents certain precise characteristics. It rests fundamentally on power-driven machinery which transcends the physical limits of its human directors, multiplying indefinitely the capacity for the production of goods. Science in all its branches—physics, chemistry, biology, and psychology—is the servant and upholder of this system. The day of crude invention being almost over, continuous research in the natural sciences is absolutely necessary to the extension of the machine and its market, thus forcing continuously the creation of new goods, new processes, and new modes of life. As the money for learning comes in increasing proportions from taxes on industry and gifts by captains of capitalism, a steady growth in scientific endowments is to be expected, and the scientific curiosity thus aroused and stimulated will hardly fail to expand—and to invade all fields of thought with a technique of ever-refining subtlety. Affording the demand for the output of industry are the vast populations of the globe; hence mass production and marketing are inevitable concomitants of the machine routine.

For the present, machine civilization is associated with capitalism, under which large-scale production has risen to its present stage, but machine civilization is by no means synonymous with capitalism—that ever-changing scheme of exploitation. While the acquisitive instinct of the capitalist who builds factories and starts mass production is particularly emphasized by economists and is, no doubt, a factor of immense moment, it must not be forgotten that the acquisitive passion of the earth's multitudes for the goods, the comforts, and the securities of the classes is an equal, if not a more important, force, and in any case is likely to survive capitalism as we know it. Few choose nakedness when they can be clothed, the frosts of winter when they can be warm, or the misery of bacterial diseases when sanitation is offered to them. In fact, the ascetics and flagellants of the world belong nowhere in the main stream of civilization—and are of dubious utility and service in any civilization.

Though machine civilization has here been treated as if it were an order, it in fact differs from all others in that it is highly dynamic, containing within itself the seeds of constant reconstruction. Everywhere agricultural civilizations of the pre-machine age have changed only slowly with the fluctuations of markets, the fortunes of governments, and the vicissitudes of knowledge, keeping their basic institutions intact from century to century. Pre-machine urban civilizations have likewise retained their essential characteristics through long lapses of time. But machine civilization based on technology, science, invention, and expanding markets must of necessity change—and rapidly. The order of steam is hardly established before electricity invades it; electricity hardly gains a fair start before the internal combustion engine overtakes it. There has never been anywhere in the world any order comparable with it, and all analogies drawn from the middle ages, classical antiquity, and the Orient are utterly inapplicable to its potentialities, offering no revelations as to its future.

Granted that these essential characteristics of so-called Western civilization, namely, its mechanical and scientific foundations are realistic, is it a mere "flash in the pan," a historical accident destined to give way to some other order based upon entirely different modes of life, lifting mankind "above the rudeness of the savage"? Now, if the term "decline" in this connection means anything concrete, it signifies the gradual or rapid abandonment of the material modes of production prevailing in any particular age and the habits and arts associated with them. Conceivably the Prussianism of the Hohenzollerns described so well in Spengler's "Prussianism and Socialism," may decline—is declining. It is highly probable that the petty tenure system of the French peasantry, the now sadly diluted aristocracy inherited from the eighteenth century, the church of little mysteries and miracles may decline, but these things are not the peculiar characteristics of the West. They are the remnants of the agricultural complex which the machine is everywhere steadily subduing. The real question is this: can and will machine society "decline"?

It is generally agreed among historians that the decay of agriculture, owing to the lack of scientific management and fertilization, was one of the chief causes for the breakdown of the Roman state. Is it to be supposed that the drive of the masses of mankind for machine-made goods will fail, that large-scale production will be abandoned, that the huge literature of natural science will disappear in the same fashion as most of the literature of ancient Egypt, that the ranks of scientific men will cease in time to be recruited, that the scientific power to meet new situations will fail? An affirmative answer requires a great deal of hardihood. The scientific order is not recruited from a class, such as the patricians of ancient Rome; nor is scientific knowledge the monopoly of a caste likely to dissolve. Unless all visible signs deceive us, there is no reason for supposing that either machinery or science will disappear or even dwindle to insignificance. And they are the basis of the modern civilization.

If Western civilization does not break down from such internal causes, is there good reason for supposing that any of the races now inhabiting Asia or Africa could overcome the machine order of the West by any process, peaceful or warlike, without themselves adopting the technical apparatus of that order? No doubt, some of them are already borrowing various features of machine society, but slowly and with indifferent success. The most efficient of them, the Japanese, still rely largely upon the West for a substantial part of their mechanical outfit—for inventiveness and creative mechanical skill. Unless there is a material decline in Western technology—and no evidence of such a slump is now in sight—then it may be safely contended that none of the agricultural civilizations of Asia or Africa will ever catch up with the scientific development of the West. As things stand at present, none of them gives any promise of being able to overrun the West as the conquerors of Rome overran the provinces of that Empire. Certainly there is not likely to be, in any future that we can foresee, such an equality of armaments as existed between the best of the Roman legions and the forces of their conquerors. Hence the downfall of the West through conquest may fairly be ruled out of the possibilities of the coming centuries. If, in due time, the East smashes the West on the battlefield, it will be because the East has completely taken over the technology of the West, gone it one better, and thus become Western in civilization. In that case machine civilization will not disappear but will make a geographical shift.

Defining civilization narrowly in terms of letters and art, are the probabilities of a "decline" more numerous? Here we approach a more debatable, more intangible, topic. With reference to letters, taking into account the evidence of the last fifty years, there is no sign of a decay—at all events, a decay like that which occurred between the first and the sixth centuries in Roman history. Indeed, there are many cautious critics who tell us that the writers of the past hundred years, with the machine system at a high pitch, may be compared in number, competence, and power without fear with the writers of any century since the appearance of the Roman grand style. Granted that we have no Horace, Shakespeare, or Goethe, we may reasonably answer that literature of their manner has little meaning for a civilization founded on a different basis. Considered in relation to their environment rather than some fictitious absolute, the best of modern writers, it may well be argued, rank with the best of the middle ages and antiquity. If poetry sinks in the scale and tragedy becomes comical, it may be because the mythology upon which they feed is simply foreign to the spirit of the machine age—not because there has been a dissolution of inherited mental powers. The imagination of an Einstein, a Bohr, or a Millikan may well transcend that of a Milton or a Virgil. Who is to decide?

The case of the arts is on a similar footing. For the sake of the argument, it may be conceded that the machine age has produced nothing comparable with the best of the painting, sculpture, and architecture of antiquity and the middle ages. What does that signify? Anything more than a decline in the arts appropriate to an agricultural and market-city era? The machine age is young. As yet it can hardly be said to have created an art of its own, although there are signs of great competence, if not genius, about us—signs of a new art appropriate to speed, mechanics, motion, railway stations, factories, office buildings, and public institutions. Using the lowest common denominator in the reckoning, there is no evidence of a decay in artistic power such as appears in the contrast between the Pantheon of Agrippa and the rude churches of Saxon England. To say that the modern age has produced no ecclesiastical architecture comparable with that of the middle ages is to utter a judgment as relevant to our situation as a statement that the mediæval times can show no aqueducts or baths equal to the noblest structures of pagan Rome. It may be that the machine age will finally prove to be poor in artistic genius—a debatable point—but it can hardly be said that it has produced its typical art, from which a decline may be expected.

Passing to a more tangible subject, is it possible that machine civilization may be destroyed by internal revolutions or civil wars such as have often wrecked great states in the past? That such disturbances will probably rise in the future from time to time cannot be denied, and the recent Bolshevik revolution in Russia is often cited as a warning to contemporary statesmen. If the revolutions of antiquity be taken as illustrations, it must be pointed out that the analogies are to be used with extreme care in all applications to the machine age. When the worst has been said about the condition of the industrial proletariat, it must be conceded that as regards material welfare, knowledge, social consideration, and political power, it is far removed from the proletariat of Rome or the slaves of a more remote antiquity. The kind of servile revolt that was so often ruinous in Greece and Rome is hardly possible in a machine civilization, even if economic distress were to pass anything yet experienced since the eighteenth century. The most radical of the modern proletariat want more of the good things of civilization—not a destruction of technology. If the example of Russia be pressed as relevant, the reply is that Russia possessed not a machine, but an agricultural civilization of the crudest sort; peasant soldiers supplied the storm troops of the November revolution, and the Bolsheviki are straining every nerve to maintain their position by promising the peasants and urban dwellers that the benefits of a machine order will surely come. There will be upheavals in machine civilizations, no doubt, and occasional dictatorships like that in the United States between 1861 and 1865, but the triumph of a party dedicated to a deliberate return to pre-machine agriculture with its low standards of life, its diseases, and its illiteracy is beyond the imagination.

Finally, we must face the assertion that wars among the various nations of machine civilization may destroy the whole order. Probably terrible wars will arise and prove costly in blood and treasure, but it is a strain upon the speculative faculties to conceive of any conflict that could destroy the population and mechanical equipment of the Western world so extensively that human vitality and science could not restore economic prosperity and even improve upon the previous order. According to J. S. Mill, the whole mechanical outfit of a capitalistic country can be reproduced in about ten years. Hence the prospect of repeated and costly wars in the future need not lead us to the pessimistic view that suicide is to be the fate of machine civilization. We may admit the reality of the perils ahead without adopting the counsel of despair. If Europe and America were absolutely devastated, Japan with her present equipment in libraries, laboratories, and technology could begin the work of occupying the vacant areas, using the machine process in the operation.

For the reasons thus adduced it may be inferred: that modern civilization founded on science and the machine will not decline after the fashion of older agricultural civilizations; that analogies drawn from ages previous to technology are inapplicable; that according to signs on every hand technology promises to extend its area and intensify its characteristics; that it will afford the substance with which all who expect to lead and teach in the future must reckon.

Such appears to be the promise of the long future, if not the grand destiny of what we call modern civilization—the flexible framework in which the human spirit must operate during the coming centuries. Yet this view by no means precludes the idea that the machine system, as tested by its present results, presents shocking evils and indeed terrible menaces to the noblest faculties of the human race. By the use of material standards for measuring achievement, it is in danger of developing a kind of ignorant complacency that would make Phidias, Sophocles, Horace, St. Augustine, Dante, Michelangelo, Shakespeare, Lord Bacon, Newton, Goethe, Ruskin, and Emerson appear to be mere trifling parasites as compared with Lord Beaverbrook, Hugo Stinnes, John Pierpont Morgan, and Henry Ford. To deny the peril that lies in any such numerical morality would be a work of supererogation. More perilous still is the concentration on the production of goods that will sell quickly at the best price the traffic will bear and fall to pieces quickly—mass production of cheap goods —rather than concentration on the manufacture and exchange of commodities with the finest intrinsic values capable of indefinite endurance. What the creed of "give as little as you can for as much as you can get" will do to the common honesty of mankind, if followed blindly for centuries, can readily be imagined. Finally, it must be admitted that the dedication of the engines of state, supported by a passionate and uninformed chauvinism, to the promotion and sale of machine-made goods is creating zones of international rivalry likely to flame up in wars more vast and destructive than any yet witnessed.

To consider for the moment merely the domestic aspects of the question, the machine civilization is particularly open to attack from three sides.

On æsthetic grounds, it has been assailed for nearly a hundred years, England, the classical home of the industrial revolution, being naturally enough the mother of the severest critics—Ruskin, Carlyle, Kingsley, and Matthew Arnold. The chief article in their indictment, perhaps, is the contention that men who work with machinery are not creative, joyous, or free, but are slaves to the monotonous routine of the inexorable wheel. In a sense it is true that, in the pre-machine age, each craftsman had a certain leeway in shaping his materials with his tools and that many a common artisan produced articles of great beauty.

Yet the point can be easily overworked. Doubtless the vast majority of mediæval artisans merely followed designs made by master workmen. This is certainly true of artisans in the Orient today. With respect to the mass of mankind, it is safe to assume that the level of monotony on which labor is conducted under the machine régime is by and large not lower but higher than in the handicraft, servile, or slave systems of the past. Let anyone who has doubts on this matter compare the life of laborers on the latifundia of Rome or in the cities of modern China with that of the workers in by far the major portion of machine industries. Those who are prepared to sacrifice the standard of living for the millions to provide conditions presumably favorable to the creative arts must assume a responsibility of the first magnitude.

Indeed, it is not certain, so primitive as yet are the beginnings of machine civilization, that there can be no substitute for the handicrafts as æsthetic stimulants, assuming that mechanical industry is not favorable to the creative life. The machine régime does not do away with the necessity for designing or reduce the opportunities for the practice of that craft: it transfers the operation from the shop to the laboratory; and it remains to be seen whether great æsthetic powers will not flourish after the first storm of capitalism has passed. In any case, it must be admitted that the "cheap and nasty" character of machine-made goods, so marked everywhere, may really be due to the profit-making lust and the desire of the multitude to have imitations of the gew-gaws loved by the patricians, not to the inherent nature of machine industry. Possibly what is lost in the merits of individual objects of beauty may be more than offset by city and community planning, realizing new types of æsthetic ideals on a vast, democratic basis. Certainly the worst of the æsthetic offences created by the machine—the hideous factory town—can be avoided by intelligent co-operative action, as the garden-city movement faintly foreshadows. In a hundred years the coal-consuming engine may be as obsolete as the Dodo and the Birminghams, Pittsburghs, and Essens of the modern world live only in the records of the historians. However this may be, the æsthetes of the future will have to work within the limitations and opportunities created by science and the machine, directed, it may be hoped, by a more intelligent economy and nobler concepts of human values.

Frequently affiliated with æsthetic criticism of the machine and science is the religious attack. With endless reiteration, the charge is made that industrial civilization is materialistic. In reply, the scornful might say, "Well, what of it?" But the issue deserves consideration on its merits, in spite of its illusive nature. As generally used, the term "materialistic" has some of the qualities of moonshine; it is difficult to grasp. It is the fashion of certain Catholic writers to call Protestantism materialistic, on account of its emphasis on thrift and business enterprise—a fashion which some radicals have adopted: Max Weber in Germany and R. H. Tawney in England, for example. With something akin to the same discrimination, Oswald Spengler calls all England materialistic, governed by pecuniary standards—as contrasted with old Prussia where "duty," "honor," and "simple piety" reigned supreme. More recently, André Siegfried, following a hundred English critics, with Matthew Arnold in the lead, has found materialism to be one of the chief characteristics of the United States, as contrasted with the richer and older civilizations of Europe, particularly France. And Gandhi consigns every one of them—England, Prussia, France, and America—to the same bottomless pit of industrial materialism. When all this verbiage is sifted, it usually means that charge arises from emotions that have little or no relation to religion or philosophy—from the quarrels of races, sects, and nations.

If religion is taken in a crude, anthropomorphic sense, filling the universe with gods, spirits, and miraculous feats, then beyond question the machine and science are the foes of religion. If it is materialistic to disclose the influence of technology and environment in general upon humanity, then perhaps the machine and science are materialistic. But it is one of the ironies of history that science has shown the shallowness of the old battle between materialist and spiritist and through the mouths of physicists has confessed that it does not know what matter and force are. Matter is motion; motion is matter; both elude us, we are told. Doubtless science does make short shrift of a thousand little mysteries once deemed as essential to Christianity as were the thousand minor gods to the religion of old Japan, but for these little mysteries it has substituted a higher and sublimer mystery.

To descend to the concrete, is the prevention of disease by sanitation more materialistic than curing it by touching saints' bones? Is feeding the multitude by mass production more materialistic than feeding it by a miracle? Is the elimination of famines by a better distribution of goods more materialistic than prevention by the placation of the rain gods? At any rate, it is not likely that science and machinery will be abandoned because the theologian (who seldom refuses to partake of their benefits) wrings his hands and cries out against materialism. After all, how can he consistently maintain that Omnipotent God ruled the world wisely and well until the dawn of the modern age and abandoned it to the Evil One because Henry VIII or Martin Luther quarrelled with the Pope and James Watt invented the steam engine?

Arising, perhaps, from the same emotional source as æsthetic and religious criticisms, is the attack on the machine civilization as lacking in humanitarianism. Without commenting on man's inhumanity to man as an essential characteristic of the race, we may fairly ask on what grounds can anyone argue that the masses were more humanely treated in the agricultural civilization of antiquity or the middle ages than in the machine order of modern times. Tested by the mildness of its laws (brutal as many of them are), by its institutions of care and benevolence, by its death rate (that tell-tale measurement of human welfare), by its standards of life, and by every conceivable measure of human values, machine civilization, even in its present primitive stage, need fear no comparison with any other order on the score of general well-being.

Under the machine and science, the love of beauty, the sense of mystery, and the motive of compassion—sources of æsthetics, religion, and humanism—are not destroyed. They remain essential parts of our nature. But the conditions under which they must operate, the channels they must take, the potentialities of their action are all changed. These ancient forces will become powerful in the modern age just in the proportion that men and women accept the inevitability of science and the machine, understand the nature of the civilization in which they must work, and turn their faces resolutely to the future.

QUESTIONS AND TOPICS

1. Do you agree with Beard that the kind of civilization he is defending "is by no means synonymous with capitalism"?
2. If there were no hydrogen bomb today, would Beard be correct in his claims that machine civilization would persist indefinitely?
3. Do you agree with Beard that machine civilization is basically beneficial to the multitude?
4. Has Beard neglected to consider the fact that people can be well-fed and well-clothed, yet unhappy? Should he have considered this aspect of human behavior?
5. Does Beard dismiss religion and art too easily?

Nathanael West

from
THE DAY
OF THE
LOCUST

Nathanael West, 1902–1940, lived much of his professional life in Hollywood as a screen writer and film critic. In this selection from The Day of the Locust, *1939, a savage attack against Hollywood values, West brings to life the crowd Ortega y Gasset feared so much.*

When Tod reached the street, he saw a dozen great violet shafts of light moving across the evening sky in wide crazy sweeps. Whenever one of the fiery columns reached the lowest point of its arc, it lit for a moment the rose-colored domes and delicate minarets of Kahn's Persian Palace Theatre. The purpose of this display was to signal the world premiere of a new picture.

Turning his back on the searchlights, he started in the opposite direction, toward Homer's place. Before he had gone very far, he saw a clock that read a quarter past six and changed his mind about going back just yet. He might as well let the poor fellow sleep for another hour and kill some time by looking at the crowds.

When still a block from the theatre, he saw an enormous electric sign that hung over the middle of the street. In letters ten feet high he read that—

MR. KAHN A PLEASURE DOME DECREED

Although it was still several hours before the celebrities would arrive, thousands of people had already gathered. They stood facing the theatre with their backs toward the gutter in a thick line hundreds of feet long.

A big squad of policemen was trying to keep a lane open between the front rank of the crowd and the façade of the theatre.

Tod entered the lane while the policeman guarding it was busy with a woman whose parcel had torn open, dropping oranges all over the place. Another policeman shouted for him to get the hell across the street, but he took a chance and kept going. They had enough to do without chasing him. He noticed how worried they looked and how careful they tried to be. If they had to arrest someone, they joked good-naturedly with the culprit, making light of it until they got him around the corner, then they whaled him with their clubs. Only so long as the man was actually part of the crowd did they have to be gentle.

Tod had walked only a short distance along the narrow lane when he began to get frightened. People shouted, commenting on his hat, his carriage, and his clothing. There was a continuous roar of catcalls, laughter and yells, pierced occasionally by a scream. The scream was usually followed by a sudden movement in the dense mass and part of it would surge forward wherever the police line was weakest. As soon as that part was rammed back, the bulge would pop out somewhere else.

The police force would have to be doubled when the stars started to arrive. At the sight of their heroes and heroines, the crowd would turn demoniac. Some little gesture, either too pleasing or too offensive, would start it moving and then nothing but machine guns would stop it. Individually the purpose of its members might simply be to get a souvenir, but collectively it would grab and rend.

A young man with a portable microphone was describing the scene. His rapid, hysterical voice was like that of a revivalist preacher whipping his congregation toward the ecstasy of fits.

"What a crowd, folks! What a crowd! There must be ten thousand excited, screaming fans outside Kahn's Persian tonight. The police can't hold them. Here, listen to them roar."

He held the microphone out and those near it obligingly roared for him.

"Did you hear it? It's a bedlam, folks. A veritable bedlam! What excitement! Of all the premières I've attended, this is the most . . . the most . . . stupendous, folks. Can the police hold them? Can they? It doesn't look so, folks . . ."

Another squad of police came charging up. The sergeant pleaded with the announcer to stand further back so the people couldn't hear him.

His men threw themselves at the crowd. It allowed itself to be hustled and shoved out of habit and because it lacked an objective. It tolerated the police, just as a bull elephant does when he allows a small boy to drive him with a light stick.

Tod could see very few people who looked tough, nor could he see any working men. The crowd was made up of the lower middle classes, every other person one of his torchbearers.

Just as he came near the end of the lane, it closed in front of him with a heave, and he had to fight his way through. Someone knocked his hat off and when he stooped to pick it up, someone kicked him. He whirled around angrily and found himself surrounded by people who were laughing at him. He knew enough to laugh with them. The crowd became sympathetic. A stout woman slapped him on the back, while a man handed him his hat, first brushing it carefully with his sleeve. Still another man shouted for a way to be cleared.

By a great deal of pushing and squirming, always trying to look as though he were enjoying himself, Tod finally managed to break into the open. After rearranging his clothes, he went over to a parking lot and sat down on the low retaining wall that ran along the front of it.

New groups, whole families, kept arriving. He could see a change come over them as soon as they had become part of the crowd. Until they reached the line, they looked difficult, almost furtive, but the moment they had become part of it, they turned arrogant and pugnacious. It was a mistake to think them harmless curiosity seekers. They were savage and bitter, especially the middle-aged and the old, and had been made so by boredom and disappointment.

All their lives they had slaved at some kind of dull, heavy labor, behind desks and counters, in the fields and at tedious machines of all sorts, saving their pennies and dreaming of the leisure that would be theirs when they had enough. Finally that day came. They could draw a weekly income of ten or fifteen dollars. Where else should they go but California, the land of sunshine and oranges?

Once there, they discover that sunshine isn't enough. They get tired of oranges, even of avocado pears and passion fruit. Nothing happens. They don't know what to do with their time. They haven't the mental equipment for leisure, the money nor the physical equipment for pleasure. Did they slave so long just to go to an occasional Iowa picnic? What else is there? They watch the waves come in at Venice. There wasn't any ocean where most of them came from, but after you've seen one wave, you've seen them all. The same is true of the airplanes at Glendale. If only a plane would crash once in a while so that they could watch the passengers being consumed in a "holocaust of flame," as the newspapers put it. But the planes never crash.

Their boredom becomes more and more terrible. They realize that they've been tricked and burn with resentment. Every day of their lives they read the newspapers and went to the movies. Both fed them on lynchings, murder, sex crimes, explosions, wrecks, love nests, fires, miracles, revolutions, war. This daily diet made sophisticates of them. The sun is a joke. Oranges can't titillate their jaded palates. Nothing can ever be violent enough to make taut their slack minds and bodies. They have been cheated and betrayed. They have slaved and saved for nothing.

Tod stood up. During the ten minutes he had been sitting on the wall, the crowd had grown thirty feet and he was afraid that his escape might be cut off if he loitered much longer. He crossed to the other side of the street and started back.

He was trying to figure what to do if he were unable to wake Homer when, suddenly he saw his head bobbing above the crowd. He hurried toward him. From his appearance, it was evident that there was something definitely wrong.

Homer walked more than ever like a badly made automaton and his features were set in a rigid, mechanical grin. He had his trousers on over his nightgown and part of it hung out of his open fly. In both of his hands were suitcases. With each step, he lurched to one side then the other, using the suitcases for balance weights.

Tod stopped directly in front of him, blocking his way.

"Where're you going?"

"Wayneville," he replied, using an extraordinary amount of jaw movement to get out this single word.

"That's fine. But you can't walk to the station from here. It's in Los Angeles."

Homer tried to get around him, but he caught his arm.

"We'll get a taxi. I'll go with you."

The cabs were all being routed around the block because of the preview. He explained this to Homer and tried to get him to walk to the corner.

"Come on, we're sure to get one on the next street."

Once Tod got him into a cab, he intended to tell the driver to go to the nearest hospital. But Homer wouldn't budge, no matter how hard he yanked and pleaded. People stopped to watch them, others turned their heads curiously. He decided to leave him and get a cab.

"I'll come right back," he said.

He couldn't tell from either Homer's eyes or expression whether he heard, for they both were empty of everything, even annoyance. At the corner he looked around and saw that Homer had started to cross the street, moving blindly. Brakes screeched and twice he was almost run over, but he didn't swerve or hurry. He moved in a straight diagonal. When he reached the other curb, he tried to get on the sidewalk at a point where the crowd was very thick and was shoved violently back. He made another attempt and this time a policeman grabbed him by the back of the neck and hustled him to the end of the line. When the policeman let go of him, he kept on walking as though nothing had happened.

Tod tried to get over to him, but was unable to cross until the traffic lights changed. When he reached the other side, he found Homer sitting on a bench, fifty or sixty feet from the outskirts of the crowd.

He put his arm around Homer's shoulder and suggested that they walk a few blocks further. When Homer didn't answer, he reached over to pick up one of the valises. Homer held on to it.

"I'll carry it for you," he said, tugging gently.

"Thief!"

Before Homer could repeat the shout, he jumped away. It would be extremely embarrassing if Homer shouted thief in front of a cop. He thought of phoning for an ambulance. But then, after all, how could he be sure that Homer was crazy? He was sitting quietly on the bench, minding his own business.

Tod decided to wait, then try again to get him into a cab. The crowd was growing in size all the time, but it would be at least half an hour before it over-ran the bench. Before that happened, he would think of some plan. He moved a short distance away and stood with his back to a store window so that he could watch Homer without attracting attention.

About ten feet from where Homer was sitting grew a large eucalyptus tree and behind the trunk of the tree was a little boy. Tod saw him peer around it with great caution, then suddenly jerk his head back. A minute later he repeated the maneuver. At first Tod thought he was playing hide and seek, then noticed that he had a string in his hand which was attached to an old purse that lay in front of Homer's bench. Every once in a while the child would jerk the string, making the purse hop like a sluggish toad. Its torn lining hung from its iron mouth like a furry tongue and a few uncertain flies hovered over it.

Tod knew the game the child was playing. He used to play it himself when he was small. If Homer reached to pick up the purse, thinking there was money in it, he would yank it away and scream with laughter.

When Tod went over to the tree, he was surprised to discover that it was Adore Loomis, the kid who lived across the street from Homer. Tod tried to chase him, but he dodged around the tree, thumbing his nose. He gave up and went back to his original position. The moment he left, Adore got busy with his purse again. Homer wasn't paying any attention to the child, so Tod decided to let him alone.

Mrs. Loomis must be somewhere in the crowd, he thought. Tonight when she found Adore, she would give him a hiding. He had torn the pocket of his jacket and his Buster Brown collar was smeared with grease.

Adore had a nasty temper. The completeness with which Homer ignored both him and his pocketbook made him frantic. He gave up dancing it at the end of the string and approached the bench on tiptoes, making ferocious faces, yet ready to run at Homer's first move. He stopped when about four feet away and stuck his tongue out. Homer ignored him. He took another step forward and ran through a series of insulting gestures.

If Tod had known that the boy held a stone in his hand, he would have interfered. But he felt sure that Homer wouldn't hurt the child and was waiting to see if he wouldn't move because of his pestering. When Adore raised his arm, it was too late. The stone hit Homer in the face. The boy turned to flee, but tripped and fell. Before he could scramble away, Homer landed on his back with both feet, then jumped again.

Tod yelled for him to stop and tried to yank him away. He shoved Tod and went on using his heels. Tod hit him as hard as he could, first in the belly, then in the face. He ignored the blows and continued to stamp on the boy. Tod hit him again and again, then threw both arms around him and tried to pull him off. He couldn't budge him. He was like a stone column.

The next thing Tod knew, he was torn loose from Homer and sent to his knees by a blow in the back of the head that spun him sideways. The crowd in front of the theatre had charged. He was surrounded by churning legs and feet. He pulled himself erect by grabbing a man's coat, then let himself be carried along backwards in a long, curving swoop. He saw Homer rise above the mass for a moment, shoved against the sky, his jaw hanging as though he wanted to scream but couldn't. A hand reached up and caught him by his open mouth and pulled him forward and down.

There was another dizzy rush. Tod closed his eyes and fought to keep upright. He was jostled about in a hacking cross surf of shoulders and backs, carried rapidly in one direction and then in the opposite. He kept pushing and hitting out at the people around him, trying to face in the direction he was going. Being carried backwards terrified him.

Using the eucalyptus tree as a landmark, he tried to work toward it by slipping sideways against the tide, pushing hard when carried away from it and riding the current when it moved toward his objective. He was within only a few feet of the tree when a sudden, driving rush carried him far past it. He struggled desperately for a moment, then gave up and let himself be swept along. He was the spearhead of a flying wedge when it collided with a mass going in the opposite direction. The impact turned him around. As the two forces ground against each other, he was turned again and again, like a grain between millstones. This didn't stop until he became part of the opposing force. The pressure continued to increase until he thought he must collapse. He was slowly being pushed into the air. Although relief for his cracking ribs could be gotten by continuing to rise, he fought to keep his feet on the ground. Not being able to touch was an even more dreadful sensation than being carried backwards.

There was another rush, shorter this time, and he found himself in a dead spot where the pressure was less and equal. He became conscious of a terrible pain in his left leg, just above the ankle, and tried to work it into a more comfortable position. He couldn't turn his body, but managed to get his head around. A very skinny boy, wearing a Western Union cap, had his back wedged against his shoulder. The pain continued to grow and his whole leg as high as the groin throbbed. He finally got his left arm free and took the back of the boy's neck in his fingers. He twisted as hard as he could. The boy began to jump up and down in his clothes. He managed to straighten his elbow, by pushing at the back of the boy's head, and so turn halfway around and free his leg. The pain didn't grow less.

There was another wild surge forward that ended in another dead spot. He now faced a young girl who was sobbing steadily. Her silk print dress had been torn down the front and her tiny brassiere hung from one strap.

He tried by pressing back to give her room, but she moved with him every time he moved. Now and then, she would jerk violently and he wondered if she was going to have a fit. One of her thighs was between his legs. He struggled to get free of her, but she clung to him, moving with him and pressing against him.

She turned her head and said, "Stop, stop," to someone behind her.

He saw what the trouble was. An old man, wearing a Panama hat and horn-rimmed glasses, was hugging her. He had one of his hands inside her dress and was biting her neck.

Tod freed his right arm with a heave, reached over the girl and brought his fist down on the man's head. He couldn't hit very hard but managed to knock the man's hat off, also his glasses. The man tried to bury his face in the girl's shoulder, but Tod grabbed one of his ears and yanked. They started to move again. Tod held on to the ear as long as he could hoping that it would come away in his hand. The girl managed to twist under his arm. A piece of her dress tore, but she was free of her attacker.

Another spasm passed through the mob and he was carried toward the curb. He fought toward a lamp-post, but he was swept by before he could grasp it. He saw another man catch the girl with the torn dress. She screamed for help. He tried to get to her, but was carried in the opposite direction. This rush also ended in a dead spot. Here his neighbors were all shorter than he was. He turned his head upward toward the sky and tried to pull some fresh air into his aching lungs, but it was all heavily tainted with sweat.

In this part of the mob no one was hysterical. In fact, most of the people seemed to be enjoying themselves. Near him was a stout woman with a man pressing hard against her from in front. His chin was on her shoulder, and his arms were around her. She paid no attention to him and went on talking to the woman at her side.

"The first thing I knew," Tod heard her say, "there was a rush and I was in the middle."

"Yeah. Somebody hollered, 'Here comes Gary Cooper,' and then wham!"

"That ain't it," said a little man wearing a cloth cap and pullover sweater. "This is a riot you're in."

"Yeah," said a third woman, whose snaky gray hair was hanging over her face and shoulders. "A pervert attacked a child."

"He ought to be lynched."

Everybody agreed vehemently.

"I come from St. Louis," announced the stout woman, "and we had one of them pervert fellers in our neighborhood once. He ripped up a girl with a pair of scissors."

"He must have been crazy," said the man in the cap. "What kind of fun is that?"

Everybody laughed. The stout woman spoke to the man who was hugging her.

"Hey, you," she said. "I ain't no pillow."

The man smiled beatifically but didn't move. She laughed, making no effort to get out of his embrace.

"A fresh guy," she said.

The other woman laughed.

"Yeah," she said, "this is a regular free-for-all."

The man in the cap and sweater thought there was another laugh in his comment about the pervert.

"Ripping up a girl with scissors. That's the wrong tool."

He was right. They laughed even louder than the first time.

"You'd a done it different, eh, kid?" said a young man with a kidney-shaped head and waxed mustaches.

The two women laughed. This encouraged the man in the cap and he reached over and pinched the stout woman's friend. She squealed.

"Lay off that," she said good-naturedly.

"I was shoved," he said.

An ambulance siren screamed in the street. Its wailing moan started the crowd moving again and Tod was carried along in a slow, steady push. He closed his eyes and tried to protect his throbbing leg. This time, when the movement ended, he found himself with his back to the theatre wall. He kept his eyes closed and stood on his good leg. After what seemed like hours, the pack began to loosen and move again with a churning motion. It gathered momentum and rushed. He rode it until he was slammed against the base of an iron rail which fenced the driveway of the theatre from the street. He had the wind knocked out of him by the impact, but managed to cling to the rail. He held on desperately, fighting to keep from being sucked back. A woman caught him around the waist and tried to hang on. She was sobbing rhythmically. Tod felt his fingers slipping from the rail and kicked backwards as hard as he could. The woman let go.

Despite the agony in his leg, he was able to think clearly about his picture, "The Burning of Los Angeles." After his quarrel with Faye, he had worked on it continually to escape tormenting himself, and the way to it in his mind had become almost automatic.

As he stood on his good leg, clinging desperately to the iron rail, he could see all the rough charcoal strokes with which he had blocked it out on the big canvas. Across the top, parallel with the frame, he had drawn the burning city, a great bonfire of architectural styles, ranging from Egyptian to Cape Cod colonial. Through the center, winding from left to right, was a long hill street and down it, spilling into the middle foreground, came the mob carrying baseball bats and torches. For the faces of its members, he was using the innumerable sketches he had made of the people who come to California to die; the cultists of all sorts, economic as well as religious, the wave, airplane, funeral and preview watchers—all those poor devils who can only be stirred by the promise of miracles and then only to violence. A super "Dr. Know-All Pierce-All" had made the necessary promise and they were marching behind his banner in a great united front of screwballs and screwboxes to purify the land. No longer bored, they sang and danced joyously in the red light of the flames.

In the lower foreground, men and women fled wildly before the vanguard of the crusading mob. Among them were Faye, Harry, Homer, Claude and himself. Faye ran proudly, throwing her knees high. Harry stumbled along behind her, holding on to his beloved derby hat with both hands. Homer seemed to be falling out of the canvas, his face half-asleep, his big hands clawing the air in anguished pantomime. Claude turned his head as he ran to thumb his nose at his pursuers. Tod himself picked up a small stone to throw before continuing his flight.

He had almost forgotten both his leg and his predicament, and to make his escape still more complete he stood on a chair and worked at the flames in an upper corner of the canvas, modeling the tongues of fire so that they licked even more avidly at a Corinthian column that held up the palmleaf roof of a nutburger stand.

He had finished one flame and was starting on another when he was brought back by someone shouting in his ear. He opened his eyes and saw a policeman trying to reach him from behind the rail to which he was clinging. He let go with his left hand and raised his arm. The policeman caught him by the wrist, but couldn't lift him. Tod was afraid to let go until another man came to aid the policeman and caught him by the back of his jacket. He let go of the rail and they hauled him up and over it.

When they saw that he couldn't stand, they let him down easily to the ground. He was in the theatre driveway. On the curb next to him sat a woman crying into her skirt. Along the wall were groups of other disheveled people. At the end of the driveway was an ambulance. A policeman asked him if he wanted to go to the hospital. He shook his head no. He then offered him a lift home. Tod had the presence of mind to give Claude's address.

He was carried through the exit to the back street and lifted into a police car. The siren began to scream and at first he thought he was making the noise himself. He felt his lips with his hands. They were clamped tight. He knew then it was the siren. For some reason this made him laugh and he began to imitate the siren as loud as he could.

QUESTIONS AND TOPICS

1. Why do people in general like to flock together in crowds? What changes take place in their behavior when in a crowd?
2. What is the social composition of the crowd? Why are they disillusioned? Do you agree with West that most older people who come to California become ugly and embittered?
3. Are ordinary Americans of lower-middle-class origin apt to join in crowds such as the one described? Is the quality of their lives as empty as West suggests?
4. Do you think that such people influence California society and politics? United States society and politics?

5

YOUTH
IN
AMERICA

THOUGH MANY OF OUR YOUNG PEOPLE must still suffer the "culture of poverty" described by Harrington, more and more youngsters are growing up in affluence. Yet a great number of them feel that the quality of their lives has not thereby been improved. For them affluence has not brought the fulfillment that their parents, many of them once poor and struggling, had desired. Because their elders experienced insecurity and danger, they are urged to adopt the ethic of security and achievement. The approved path is clear: college, a job, marriage, children. Yet many young people wonder. Some always have found schooling intolerable; probably more do now. Searching for excitement which school cannot give them, they decline to work for the usual rewards. Some protest; others drop out; many just coast along.

Others do well at school, yet seem to find life deadening and mechanical, the expected goals uninteresting. Some of these join the New Left. Above all, the young people in question are disaffiliated. They no longer identify themselves with the goals of American society. And they make the headlines increasingly. In the 1960's college riots often shared newspaper headlines with race riots.

Yet most young people, to use Gold's phrase, are "allrightniks." Though bothered by emanations from their disaffiliated neighbors, they follow, more or less, the paths of their forebears. Many seek, as William H.

Whyte, Jr., tells us, not to become pioneers, or to form businesses of their own, but to affiliate themselves with a larger organization, in which decisions are made for them. The choice may not even be their own, since more and more of our economy is controlled by large organizations. The great majority marry early, beget children, and are surprised at the violence prevalent in the world about them. Most simply believe what they have been told and live quite happily, as people have for ages, until, on occasion, some catastrophe disrupts the surface of their lives.

But, in general, even if the question of disaffiliation is ignored, youth is not a comfortable time in Western culture. Adolescence, Ruth Benedict writes, "is in our tradition a physiological state as definitely characterized by domestic explosions and rebellion as typhoid is marked by fever." Men must find professions; both sexes seek an end to sexual uncertainty. Though some young people march through adolescence triumphantly, most, even those who are not rebellious, find it a time of confusion and stress.

Arthur Miller

THE BORED
AND THE
VIOLENT

Arthur Miller, 1915–, the well-known playwright, has also written excellent short stories and essays. The following essay on juvenile delinquency, written in 1962, refuses to offer easy solutions and is an example of his penetration and insight into the problems of ordinary people.

If my own small experience is any guide, the main difficulty in approaching the problem of juvenile delinquency is that there is very little evidence about it and very many opinions as to how to deal with it. By evidence I do not mean the news stories telling of gang fights and teenage murders—there are plenty of those. But it is unknown, for instance, what the actual effects are on the delinquent of prison sentences, psychotherapy, slum-clearance projects, settlement-house programs, tougher or more lenient police attitudes, the general employment situation, and so on. Statistics are few and not generally reliable. The narcotics problem alone is an almost closed mystery.

Not that statistical information in itself can solve anything, but it might at least outline the extent of the disease. I have it, for instance, from an old and deservedly respected official—it is his opinion anyway—that there is really no great increase in delinquent acts but a very great intensification of our awareness of them. He feels we are more nervous now about infractions of the social mores than our ancestors, and he likes to point out that Shakespeare, Boccaccio, and other writers never brought on stage a man of wealth or station without his bravos, who were simply his private police force, necessary to him when he ventured out of his house, especially at night. He would have us read *Great Expectations, Oliver Twist,*

Huckleberry Finn, and other classics, not in a romantic mood but in the way we read about our own abandoned kids and their depredations. The difference lies mainly in the way we look at the same behavior.

The experts have only a little more to go on than we have. Like the surgeon whose hands are bloody a good part of the day, the social worker is likely to come to accept the permanent existence of the delinquency disease without the shock of the amateur who first encounters it.

A new book on the subject, *All the Way Down,** reports the experience of a social worker—of sorts—who never got used to the experience, and does not accept its inevitability. It is an easy book to attack on superficial grounds because it has no evident sociological method, it rambles and jumps and shouts and curses. But it has a virtue, a very great and rare one, I think, in that it does convey the endless, leaden, mind-destroying boredom of the delinquent life. Its sex is without romance or sexuality, its violence is without release or gratification—exactly like the streets— movies and plays about delinquency notwithstanding.

Unlike most problems which sociology takes up, delinquency seems to be immune to the usual sociological analyses or cures. For instance, it appears in all technological societies, whether Latin or Anglo-Saxon or Russian or Japanese. It has a very slippery correlation with unemployment and the presence or absence of housing projects. It exists among the rich in Westchester and the poor in Brooklyn and Chicago. It has spread quickly into the rural areas and the small towns. Now according to Harrison Salisbury, it is the big problem in the Soviet Union. So that any single key to its causation is nowhere visible. If one wants to believe it to be essentially a symptom of unequal opportunity—and certainly this factor operates—one must wonder about the Russian problem, for the Soviet youngster can, in fact, go right up through the whole school system on his ability alone, as many of ours cannot. Yet the gangs are roaming the Russian streets, just as they do in our relatively permissive society.

So no one knows what "causes" delinquency. Having spent some months in the streets with boys of an American gang, I came away with certain impressions, all of which stemmed from a single, overwhelming conviction —that the problem underneath is boredom. And it is not strange, after all, that this should be so. It is the theme of so many of our novels, our plays, and especially our movies in the past twenty years, and is the hall-

---

* Vincent Riccio and Bill Slocum (New York: Simon and Schuster, 1962).

mark of society as a whole. The outcry of Britain's so-called Angry Young Men was against precisely this seemingly universal sense of life's point-lessness, the absence of any apparent aim to it all. So many American books and articles attest to the same awareness here. The stereotype of the man coming home from work and staring dumbly at a television set is an expression of it, and the "New Wave" of movies in France and Italy propound the same fundamental theme. People no longer seem to know why they are alive; existence is simply a string of near-experiences marked off by periods of stupefying spiritual and psychological stasis, and the good life is basically an amused one.

Among the delinquents the same kind of mindlessness prevails, but without the style—or stylishness—which art in our time has attempted to give it. The boredom of the delinquent is remarkable mainly because it is so little compensated for, as it may be among the middle classes and the rich who can fly down to the Caribbean or to Europe, or refurnish the house, or have an affair, or at least go shopping. The delinquent is stuck with his boredom, stuck inside it, stuck to it, until for two or three minutes he "lives"; he goes on a raid around the corner and feels the thrill of risk-ing his skin or his life as he smashes a bottle filled with gasoline on some other kid's head. In a sense, it is his trip to Miami. It makes his day. It is his shopping tour. It gives him something to talk about for a week. It is *life*. Standing around with nothing coming up is as close to dying as you can get. Unless one grasps the power of boredom, the threat of it to one's existence, it is impossible to "place" the delinquent as a member of the human race.

With boredom in the forefront, one may find some perspective in the mélange of views which are repeated endlessly about the delinquent. He is a rebel without a cause, or a victim of poverty, or a victim of undue privilege, or an unloved child, or an overloved child, or a child looking for a father, or a child trying to avenge himself on an uncaring society, or whatnot. But face to face with one of them, one finds these criteria use-less, if only because no two delinquents are any more alike than other people are. They do share one mood, however. They are drowning in boredom. School bores them, preaching bores them, even television bores them. The word rebel is inexact for them because it must inevitably imply a purpose, an end.

Other people, of course, have known boredom. To get out of it, they go to the movies, or to a bar, or read a book, or go to sleep, or turn on TV or a girl, or make a resolution, or quit a job. Younger persons who are not delinquents may go to their room and weep, or write a poem, or call up a friend until they get tired talking. But note that each of these escapes can only work if the victim is sure somewhere in his mind, or reasonably hopeful, that by so doing he will overthrow his boredom and with luck may come out on the other side where something hopeful or interesting waits. But the delinquent has no such sense of an imminent improvement. Most of the kids in the Riccio and Slocum book have never known a single good day. How can they be expected to project one and restrain themselves in order to experience such joy once more?

The word rebel is wrong, too, in that it implies some sort of social criticism in the delinquent. But that would confuse him with the bourgeois Beatnik. The delinquent has only respect, even reverence, for certain allegedly bourgeois values. He implicitly believes that there are good girls and bad girls, for instance. Sex and marriage are two entirely separate things. He is, in my experience anyway, deeply patriotic. Which is simply to say that he respects those values he never experienced, like money and good girls and the Army and Navy. What he has experienced has left him with absolute contempt, or more accurately, an active indifference. Once he does experience decency—as he does sometimes in a wife—he reacts decently to it. For to this date the only known cure for delinquency is marriage.

The delinquent, far from being the rebel, is the conformist par excellence. He is actually incapable of doing anything alone, and a story may indicate how incapable he is. I went along with Riccio and the gang in his book to a YMCA camp outside New York City for an overnight outing. In the afternoon we started a baseball game, and everything proceeded normally until somebody hit a ball to the outfield. I turned to watch the play and saw ten or twelve kids running for the catch. It turned out that not one of them was willing to play the outfield by himself, insisting that the entire group hang around out there together. The reason was that a boy alone might drop a catch and would not be able to bear the humiliation. So they ran around out there in a drove all afternoon, creating a stampede every time a ball was hit.

They are frightened kids, and that is why they are so dangerous. But again, it will not do to say—it is simply not true—that they are therefore unrelated to the rest of the population's frame of mind. Like most of us, the delinquent is simply doing as he was taught. This is often said but rarely understood. Only recently a boy was about to be executed for murder in New York State. Only after he had been in jail for more than a year after sentencing did a campaign develop to persuade the Governor to commute his sentence to life imprisonment, for only then was it discovered that he had been deserted by his father in Puerto Rico, left behind when his mother went to New York, wandered about homeless throughout his childhood, and so on. The sentencing judge only learned his background a week or two before he was to be officially murdered. And then what shock, what pity! I have to ask why the simple facts of his deprivation were not brought out in court, if not before. I am afraid I know the answer. Like most people, it was probably beyond the judge's imagination that small children sometimes can be treated much worse than kittens or puppies in our cities.

Gangs in Suburbia It is only in theory that the solution seems purely physical—better housing, enlightened institutions for deserted kids, psychotherapy, and the rest. The visible surfaces of the problem are easy to survey—although we have hardly begun even to do that.

More difficult is the subterranean moral question which every kind of delinquency poses. Not long ago a gang was arrested in a middle-class section of Brooklyn, whose tack was to rob homes and sell the stuff to professional fences. Many of these boys were top students, and all of them were from good, middle-class backgrounds. Their parents were floored by the news of their secret depredations, and their common cry was that they had always given their sons plenty of money, that the boys were secure at home, that there was no conceivable reason for this kind of aberration. The boys were remorseful and evidently as bewildered as their parents.

Greenwich, Connecticut, is said to be the wealthiest community in the United States. A friend of mine who lives there let his sons throw a party for their friends. In the middle of the festivities a gang of boys arrived— their own acquaintances who attend the same high school. They tore the house apart, destroyed the furniture, pulled parts off the automobile and left them on the lawn, and split the skulls of two of the guests with beer cans.

Now if it is true that the slum delinquent does as he is taught, it must be true that the Greenwich delinquent does the same. But obviously the lines of force from example to imitation are subtler and less easily traced here. It is doubtful that the parents of this marauding gang rip up the furniture in the homes to which they have been invited. So that once again it is necessary to withhold one's cherished theories. Rich delinquency is delinquency but it is not the same as slum delinquency. But there is one clear common denominator, I think. They do not know how to live when alone. Most boys in Greenwich do not roam in gangs but a significant fraction in both places find that counterfeit sense of existence which the gang life provides.

Again, I think it necessary to raise and reject the idea of rebellion, if one means by that word a thrust of any sort. For perspective's sake it may be wise to remember another kind of youthful reaction to a failed society in a different era. In the 'thirties, for instance, we were also contemptuous of the given order. We had been brought up to believe that if you worked hard, saved your money, studied, kept your nose clean, you would end up made. We found ourselves in the Depression, when you could not get a job, when all the studying you might do would get you a chance, at best, to sell ties in Macy's. Our delinquency consisted in joining demonstrations of the unemployed, pouring onto campuses to scream against some injustice by college administrations, and adopting to one degree or another a Socialist ideology. This, in fact, was a more dangerous kind of delinquency than the gangs imply, for it was directed against the social structure of capitalism itself. But, curiously, it was at the same time immeasurably more constructive, for the radical youth of the 'thirties, contemptuous as he was of the social values he had rejected, was still bent upon instituting human values in their place. He was therefore a conserver, he believed in *some* society.

Gide wrote a story about a man who wanted to get on a train and shoot a passenger. Any train, any passenger. It would be a totally gratuitous act, an act devoid of any purpose whatever, an act of "freedom" from purpose. To kill an unknown man without even anger, without unrequited love, without love at all, with nothing in his heart but the sheerly physical contemplation of the gun barrel and the target. In doing this one would partake of Death's irreproachable identity and commit an act in revolt against meaning itself, just as Death is, in the last analysis, beyond analysis.

To think of contemporary delinquency in the vein of the 'thirties, as a rebellion toward something, is to add a value to it which it does not have. To give it even the dignity of cynicism run rampant is also overelaborate. For the essence is not the individual at all; it is the gang, the herd, and we should be able to understand its attractions ourselves. It is not the thrust toward individual expression but a flight from self in any defined form. Therefore, to see it simply as a protest against conformism is to stand it on its head; it is profoundly conformist but without the mottoes, the entablature of recognizable, "safe" conformism and its liturgy of religious, patriotic, socially conservative credos.

The Greenwich gang, therefore, is also doing as it was taught, just as the slum gang does, but more subtly. The Greenwich gang is conforming to the hidden inhumanity of conformism, to the herd quality in conformism; it is acting out the terror-fury that lies hidden under father's acceptable conformism. It is simply conformity sincere, conformity revealing its true content, which is hatred of others, a stunted wish for omnipotence, and the conformist's secret belief that nothing outside his skin is real or true. For which reason he must redouble his obeisance to institutions lest, if the act of obeisance be withheld, the whole external world will vanish, leaving him alone. And to be left alone when you do not sense any existence in yourself is the ultimate terror. But this loneliness is not the poet's, not the thinker's, not the loneliness that is filled with incommunicable feeling, insufficiently formed thought. It is nonexistence and must not be romanticized as it has been in movies and some of the wishful Beat literature. It is a withdrawal not from the world but from oneself. It is boredom, the subsidence of inner impulse, and it threatens true death unless it is overthrown.

All of which is said in order to indicate that delinquency is not the kind of "social problem" it is generally thought to be. That is, it transcends even as it includes the need for better housing, medical care, and the rest. It is our most notable and violent manifestation of social nihilism. In saying this, however, it is necessary to short-circuit any notion that it is an attempt by the youth to live "sincerely." The air of "sincerity" which so many writers have given the delinquent is not to be mistaken as his "purpose." This is romanticism and solves nothing except to sentimentalize brutality. The gang kid can be sincere; he can extend himself for a buddy and risk himself for others but he is just as liable, if not more so than others, to desert his buddies in need and to treat his friends disloyally. Gang boys rarely go to visit a buddy in jail excepting in the movies. They forget about him. The cult of sincerity, of true human relations uncontaminated by money and the social rat race, is not the hallmark of the gang. The only moment of truth comes when the war starts. Then the brave show themselves, but few of these boys know how to fight alone, and hardly any without a knife or a gun. They are not to be equated with matadors or boxers or Hemingway heroes. They are dangerous pack hounds who will not even expose themselves singly in the outfield.

Flight from Nothingness   If, then, one begins to put together all the elements, this "social problem" takes on not merely its superficial welfare aspects but its philosophical depths, which I think are the controlling ones. It is not a problem of big cities alone but of rural areas too; not of capitalism alone but of socialism as well; not restricted to the physically deprived but shared by the affluent; not a racial problem alone or a problem of recent immigrants, or a purely American problem. I believe it is in its present form the product of technology destroying the very concept of man as a value in himself.

I hesitate to say what I think the cure might be, if only because I cannot prove it. But I have heard most of the solutions men have offered, and they are spiritless, they do not assume that the wrong is deep and terrible and general among us all. There is, in a word, a spirit gone. Perhaps two world wars, brutality immeasurable, have blown it off the earth; perhaps the very processes of technology have sucked it out of man's soul; but it is gone. Many men rarely relate to one another excepting as customer to seller, worker to boss, the affluent to the deprived and vice versa—in short, as factors to be somehow manipulated and not as intrinsically valuable persons.

Power was always in the world, to be sure, and its evils, but with us now it is strangely, surrealistically masked and distorted. Time was, for example, when the wealthy and the politically powerful flaunted themselves, used power openly as power, and were often cruel. But this openness had the advantage for man of clarity; it created a certain reality in the world, an environment that was defined, with hard but touchable barriers. Today power would have us believe—everywhere—that it is purely beneficent. The bank is not a place which makes more money with your deposits than it returns to you in the form of interest; it is not a sheer economic necessity, it is not a business at all. It is "Your Friendly Bank," a kind of welfare institution whose one prayer, day and night, is to serve your whims or needs. A school is no longer a place of mental discipline but a kind of day-care center, a social gathering where you go through a ritual of games and entertainments which insinuate knowledge and the crafts of the outside world. Business is not the practice of buying low and selling high, it is a species of public service. The good life itself is not the life of struggle for meaning, not the quest for union with the past, with God, with man that it traditionally was. The good life is the life of ceaseless entertainment, effortless joys, the air-conditioned, dust-free languor beyond the Mussulman's most supine dream. Freedom is, after all, comfort; sexuality is a photograph. The enemy of it all is the real. The enemy is conflict. The enemy, in a word, is life.

My own view is that delinquency is related to this dreamworld from two opposing sides. There are the deprived who cannot take part in the dream; poverty bars them. There are the oversated who are caught in its indefiniteness, its unreality, its boring hum, and strike for the real now and then—they rob, they hurt, they kill. In flight from the nothingness of this comfort they have inherited, they butt against its rubber walls in order to feel a real pain, a genuine consequence. For the world in which comfort rules is a delusion, whether one is within it or deprived of it.

There are a few social theorists who look beyond poverty and wealth, beyond the time when men will orient themselves to the world as breadwinners, as accruers of money power. They look to the triumph of technology, when at least in some countries the physical struggle to survive will no longer be the spine of existence. Then, they say, men will define themselves through varying "styles of life." With struggles solved, nature tamed and abundant, all that will be left to do will be the adornment of existence, a novel-shaped swimming pool, I take it, or an outburst of artistic work.

It is not impossible, I suppose. Certainly a lot of people are already living that way—when they are not at their psychiatrists'. But there is still a distance to go before life's style matters very much to most of humanity in comparison to next month's rent. I do not know how we ought to reach for the spirit again but it seems to me we must flounder without it. It is the spirit which does not accept injustice complacently and yet does not betray the poor with sentimentality. It is the spirit which seeks not to flee the tragedy which life must always be, but seeks to enter into it, thereby to be strengthened by the fullest awareness of its pain, its ultimate non sequitur. It is the spirit which does not mask but unmasks the true function of a thing, be it business, unionism, architecture, or love.

Riccio's and Slocum's book, with all its ugliness, its crudeness, its lack of polish and design, is good because it delivers up the real. It is only as hopeless as the situation is. Its implied solutions are good ones: reform of idiotic narcotics laws, a real attempt to put trained people at the service of bewildered, desperate families, job-training programs, medical care, reading clinics—all of it is necessary and none of it would so much as strain this economy. But none of it will matter, none of it will reach further than the spirit in which it is done. Not the spirit of fear with which so many face delinquency, nor the spirit of sentimentality which sees in it some virtue of rebellion against a false and lying society. The spirit has to be that of those people who know that delinquents are a living expression of our universal ignorance of what life ought to be, even of what it is, and of what it truly means to live. Bad pupils they surely are. But who from his own life, from his personal thought has come up with the good teaching, the way of life that is joy? This book shows how difficult it is to reach these boys; what the country has to decide is what it is going to say if these kids should decide to listen.

QUESTIONS AND TOPICS

1. Have you known any delinquents? Describe their behavior and activities.
2. Do you agree with Miller that simple boredom is the most important cause of delinquency?
3. Miller denies that delinquents are rebels. Do you agree? (Be sure to define the term *rebel*.)
4. Miller writes that delinquency "is profoundly conformist but without the mottoes, the entablature of recognizable 'safe' conformism and its liturgy of religious, patriotic, socially conservative credos." Do you think Miller is grouping disparate phenomena under the all-inclusive term *conformism*? Is normal conformism as empty and violent as Miller seems to imply?
5. Do you agree with Miller that delinquency in its present form is a product of technological society? State your own views on this issue.

Paul Goodman

A USUAL CASE—
NOTHING FANCY

Paul Goodman, 1911–, is a social critic who advocates a society that is not only communal but centered on the individual. Goodman wants society to be split into small units so that the individual's desires play a greater part in the management of institutions. This essay, an excerpt from Compulsory Mis-Education, *1964, attacks the university system because it does not fulfill the personal needs of young people. The essay exposes the dilemma of many students who must satisfy requirements they neither want nor, in their opinion, need.*

To sum up these dour remarks about American schools in the middle of the twentieth century, consider a usual case. Here is a young fellow in a college classroom. *He* is not usual, for everybody is unique, but his case is usual. His face is pretty blank but he is sitting in a middle row, not, like some, in the rear near the door, ready to bolt. Let me review a dozen important facts about his situation—they are obvious, nothing fancy.

He is in his junior year. So, omitting kindergarten, he has been in an equivalent classroom for nearly fifteen continuous years, intermitted only by summer vacations for play. Schooling has been the serious part of his life, and it has consisted of listening to some grown-up talking and of doing assigned lessons. The young man has almost never seriously assigned himself a task. Sometimes, as a child, he thought he was doing something earnest on his own, but the adults interrupted him and he became discouraged.

He's bright—he can manipulate formulas and remember sentences, and he has made a well-known college. During his last year in high school, he made good grades on a series of gruelling State and National Tests, Regents, College Boards, National Merits, Scholastic Aptitudes. And in this college, which is geared to process Ph.D.'s, he has survived, though the attrition is nearly 40 per cent. He has even gotten a partial scholarship on the National Defense Education Act. Yet, as it happens, he doesn't like books or study at all. He gets no flashes of insight into the structure or the methods of the academic subjects. This isn't the field in which his intelligence, grace, and strength of mind and body show to best advantage. He just learns the answers or figures out the puzzles. Needless to say he has already forgotten most of the answers that he once "knew" well enough to pass, sometimes brilliantly.

The academic subject being taught in this particular classroom is intrinsically interesting; most arts and sciences are intrinsically interesting. The professor and even the section-man know a good deal about it, and it is interesting to watch their minds work. But it is one of the social sciences and our young man does not grasp that it is *about* something; it has no connection for him. He has had so little experience of society or institutions. He has not practiced a craft, been in business, tried to make a living, been married, had to cope with children. He hasn't voted, served on a jury, been in politics, nor even in a youth movement for civil rights or peace or Goldwater. Coming from a modest middle class suburb, he has never really seen poor people or foreigners. His emotions have been carefully limited by the conventions of his parents and the conformism of his gang. What, for him, could history, sociology, political science, psychology, classical music or literature, possibly be about? (In the *Republic*, Plato forbids teaching most of our academic subjects until the student is thirty years old! Otherwise the lessons will be mere sophistry, emptily combative.)

Our young man is not verbally combative, and he's not a hipster who talks out to show that he knows the score, in order to put you down. But sometimes he is teased by something that the teacher or the book says, and he wants to demur, argue, ask a question. But the class is too crowded for any dialogue. When the format is a lecture, one cannot interrupt. Perhaps the chief obstacle to discussion, however, is the other students. In their judgment, discussion is irrelevant to the finals and the grades, and they resent wasting time. Also, they resent it if a student "hogs attention."

From time to time, the teacher, especially the young section-man, is heartened by a sign of life and does want to pursue the discussion. He is himself given to expressing dissenting opinions, questioning the justification of an institution or asking a student for evidence from personal experience. At once a wall of hostility rises against the teacher as well as the questioning student. Surely he must be a communist, pacifist, or homosexual. Maybe he is ridiculing the class. Feeling the hostility and being a rather timid academic, worried about advancement and ultimate tenure, the teacher signs off: "Well, let's get back to the meat of the course . . . that's beyond our scope here, why don't you take Sosh 403? . . . that's really anthropology, young man, and you'd better ask Professor O'Reilly, heh heh."

Indeed, little of the teaching makes our student see the relevance, necessity, or beauty of the subject. The professor, especially, is interested in the latest findings and in the ingenuity of a new technique, but the student is at sea as to why he is studying it at all, except that it's part of sequence B toward a Bachelor's. The confusion is made worse, as I have said, by the fact that the present young generation, including the young teachers, has at most a tenuous loyalty to the culture of the Western world, the Republic of Letters, the ideal of disinterested Science. But apart from this tradition, the University is nothing but a factory to train apprentices and process academic union-cards.

Yet a college is a poor environment in which to train apprentices, except in lab sciences where one works at real problems with the real apparatus. Most of the academic curriculum, whether in high school or college, is abstract in a bad sense. It must be so. A structure of ideas is abstracted from the on-going professions, civic and business activities, social institutions; and these ideas are again thinned out and processed to be imported into classrooms and taught as the curriculum. To be sure, this ancient procedure often makes sense. It makes sense for aspiring professionals who know what they are after and want a briefing; and it makes sense for the scholarly who have a philosophical interest in essences and their relationship, and want to chart the whole field. But for most, the abstractness of the curricular subjects, especially if the teaching is pedantic, can be utterly barren. The lessons are only exercises, with no relation to the real world. They are never for keeps. And many of the teachers are merely academics, not practicing professionals; they are interested in the words and the methodology, not the thing and the task.

II

The young man respects his teachers and he knows it is a good school, almost a prestige school, but he cannot help feeling disappointed. He had hoped in a vague way that when he came to college it would be different from high school. He would be a kind of junior friend of learned men who had succeeded; he could model himself on them. After all, except for parents and school-teachers—and the school-teachers have been prissy— he has had little contact with any adults in his whole life.

He thought, too, that the atmosphere of learning in college would, somehow, be free, liberating, a kind of wise bull-session that would reveal a secret. But it has proved to be the same cash-accounting of hours, tests, credits, grades. The professor is, evidently, preoccupied with his own research and publishing. In both class and office-hours he is formal and stand-offish. He never appears in the coffee-shop, never invites one home. He certainly never exposes himself as a human being. He is rather meticulous about the assignments being on time and he is a "tough" grader, but this seems to be his way of keeping the students under control, rather than due to belief in the system. He does not seem to realize that they respect him anyway.

So, just as in high school, the youth are driven back on their exclusive "sub-culture," which only distracts further from any meaning that academic life might have. As Riesman and others have pointed out, the students and faculty confront one another like hostile, or at least mutually suspicious, tribes.

Also, this past decade, the lack of community has been vastly exacerbated by the state of chaotic transition in which almost every college in the country exists. The grounds are torn up by bulldozers; the enrollment is excessive; the classes are too large; the students are housed three and four in a room meant for two. The curriculum is continually in process of readjustment. Professors are on the move, following the contracted research, or pirated away by salary hikes. These conditions are supposed to be temporary, but I have seen them now for ten years and the immediate future will be worse. A whole generation is being sacrificed.

An even deadlier aspect of the expansion is the unabashed imperialism of the administrators. This leads to entirely phony operations. Excellent teachers and scholars are scuttled for spectacular names that will never teach. A reputation for innovation and daring is sought, but student publications are censored in order to protect the Image. Scores of millions of new endowments are boasted of, but there is unbelievable penny-pinching about deficits in the cafeteria, rent for the dormitories, tuition, instructors' salaries.

Another aspect of transition is the Knowledge Explosion. New approaches and altogether new subjects must be taught, yet the entrenched faculty are by no means willing to give up any of the old prescribed subjects. It is peculiar; one would expect that, since the professors have tenure, they would welcome dropping some of the course load; but their imperialism is strong too, and they will give up nothing. So our student is taking five or even six subjects, when the maximum should be three. Whenever he begins to be interested in a subject, he is interrupted by other chores. Rushed, he gives token performances, which he has learned to fake. No attention is paid to what suits *him*. The only time a student is treated as a person is when he breaks down and is referred to Guidance.

In place of reliance on intrinsic motives, respect for individuality, leisurely exploration, there is a stepped-up pressure of extrinsic motivations, fear and bribery. The student cannot help worrying about his father's money, the fantastic tuition and other fees that will go down the drain if he flunks out; and he must certainly keep his scholarship. On the other hand, the talent scouts of big corporations hover around with lavish offers. In this atmosphere are supposed to occur disinterested scrutiny of the nature of things, the joy of discovery, moments of creativity, the finding of identity and vocation. It is sickening to watch.

III

Finally, we must say something about the animal and community life from which our collegian has come into this classroom. The college has spent government and foundation money in pretentious buildings with plushy lounges, but the food is lousy and the new dormitories are like bedlam for want of sound-proofing. The values of college presidents are incredibly petty-bourgeois; their world is made for photographs, not to live in.

The Administration has set itself strongly against fraternity-houses because of the exclusion-clauses and to promote cohesiveness of the community. These are excellent reasons, but one sometimes has a strong suspicion that the reality is to fill the new dormitories, built with Urban Renewal funds. If students want to live off-campus in their own cooperatives, they are avuncularly told that, at 20 years old, they are not mature enough to feed their faces and make their beds.

No attempt is made by the University to come to terms with its neighbors. Rather, to expand, it has the neighborhood condemned as a slum and it dislocates residents of many years. Then it asks for police protection because of the social tension. Some students vanish into the condemnable or condemned neighborhood and the campus sees little of them except for classes. Other students more hospitably invite the neighbors to Saturday night dances, with a local jazz combo, but the Dean breaks it up by having a cop ask for ID cards.

There are exquisitely elaborate regulations for sexual and convivial behavior—days and hours and how many inches the door must be open and whose feet must be on the ground. The Administration claims to be *in loco parentis*, yet half the young men and women had more freedom at home, when they were kids in high school. One has more than a strong suspicion, and not sometimes but usually, that all the parental concern is merely for Public Relations. The college motto is *Lux et Veritas,* but there is a strong smell of hypocrisy in the air.

Maybe the most galling thing of all is that there is a Student Government, with political factions and pompous elections. It is empowered to purchase the class rings and organize the Prom and the boatride. Our young man no longer bothers to vote. But when there is a need to censor the student paper or magazine, the Administration appoints these finks to be on a joint faculty-student board of review, so that the students are made responsible for their own muzzling.

QUESTIONS AND TOPICS

1. Do you believe in the reality of Goodman's young man? Would he be going to college if society did not require a bachelor's degree for a decent job?
2. Should colleges only admit those who are highly motivated and possess superior qualifications?
3. Goodman blames in part the "cash-accounting of hours, tests, credits, grades" for student dissatisfaction. Do you agree? Can a university carry out its educational functions without "cash-accounting"? Can you suggest a substitute system?

4. Are your professors uninterested in their students? If so, why? Does the university encourage such lack of interest?

5. Do you think that college education is too abstract? Should scholarly discipline be reserved for the few, while the majority receive more practical training?

6. Goodman implies that professors should appear in the coffee shops. Would most students be interested in talking with them?

7. Would education improve if courses were reduced in number? Would students study more or would they simply "goof off"?

8. Goodman claims that the university drives students "back on their exclusive 'sub-culture,' which only distracts further from any meaning that academic life might have." Is the "sub-culture" in your university hostile to education and intellectual growth? If so, is there any way to change student attitudes?

Christopher Jencks

LIMITS
OF THE
NEW LEFT

Combining sympathy and objectivity, Christopher Jencks has written one of the best pieces on the controversial New Left. (The essay appeared in the fall of 1967.)

Week before last, I reported on a meeting in Czechoslovakia between 40 Americans and two delegations of Vietnamese revolutionaries. That report concentrated on the Vietnamese side of the dialogue; now I want to say something about the Americans there. The majority were young and came from what is now irrevocably christened the "New Left." Some were active in the antiwar movement, organizing teach-ins, writing, helping set up protest groups and fomenting draft resistance. Others were working with poor whites and blacks on grievances only obliquely related to the war; they knew relatively little about Vietnam when they arrived in Bratislava. But they all saw the war as an inevitable by-product of some ill-defined sickness in the American system, which could only be cured by radical political remedies. They were contemptuous of liberals who regard the war as a colossal blunder and who think that when the war is over America will get on with rehabilitating a flawed but redeemable society. For this reason almost all the young radicals at Bratislava were slightly scornful of the traditional "peace movement," which they regard as ideologically naïve and politically ineffective. They had little in common with the clergymen and pacifists from the pre-Vietnam peace movement who were also in Bratislava, except distaste for the war.

To me, the most striking fact about the young radicals was the extent to which they identified with the Viet Cong. This identification was almost entirely confined to people born after the outbreak of World War II. I myself am only a few years older, have been bitterly critical of the war and support the National Liberation Front in the limited sense that I would rather let it take power than continue either the war or the present Thieu-Ky regime. Yet I do not feel instinctively allied to the NLF, and I know hardly anyone else my age who does. Indeed, I would say that inability to identify with the Viet Cong is one of the obvious differences between the generation which came to political consciousness under Eisenhower, as I did, and the generation which worked out its political position under John Kennedy and Lyndon Johnson, as the young radicals at Bratislava had.

This New Left sympathy for the NLF is not based on any similarity of style or of temperament. The Vietnamese revolutionaries we met were not the joyless communist *aparachiks* whom the Soviet Union would send to such a meeting, but they were dignified, restrained, disciplined and apparently selfless—about as unlike the loose-tongued, anarchistic, spontaneous Americans as any group could conceivably be. It was easy to respect their courage and patience under incredibly difficult conditions, and to find them personally charming, but it would not be very easy for a young American to establish an intimate personal friendship with or psychological understanding of such strangers. Nor do I think most of the Americans at Bratislava would find life in post-revolutionary Vietnam congenial; on the contrary, I suspect most would find themselves in opposition fairly soon. The common bond between the New Left and the NLF is not, then, a common dream or a common experience but a common enemy: the US government, the system, the Establishment. The young radicals' admiration for the NLF stems from the feeling that the NLF is resisting The Enemy successfully, whereas they are not.

Speaking for the older generation at Bratislava, David Dellinger said to the Vietnamese at one point, "You are Vietnamese and you love Vietnam. You must remember that we are Americans and we love America too, even though we oppose our government's policies with all our strength." The young man next to me groaned at this expression of patriotic sentiment, and as I looked around the room at other American faces I got the impression that he was not alone in his embarrassment. Certainly he was not alone in his feeling that almost anything non-American was likely to be better than almost anything American.

The historical failures of American radicalism are, I think, linked in important ways to this distaste for American culture and American institutions. One reason why the radical revival of the early 1960's captured the

American imagination and achieved modest successes was that it seemed so completely native, so true to the professed high purposes of the Republic. It appealed to the Constitution, to schoolbook stories of what America should be, to injustices which troubled millions of decent citizens.

But the New Left has never numbered patience among its virtues; it soured on America once it became clear that radical change, rather amorphously defined, would be neither quick nor easy. If America could not undo the evil consequences of racism in a few years, then America was hopeless. If America could not restrain its military, if it would not support revolutions in the underdeveloped countries, then America was a positive menace and the primary task of our time was to contain American power. Having begun a few years earlier with great residual faith in the American people, and a conviction that "the people" had strengths from which a new and better society might be built, many of the young radicals moved to the conclusion that Americans as a whole were hopelessly complacent, corrupt and self-centered. This view is not yet universal in the New Left, but it seems to be gaining ground. The result was a dramatic contrast at Bratislava between optimistic, confident Vietnamese and pessimistic, self-deprecating Americans. They sang "We Shall Overcome," but it was a nostalgic tribute to an earlier era, not an expression of confidence in the future.

The central weakness of the New Left, it seems to me, is its attitude toward authority. This came out clearly two years ago when this journal asked a number of young radicals to describe what they thought was wrong with America and what should be done about it. The essays were almost monotonous in their insistence that the people have no voice in decisions which affect their lives; that they are powerless.

That is true, but it is by no means a universal complaint. The toiling masses of Marxist memory still toil, but they do not seem to feel oppressed by the institutions within which they live. On the contrary, most defend these institutions staunchly. If, for example, you ask poor people what is wrong with America, they will usually complain about the *results* of decisions which affect their lives, not the *process* by which the decisions are made. They want good schools or good housing; relatively few of them want a voice in the operation of these facilities if the results are satisfactory. The New Left, however, cares more about how a decision gets made than about what the decision is. The Free Speech Movement at Berkeley exemplified this outlook. Very few Berkeley students had any real interest in whether the university allowed political advocacy on its property. But many came to resent the university's making such decisions arbitrarily without consulting anyone, and thousands enjoyed participating in the struggle to alter the rules.

An allergy to paternalism is not unique to the New Left, but young radicals of the kind who went to Bratislava have taken it more seriously than almost anyone in my generation and more seriously than most of their peers. It is this which has driven many into total opposition to the American way of life, which, they say, is largely shaped by big organizations and involves passive dependence on enormous numbers of remote experts, bureaucracies and commercial enterprises. Their opposition has led a growing minority to talk about the need for a revolution in America— though no one has any clear idea who would organize such a revolution, or whom it would bring to power, or how post-revolutionary America would be organized. It is this opposition, too, which has made the young radicals cynical about the anti-communism of their elders, forgetting that many liberal anti-communists were also anti-authoritarian. They are ready to support any sort of attack on the American establishment, even if it is launched by Vietnamese guerrillas with whom the New Left has only the most remote ideological or cultural kinship.

How widespread is this readiness to identify with "the enemy"? The militant, embittered sentiments described above are probably confined to one or two percent of the younger generation. But I think the basic attitudes which lead the activists to sympathy for the Viet Cong are quite general among the young, and that their impact is only beginning to be felt.

These are children of the 1940's, raised in relatively permissive middle-class homes where authority was supposed to be rational rather than arbitrary. Unlike earlier generations of Americans, their parents were reluctant to take advantage of their monopoly on physical, economic and legal power. Their youngsters were free to challenge the legitimacy of parental authority from an early age, by arguing that their parents were not using their power reasonably or wisely. Not only that, but such challenges often succeeded. Even when they failed, the children often curbed their parents' power indirectly by refusing to join in a consensus which defined certain rules as sensible and just. Without such a consensus many parents felt reluctant to impose their will, and in many cases found it impossible even when they tried.

The emphasis on consensus and rationality in these young people's upbringing was accompanied by reliance on new forms of discipline. The distinctive feature of a "permissive" home is not that "anything goes." It is that the limits are supposed to be set by the child's internalized sense of what is reasonable and unreasonable. In order to keep up this pretense, overt sanctions and punishments are frowned on. Instead, if the child behaves in what the parents regard as an unreasonable fashion, they retaliate by making the child feel he has hurt them, has let them down. Such a threat was doubtless terrifying to the very young. As they grew older, however, children discovered that they too could use such weapons. Children fear rejection, but so do parents, at least in modern America. A child who acted as if he hated his mother could frequently reduce her to tears. This leads to a system of mutual deterrence, which makes parents hesitate to use their ultimate power and produces an unprecedented equality in relations between the generations.

Such children emerged into the larger society with relatively little experience of authority structures based solely on superior force. Yet this is almost always the ultimate source of authority in large groups and organizations. Confronted with such authority these young people's first reaction was to resort to the tricks they had learned at home. First they tried reason. Racism, they argued, was a violation of the Constitution; the Saigon government was founded on a violation of the Geneva Agreements; and so forth. Such arguments had some success on the racial front, but virtually none on foreign policy. When this tactic failed the young radicals tried withholding love and approval from their elders. This was both the origin and the effect of the protest marches and of civil disobedience—a technique known to all children in all times. Like reason and legalism, emotional confrontations proved moderately effective as weapons against racism. The liberal leaders of the national establishment wanted the young to love and admire them. They did not want to play the tyrannical father and enforce order with a paddle. (Small-town Southern elites came from an older tradition, and felt no more embarrassed by using force against protesters than they did about spanking their children.) . . .

The failure of the techniques learned in permissive, middle-class homes has brought a crisis in America's radical movement. Ghetto Negroes have turned naturally to violence, for they have mostly been raised on it. Young middle-class whites, on the other hand, find violence almost impossible.

The radicals must, therefore, either abandon the struggle and retreat into cynicism and privatism or else compete with other adults for control over the apparatus of the state—which means, ultimately, control over the apparatus of violence and coercion. One way to do this might theoretically be violent revolution, but as a practical matter this seems infeasible, undesirable, and an escape from reality. America is not Vietnam. The only real alternative seems to be creating political organizations capable of taking power, first locally and eventually nationally.

Yet it is precisely here that the young radicals' distrust of all authority becomes an apparently insuperable problem. They are allergic to leadership, hierarchy and discipline. They want a movement of small insurgent "cells," organized around mutual trust, equality and respect for every man's individuality. These are appealing values. They are, indeed, my own. But I doubt that they can lead to the creation of political organizations capable of winning and wielding power.

If the children of permissive, middle-class parents are unwilling or unable to participate in established political institutions, or if their distaste and alienation from the whole pattern of American life makes it difficult for them to communicate with a relatively complacent and chauvinistic majority, who *will* exercise power in America? The most likely answer is that power will go by default to conservatives and reactionaries from more traditional backgrounds, who are less allergic to leadership, more willing to submit to the discipline of political organization, readier to make the compromises inherent in the assumption and exercise of power. . . .

QUESTIONS AND TOPICS

1. According to Jencks, what is the attitude of the New Left toward patriotism? Do you share this attitude?
2. Do you believe, along with the New Left, that most Americans are "hopelessly complacent, corrupt and self-centered"?
3. According to Jencks, the New Left strongly criticizes American society but offers no solutions. Do you feel that anyone espousing a political cause should offer a solution for the ills he attacks? Do you think that political action can alleviate our most pressing problems?
4. Do you agree with Jencks that "the basic attitudes which lead the activists

to sympathy for the Viet Cong are quite general among the young, and that their impact is only beginning to be felt"? To what degree are most young people disenchanted with the Establishment?

5. Do you believe that the type of permissive upbringing experienced by many young people weakens them in their confrontation with authority?

6. Can any group which is "allergic to leadership, hierarchy and discipline" create a meaningful political movement?

William H. Whyte, Jr.

A GENERATION
OF
BUREAUCRATS

This essay by William H. Whyte, Jr., 1917–, is taken from his book, The Organization Man, *published in 1956. Though some of his facts are dated, and today we hear mostly of radical dissent on campus, Whyte's organization men still exist.*

When I was a college senior in 1939, we used to sing a plaintive song about going out into the "cold, cold world." It wasn't really so very cold then, but we did enjoy meditating on the fraughtness of it all. It was a big break we were facing, we told ourselves, and those of us who were going to try our luck in the commercial world could be patronizing toward those who were going on to graduate work or to academic life. We were taking the leap.

Seniors still sing the song, but somehow the old note of portent is gone. There is no leap left to take. The union between the world of organization and the college has been so cemented that today's seniors can see a continuity between the college and the life thereafter that we never did. Come graduation, they do not go outside to a hostile world; they transfer.

For the senior who is headed for the corporation it is almost as if it were part of one master scheme. The locale shifts; the training continues, for at the same time that the colleges have been changing their curriculum to suit the corporation, the corporation has responded by setting up its own campuses and classrooms. By now the two have been so well molded that it's difficult to tell where one leaves off and the other begins.

The descent, every spring, of the corporations' recruiters has now become a built-in feature of campus life. If the college is large and its placement director efficient, the processing operation is visibly impressive.

I have never been able to erase from my mind the memory of an ordinary day at Purdue's placement center. It is probably the largest and most effective placement operation in the country, yet, much as in a well-run group clinic, there seemed hardly any activity. In the main room some students were quietly studying company literature arranged on the tables for them; others were checking the interview timetables to find what recruiter they would see and to which cubicle he was assigned; at the central filing desk college employees were sorting the hundreds of names of men who had registered for placement. Except for a murmur from the row of cubicles there was little to indicate that scores of young men were, every hour on the half hour, making the decisions that would determine their whole future life.

Someone from a less organized era might conclude that the standardization of this machinery—and the standardized future it portends—would repel students. It does not. For the median senior this is the optimum future; it meshes so closely with his own aspirations that it is almost as if the corporation was planned in response to an attitude poll.

Because they are the largest single group, the corporation-bound seniors are the most visible manifestation of their generation's values. But in essentials their contemporaries headed for other occupations respond to the same urges. The lawyers, the doctors, the scientists—their occupations are also subject to the same centralization, the same trend to group work and to bureaucratization. And so are the young men who will enter them. Whatever their many differences, in one great respect they are all of a piece: more than any generation in memory, theirs will be a generation of bureaucrats.

They are, above all, conservative. Their inclination to accept the status quo does not necessarily mean that in the historic sweep of ideas they are conservative—in the more classical sense of conservatism, it could be argued that the seniors will be, in effect if not by design, agents of revolution. But this is a matter we must leave to later historians. For the immediate present, at any rate, what ideological ferment college men exhibit is not in the direction of basic change.

This shows most clearly in their attitude toward politics. It used to be axiomatic that young men moved to the left end of the spectrum in revolt against their fathers and then, as the years went on, moved slowly to the right. A lot of people still believe this is true, and many businessmen fear that twenty years of the New Deal hopelessly corrupted our youth into radicalism. After the election of 1952 businessmen became somewhat more cheerful, but many are still apprehensive, and whenever a poll indicates that students don't realize that business makes only about 6 per cent profit, there is a flurry of demands for some new crusade to rescue our youth from socialistic tendencies.

If the seniors do any moving, however, it will be from dead center. Liberal groups have almost disappeared from the campus, and what few remain are anemic. There has been no noticeable activity at the other end of the spectrum either. When William Buckley, Jr., produced *God and Man at Yale*, some people thought this signaled the emergence of a strong right-wing movement among the young men. The militancy, however, has not proved particularly contagious; when the McCarthy issue roused and divided their elders, undergraduates seemed somewhat bored with it all.

Their conservatism is passive. No cause seizes them, and nothing so exuberant or willfully iconoclastic as the Veterans of Future Wars has reappeared. There are Democrats and Republicans, and at election time there is the usual flurry of rallies, but in comparison with the agitation of the thirties no one seems to care too much one way or the other. There has been personal unrest—the suspense over the prospect of military service assures this—but it rarely gets resolved into a thought-out protest. Come spring and students may start whacking each other over the head or roughing up the townees and thereby cause a rush of concern over the wild younger generation. But there is no real revolution in them, and the next day they likely as not will be found with their feet firmly on the ground in the recruiters' cubicles.

Some observers attribute the disinterest to fear. I heard one instructor tell his colleagues that in his politics classes he warned students to keep their noses clean. "I tell them," he said, "that they'd better realize that what they say might be held against them, especially when we get to the part about Marx and Engels. Someday in the future they might find their comments bounced back at them in an investigation."

The advice, as his colleagues retorted, was outrageously unnecessary. The last thing students can be accused of now is dangerous discussion; they are not interested in the kind of big questions that stimulate heresy and whatever the subject—the corporation, government, religion—students grow restive if the talk tarries on the philosophical. Most are interested in the philosophical only to the extent of finding out what the accepted view is in order that they may accept it and get on to the practical matters. This spares the bystander from the lofty bulling and the elaborate pose of unorthodoxy that my contemporaries often used to affect, but it does make for a rather stringent utilitarianism.

Even in theological seminaries, this impatience to be on with the job has been evident. Writes Norman Pittenger, professor at General Theological Seminary:

> It is a kind of authoritarianism in reverse. Theological students today, in contrast to their fellows of twenty years ago, want "to be told." I have gone out of my way to ask friends who teach in seminaries of other denominations whether they have recognized the new tendency. Without exception they have told me that they find the present generation of students less inquiring of mind, more ready to accept an authority, and indeed most anxious to have it "laid on the line."
>
> In the seminary this means that the lecturer or teacher must be unusually careful lest his opinion, or what "the Bible says" or "the church teaches," shall be taken as the last word. . . . What troubles many of us is that students today are not willing enough to think things through for themselves. If this is what the Bible says, then how does it say it and why, and how do we know that this is indeed the teaching of Scripture? If this is what the church teaches, why does it teach it, what evidence can be given for the teaching and what right has the church to teach at all? Or if a professor says that such-and-such a view is correct, why does he say it and what real evidence can he produce that his statement is true? It would be better and healthier if the new respect for authority were more frequently found in combination with a spirit of inquiry, a ready willingness to think through what is authoritatively declared, and a refusal ever to accept anything simply because some reputable expert makes the statement.

In judging a college generation, one usually bases his judgment on how much it varies from one's own, and presumably superior, class, and I must confess that I find myself tempted to do so. Yet I do not think my generation has any license to damn the acquiescence of seniors as a weakening of intellectual fiber. It is easy for us to forget that if earlier generations were less content with society, there was a great deal less to be contented about. In the intervening years the economy has changed enormously, and even in retrospect the senior can hardly be expected to share former discontents. Society is not out of joint for him, and if he acquiesces it is not out of fear that he does so. He does not want to rebel against the status quo because he really likes it—and his elders, it might be added, are not suggesting anything bold and new to rebel *for*.

Perhaps contemporaryism would be a better word than conservatism to describe their posture. The present, more than the past, is their model; while they share the characteristic American faith in the future also, they see it as more of same. As they paraphrase what they are now reading about America, they argue that at last we have got it. The big questions are all settled; we know the direction, and while many minor details remain to be cleared up, we can be pretty sure of enjoying a wonderful upward rise.

While the degree of their optimism is peculiarly American, the spirit of acquiescence, it should be noted, is by no means confined to the youth of this country. In an Oxford magazine, called, aptly enough, *Couth,* one student writes this of his generation:

> It is true that over the last thirty years it has been elementary good manners to be depressed. . . . But . . . we are not, really, in the least worried by our impending, and other people's present, disasters. This is not the Age of Anxiety. What distinguishes the comfortable young men of today from the uncomfortable young men of the last hundred years . . . is that for once the younger generation is not in revolt against anything. . . . We don't want to rebel against our elders. They are much too nice to be rebella-ble-against. Old revolutionaries as they are, they get rather cross with us and tell us we are stuffy and prudish, but even this can't provoke us into hostility. . . . Our fathers . . . brought us up to see them not as the representatives of ancient authority and unalterable law but as rebels against our grand-fathers. So naturally we have grown up to be on their side, even if we feel on occasion that they were a wee bit hard on their fathers, or even a little naïve.*

More than before, there is a tremendous interest in techniques. Having no quarrel with society, they prefer to table the subject of ends and concentrate instead on means. Not what or why but *how* interests them, and any evangelical strain they have they can sublimate; once they have equated the common weal with organization—a task the curriculum makes easy—they will let the organization worry about goals. "These men do not question the system," an economics professor says of them, approvingly. "They want to get in there and lubricate and make them run better. They will be technicians of the society, not innovators."

* Similar tendencies have been noticed among German youth. In *Der Junge Arbeiter von Heute,* Karl Bednarik, a former leader in the socialist youth move-ment, has commented on the "bourgeoisification" of younger workers as a response to the postwar situation.

The attitude of men majoring in social science is particularly revealing on this score. Not so very long ago, the younger social scientist was apt to see his discipline as a vehicle for protest about society as well as the study of it. The seniors that set the fashion for him were frequently angry men, and many of the big studies of the twenties and thirties—Robert and Helen Lynd's *Middletown,* for example—did not conceal strong opinions about the inequities in the social structure. But this is now old hat: it is the "bleeding-heart" school to the younger men (and to some not so young, too), for they do not wish to protest; they wish to collaborate. Reflecting the growing reconciliation with middle-class values that has affected all types of intellectuals, they are turning more and more to an interest in methodology, particularly the techniques of measurement. Older social scientists who have done studies on broad social problems find that the younger men are comparatively uninterested in the problems themselves. When the discussion period comes, the questions the younger men ask are on the technical points; not the what, or why, but the how.

The urge to be a technician, a collaborator, shows most markedly in the kind of jobs seniors prefer. They want to work for somebody else. Paradoxically, the old dream of independence through a business of one's own is held almost exclusively by factory workers—the one group, as a number of sociologists have reported, least able to fulfill it. Even at the bull-session level college seniors do not affect it, and when recruiting time comes around they make the preference clear. Consistently, placement officers find that of the men who intend to go into business—roughly one half of the class—less than 5 per cent express any desire to be an entrepreneur. About 15 to 20 per cent plan to go into their fathers' business. Of the rest, most have one simple goal: the big corporation.

And not just as a stopgap either. When I was a senior many of us liked to rationalize that we were simply playing it smart; we were going with big companies merely to learn the ropes the better to strike out on our own later. Today, seniors do not bother with this sort of talk; once the tie has been established with the big company, they believe, they will not switch to a small one, or, for that matter, to another big one. The relationship is to be for keeps.*

* One reason why seniors prefer big business is that the big companies go after them and the small ones don't. Of the 450,000 incorporated firms in the U.S.,

It is not simply for security that they take the vows. Far more than their predecessors they understand bigness. My contemporaries, fearful of anonymity, used to talk of "being lost" in a big corporation. This did not prevent us from joining corporations, to be sure, but verbally, at least, it was fashionable to view the organization way with misgivings. Today this would show a want of sophistication. With many of the liberals who fifteen years ago helped stimulate the undergraduate distrust of bigness now busy writing tracts in praise of bigness, the ideological underpinnings for the debate have crumbled.

The fact that a majority of seniors headed for business shy from the idea of being entrepreneurs is only in part due to fear of economic risk. Seniors can put the choice in moral terms also, and the portrait of the entrepreneur as a young man detailed in postwar fiction preaches a sermon that seniors are predisposed to accept. What price bitch goddess Success? The entrepreneur, as many see him, is a selfish type motivated by greed, and he is, furthermore, unhappy. The big-time operator as sketched in fiction eventually so loses stomach for enterprise that he finds happiness only when he stops being an entrepreneur, forsakes "21," El Morocco, and the boss's wife and heads for the country. Citing such fiction, the student can moralize on his aversion to entrepreneurship. His heel quotient, he explains, is simply not big enough.

Not that he is afraid of risk, the senior can argue. Far from being afraid of taking chances, he is simply looking for the *best* place to take them in.* Small business is small because of nepotism and the roll-top desk outlook, the argument goes; big business, by contrast, has borrowed the tools of science and made them pay off. It has its great laboratories,

---

only about 1,000 actually recruit on the campuses, and it is these active 1,000 firms—generally the biggest—that get the cream. Sometimes college placement directors do line up the small company position, but even then they find the students apathetic. "Frankly," says one placement director, echoing many another, "the only kind I can interest in the small company job is the dynamic sort— the one type that is least likely to get lost in a big company. I would sooner interest the other kind; I point out to the shy, diffident fellows that in a small outfit they'd be something of a jack-of-all-trades, that they'd get a better chance to express themselves, to grow out of their shell. They still don't want it."

* A Youth Institute Survey of 4,660 young men indicated that only 20 per cent felt that they could not achieve all their economic desires by working for someone else.

its market-research departments, and the time and patience to use them. The odds, then, favor the man who joins big business. "We wouldn't hesitate to risk adopting new industrial techniques and products," explains a proponent of this calculated-risk theory, "but we would do it only after we had subjected it to tests of engineers, pre-testing in the market and that kind of thing." With big business, in short, risk-taking would be a cinch.

In turning their back on the Protestant Ethic they are consistent; if they do not cherish venture, neither do they cherish what in our lore was its historic reward. They are without avarice. Reflecting on the difference between the postwar classes and his own class of 1928, an erstwhile Yale history professor confessed that the former were so unmercenary he was almost a little homesick for his own. "We were a terrible class. It was the days of the roasted lark, Hell's entries, of the white-shoe boys. Everyone was playing the stock market—they even had a ticker down at the Hotel Taft—and I wound up for a while in a bucket shop down in Wall Street. But today you don't hear that kind of talk. They don't want a million. They are much more serious, much more worth while." He shook his head nostalgically.

Others have been similarly impressed. One recruiter went through three hundred interviews without one senior's mentioning salary, and the experience is not unusual. Indeed, sometimes seniors react as if a large income and security were antithetical. As some small companies have found to their amazement, the offer of a sales job netting $15,000 at the end of two years is often turned down in favor of an equivalent one with a large company netting $8,000. Along with the $8,000 job, the senior says in justification, goes a pension plan and other benefits. He could, of course, buy himself some rather handsome annuities with the extra $7,000 the small company offers, but this alternative does not suggest itself readily.

When seniors are put to speculating how much money they would like to make twenty or thirty years hence, they cite what they feel are modest figures. Back in forty-nine it was $10,000. Since then the rising cost of living has taken it up higher, but the median doesn't usually surpass $15,000.* For the most part seniors do not like to talk of the future in

---

* The figures depend a great deal on the college. In the study done by the Youth Research Institute on a cross section of college seniors, the median figure is about $8,000. At Princeton and Williams, by contrast, the figure is about double. [Note that Mr. Whyte's book was published in 1956. All figures would now be markedly higher. Ed.]

terms of the dollar—on several occasions I have been politely lectured by someone for so much as bringing the point up.

In popular fiction, as I will take up later, heroes aren't any less materialistic than they used to be, but they are decidedly more sanctimonious about it. So with seniors. While they talk little about money, they talk a great deal about the good life. This life is, first of all, calm and ordered. Many a senior confesses that he's thought of a career in teaching, but as he talks it appears that it is not so much that he likes teaching itself as the sort of life he associates with it—there is a touch of elms and quiet streets in the picture. For the good life is equable; it is a nice place out in the suburbs, a wife and three children, one, maybe two cars (you know, a little knock-about for the wife to run down to the station in), and a summer place up at the lake or out on the Cape, and, later, a good college education for the children. It is not, seniors explain, the money that counts.

QUESTIONS AND TOPICS

1. Which of Whyte's facts are now out of date?
2. Does present campus unrest represent a real change from the college atmosphere Whyte describes or simply a surface phenomenon exaggerated by the mass media?
3. Do business students still prefer the large corporation to the small corporation? Why?
4. Do seniors still think of the entrepreneur as a man who pursues the "bitch goddess Success"? Do they still believe that most risk-taking businessmen are "motivated by greed, and . . . [are] furthermore, unhappy"?
5. Do current negative attitudes toward business imply a revolution of sorts among students? Do businessmen have real reason to worry?
6. Do you still notice student reluctance to talk about controversial social and philosophical issues?

Sherwood Anderson

SOPHISTICATION

In Winesburg, Ohio, *1919, Sherwood Anderson, 1876–1941, portrays a typical American town of the early twentieth century. The following short story from that work deals with the problem of maturation.*

It was early evening of a day in the late fall and the Winesburg County Fair had brought crowds of country people into town. The day had been clear and the night came on warm and pleasant. On the Trunion Pike, where the road after it left town stretched away between berry fields now covered with dry brown leaves, the dust from passing wagons arose in clouds. Children, curled into little balls, slept on the straw scattered on wagon beds. Their hair was full of dust and their fingers black and sticky. The dust rolled away over the fields and the departing sun set it ablaze with colors.

In the main street of Winesburg crowds filled the stores and the sidewalks. Night came on, horses whinnied, the clerks in the stores ran madly about, children became lost and cried lustily, an American town worked terribly at the task of amusing itself.

Pushing his way through the crowds in Main Street, young George Willard concealed himself in the stairway leading to Doctor Reefy's office and looked at the people. With feverish eyes he watched the faces drifting past under the store lights. Thoughts kept coming into his head and he did not want to think. He stamped impatiently on the wooden steps and looked sharply about. "Well, is she going to stay with him all day? Have I done all this waiting for nothing?" he muttered.

George Willard, the Ohio village boy, was fast growing into manhood and new thoughts had been coming into his mind. All that day, amid the jam of people at the Fair, he had gone about feeling lonely. He was about to leave Winesburg to go away to some city where he hoped to get work on a city newspaper and he felt grown up. The mood that had taken possession of him was a thing known to men and unknown to boys. He felt old and a little tired. Memories awoke in him. To his mind his new sense of maturity set him apart, made of him a half-tragic figure. He wanted someone to understand the feeling that had taken possession of him after his mother's death.

There is a time in the life of every boy when he for the first time takes the backward view of life. Perhaps that is the moment when he crosses the line into manhood. The boy is walking through the street of his town. He is thinking of the future and of the figure he will cut in the world. Ambitions and regrets awake within him. Suddenly something happens; he stops under a tree and waits as for a voice calling his name. Ghosts of old things creep into his consciousness; the voices outside of himself whisper a message concerning the limitations of life. From being quite sure of himself and his future he becomes not at all sure. If he be an imaginative boy a door is torn open and for the first time he looks out upon the world, seeing, as though they marched in procession before him, the countless figures of men who before his time have come out of nothingness into the world, lived their lives and again disappeared into nothingness. The sadness of sophistication has come to the boy. With a little gasp he sees himself as merely a leaf blown by the wind through the streets of his village. He knows that in spite of all the stout talk of his fellows he must live and die in uncertainty, a thing blown by the winds, a thing destined like corn to wilt in the sun. He shivers and looks eagerly about. The eighteen years he has lived seem but a moment, a breathing space in the long march of humanity. Already he hears death calling. With all his heart he wants to come close to some other human, touch someone with his hands, be touched by the hand of another. If he prefers that the other be a woman, that is because he believes that a woman will be gentle, that she will understand. He wants, most of all, understanding.

When the moment of sophistication came to George Willard his mind turned to Helen White, the Winesburg banker's daughter. Always he had been conscious of the girl growing into womanhood as he grew into manhood. Once on a summer night when he was eighteen, he had walked with her on a country road and in her presence had given way to an impulse to boast, to make himself appear big and significant in her eyes. Now he wanted to see her for another purpose. He wanted to tell her of the new impulses that had come to him. He had tried to make her think of him as a man when he knew nothing of manhood and now he wanted to be with her and to try to make her feel the change he believed had taken place in his nature.

As for Helen White, she also had come to a period of change. What George felt, she in her young woman's way felt also. She was no longer a girl and hungered to reach into the grace and beauty of womanhood. She had come home from Cleveland, where she was attending college, to spend a day at the Fair. She also had begun to have memories. During the day she sat in the grandstand with a young man, one of the instructors from the college, who was a guest of her mother's. The young man was of a pedantic turn of mind and she felt at once he would not do for her purpose. At the Fair she was glad to be seen in his company as he was well dressed and a stranger. She knew that the fact of his presence would create an impression. During the day she was happy, but when night came on she began to grow restless. She wanted to drive the instructor away, to get out of his presence. While they sat together in the grand-stand and while the eyes of former schoolmates were upon them, she paid so much attention to her escort that he grew interested. "A scholar needs money. I should marry a woman with money," he mused.

Helen White was thinking of George Willard even as he wandered gloomily through the crowds thinking of her. She remembered the summer evening when they had walked together and wanted to walk with him again. She thought that the months she had spent in the city, the going to theatres and the seeing of great crowds wandering in lighted thoroughfares, had changed her profoundly. She wanted him to feel and be conscious of the change in her nature.

The summer evening together that had left its mark on the memory of both the young man and woman had, when looked at quite sensibly, been rather stupidly spent. They had walked out of town along a country road. Then they had stopped by a fence near a field of young corn and George had taken off his coat and let it hang on his arm. "Well, I've stayed here in Winesburg—yes—I've not yet gone away but I'm growing up," he had said. "I've been reading books and I've been thinking. I'm going to try to amount to something in life.

"Well," he explained, "that isn't the point. Perhaps I'd better quit talking."

The confused boy put his hand on the girl's arm. His voice trembled. The two started to walk back along the road toward town. In his desperation George boasted, "I'm going to be a big man, the biggest that ever lived here in Winesburg," he declared. "I want you to do something, I don't know what. Perhaps it is none of my business. I want you to try to be different from other women. You see the point. It's none of my business I tell you. I want you to be a beautiful woman. You see what I want."

The boy's voice failed and in silence the two came back into town and went along the street to Helen White's house. At the gate he tried to say something impressive. Speeches he had thought out came into his head, but they seemed utterly pointless. "I thought—I used to think—I had it in my mind you would marry Seth Richmond. Now I know you won't," was all he could find to say as she went through the gate and toward the door of her house.

On the warm fall evening as he stood in the stairway and looked at the crowd drifting through Main Street, George thought of the talk beside the field of young corn and was ashamed of the figure he had made of himself. In the street the people surged up and down like cattle confined in a pen. Buggies and wagons almost filled the narrow thoroughfare. A band played and small boys raced along the sidewalk, diving between the legs of men. Young men with shining red faces walked awkwardly about with girls on their arms. In a room above one of the stores, where a dance was to be held, the fiddlers tuned their instruments. The broken sounds floated down through an open window and out across the murmur of voices and the loud blare of the horns of the band. The medley of sounds got on young Willard's nerves. Everywhere, on all sides, the sense of crowding, moving life closed in about him. He wanted to run away by himself and think. "If she wants to stay with that fellow she may. Why should I care? What difference does it make to me?" he growled and went along Main Street and through Hern's grocery into a side street.

George felt so utterly lonely and dejected that he wanted to weep but pride made him walk rapidly along, swinging his arms. He came to Westley Moyer's livery barn and stopped in the shadows to listen to a group of men who talked of a race Westley's stallion, Tony Tip, had won at the Fair during the afternoon. A crowd had gathered in front of the barn and before the crowd walked Westley, prancing up and down and boasting. He held a whip in his hand and kept tapping the ground. Little puffs of dust arose in the lamplight. "Hell, quit your talking,"

Westley exclaimed. "I wasn't afraid, I knew I had 'em beat all the time. I wasn't afraid."

Ordinarily George Willard would have been intensely interested in the boasting of Moyer, the horseman. Now it made him angry. He turned and hurried away along the street. "Old windbag," he sputtered. "Why does he want to be bragging? Why don't he shut up?"

George went into a vacant lot and as he hurried along, fell over a pile of rubbish. A nail protruding from an empty barrel tore his trousers. He sat down on the ground and swore. With a pin he mended the torn place and then arose and went on. "I'll go to Helen White's house, that's what I'll do. I'll walk right in. I'll say that I want to see her. I'll walk right in and sit down, that's what I'll do," he declared, climbing over a fence and beginning to run.

• • •

On the veranda of Banker White's house Helen was restless and distraught. The instructor sat between the mother and daughter. His talk wearied the girl. Although he had also been raised in an Ohio town, the instructor began to put on the airs of the city. He wanted to appear cosmopolitan. "I like the chance you have given me to study the background out of which most of our girls come," he declared. "It was good of you, Mrs. White, to have me down for the day." He turned to Helen and laughed. "Your life is still bound up with the life of this town?" he asked. "There are people here in whom you are interested?" To the girl his voice sounded pompous and heavy.

Helen arose and went into the house. At the door leading to a garden at the back she stopped and stood listening. Her mother began to talk. "There is no one here fit to associate with a girl of Helen's breeding," she said.

Helen ran down a flight of stairs at the back of the house and into the garden. In the darkness she stopped and stood trembling. It seemed to her that the world was full of meaningless people saying words. Afire with eagerness she ran through a garden gate and turning a corner by the banker's barn, went into a little side street. "George! Where are you, George?" she cried, filled with nervous excitement. She stopped running, and leaned against a tree to laugh hysterically. Along the dark little street came George Willard, still saying words. "I'm going to walk right into her house. I'll go right in and sit down," he declared as he came up to her.

He stopped and stared stupidly. "Come on," he said and took hold of her hand. With hanging heads they walked away along the street under the trees. Dry leaves rustled under foot. Now that he had found her George wondered what he had better do and say.

• • •

At the upper end of the fair ground, in Winesburg, there is a half decayed old grand-stand. It has never been painted and the boards are all warped out of shape. The fair ground stands on top of a low hill rising out of the valley of Wine Creek and from the grand-stand one can see at night, over a cornfield, the lights of the town reflected against the sky.

George and Helen climbed the hill to the fair ground, coming by the path past Waterworks Pond. The feeling of loneliness and isolation that had come to the young man in the crowded streets of his town was both broken and intensified by the presence of Helen. What he felt was reflected in her.

In youth there are always two forces fighting in people. The warm unthinking little animal struggles against the thing that reflects and remembers, and the older, the more sophisticated thing had possession of George Willard. Sensing his mood, Helen walked beside him filled with respect. When they got to the grand-stand they climbed up under the roof and sat down on one of the long bench-like seats.

There is something memorable in the experience to be had by going into a fair ground that stands at the edge of a Middle Western town on a night after the annual fair has been held. The sensation is one never to be forgotten. On all sides are ghosts, not of the dead, but of living people. Here, during the day just passed, have come the people pouring in from the town and the country around. Farmers with their wives and children and all the people from the hundreds of little frame houses have gathered within these board walls. Young girls have laughed and men with beards have talked of the affairs of their lives. The place has been filled to overflowing with life. It has itched and squirmed with life and now it is night and the life has all gone away. The silence is almost terrifying. One conceals oneself standing silently beside the trunk of a tree and what there is of a reflective tendency in his nature is intensified. One shudders at the thought of the meaninglessness of life while at the same instant, and if the people of the town are his people, one loves life so intensely that tears come into the eyes.

In the darkness under the roof of the grand-stand, George Willard sat beside Helen White and felt very keenly his own insignificance in the scheme of existence. Now that he had come out of town where the presence of the people stirring about, busy with a multitude of affairs, had been so irritating the irritation was all gone. The presence of Helen renewed and refreshed him. It was as though her woman's hand was assisting him to make some minute readjustment of the machinery of his life. He began to think of the people in the town where he had always lived with something like reverence. He had reverence for Helen. He wanted to love and to be loved by her, but he did not want at the moment to be confused by her womanhood. In the darkness he took hold of her hand and when she crept close put a hand on her shoulder. A wind began to blow and he shivered. With all his strength he tried to hold and to understand the mood that had come upon him. In that high place in the darkness the two oddly sensitive human atoms held each other tightly and waited. In the mind of each was the same thought. "I have come to this lonely place and here is this other," was the substance of the thing felt.

In Winesburg the crowded day had run itself out into the long night of the late fall. Farm horses jogged away along lonely country roads pulling their portion of weary people. Clerks began to bring samples of goods in off the sidewalks and lock the doors of stores. In the Opera House a crowd had gathered to see a show and further down Main Street the fiddlers, their instruments tuned, sweated and worked to keep the feet of youth flying over a dance floor.

In the darkness in the grand-stand Helen White and George Willard remained silent. Now and then the spell that held them was broken and they turned and tried in the dim light to see into each others eyes. They kissed but that impulse did not last. At the upper end of the fair ground a half dozen men worked over horses that had raced during the afternoon. The men had built a fire and were heating kettles of water. Only their legs could be seen as they passed back and forth in the light. When the wind blew the little flames of the fire danced crazily about.

George and Helen arose and walked away into the darkness. They went along a path past a field of corn that had not yet been cut. The wind whispered among the dry corn blades. For a moment during the walk back into town the spell that held them was broken. When they had come to the crest of Waterworks Hill they stopped by a tree and George again put his hands on the girl's shoulders. She embraced him eagerly and then again they drew quickly back from that impulse. They stopped kissing and stood a little apart. Mutual respect grew big in them. They were both embarrassed and to relieve their embarrassment dropped into the animalism of youth. They laughed and began to pull and haul at each other. In some way chastened and purified by the mood they had been in they became, not man and woman, not boy and girl, but excited little animals.

It was so they went down the hill. In the darkness they played like two splendid young things in a young world. Once, running swiftly forward, Helen tripped George and he fell. He squirmed and shouted. Shaking with laughter, he rolled down the hill. Helen ran after him. For just a moment she stopped in the darkness. There is no way of knowing what woman's thoughts went through her mind but, when the bottom of the hill was reached and she came up to the boy, she took his arm and walked beside him in dignified silence. For some reason they could not have explained they had both got from their silent evening together the thing needed. Man or boy, woman or girl, they had for a moment taken hold of the thing that makes the mature life of men and women in the modern world possible.

QUESTIONS AND TOPICS

1. Why does George feel that he has achieved sophistication? Are your own concepts of sophistication and maturity different?
2. Is the theme of the story too vague and undefined? Must one use vague, almost mystical terms to describe George Willard's state of mind?
3. Write a theme on a similar experience in your own life.
4. Do you feel that Anderson romanticizes George Willard?

Lawrence Ferlinghetti

TWO POEMS

*The poetry of Lawrence Ferlin-
ghetti, 1920–, appeals to many
young people, partly because of his
use of jazz rhythms, and partly because of his refusal to take anything
too seriously. Actually he has serious messages to convey but lightens
them with a sense of humor.*

Just as I used to say
    love comes harder to the aged
because they've been running
     on the same old rails too long
  and then when the sly switch comes along
       they miss the turn
   and burn up the wrong rail while
      the gay caboose goes flying
  and the steamengine driver don't recognize
      them new electric horns
and the aged run out on the rusty spur
      which ends up in
    the dead grass where
the rusty tincans and bedsprings and old razor
    blades and moldy mattresses
       lie
  and the rail breaks off dead
      right there
   though the ties go on awhile
      and the aged
say to themselves
   Well
    this must be the place
we were supposed to lie down

And they do

           while the bright saloon careens along away
on a high
      hilltop
          its windows full of bluesky and lovers
    with flowers
            their long hair streaming
                  and all of them laughing
       and waving and
              whispering to each other
  and looking out and
            wondering what that graveyard
    where the rails end
          is

QUESTIONS AND TOPICS

1. Why does Ferlinghetti use the basic metaphor of the poem?
2. The young seem unaware of the fate of the aged. Is this true of the young people you know? Should they be aware?
3. What seems to be society's attitude toward the aged?
4. Write a theme about the treatment of the old in your family or in that of a friend.

The pennycandystore beyond the El
is where I first
      fell in love
          with unreality
Jellybeans glowed in the semi-gloom
of that september afternoon
A cat upon the counter moved among
           the licorice sticks
   and tootsie rolls
  and Oh Boy Gum

Outside the leaves were falling as they died

A wind had blown away the sun

A girl ran in
Her hair was rainy
Her breasts were breathless in the little room

Outside the leaves were falling
                and they cried
                        Too soon! too soon!

QUESTIONS AND TOPICS

1. What is the significance of the girl's appearance in the candystore? Why does Ferlinghetti use the leaf image?
2. Do you think Ferlinghetti sentimentalizes childhood?
3. Do you feel a sense of loss toward your childhood? Write a theme on the topic.

6

THE QUESTION OF SEXUAL MORALITY

THE QUESTION OF SEXUAL MORALITY poses especially difficult problems for young people. Their normal problems of sexual awareness and adjustment are aggravated today by changing social values and mores. In fact, the term *sexual revolution* has become commonplace among journalists and television commentators. Of course, students will react differently to the subject, depending on their backgrounds, experiences, and locations. For some, a sexual revolution might scarcely be a reality.

Student papers on sex are usually complicated by careless use of the terms *morality* and *immorality*. To adequately define either word in an era of shifting values might very well be beyond the possibility of a freshman theme. One must avoid the assumption that man has always known what is moral and immoral. The student who thinks that way substitutes second-hand standards for real ones. Yet it is equally unreasonable to think that no such thing as morality exists in the sphere of sexual relations, or that no one can ever determine right and wrong in regard to his behavior towards other people.

The student should also try to understand the feelings and problems of the opposite sex. Such understanding is usually made difficult by the unthinking acceptance of the "double standard," which provides different sexual codes for men and women. Though this standard has existed for ages and is sometimes defended by writers as different as Dr. Clendening and George Bernard Shaw, it has lately come under a great deal of attack. The advent of more effective birth control, for instance, has permitted some men and women, not restricted by religious scruples, to believe that both parties come to the sex act with equal freedom.

In fact, some students, inspired by the growing freedom of mass entertainment, believe that modern trends toward greater sexual freedom cannot be reversed. Yet history points out many instances in which sexually liberal societies were replaced by those which were more conservative. The argument one finds in some student papers, that all young people ought to embrace the sexual revolution because its triumph is inevitable, is based on inexact historical reasoning.

Another suspicious argument assumes that freedom is good in all circumstances. Almost all societies, Ruth Benedict tells us in *Patterns of Culture,* have seen fit to regulate sex in some way. Perhaps a new society can be created in which regulation is not necessary. We know, however, that certain freedoms deprive others of freedom, that when certain liberties become widespread, an entire society may be upset. One can argue for perfect freedom only if he can demonstrate that the present society or one in the near future will be able to absorb the consquences of that freedom.

Logan Clendening

from
THE
HUMAN BODY

Logan Clendening, 1884–1945, a well-known physician for many years, wrote the following speculations in The Human Body, *1927, a popular book on medical matters. Dr. Clendening explains relations between the sexes in terms of mammalian biology.*

To reproduce a new and distinct human body requires the co-operation of two other matured human bodies, differing slightly in structure from one another and known technically among biologists as male and female.

On the whole it seems rather a clumsy arrangement. It is difficult to discover any unusual perspicacity on the part of deity in such a scheme. It does not, moreover, appear to be an inescapable rule of biology. A unicellular organism regularly reproduces another individual by the simple expedient of dividing into two. Even much higher up in the structural tree such animals as the sea-worm, *Planaria maculata,* are able to reproduce or at least regenerate after being divided either horizontally or vertically, each half regenerating a head, a tail, or another eye as the occasion demands.

Among vertebrates, of course, such things do not happen at all. Among vertebrates the absence of the necessity for male parents is found only in research laboratories and the Gospel according to St. Luke. Jacques Loeb was able to fertilize with chemical salts the eggs of a female frog, so that adult living frogs resulted. The explanation of this, as advanced by competent biologists, is that to fertilization there are two elements. When the sperm, as the male element of reproduction is called, enters the female element, the ovum, it brings first its contribution of nuclear chromosomes and secondly a chemical change somewhat as if it were a catalyst. Previous to fertilization the egg membrane is very impervious to any salts in the medium surrounding it. The entrance of the sperm seems to allow certain salts to enter the egg cytoplasm. It is these salts, rather than the union of the chromosomes of sperm and ovum, that initiate the rapid growth and multiplication of the germinating cells. By changing the chemical content of the solution in which the frog and sea-urchin eggs were kept, Loeb could instigate a development unquestionably, but one never imitated in nature.

Nature seems certain, however, that the plan of having two parents is a success. And we must try to explain or understand the advantages which her experience has taught her. One reason suggests itself immediately. In a wild state the danger to any animal's life is constant and imminent. If the destinies of the unborn individual were invested in one animal and that animal killed, the next generation, so far as that unit was concerned, would be completely wiped out. As it is, the male can guard the female, bear the brunt of any attack, even be destroyed, without affecting the unborn at all.

The great advantage of bisexual parentage, however, lies in the enormous possibility of variation. A single individual reproducing passes over to its offspring only its own somatic characteristics. A terrific monotony would result. But with bisexual parentage the male element, the sperm, as well as the female element, the ovum, bears all the possibilities of all its ancestors in its chromosomes. These divergent strains joining are bound to result in fresh and new combinations which furnish a constant set of variations, upon which natural selection can fasten.

Mammals, to which class the order of primates, including the species man, belongs, are distinguished by the facts that during the early stages of development the offspring is harboured inside the body of the female in an organ called the womb or uterus, and that after it is extruded from the mother's body, the mother nourishes it by elaborating a nutritious fluid, milk, in certain glands, the breasts or mammæ. This general plan has been much praised and is supposed to represent a great improvement over other methods of reproduction in the animal kingdom and a particular solicitation towards man and especially woman on the part of that force external to ourselves which makes for righteousness. I am not sure that such praise is entirely deserved. The most sensible arrangement, I submit, is that developed in another branch of the tree of evolution—the birds, reptiles, and fishes. If I were picking out the animal mothers which seem to have had the advantage of the greatest amount of foresight on the part of that force external to ourselves which makes for righteousness, I should most unquestionably give my vote to an egg-laying order. The hen, it seems to me, has it all over the woman in this respect.

The hen is able to extrude the fertilized egg from her body with no more discomfort than arises from the writing of a sonnet.* From prevalent complaints on the subject which reach me from time to time I deduce that this is a distinct advantage over the human manœuvre. Nor is this virtuosity of the hen's attended with any decompensating lack of efficiency in the product. Her egg after extrusion is endowed with the ability to develop and produce an individual quite as complex as any human prototype: its liver when put under the microscope has cells and structure as intricate and praiseworthy as the liver of the infant daughter of a congressman. Its eye can hardly be distinguished from a human eye; it has retina, iris, rods and cones, sclera—all the same, all equally perfect. It is true that there are more creases in the brain of the human infant than in the brain of the chick, but in rebuttal it can be advanced that there are more feathers on the chick, and whether one is more important than the other is distinctly debatable. Plainly, however, argument is useless: the human female is a mammal and not a bird, and there is no way to change her methods of reproduction. But equally plainly, however superior we may feel about other instances of omnipotent grace so far as our structure and function are concerned, there is no use in assuming an air of false pride and preeminence over the hen in the special matter of our divergent modes of reproduction.

Platitudinous as these statements may seem and indeed are, they nevertheless are, and always have been, fraught with a deep significance to the human race, particularly on the basis of such social problems as are usually encompassed by the term "the Woman Question." The position of woman, the equality or inequality of the sexes, woman's place in the sun, the

* I wrote this ten years ago purely on the basis of personal observation. All the hens I ever saw lay an egg did so with the same painless ease that I have indicated. But nothing in this world seems to be perfected and I was informed soon after this sentence was first seen in print that hens frequently have to be assisted, at least in the delivery of their first egg, by the farmer's wife, who greases her finger and inserts it in the cloaca, divulsing it. Hens have even been known to die without this aid. However, the experience is comparatively rare and confined to the first delivery, so for all practical purposes my comparison stands.

double standard of morals, about all of which young dramatists and sociologists have perspired for so many æons, are at bottom biological problems, and not social or moral or economic problems at all. At times this is faintly recognized and even mildly mentioned; in most discussions of the subject, however, the biology and psychology of sex are treated as if they did not exist. But from the time when the morning stars sang together and until the period when the last representatives of animal life on the chilly remains of this planet are crawling along the shores of the still faintly warm rivulets at the equator, males will look at the phenomena of existence from one view-point and females from another. And that is one of the things I always tell my young candidates for ordination when they are sent to me for advice.

Instances are on every hand, but I will choose one of a totally impersonal nature from a volume of fiction—*The Painted Veil*, by W. Somerset Maugham. For purposes of experiment I have set a large number of women, fairly representative as to intelligence, to the perusal of a highly significant passage in this not otherwise notable book. I have directed their particular attention to a scene in which a woman has a very important conversation with a man.

The opening chapter of the novel depicts a bedchamber in the home of a British Government bacteriologist stationed in China. The time is early afternoon. His wife is entertaining her clandestine lover, who happens to be lieutenant-governor of the province. Their seance is interrupted by hearing someone trying to turn the knob of the door to the room. It is noted that the lieutenant-governor hastily attempts to put on his shoes. The intruder, however, goes away and the lovers convince themselves that it was merely a servant.

The next day the woman's husband discloses the fact that he himself was the intruder and that he thus assured himself of positive knowledge of the intrigue. The woman admits it frankly and says that if she is divorced, her lover will divorce his own wife and marry her. At this the husband is highly amused. His amusement provokes her to the most positive reiteration of faith in her lover. Whereupon the husband announces that he has been ordered to an inland city where cholera is raging; if he takes her with him, it means very probable death for both. If he goes alone, it means very probable death for him. He generously proposes that if her lover will make a statement in writing to the effect that when she becomes a widow, the lover will divorce his own wife and marry her, the husband will go to the cholera-infested city alone. If the lover refuses, she must either go with her husband into the danger zone or submit to divorce under conditions amounting to disgrace. Certain of the loyalty of her lover, she goes to interview him. It is this interview to which I have directed the attention of my female friends.

The lover, of course, upon hearing the terms of the proposal, is thoroughly upset, fumbles round in a very inglorious manner, and finally flatly refuses. The woman sits before him aghast, with true astonishment. She has believed every one of his professions. He points out to her gravely and carefully how such a proceeding would jeopardize all his chances of advancement in the Civil Service, and that even on the chance that he did all this and married her, they would be ruined and penniless. She replies merely by saying: "But you said you loved me and would do anything for me." He acknowledges this, submits it was a justifiable overstatement under the circumstances, and hurries on to show that his wife is a perfectly innocent party and should not be required to suffer for their misdeeds. She replies merely by saying: "But you made me believe you loved me and promised to do anything for me." He turns from this to bring into her focus his children; he reminds her that she has no children to consider; his children require his care and also have a reasonable right to be protected from a legacy of disgrace. She merely repeats monotonously: "Why did you make me believe you really were mad about me?" So he has to reply shamefacedly that probably that is the kind of person he is. She then wants to know whether he is willing to allow her to go to her death. And he takes her in his arms and kisses her and says, in effect, that he is afraid he is willing to do just that.

Every woman to whom I have submitted this document has without exception applied exactly the same word to the lover. He is a *"cad."* This, of course, is a female word, carrying with its use all the force and despotism of a shibboleth. The truth being that whether or not there is any word for him, the man is, under duress, exhibiting the quintessence of the male view-point. He is doing exactly what all wives, all safe women, all vested authority, have planned through all the ages that he should do.

It is because the women to whom I have submitted this problem fail so totally to grasp these elementary truths that I venture to elaborate the theme at such length. Let us get down to fundamentals. What is the female view-point? The female view-point is dependent upon an instinctive inner knowledge of the role the female plays in the process of reproduction. The female knows perfectly well that she must attract a male mate. She also knows that after she has attracted one, if she accepts him and submits to him, the legitimate result of the adventure for her will be pregnancy. During that period of pregnancy and even more so during labour and the period of the puerperium she knows that she will be help-less and relatively defenceless, that she will require guardianship, pro-tection, and service. She will depend upon the male to furnish these. Therefore she will instinctively make perfectly sure of such things before she submits herself to him. In a state of nature among lower animals this is accomplished in many subtle ways. In a state of civilization the females from the earliest time have ranged Church, State, home, and Rotary on their side in order to compel its assurance. If some foolish one like the lady in my fable chooses to disregard these plain guide-posts, she has, if she comes to grief, only herself to blame.

The male, in fact, has no such preoccupations as beset the female. He has no period of pregnancy in contemplation. He has no puerperium or feeding of the young to consider. He is scourged by another inexorable law of nature—the urge for reproduction, the will to live. He is expressly made to roam over the earth impregnating as many females as he possibly can. It is the deepest instinct in his heart, except the instinct for self-preserva-tion. It is the deepest desire of nature, or, if you prefer the term, the deepest desire of God. It is simply silly to pretend that it is not, or to try to control it by moral admonitions. The only thing that can control him is the common sense of the female. The sense to lead him to the altar or the justice court, the sense to use the means her old mothers fashioned for her to bind him with hoops of steel. And he, too, uses wiles. He will bow his neck to matrimony only if that is the only way out. He wonders all the rest of his life why he did it. He never submits tamely. He promises to love her for ever if she will accede to him. He lies, he coaxes, he fawns in order to accomplish his purpose. And after it is accomplished he is alertly ready for the next candidate, and to remind him of the means he used to accomplish it or to call him names for using them is as unworldly as to rebuke the flowers for blooming or the bees for visiting them.

And all these things, I think, I should tell to everyone's daughter. Ex-cept for the sly fact that she knows them already.

Of course, in a state of civilization certain modifications are imposed upon biologic laws. But the fundamentals remain. Love is a trick of nature —a trick to carry out her insatiable lust for reproduction. For Schopenhauer, you know, was right—the only God you can discern in nature is a "will to live." * I go into my garden—the shrubs, the flowers, and even more energetically the dandelions are reproducing as fast as ever they can. In my pool the little gold-fish are making new little gold-fish until the water swarms with them. Why? I haven't the slightest idea. At least I do not know the ultimate reason—the general scheme. Why they do it— the immediate impulse—is, I have no doubt, just as sweet and as irresistible to the gold-fish as to the boy and girl over the garden gate. Love is concocted of its unbearable ecstasy and its poignant sweetness because in no other way can the crafty old schemer, nature, carry out her purpose. The boy thinks it a specially dispensed miracle that he should be born in the same village with the one girl who is completely desirable. The poor dear does not know that he would have found one no matter where he was born. It is nature's way of getting her world populated. If either the boy or the girl realized the stifling responsibilities they were assuming, the last representative of the human race would ere long be sitting by the empty shores of the eternal ocean.

But they do not know, and society has wisely built up another trick, called marriage, because it found out that such things were necessary if nature's purposes were to be adequately fulfilled. The boy and girl enter this state two utterly unfamiliar elements. They enter it in a state of delirious ecstasy. They enter it because it seems to be the one way to carry out their most cherished and most selfish objects. Is it any wonder they so often find that instead of a paradise it is a prison? Is it any wonder that they find the two strange elements unassimilable? Is it any wonder that after a time they find themselves pulling to get asunder? They went in, as every human creature goes into everything, he to please himself, she to please herself. After marriage, in most instances, they each continue to try to please the one person they most wish to gratify—himself or herself. These two objects may conflict. And by that time there are the children to be considered. And the hoarse chuckle of Mother Nature and of Mother Church is heard in the wings. No, the wonder is that in so many instances it turns out well at all. For sometimes in spite of all the cynics and all the natural philosophers it does do that. Sometimes by some curious

---

* A great physicist with whom I was once discussing this eternally fascinating question said: "My idea of the nature of God is energy." I am inclined to think his definition is more comprehensive. But in the world of living creatures it amounts to will.

alchemy it becomes that very state which the marriage service so wistfully describes, "like unto the mystical union that is between Christ and His Church." How I do not know. Some union of purpose and of thought, some strange anabolism of human spirits, some mystical method by which two people can work out their separate destinies, yet work them out together.

QUESTIONS AND TOPICS

1. Why does Dr. Clendening find human procreation a clumsy process? Imagine that the human race were replenished by simple cellular division, or by the laying of eggs. What effects would this have on marriage? On society?
2. Do you think Dr. Clendening accurately describes the roles of woman and man in mating? How would you define their roles?
3. Do you think Dr. Clendening has stated properly the reason for sex and has analyzed justly the sex drive in man and woman? What different reasons, if any, would you give?
4. How would you define "the double standard"? What do you think of this standard? If man is driven by the "insatiable lust for reproduction," can he be blamed for wanting, consciously or unconsciously, to replenish the species with as many women as possible?
5. Relate advancements in birth control to Dr. Clendening's analysis. Do these advancements seem to work against the biological functions he discusses? Is this good or bad? Why?
6. Read George Bernard Shaw's *Man and Superman* (especially the "Don Juan in Hell" section) and compare Shaw's analysis of mating with that of Dr. Clendening.
7. In your opinion, is there a mystical element in sex? Read Lawrence's short story on p. 299.

W. H. Auden

VICTOR,
A BALLAD

In the following poem W. H. Auden, 1907–, uses representative characters to attack certain stereotyped attitudes towards sex.

Victor was a little baby,
    Into this world he came;
His father took him on his knee and said:
    'Don't dishonour the family name.'

Victor looked up at his father
    Looked up with big round eyes:
His father said; 'Victor, my only son,
    Don't you ever ever tell lies.'

Victor and his father went riding
    Out in a little dog-cart;
His father took a Bible from his pocket and read;
    'Blessed are the pure in heart.'

It was a frosty December
    Victor was only eighteen,
But his figures were neat and his margins straight
    And his cuffs were always clean.

He took a room at the Peveril,
    A respectable boarding-house;
And Time watched Victor day after day
    As a cat will watch a mouse.

The clerks slapped Victor on the shoulder;
    'Have you ever had a woman?' they said,
'Come down town with us on Saturday night.'
    Victor smiled and shook his head.

The manager sat in his office,
    Smoked a Corona cigar:
Said; 'Victor's a decent fellow but
    He's too mousey to go far.'

Victor went up to his bedroom,
    Set the alarum bell;
Climbed into bed, took his Bible and read
    Of what happened to Jezebel.

It was the First of April,
    Anna to the Peveril came;
Her eyes, her lips, her breast, her hips
    And her smile set men aflame.

She looked as pure as a schoolgirl
    On her First Communion day,
But her kisses were like the best champagne
    When she gave herself away.

It was the Second of April,
    She was wearing a coat of fur;
Victor met her upon the stairs
    And he fell in love with her.

The first time he made his proposal,
    She laughed, said; 'I'll never wed;'
The second time there was a pause;
    Then she smiled and shook her head.

Anna looked into her mirror,
    Pouted and gave a frown:
Said; 'Victor's as dull as a wet afternoon
    But I've got to settle down.'

The third time he made his proposal,
 As they walked by the Reservoir:
She gave him a kiss like a blow on the head,
 Said; 'You are my heart's desire.'

They were married early in August,
 She said; 'Kiss me, you funny boy:'
Victor took her in his arms and said;
 'O my Helen of Troy.'

It was the middle of September,
 Victor came to the office one day;
He was wearing a flower in his buttonhole,
 He was late but he was gay.

The clerks were talking of Anna,
 The door was just ajar:
One said; 'Poor old Victor, but where ignorance
 Is bliss, et cetera.'

Victor stood still as a statue,
 The door was just ajar:
One said; 'God, what fun I had with her
 In that Baby Austin car.'

Victor walked out into the High Street,
 He walked to the edge of the town;
He came to the allotments and the rubbish heap
 And his tears came tumbling down.

Victor looked up at the sunset
 As he stood there all alone;
Cried: 'Are you in Heaven, Father?'
 But the sky said 'Address not known'.

Victor looked up at the mountains,
 The mountains all covered with snow
Cried; 'Are you pleased with me, Father?'
 And the answer came back, No.

Victor came to the forest,
    Cried: 'Father, will she ever be true?'
And the oaks and the beeches shook their heads
    And they answered: 'Not to you.'

Victor came to the meadow
    Where the wind went sweeping by:
Cried; 'O Father, I love her so,'
    But the wind said, 'She must die.'

Victor came to the river
    Running so deep and so still:
Crying; 'O Father, what shall I do?'
    And the river answered, 'Kill.'

Anna was sitting at table,
    Drawing cards from a pack;
Anna was sitting at table
    Waiting for her husband to come back.

It wasn't the Jack of Diamonds
    Nor the Joker she drew at first;
It wasn't the King or the Queen of Hearts
    But the Ace of Spades reversed.

Victor stood in the doorway,
    He didn't utter a word:
She said; 'What's the matter, darling?'
    He behaved as if he hadn't heard.

There was a voice in his left ear,
    There was a voice in his right,
There was a voice at the base of his skull
    Saying, 'She must die tonight.'

Victor picked up a carving-knife,
    His features were set and drawn,
Said; 'Anna, it would have been better for you
    If you had not been born.'

Anna jumped up from the table,
    Anna started to scream,
But Victor came slowly after her
    Like a horror in a dream.

She dodged behind the sofa,
    She tore down a curtain rod,
But Victor came slowly after her:
    Said; 'Prepare to meet thy God.'

She managed to wrench the door open,
    She ran and she didn't stop.
But Victor followed her up the stairs
    And he caught her at the top.

He stood there above the body,
    He stood there holding the knife;
And the blood ran down the stairs and sang,
    'I'm the Resurrection and the Life.'

They tapped Victor on the shoulder,
    They took him away in a van;
He sat as quiet as a lump of moss
    Saying, 'I am the Son of Man.'

Victor sat in a corner
    Making a woman of clay:
Saying; 'I am Alpha and Omega, I shall come
    To judge the earth one day.'

QUESTIONS AND TOPICS

1. What seems to be Victor's problem? Is he a sympathetic figure? A tragic figure? Why?
2. What is the attitude towards sex held by the clerks? Is this the usual attitude of most men?

3. What is Anna's attitude towards sex? Does Auden intend her to be condemned? What would be your reaction if you discovered that you had married an Anna? Or a Victor?

4. Why is there so much reference to religion in the poem? Can religion and sexual promiscuity be reconciled?

5. There are several attitudes towards sex explored, then, in the poem. What seems to be the attitude that the poet espouses, if he espouses one?

W. Somerset Maugham

THE
COLONEL'S
LADY

During a long and popular career, W. Somerset Maugham, 1874– 1965, the British writer, produced numerous novels and plays, and a number of witty and urbane books about himself and sundry topics. One of the frequent criticisms of Maugham's works is that they are philosophically and morally superficial. The following story, however, attests to the fact that he had something to say to a great many people about personal relationships and moral values.

All this happened two or three years before the outbreak of the war.

The Peregrines were having breakfast. Though they were alone and the table was long they sat at opposite ends of it. From the walls George Peregrine's ancestors, painted by the fashionable painters of the day, looked down upon them. The butler brought in the morning post. There were several letters for the colonel, business letters, *The Times* and a small parcel for his wife Evie. He looked at his letters and then, opening *The Times*, began to read it. They finished breakfast and rose from the table. He noticed that his wife hadn't opened the parcel.

"What's that?" he asked.

"Only some books."

"Shall I open it for you?"

"If you like."

He hated to cut string and so with some difficulty untied the knots.

"But they're all the same," he said when he had unwrapped the parcel. "What on earth d'you want six copies of the same book for?" He opened one of them. "Poetry." Then he looked at the title page. *When Pyramids Decay,* he read, by E. K. Hamilton. Eva Katherine Hamilton: that was his wife's maiden name. He looked at her with smiling surprise. "Have you written a book, Evie? You are a slyboots."

"I didn't think it would interest you very much. Would you like a copy?"

"Well, you know poetry isn't much in my line, but—yes, I'd like a copy; I'll read it. I'll take it along to my study. I've got a lot to do this morning."

He gathered up *The Times,* his letters and the book, and went out. His study was a large and comfortable room, with a big desk, leather armchairs and what he called "trophies of the chase," on the walls. On the bookshelves were works of reference, books on farming, gardening, fishing and shooting, and books on the last war, in which he had won an M.C. and D.S.O. For before his marriage he had been in the Welsh Guards. At the end of the war he retired and settled down to the life of a country gentleman in the spacious house, some twenty miles from Sheffield, which one of his forebears had built in the reign of George III. George Peregrine had an estate of some fifteen hundred acres which he managed with ability; he was a Justice of the Peace and performed his duties conscientiously. During the season he rode to hounds two days a week. He was a good shot, a golfer and though now a little over fifty could still play a hard game of tennis. He could describe himself with propriety as an all-round sportsman.

He had been putting on weight lately, but was still a fine figure of a man; tall, with grey curly hair, only just beginning to grow thin on the crown, frank blue eyes, good features and a high colour. He was a public-spirited man, chairman of any number of local organizations and, as became his class and station, a loyal member of the Conservative party. He looked upon it as his duty to see to the welfare of the people on his estate and it was a satisfaction to him to know that Evie could be trusted to tend the sick and succour the poor. He had built a cottage hospital on the outskirts of the village and paid the wages of a nurse out of his own pocket. All he asked of the recipients of his bounty was that at elections, county or general, they should vote his candidate. He was a friendly man, affable to his inferiors, considerate with his tenants and popular with the neighbouring gentry. He would have been pleased and at the same time slightly embarrassed if someone had told him he was a jolly good fellow. That was what he wanted to be. He desired no higher praise.

It was hard luck that he had no children. He would have been an excellent father, kindly but strict, and would have brought up his sons as gentlemen's sons should be brought up, sent them to Eton, you know, taught them to fish, shoot and ride. As it was, his heir was a nephew, son of his brother killed in a motor accident, not a bad boy, but not a chip off the old block, no, sir, far from it; and would you believe it, his fool of a mother was sending him to a co-educational school. Evie had been a sad disappointment to him. Of course she was a lady, and she had a bit of money of her own; she managed the house uncommonly well and she was a good hostess. The village people adored her. She had been a pretty little thing when he married her, with a creamy skin, light brown hair and a trim figure, healthy too and not a bad tennis player; he couldn't understand why she'd had no children; of course she was faded now, she must be getting on for five and forty; her skin was drab, her hair had lost its sheen and she was as thin as a rail. She was always neat and suitably dressed, but she didn't seem to bother how she looked, she wore no make-up and didn't even use lipstick; sometimes at night when she dolled herself up for a party you could tell that once she'd been quite attractive, but ordinarily she was—well, the sort of woman you simply didn't notice. A nice woman, of course, a good wife, and it wasn't her fault if she was barren, but it was tough on a fellow who wanted an heir of his own loins; she hadn't any vitality, that's what was the matter with her. He supposed he'd been in love with her when he asked her to marry him, at least sufficiently in love for a man who wanted to marry and settle down, but with time he discovered that they had nothing much in common. She didn't care about hunting, and fishing bored her. Naturally they'd drifted apart. He had to do her the justice to admit that she'd never bothered him. There'd been no scenes. They had no quarrels. She seemed to take it for granted that he should go his own way. When he went up to London now and then she never wanted to come with him. He had a girl there, well, she wasn't exactly a girl, she was thirty-five if she was a day, but she was blonde and luscious and he only had to wire ahead of time and they'd dine, do a show and spend the night together. Well, a man, a healthy normal man had to have some fun in his life. The thought crossed his mind that if Evie hadn't been such a good woman she'd have been a better wife; but it was not the sort of thought that he welcomed and he put it away from him.

George Peregrine finished his *Times* and being a considerate fellow rang the bell and told the butler to take it to Evie. Then he looked at his watch. It was half-past ten and at eleven he had an appointment with one of his tenants. He had half an hour to spare.

"I'd better have a look at Evie's book," he said to himself.

He took it up with a smile. Evie had a lot of highbrow books in her sitting-room, not the sort of books that interested him, but if they amused her he had no objection to her reading them. He noticed that the volume he now held in his hand contained no more than ninety pages. That was all to the good. He shared Edgar Allan Poe's opinion that poems should be short. But as he turned the pages he noticed that several of Evie's had long lines of irregular length and didn't rhyme. He didn't like that. At his first school, when he was a little boy, he remembered learning a poem that began: *The boy stood on the burning deck,* and later, at Eton, one that started: *Ruin seize thee, ruthless king;* and then there was Henry V; they'd had to take that one half. He stared at Evie's pages with consternation.

"That's not what I call poetry," he said.

Fortunately it wasn't all like that. Interspersed with the pieces that looked so odd, lines of three or four words and then a line of ten or fifteen there were little poems, quite short, that rhymed, thank God, with the lines all the same length. Several of the pages were just headed with the word *Sonnet,* and out of curiosity he counted the lines; there were four-teen of them. He read them. They seemed all right, but he didn't quite know what they were all about. He repeated to himself: *Ruin seize thee, ruthless king.*

"Poor Evie," he sighed.

At that moment the farmer he was expecting was ushered into the study, and putting the book down he made him welcome. They embarked on their business.

"I read your book, Evie," he said as they sat down to lunch. "Jolly good. Did it cost you a packet to have it printed?"

"No, I was lucky. I sent it to a publisher and he took it."

"Not much money in poetry, my dear," he said in his good-natured hearty way.

"No, I don't suppose there is. What did Bannock want to see you about this morning?"

Bannock was the tenant who had interrupted his reading of Evie's poems.

"He's asked me to advance the money for a pedigree bull he wants to buy. He's a good man and I've half a mind to do it."

George Peregrine saw that Evie didn't want to talk about her book and he was not sorry to change the subject. He was glad she had used her maiden name on the title page; he didn't suppose anyone would ever hear about the book, but he was proud of his unusual name and he wouldn't have liked it if some damned penny-a-liner had made fun of Evie's effort in one of the papers.

During the few weeks that followed he thought it tactful not to ask Evie any questions about her venture in verse, and she never referred to it. It might have been a discreditable incident that they had silently agreed not to mention. But then a strange thing happened. He had to go to London on business and he took Daphne out to dinner. That was the name of the girl with whom he was in the habit of passing a few agreeable hours whenever he went to town.

"Oh, George," she said, "is that your wife who's written a book they're all talking about?"

"What on earth d'you mean?"

"Well, there's a fellow I know who's a critic. He took me out to dinner the other night and he had a book with him. 'Got anything for me to read?' I said. 'What's that?' 'Oh, I don't think that's your cup of tea,' he said. 'It's poetry. I've just been reviewing it.' 'No poetry for me,' I said. 'It's about the hottest stuff I ever read,' he said. 'Selling like hot cakes. And it's damned good.'"

"Who's the book by?" asked George.

"A woman called Hamilton. My friend told me that wasn't her real name. He said her real name was Peregrine. 'Funny,' I said, 'I know a fellow called Peregrine.' 'Colonel in the army,' he said. 'Lives near Sheffield.'"

"I'd just as soon you didn't talk about me to your friends," said George with a frown of vexation.

"Keep your shirt on, dearie. Who d'you take me for? I just said: 'It's not the same one.'" Daphne giggled. "My friend said: 'They say he's a regular Colonel Blimp.'"

George had a keen sense of humour.

"You could tell them better than that," he laughed. "If my wife had written a book I'd be the first to know about it, wouldn't I?"

"I suppose you would."

Anyhow the matter didn't interest her and when the colonel began to talk of other things she forgot about it. He put it out of his mind too. There was nothing to it, he decided, and that silly fool of a critic had just been pulling Daphne's leg. He was amused at the thought of her tackling that book because she had been told it was hot stuff and then finding it just a lot of bosh cut up into unequal lines.

He was a member of several clubs and next day he thought he'd lunch at one in St. James's Street. He was catching a train back to Sheffield early in the afternoon. He was sitting in a comfortable armchair having a glass of sherry before going into the dining-room when an old friend came up to him.

"Well, old boy, how's life?" he said. "How d'you like being the husband of a celebrity?"

George Peregrine looked at his friend. He thought he saw an amused twinkle in his eyes.

"I don't know what you're talking about," he answered.

"Come off it, George. Everyone knows E. K. Hamilton is your wife. Not often a book of verse has a success like that. Look here, Henry Dashwood is lunching with me. He'd like to meet you."

"Who the devil is Henry Dashwood and why should he want to meet me?"

"Oh, my dear fellow, what do you do with yourself all the time in the country? Henry's about the best critic we've got. He wrote a wonderful review of Evie's book. D'you mean to say she didn't show it to you?"

Before George could answer his friend had called a man over. A tall, thin man, with a high forehead, a beard, a long nose and a stoop, just the sort of man whom George was prepared to dislike at first sight. Introductions were effected. Henry Dashwood sat down.

"Is Mrs. Peregrine in London by any chance? I should very much like to meet her," he said.

"No, my wife doesn't like London. She prefers the country," said George stiffly.

"She wrote me a very nice letter about my review. I was pleased. You know, we critics get more kicks than half-pence. I was simply bowled over by her book. It's so fresh and original, very modern without being obscure. She seems to be as much at her ease in free verse as in the classical metres." Then because he was a critic he thought he should criticize. "Sometimes her ear is a trifle at fault, but you can say the same of Emily

Dickinson. There are several of those short lyrics of hers that might have been written by Landor."

All this was gibberish to George Peregrine. The man was nothing but a disgusting highbrow. But the colonel had good manners and he answered with proper civility: Henry Dashwood went on as though he hadn't spoken.

"But what makes the book so outstanding is the passion that throbs in every line. So many of these young poets are so anæmic, cold, bloodless, dully intellectual, but here you have real naked, earthy passion; of course deep, sincere emotion like that is tragic—ah, my dear Colonel, how right Heine was when he said that the poet makes little songs out of his great sorrows. You know, now and then, as I read and re-read those heart-rending pages I thought of Sappho."

This was too much for George Peregrine and he got up.

"Well, it's jolly nice of you to say such nice things about my wife's little book. I'm sure she'll be delighted. But I must bolt, I've got to catch a train and I want to get a bite of lunch."

"Damned fool," he said irritably to himself as he walked upstairs to the dining-room.

He got home in time for dinner and after Evie had gone to bed he went into his study and looked for her book. He thought he'd just glance through it again to see for himself what they were making such a fuss about, but he couldn't find it. Evie must have taken it away.

"Silly," he muttered.

He'd told her he thought it jolly good. What more could a fellow be expected to say? Well, it didn't matter. He lit his pipe and read the *Field* till he felt sleepy. But a week or so later it happened that he had to go into Sheffield for the day. He lunched there at his club. He had nearly finished when the Duke of Haverel came in. This was the great local magnate and of course the colonel knew him, but only to say how d'you do to; and he was surprised when the Duke stopped at his table.

"We're so sorry your wife couldn't come to us for the week-end," he said, with a sort of shy cordiality. "We're expecting rather a nice lot of people."

George was taken aback. He guessed that the Haverels had asked him and Evie over for the week-end and Evie, without saying a word to him about it, had refused. He had the presence of mind to say he was sorry too.

"Better luck next time," said the Duke pleasantly and moved on.

Colonel Peregrine was very angry and when he got home he said to his wife:

"Look here, what's this about our being asked over to Haverel? Why on earth did you say we couldn't go? We've never been asked before and it's the best shooting in the county."

"I didn't think of that. I thought it would only bore you."

"Damn it all, you might at least have asked me if I wanted to go."

"I'm sorry."

He looked at her closely. There was something in her expression that he didn't quite understand. He frowned.

"I suppose *I* was asked?" he barked.

Evie flushed a little.

"Well, in point of fact you weren't."

"I call it damned rude of them to ask you without asking me."

"I suppose they thought it wasn't your sort of party. The Duchess is rather fond of writers and people like that, you know. She's having Henry Dashwood, the critic, and for some reason he wants to meet me."

"It was damned nice of you to refuse, Evie."

"It's the least I could do," she smiled. She hesitated a moment. "George, my publishers want to give a little dinner party for me one day towards the end of the month and of course they want you to come too."

"Oh, I don't think that's quite my mark. I'll come up to London with you if you like. I'll find someone to dine with."

Daphne.

"I expect it'll be very dull, but they're making rather a point of it. And the day after, the American publisher who's taken my book is giving a cocktail party at Claridge's. I'd like you to come to that if you wouldn't mind."

"Sounds like a crashing bore, but if you really want me to come I'll come."

"It would be sweet of you."

George Peregrine was dazed by the cocktail party. There were a lot of people. Some of them didn't look so bad, a few of the women were decently turned out, but the men seemed to him pretty awful. He was introduced to everyone as Colonel Peregrine, E. K. Hamilton's husband, you know. The men didn't seem to have anything to say to him, but the women gushed.

"You *must* be proud of your wife. Isn't it *wonderful?* You know, I read it right through at a sitting. I simply couldn't put it down, and when I'd finished I started again at the beginning and read it right through a second time. I was simply *thrilled.*"

The English publisher said to him:

"We've not had a success like this with a book of verse for twenty years. I've never seen such reviews."

The American publisher said to him:

"It's swell. It'll be a smash hit in America. You wait and see."

The American publisher had sent Evie a great spray of orchids. Damned ridiculous, thought George. As they came in, people were taken up to Evie, and it was evident that they said flattering things to her, which she took with a pleasant smile and a word or two of thanks. She was a trifle flushed with the excitement, but seemed quite at her ease. Though he thought the whole thing a lot of stuff and nonsense George noted with approval that his wife was carrying if off in just the right way.

"Well, there's one thing," he said to himself, "you can see she's a lady and that's a damned sight more than you can say of anyone else here."

He drank a good many cocktails. But there was one thing that bothered him. He had a notion that some of the people he was introduced to looked at him in rather a funny sort of way, he couldn't quite make out what it meant, and once when he strolled by two women, who were sitting together on a sofa he had the impression that they were talking about him, and after he passed he was almost certain they tittered. He was very glad when the party came to an end.

In the taxi on their way back to their hotel Evie said to him:

"You were wonderful, dear. You made quite a hit. The girls simply raved about you; they thought you so handsome."

"Girls," he said bitterly. "Old hags."

"Were you bored, dear?"

"Stiff."

She pressed his hand in a gesture of sympathy.

"I hope you won't mind if we wait and go down by the afternoon train. I've got some things to do in the morning."

"No, that's all right. Shopping?"

"I do want to buy one or two things, but I've got to go and be photographed. I hate the idea, but they think I ought to be. For America, you know."

He said nothing. But he thought. He thought it would be a shock to the American public when they saw the portrait of the homely, desiccated little woman who was his wife. He'd always been under the impression that they liked glamour in America.

He went on thinking, and next morning when Evie had gone out he went to his club and up to the library. There he looked up recent numbers of *The Times Literary Supplement,* the *New Statesman* and the *Spectator.* Presently he found reviews of Evie's book. He didn't read them very carefully, but enough to see that they were extremely favourable. Then he went to the bookseller's in Piccadilly where he occasionally bought books. He'd made up his mind that he had to read this damned thing of Evie's properly, but he didn't want to ask her what she'd done with the copy she'd given him. He'd buy one for himself. Before going in he looked in the window and the first thing he saw was a display of *When Pyramids Decay.* Damned silly title! He went in. A young man came forward and asked if he could help him.

"No, I'm just having a look round." It embarrassed him to ask for Evie's book and he thought he'd find it for himself and then take it to the salesman. But he couldn't see it anywhere and at last, finding the young man near him, he said in a carefully casual tone: "By the way, have you got a book called *When Pyramids Decay?*"

"The new edition came in this morning. I'll get a copy."

In a moment the young man returned with it. He was a short, rather stout young man, with a shock of untidy carroty hair and spectacles. George Peregrine, tall, upstanding, very military, towered over him.

"Is this a new edition then?" he asked.

"Yes, sir. The fifth. It might be a novel the way it's selling."

George Peregrine hesitated a moment.

"Why d'you suppose it's such a success? I've always been told no one reads poetry."

"Well, it's good, you know. I've read it meself." The young man, though obviously cultured, had a slight Cockney accent, and George quite instinctively adopted a patronising attitude. "It's the story they like. Sexy, you know, but tragic."

George frowned a little. He was coming to the conclusion that the young man was rather impertinent. No one had told him anything about there being a story in the damned book and he had not gathered that from reading the reviews. The young man went on.

"Of course it's only a flash in the pan, if you know what I mean. The way I look at it, she was sort of inspired like by a personal experience, like Housman was with *A Shropshire Lad*. She'll never write anything else."

"How much is the book?" said George coldly to stop his chatter. "You needn't wrap it up, I'll just slip it into my pocket."

The November morning was raw and he was wearing a greatcoat.

At the station he bought the evening papers and magazines and he and Evie settled themselves comfortably in opposite corners of a first-class carriage and read. At five o'clock they went along to the restaurant car to have tea and chatted a little. They arrived. They drove home in the car which was waiting for them. They bathed, dressed for dinner, and after dinner Evie, saying she was tired out, went to bed. She kissed him, as was her habit, on the forehead. Then he went into the hall, took Evie's book out of his greatcoat pocket and going into the study began to read it. He didn't read verse very easily and though he read with attention, every word of it, the impression he received was far from clear. Then he began at the beginning again and read it a second time. He read with increasing malaise, but he was not a stupid man and when he had finished he had a distinct understanding of what it was all about. Part of the book was in free verse, part in conventional metres, but the story it related was coherent and plain to the meanest intelligence. It was the story of a passionate love affair between an older woman, married, and a young man. George Peregrine made out the steps of it as easily as if he had been doing a sum in simple addition.

Written in the first person, it began with the tremulous surprise of the woman, past her youth, when it dawned upon her that the young man was in love with her. She hesitated to believe it. She thought she must be deceiving herself. And she was terrified when on a sudden she discovered that she was passionately in love with him. She told herself it was absurd; with the disparity of age between them nothing but unhappiness could come to her if she yielded to her emotion. She tried to prevent him from speaking, but the day came when he told her that he loved her and forced her to tell him that she loved him too. He begged her to run away with him. She couldn't leave her husband, her home; and what life could they look forward to, she an ageing woman, he so young? How could she expect his love to last? She begged him to have mercy on her. But his love was impetuous. He wanted her, he wanted her with all his heart, and at last trembling, afraid, desirous, she yielded to him. Then there was a period of ecstatic happiness. The world, the dull, humdrum world of every day, blazed with glory. Love songs flowed from her pen. The woman worshipped the young, virile body of her lover. George flushed darkly when she praised his broad chest and slim flanks, the beauty of his legs and the flatness of his belly.

Hot stuff, Daphne's friend had said. It was that all right. Disgusting.

There were sad little pieces in which she lamented the emptiness of her life when as must happen he left her, but they ended with a cry that all she had to suffer would be worth it for the bliss that for a while had been hers. She wrote of the long, tremulous nights they passed together and the languor that lulled them to sleep in one another's arms. She wrote of the rapture of brief stolen moments when, braving all danger, their passion overwhelmed them and they surrendered to its call.

She thought it would be an affair of a few weeks, but miraculously it lasted. One of the poems referred to three years having gone by without lessening the love that filled their hearts. It looked as though he continued to press her to go away with him, far away, to a hill town in Italy, a Greek island, a walled city in Tunisia, so that they could be together always, for in another of the poems she besought him to let things be as they were. Their happiness was precarious. Perhaps it was owing to the difficulties they had to encounter, and the rarity of their meetings that their love had retained for so long its first enchanting ardour. Then on a sudden the young man died. How, when or where George could not discover. There followed a long, heartbroken cry of bitter grief, grief she could not indulge in, grief that had to be hidden. She had to be cheerful, give dinner-parties and go out to dinner, behave as she had always behaved, though the light had gone out of her life and she was bowed down with anguish. The last poem of all was a set of four short stanzas in which the writer, sadly resigned to her loss, thanked the dark powers that rule man's destiny that she had been privileged at least for a while to enjoy the greatest happiness that we poor human beings can ever hope to know.

It was three o'clock in the morning when George Peregrine finally put the book down. It had seemed to him that he heard Evie's voice in every line, over and over again he came upon turns of phrase he had heard her use, there were details that were as familiar to him as to her: there was no doubt about it; it was her own story she had told, and it was as plain as anything could be that she had had a lover and her lover had died. It was not anger so much that he felt, nor horror or dismay, though he was dismayed and he was horrified, but amazement. It was as inconceivable that Evie should have had a love affair, and a wildly passionate one at that, as that the trout in a glass case over the chimney piece in his study, the finest he had ever caught, should suddenly wag its tail. He understood now the meaning of the amused look he had seen in the eyes of that man he had spoken to at the club, he understood why Daphne when she was talking about the book had seemed to be enjoying a private joke, and why those two women at the cocktail-party had tittered when he strolled past them.

He broke out into a sweat. Then on a sudden he was seized with fury and he jumped up to go and awake Evie and ask her sternly for an explanation. But he stopped at the door. After all what proof had he? A book. He remembered that he'd told Evie he thought it jolly good. True, he hadn't read it, but he'd pretended he had. He would look a perfect fool if he had to admit that.

"I must watch my step," he muttered.

He made up his mind to wait for two or three days and think it all over. Then he'd decide what to do. He went to bed, but he couldn't sleep for a long time.

"Evie," he kept on saying to himself. "Evie, of all people."

They met at breakfast next morning as usual. Evie was as she always was, quiet, demure and self-possessed, a middle-aged woman who made no effort to look younger than she was, a woman who had nothing of what he still called It. He looked at her as he hadn't looked at her for years. She had her usual placid serenity. Her pale blue eyes were untroubled. There was no sign of guilt on her candid brow. She made the same little casual remarks she always made.

"It's nice to get back to the country again after those two hectic days in London. What are you going to do this morning?"

It was incomprehensible.

Three days later he went to see his solicitor. Henry Blane was an old friend of George's as well as his lawyer. He had a place not far from Peregrine's and for years they had shot over one another's preserves. For two days a week he was a country gentleman and for the other five a busy lawyer in Sheffield. He was a tall, robust fellow, with a boisterous manner and a jovial laugh, which suggested that he liked to be looked upon essentially as a sportsman and a good fellow and only incidentally as a lawyer. But he was shrewd and worldly-wise.

"Well, George, what's brought you here today?" he boomed as the colonel was shown into his office. "Have a good time in London? I'm taking my missus up for a few days next week. How's Evie?"

"It's about Evie I've come to see you," said Peregrine, giving him a suspicious look. "Have you read her book?"

His sensitivity had been sharpened during those last days of troubled thought and he was conscious of a faint change in the lawyer's expression. It was as though he were suddenly on his guard.

"Yes, I've read it. Great success, isn't it? Fancy Evie breaking out into poetry. Wonders will never cease."

George Peregrine was inclined to lose his temper.

"It's made me look a perfect damned fool."

"Oh, what nonsense, George! There's no harm in Evie's writing a book. You ought to be jolly proud of her."

"Don't talk such rot. It's her own story. You know it and everyone else knows it. I suppose I'm the only one who doesn't know who her lover was."

"There is such a thing as imagination, old boy. There's no reason to suppose the whole thing isn't just made up."

"Look here, Henry, we've known one another all our lives. We've had all sorts of good times together. Be honest with me. Can you look me in the face and tell me you believe it's a made-up story?"

Harry Blane moved uneasily in his chair. He was disturbed by the distress in old George's voice.

"You've got no right to ask me a question like that. Ask Evie."

"I daren't," George answered after an anguished pause. "I'm afraid she'd tell me the truth."

There was an uncomfortable silence.

"Who was the chap?"

Harry Blane looked at him straight in the eye.

"I don't know, and if I did I wouldn't tell you."

"You swine. Don't you see what a position I'm in? Do you think it's very pleasant to be made absolutely ridiculous?"

The lawyer lit a cigarette and for some moments silently puffed it.

"I don't see what I can do for you," he said at last.

"You've got private detectives you employ, I suppose. I want you to put them on the job and let them find everything out."

"It's not very pretty to put detectives on one's wife, old boy; and besides, taking for granted for a moment that Evie had an affair, it was a good many years ago and I don't suppose it would be possible to find out a thing. They seem to have covered their tracks pretty carefully."

"I don't care. You put the detectives on. I want to know the truth."

"I won't, George. If you're determined to do that you'd better consult someone else. And look here, even if you got evidence that Evie had been unfaithful to you what would you do with it? You'd look rather silly divorcing your wife because she'd committed adultery ten years ago."

"At all events I could have it out with her."

"You can do that now, but you know just as well as I do, that if you do she'll leave you. D'you want her to do that?"

George gave him an unhappy look.

"I don't know. I always thought she'd been a damned good wife to me. She runs the house perfectly, we never have any servant trouble; she's done wonders with the garden and she's splendid with all the village people. But damn it, I have my self-respect to think of. How can I go on living with her when I know that she was grossly unfaithful to me?"

"Have you always been faithful to her?"

"More or less, you know. After all we've been married for nearly twenty-four years and Evie was never much for bed."

The solicitor slightly raised his eyebrows, but George was too intent on what he was saying to notice.

"I don't deny that I've had a bit of fun now and then. A man wants it. Women are different."

"We only have men's word for that," said Harry Blane, with a faint smile.

"Evie's absolutely the last woman I'd have suspected of kicking over the traces. I mean, she's a very fastidious, reticent woman. What on earth made her write the damned book?"

"I suppose it was a very poignant experience and perhaps it was a relief to her to get it off her chest like that."

"Well, if she had to write it why the devil didn't she write it under an assumed name?"

"She used her maiden name. I suppose she thought that was enough, and it would have been if the book hadn't had this amazing boom."

George Peregrine and the lawyer were sitting opposite one another with a desk between them. George, his elbow on the desk, his cheek resting on his hand, frowned at his thought.

"It's so rotten not to know what sort of a chap he was. One can't tell even if he was by way of being a gentleman. I mean, for all I know he may have been a farm-hand or a clerk in a lawyer's office."

Harry Blane did not permit himself to smile and when he answered there was in his eyes a kindly, tolerant look.

"Knowing Evie so well I think the probabilities are that he was all right. Anyhow I'm sure he wasn't a clerk in my office."

"It's been such a shock to me," the colonel sighed. "I thought she was fond of me. She couldn't have written that book unless she hated me."

"Oh, I don't believe that. I don't think she's capable of hatred."

"You're not going to pretend that she loves me."

"No."

"Well, what does she feel for me?"

Harry Blane leaned back in his swivel chair and looked at George reflectively.

"Indifference, I should say."

The colonel gave a little shudder and reddened.

"After all, you're not in love with her, are you?"

George Peregrine did not answer directly.

"It's been a great blow to me not to have any children, but I've never let her see that I think she's let me down. I've always been kind to her. Within reasonable limits I've tried to do my duty by her."

The lawyer passed a large hand over his mouth to conceal the smile that trembled on his lips.

"It's been such an awful shock to me," Peregrine went on. "Damn it all, even ten years ago Evie was no chicken and God knows, she wasn't much to look at. It's so ugly." He sighed deeply. "What would *you* do in my place?"

"Nothing."

George Peregrine drew himself bolt upright in his chair and he looked at Harry with the stern set face that he must have worn when he inspected his regiment.

"I can't overlook a thing like this. I've been made a laughing-stock. I can never hold up my head again."

"Nonsense," said the lawyer sharply, and then in a pleasant, kindly manner. "Listen, old boy: the man's dead; it all happened a long while back. Forget it. Talk to people about Evie's book, rave about it, tell 'em how proud you are of her. Behave as though you had so much confidence in her, you *knew* she could never have been unfaithful to you. The world moves so quickly and people's memories are so short. They'll forget."

"I shan't forget."

"You're both middle-aged people. She probably does a great deal more for you than you think and you'd be awfully lonely without her. I don't think it matters if you don't forget. It'll be all to the good if you can get it into that thick head of yours that there's a lot more in Evie than you ever had the gumption to see."

"Damn it all, you talk as if *I* was to blame."

"No, I don't think you were to blame, but I'm not so sure that Evie was either. I don't suppose she wanted to fall in love with this boy. D'you remember those verses right at the end? The impression they gave me was that though she was shattered by his death, in a strange sort of way she welcomed it. All through she'd been aware of the fragility of the tie that bound them. He died in the full flush of his first love and had never known that love so seldom endures; he'd only known its bliss and beauty. In her own bitter grief she found solace in the thought that he'd been spared all sorrow."

"All that's a bit above my head, old boy. I see more or less what you mean."

George Peregrine stared unhappily at the inkstand on the desk. He was silent and the lawyer looked at him with curious, yet sympathetic, eyes.

"Do you realize what courage she must have had never by a sign to show how dreadfully unhappy she was?" he said gently.

Colonel Peregrine sighed.

"I'm broken. I suppose you're right; it's no good crying over spilt milk and it would only make things worse if I made a fuss."

"Well?"

George Peregrine gave a pitiful little smile.

"I'll take your advice. I'll do nothing. Let them think me a damned fool and to hell with them. The truth is, I don't know what I'd do without Evie. But I'll tell you what, there's one thing I shall never understand till my dying day: What in the name of heaven did the fellow see in her?"

QUESTIONS AND TOPICS

1. What kind of man is Colonel Peregrine? Can you blame him for ignoring his wife all those years? How would you behave if you found yourself married to a woman or man who seemed unattractive and uninteresting?
2. Is the Colonel's wife unattractive and uninteresting?
3. Do you think it significant that the Colonel and his wife have no children? Explain (you might want to use Dr. Clendening's essay).
4. Do you think that the Colonel's wife actually had a lover? Would you justify her? Do you justify him for having another woman? Compare Maugham's treatment of the double standard with that of Clendening (pp. 261–268).
5. What could Colonel and Mrs. Peregrine do that would improve their relationship? Is this kind of breakdown inevitable in a marriage of this sort? Is a lessening of passion inevitable in most marriages?

Edna St. Vincent Millay

I, BEING BORN
A WOMAN

In this sonnet Edna St. Vincent Millay, 1892–1950, presents an unconventional and highly rationalistic response to sexual passion.

I, being born a woman and distressed
By all the needs and notions of my kind,
Am urged by your propinquity to find
Your person fair, and feel a certain zest
To bear your body's weight upon my breast:
So subtly is the fume of life designed,
To clarify the pulse and cloud the mind,
And leave me once again undone, possessed.
Think not for this, however, the poor treason
Of my stout blood against my staggering brain,
I shall remember you with love, or season
My scorn with pity,—let me make it plain:
I find this frenzy insufficient reason
For conversation when we meet again.

QUESTIONS AND TOPICS

1. What is the poet saying about her feminine urges? About love in general? Do you find her attitude shocking?
2. Is the poet being humorous? Do you find humor applicable to the subject?
3. Can you write a poem or an essay written by the man in response to the poet?
4. Read more of Miss Millay's sonnets. Find others that deal with love. Do they reinforce or contradict the feeling expressed in this poem?

Harvey Cox

THE
PLAYBOY

In this excerpt from The Secular City, *1965, Harvey Cox, 1929–, a contemporary theologian, discusses one manifestation of America's sexual revolution,* Playboy *magazine.*

The Playboy, illustrated by the monthly magazine of that name, does for the boys what Miss America does for the girls. Despite accusations to the contrary, the immense popularity of this magazine is not solely attributable to pin-up girls. For sheer nudity its pictorial art cannot compete with such would-be competitors as *Dude* and *Escapade*. *Playboy* appeals to a highly mobile, increasingly affluent group of young readers, mostly between eighteen and thirty, who want much more from their drugstore reading than bosoms and thighs. They need a total image of what it means to be a man. And Mr. Hefner's *Playboy* has no hesitation in telling them.

Why should such a need arise? David Riesman has argued that the responsibility for character formation in our society has shifted from the family to the peer group and to the mass-media peer-group surrogates. Things are changing so rapidly that one who is equipped by his family with inflexible, highly internalized values becomes unable to deal with the accelerated pace of change and with the varying contests in which he is called upon to function. This is especially true in the area of consumer values toward which the "other-directed person" is increasingly oriented.

Within the confusing plethora of mass-media signals and peer-group values, *Playboy* fills a special need. For the insecure young man with newly acquired free time and money who still feels uncertain about his consumer skills, *Playboy* supplies a comprehensive and authoritative guidebook to this forbidding new world to which he now has access. It tells him not only who to be; it tells him *how* to be it, and even provides consolation outlets for those who secretly feel that they have not quite made it.

In supplying for the other-directed consumer of leisure both the normative identity image and the means for achieving it, *Playboy* relies on a careful integration of copy and advertising material. The comic book that appeals to a younger generation with an analogous problem skillfully intersperses illustrations of incredibly muscled men and excessively mammalian women with advertisements for body-building gimmicks and foam-rubber brassière supplements. Thus the thin-chested comic-book readers of both sexes are thoughtfully supplied with both the ends and the means for attaining a spurious brand of maturity. *Playboy* merely continues the comic-book tactic for the next age group. Since within every identity crisis, whether in teens or twenties, there is usually a sexual-identity problem, *Playboy* speaks to those who desperately want to know what it means to be a man, and more specifically a *male*, in today's world.

Both the image of man and the means for its attainment exhibit a remarkable consistency in *Playboy*. The skilled consumer is cool and unruffled. He savors sports cars, liquor, high fidelity, and book-club selections with a casual, unhurried aplomb. Though he must certainly *have* and *use* the latest consumption item, he must not permit himself to get too attached to it. The style will change and he must always be ready to adjust. His persistent anxiety that he may mix a drink incorrectly, enjoy a jazz group that is passé, or wear last year's necktie style is comforted by an authoritative tone in *Playboy* beside which papal encyclicals sound irresolute.

"Don't hesitate," he is told, "this assertive, self-assumed weskit is what every man of taste wants for the fall season." Lingering doubts about his masculinity are extirpated by the firm assurance that "real men demand this ruggedly masculine smoke" (cigar ad). Though "the ladies will swoon for you, no matter what they promise, don't give them a puff. This cigar is for men only." A fur-lined canvas field jacket is described as "the most masculine thing since the cave man." What to be and how to be it are both made unambiguously clear.

Since being a male necessitates some kind of relationship to females, *Playboy* fearlessly confronts this problem too, and solves it by the consistent application of the same formula. Sex becomes one of the items of leisure activity that the knowledgeable consumer of leisure handles with his characteristic skill and detachment. The girl becomes a desirable—indeed an indispensable—"Playboy accesssory."

In a question-answering column entitled "The Playboy Adviser," queries about smoking equipment (how to break in a meerschaum pipe), cocktail preparation (how to mix a Yellow Fever), and whether or not to wear suspenders with a vest alternate with questions about what to do with girls who complicate the cardinal principle of casualness either by suggesting marriage or by some other impulsive gesture toward a permanent relationship. The infallible answer from the oracle never varies: sex must be contained, at all costs, within the entertainment-recreation area. Don't let her get "serious."

After all, the most famous feature of the magazine is its monthly fold-out photo of a *play*mate. She is the symbol par excellence of recreational sex. When playtime is over, the playmate's function ceases, so she must be made to understand the rules of the game. As the crew-cut young man in a *Playboy* cartoon says to the rumpled and disarrayed girl he is passionately embracing, "Why speak of love at a time like this?"

The magazine's fiction purveys the same kind of severely departmentalized sex. Although the editors have recently dressed up the *Playboy* contents with contributions by Hemingway, Bemelmans, and even a Chekhov translation, the regular run of stories relies on a repetitious and predictable formula. A successful young man, either single or somewhat less than ideally married—a figure with whom readers have no difficulty identifying—encounters a gorgeous and seductive woman who makes no demands on him except sex. She is the prose duplication of the cool-eyed but hot-blooded playmate of the fold-out.

Drawing heavily on the fantasy life of all young Americans, the writers utilize for their stereotyped heroines the hero's schoolteacher, his secretary, an old girl friend, or the girl who brings her car into the garage where he works. The happy issue is always a casual but satisfying sexual experience with no entangling alliances whatever. Unlike the women he knows in real life, the *Playboy* reader's fictional girl friends know their place and ask for nothing more. They present no danger of permanent involvement. Like any good accessory, they are detachable and disposable.

Many of the advertisements reinforce the sex-accessory identification in another way—by attributing female characteristics to the items they sell. Thus a full-page ad for the MG assures us that this car is not only "the smoothest pleasure machine" on the road and that having one is a "love-affair," but most important, "you drive it—it doesn't drive you." The ad ends with the equivocal question "Is it a date?"

Playboy insists that its message is one of liberation. Its gospel frees us from captivity to the puritanical "hatpin brigade." It solemnly crusades for "frankness" and publishes scores of letters congratulating it for its unblushing "candor." Yet the whole phenomenon of which *Playboy* is only a part vividly illustrates the awful fact of a new kind of tyranny.

Those liberated by technology and increased prosperity to new worlds of leisure now become the anxious slaves of dictatorial tastemakers. Obsequiously waiting for the latest signal on what is cool and what is awkward, they are paralyzed by the fear that they may hear pronounced on them that dread sentence occasionally intoned by "The Playboy Adviser": "You goofed!" Leisure is thus swallowed up in apprehensive competitiveness, its liberating potential transformed into a self-destructive compulsion to consume only what is *à la mode*. *Playboy* mediates the Word of the most high into one section of the consumer world, but it is a word of bondage, not of freedom.

Nor will *Playboy's* synthetic doctrine of man stand the test of scrutiny. Psychoanalysts constantly remind us how deep-seated sexuality is in the human being. But if they didn't remind us, we would soon discover it ourselves anyway. Much as the human male might like to terminate his relationship with a woman as he would snap off the stereo, or store her for special purposes like a camel's-hair jacket, it really can't be done. And anyone with a modicum of experience with women knows it can't be done. Perhaps this is the reason *Playboy's* readership drops off so sharply after the age of thirty.

Playboy really feeds on the existence of a repressed fear of involvement with women, which for various reasons is still present in many otherwise adult Americans. So *Playboy's* version of sexuality grows increasingly irrelevant as authentic sexual maturity is achieved. . . .

QUESTIONS AND TOPICS

1. Discuss Cox's statement that "the responsibility for character formation in our society has shifted from the family to the peer group and the mass-media peer-group surrogates." Other mass media besides magazines shape the average man's attitudes toward sex. Do these differ much in their approach?

2. How popular is the image of manhood that *Playboy* develops? Describe and evaluate someone you know who believes in this image.
3. Is the image of the female that *Playboy* develops realistic? What impact does it have, if any, on the lives of American women?
4. What is your evaluation of *Playboy's* sexual message?

D. H. Lawrence

THE HORSE-DEALER'S DAUGHTER

D. H. Lawrence, 1885–1930, believed that sexual morality ought to be determined not by reason or society but by man's deepest impulses. Lawrence regarded the sexual passions as holy. He disdained sex for the creation of pleasure, the satisfaction of egotism, and the alleviation of boredom. He even scorned sex for the purpose of procreation. Sex, to Lawrence, was "an offering up of yourself to the very great gods, the dark ones, and nothing else." *

In his best fiction Lawrence did not overtly propagandize. Instead, he created characters who are only fulfilled when they tear away the outward forms of civilized behavior and react in accordance with their strongest desires. The overpowering sexual instincts of Lawrence's characters, though sometimes subconscious, shape their relationships with members of both sexes and determine the course of their lives.

"Well, Mabel, and what are you going to do with yourself?" asked Joe, with foolish flippancy. He felt quite safe himself. Without listening for an answer, he turned aside, worked a grain of tobacco to the tip of his

---

* D. H. Lawrence, "Benjamin Franklin," *Studies in Classic American Literature* (New York: The Viking Press, 1964), p. 18.

tongue, and spat it out. He did not care about anything, since he felt safe himself.

The three brothers and the sister sat round the desolate breakfast table, attempting some sort of desultory consultation. The morning's post had given the final tap to the family fortunes, and all was over. The dreary dining-room itself, with its heavy mahogany furniture, looked as if it were waiting to be done away with.

But the consultation amounted to nothing. There was a strange air of ineffectuality about the three men, as they sprawled at table, smoking and reflecting vaguely on their own condition. The girl was alone, a rather short, sullen-looking young woman of twenty-seven. She did not share the same life as her brothers. She would have been good-looking, save for the impassive fixity of her face, "bull-dog," as her brothers called it.

There was a confused tramping of horses' feet outside. The three men all sprawled round in their chairs to watch. Beyond the dark holly-bushes that separated the strip of lawn from the highroad, they could see a cavalcade of shire horses swinging out of their own yard, being taken for exercise. This was the last time. These were the last horses that would go through their hands. The young men watched with critical, callous look. They were all frightened at the collapse of their lives, and the sense of disaster in which they were involved left them no inner freedom.

Yet they were three fine, well-set fellows enough. Joe, the eldest, was a man of thirty-three, broad and handsome in a hot, flushed way. His face was red, he twisted his black moustache over a thick finger, his eyes were shallow and restless. He had a sensual way of uncovering his teeth when he laughed, and his bearing was stupid. Now he watched the horses with a glazed look of helplessness in his eyes, a certain stupor of downfall.

The great draught-horses swung past. They were tied head to tail, four of them, and they heaved along to where a lane branched off from the highroad, planting their great hoofs floutingly in the fine black mud, swinging their great rounded haunches sumptuously, and trotting a few sudden steps as they were led into the lane, round the corner. Every movement showed a massive, slumbrous strength, and a stupidity which held them in subjection. The groom at the head looked back, jerking the leading rope. And the cavalcade moved out of sight up the lane, the tail of the last horse, bobbed up tight and stiff, held out taut from the swinging great haunches as they rocked behind the hedges in a motion-like sleep.

Joe watched with glazed hopeless eyes. The horses were almost like his own body to him. He felt he was done for now. Luckily he was engaged to a woman as old as himself, and therefore her father, who was steward of a neighbouring estate, would provide him with a job. He would marry and go into harness. His life was over, he would be a subject animal now.

He turned uneasily aside, the retreating steps of the horses echoing in his ears. Then, with foolish restlessness, he reached for the scraps of bacon-rind from the plates, and making a faint whistling sound, flung them to the terrier that lay against the fender. He watched the dog swallow them, and waited till the creature looked into his eyes. Then a faint grin came on his face, and in a high, foolish voice he said:

"You won't get much more bacon, shall you, you little b——?"

The dog faintly and dismally wagged its tail, then lowered its haunches, circled round, and lay down again.

There was another helpless silence at the table. Joe sprawled uneasily in his seat, not willing to go till the family conclave was dissolved. Fred Henry, the second brother, was erect, clean-limbed, alert. He had watched the passing of the horses with more sang-froid. If he was an animal, like Joe, he was an animal which controls, not one which is controlled. He was master of any horse, and he carried himself with a well-tempered air of mastery. But he was not master of the situations of life. He pushed his coarse brown moustache upwards, off his lip, and glanced irritably at his sister, who sat impassive and inscrutable.

"You'll go and stop with Lucy for a bit, shan't you?" he asked. The girl did not answer.

"I don't see what else you can do," persisted Fred Henry.

"Go as a skivvy," Joe interpolated laconically.

The girl did not move a muscle.

"If I was her, I should go in for training for a nurse," said Malcolm, the youngest of them all. He was the baby of the family, a young man of twenty-two, with a fresh, jaunty *museau*.

But Mabel did not take any notice of him. They had talked at her and round her for so many years, that she hardly heard them at all.

The marble clock on the mantelpiece softly chimed the half-hour, the dog rose uneasily from the hearthrug and looked at the party at the breakfast table. But still they sat on in ineffectual conclave.

"Oh, all right," said Joe suddenly, apropos of nothing. "I'll get a move on."

He pushed back his chair, straddled his knees with a downward jerk, to get them free, in horsey fashion, and went to the fire. Still he did not go out of the room; he was curious to know what the others would do or say. He began to charge his pipe, looking down at the dog and saying, in a high, affected voice:

"Going wi' me? Going wi' me are ter? Tha'rt goin' further than tha counts on just now, dost hear?"

The dog faintly wagged its tail, the man stuck out his jaw and covered his pipe with his hands, and puffed intently, losing himself in the tobacco, looking down all the while at the dog with an absent brown eye. The dog looked up at him in mournful distrust. Joe stood with his knees stuck out, in real horsey fashion.

"Have you had a letter from Lucy?" Fred Henry asked of his sister.

"Last week," came the neutral reply.

"And what does she say?"

There was no answer.

"Does she *ask* you to go and stop there?" persisted Fred Henry.

"She says I can if I like."

"Well, then, you'd better. Tell her you'll come on Monday."

This was received in silence.

"That's what you'll do then, is it?" said Fred Henry, in some exasperation.

But she made no answer. There was a silence of futility and irritation in the room. Malcolm grinned fatuously.

"You'll have to make up your mind between now and next Wednesday," said Joe loudly, "or else find yourself lodgings on the kerbstone."

The face of the young woman darkened, but she sat on immutable.

"Here's Jack Fergusson!" exclaimed Malcolm, who was looking aimlessly out of the window.

"Where?" exclaimed Joe, loudly.

"Just gone past."

"Coming in?"

Malcolm craned his neck to see the gate.

"Yes," he said.

There was a silence. Mabel sat on like one condemned, at the head of the table. Then a whistle was heard from the kitchen. The dog got up and barked sharply. Joe opened the door and shouted:

"Come on."

After a moment a young man entered. He was muffled up in overcoat and a purple woollen scarf, and his tweed cap, which he did not remove, was pulled down on his head. He was of medium height, his face was rather long and pale, his eyes looked tired.

"Hello, Jack! Well, Jack!" exclaimed Malcolm and Joe. Fred Henry merely said, "Jack."

"What's doing?" asked the newcomer, evidently addressing Fred Henry.

"Same. We've got to be out by Wednesday. Got a cold?"

"I have—got it bad, too."

"Why don't you stop in?"

"*Me* stop in? When I can't stand on my legs, perhaps I shall have a chance." The young man spoke huskily. He had a slight Scotch accent.

"It's a knock-out, isn't it," said Joe, boisterously, "if a doctor goes round croaking with a cold. Looks bad for the patients, doesn't it?"

The young doctor looked at him slowly.

"Anything the matter with *you*, then?" he asked sarcastically.

"Not as I know of. Damn your eyes, I hope not. Why?"

"I thought you were very concerned about the patients, wondered if you might be one yourself."

"Damn it, no, I've never been patient to no flaming doctor, and hope I never shall be," returned Joe.

At this point Mabel rose from the table, and they all seemed to become aware of her existence. She began putting the dishes together. The young doctor looked at her, but did not address her. He had not greeted her. She went out of the room with the tray, her face impassive and unchanged.

"When are you off then, all of you?" asked the doctor.

"I'm catching the eleven-forty," replied Malcolm. "Are you goin' down wi' th' trap, Joe?"

"Yes, I've told you I'm going down wi' th' trap, haven't I?"

"We'd better be getting her in then. So long, Jack, if I don't see you before I go," said Malcolm, shaking hands.

He went out, followed by Joe, who seemed to have his tail between his legs.

"Well, this is the devil's own," exclaimed the doctor, when he was left alone with Fred Henry. "Going before Wednesday, are you?"

"That's the orders," replied the other.

"Where, to Northampton?"

"That's it."

"The devil!" exclaimed Fergusson, with quiet chagrin.

And there was silence between the two.

"All settled up, are you?" asked Fergusson.

"About."

There was another pause.

"Well, I shall miss yer, Freddy, boy," said the young doctor.

"And I shall miss thee, Jack," returned the other.

"Miss you like hell," mused the doctor.

Fred Henry turned aside. There was nothing to say. Mabel came in again, to finish clearing the table.

"What are *you* going to do, then, Miss Pervin?" asked Fergusson. "Going to your sister's, are you?"

Mabel looked at him with her steady, dangerous eyes, that always made him uncomfortable, unsettling his superficial ease.

"No," she said.

"Well, what in the name of fortune *are* you going to do? Say what you mean to do," cried Fred Henry, with futile intensity.

But she only averted her head, and continued her work. She folded the white table-cloth, and put on the chenille cloth.

"The sulkiest bitch that ever trod!" muttered her brother.

But she finished her task with perfectly impassive face, the young doctor watching her interestedly all the while. Then she went out.

Fred Henry stared after her, clenching his lips, his blue eyes fixing in sharp antagonism, as he made a grimace of sour exasperation.

"You could bray her into bits, and that's all you'd get out of her," he said, in a small, narrowed tone.

The doctor smiled faintly.

"What's she *going* to do, then?" he asked.

"Strike me if *I* know!" returned the other.

There was a pause. Then the doctor stirred.

"I'll be seeing you to-night, shall I?" he said to his friend.

"Ay—where's it to be? Are we going over to Jessdale?"

"I don't know. I've got such a cold on me. I'll come round to the Moon and Stars, anyway."

"Let Lizzie and May miss their night for once, eh?"

"That's it—if I feel as I do now."

"All's one——"

The two young men went through the passage and down to the back door together. The house was large, but it was servantless now, and desolate. At the back was a small bricked house-yard, and beyond that a big square, gravelled fine and red, and having stables on two sides. Sloping, dank, winter-dark fields stretched away on the open sides.

But the stables were empty. Joseph Pervin, the father of the family, had been a man of no education, who had become a fairly large horse dealer. The stables had been full of horses, there was a great turmoil and come-and-go of horses and of dealers and grooms. Then the kitchen was full of servants. But of late things had declined. The old man had married a second time, to retrieve his fortunes. Now he was dead and everything was gone to the dogs, there was nothing but debt and threatening.

For months, Mabel had been servantless in the big house, keeping the home together in penury for her ineffectual brothers. She had kept house for ten years. But previously it was with unstinted means. Then, however brutal and coarse everything was, the sense of money had kept her proud, confident. The men might be foul-mouthed, the women in the kitchen might have bad reputations, her brothers might have illegitimate children. But so long as there was money, the girl felt herself established, and brutally proud, reserved.

No company came to the house, save dealers and coarse men. Mabel had no associates of her own sex, after her sister went away. But she did not mind. She went regularly to church, she attended to her father. And she lived in the memory of her mother, who had died when she was fourteen, and whom she had loved. She had loved her father, too, in a different way, depending upon him, and feeling secure in him, until at the age of fifty-four he married again. And then she had set hard against him. Now he had died and left them all hopelessly in debt.

She had suffered badly during the period of poverty. Nothing, however, could shake the curious sullen, animal pride that dominated each member of the family. Now, for Mabel, the end had come. Still she would not cast about her. She would follow her own way just the same. She would always hold the keys of her own situation. Mindless and persistent, she endured from day to day. Why should she think? Why should she answer anybody? It was enough that this was the end, and there was no way out. She need not pass any more darkly along the main street of the small town, avoiding every eye. She need not demean herself any more, going into the shops and buying the cheapest food. This was at an end. She thought of nobody, not even of herself. Mindless and persistent, she seemed in a sort of ecstasy to be coming nearer to her fulfilment, her own glorification, approaching her dead mother, who was glorified.

In the afternoon she took a little bag, with shears and sponge and a small scrubbing brush, and went out. It was a grey, wintry day, with saddened, dark green fields and an atmosphere blackened by the smoke of foundries not far off. She went quickly, darkly along the causeway, heeding nobody, through the town to the churchyard.

There she always felt secure, as if no one could see her, although as a matter of fact she was exposed to the stare of every one who passed along under the churchyard wall. Nevertheless, once under the shadow of the great looming church, among the graves, she felt immune from the world, reserved within the thick churchyard wall as in another country.

Carefully she clipped the grass from the grave, and arranged the pinky white, small chrysanthemums in the tin cross. When this was done, she took an empty jar from a neighbouring grave, brought water, and carefully, most scrupulously sponged the marble headstone and the coping-stone.

It gave her sincere satisfaction to do this. She felt in immediate contact with the world of her mother. She took minute pains, went through the park in a state bordering on pure happiness, as if in performing this task she came into a subtle, intimate connection with her mother. For the life she followed here in the world was far less real than the world of death she inherited from her mother.

The doctor's house was just by the church. Fergusson, being a mere hired assistant, was slave to the country-side. As he hurried now to attend to the outpatients in the surgery, glancing across the graveyard with his quick eye, he saw the girl at her task at the grave. She seemed so intent and remote, it was like looking into another world. Some mystical element was touched in him. He slowed down as he walked, watching her as if spell-bound.

She lifted her eyes, feeling him looking. Their eyes met. And each looked again at once, each feeling, in some way, found out by the other. He lifted his cap and passed on down the road. There remained distinct in his consciousness, like a vision, the memory of her face, lifted from the tombstone in the churchyard, and looking at him with slow, large, portentous eyes. It *was* portentous, her face. It seemed to mesmerize him. There was a heavy power in her eyes which laid hold of his whole being, as if he had drunk some powerful drug. He had been feeling weak and done before. Now the life came back into him, he felt delivered from his own fretted, daily self.

He finished his duties at the surgery as quickly as might be, hastily filling up the bottles of the waiting people with cheap drugs. Then, in perpetual haste, he set off again to visit several cases in another part of his round, before teatime. At all times he preferred to walk if he could, but particularly when he was not well. He fancied the motion restored him.

The afternoon was falling. It was grey, deadened, and wintry, with a slow, moist, heavy coldness sinking in and deadening all the faculties. But why should he think or notice? He hastily climbed the hill and turned across the dark green fields, following the black cinder-track. In the distance, across a shallow dip in the country, the small town was clustered like smouldering ash, a tower, a spire, a heap of low, raw, extinct houses. And on the nearest fringe of the town, sloping into the dip, was Oldmeadow, the Pervins' house. He could see the stables and the outbuildings distinctly, as they lay towards him on the slope. Well, he would not go there many more times! Another resource would be lost to him, another place gone: the only company he cared for in the alien, ugly little town he was losing. Nothing but work, drudgery, constant hastening from dwelling to dwelling among the colliers and the iron-workers. It wore him out, but at the same time he had a craving for it. It was a stimulant to him to be in the homes of the working people, moving as it were through the innermost body of their life. His nerves were excited and gratified. He could come so near, into the very lives of the rough, inarticulate, powerfully emotional men and women. He grumbled, he said he hated the hellish hole. But as a matter of fact it excited him, the contact with the rough, strongly-feeling people was a stimulant applied direct to his nerves.

Below Oldmeadow, in the green, shallow, soddened hollow of fields, lay a square, deep pond. Roving across the landscape, the doctor's quick eye detected a figure in black passing through the gate of the field, down towards the pond. He looked again. It would be Mabel Pervin. His mind suddenly became alive and attentive.

Why was she going down there? He pulled up on the path on the slope above, and stood staring. He could just make sure of the small black figure moving in the hollow of the failing day. He seemed to see her in the midst of such obscurity, that he was like a clairvoyant, seeing rather with the mind's eye than with ordinary sight. Yet he could see her positively enough, whilst he kept his eye attentive. He felt, if he looked away from her, in the thick, ugly, falling dusk, he would lose her altogether.

He followed her minutely as she moved, direct and intent, like something transmitted rather than stirring in voluntary activity, straight down the field towards the pond. There she stood on the bank for a moment. She never raised her head. Then she waded slowly into the water.

He stood motionless as the small black figure walked slowly and deliberately towards the centre of the pond, very slowly, gradually moving deeper into the motionless water, and still moving forward as the water got up to her breast. Then he could see her no more in the dusk of the dead afternoon.

"There!" he exclaimed. "Would you believe it?"

And he hastened straight down, running over the wet, soddened fields, pushing through the hedges, down into the depression of callous wintry obscurity. It took him several minutes to come to the pond. He stood on the bank, breathing heavily. He could see nothing. His eyes seemed to penetrate the dead water. Yes, perhaps that was the dark shadow of her black clothing beneath the surface of the water.

He slowly ventured into the pond. The bottom was deep, soft clay, he sank in, and the water clasped dead cold round his legs. As he stirred he could smell the cold, rotten clay that fouled up into the water. It was objectionable in his lungs. Still, repelled and yet not heeding, he moved deeper into the pond. The cold water rose over his thighs, over his loins, upon his abdomen. The lower part of his body was all sunk in the hideous cold element. And the bottom was so deeply soft and uncertain, he was afraid of pitching with his mouth underneath. He could not swim, and was afraid.

He crouched a little, spreading his hands under the water and moving them round, trying to feel for her. The dead cold pond swayed upon his chest. He moved again, a little deeper, and again, with his hands underneath, he felt all around under the water. And he touched her clothing. But it evaded his fingers. He made a desperate effort to grasp it.

And so doing he lost his balance and went under, horribly, suffocating in the foul earthy water, struggling madly for a few moments. At last, after what seemed an eternity, he got his footing, rose again into the air and looked around. He gasped, and knew he was in the world. Then he looked at the water. She had risen near him. He grasped her clothing, and drawing her nearer, turned to take his way to land again.

He went very slowly, carefully, absorbed in the slow progress. He rose higher, climbing out of the pond. The water was now only about his legs; he was thankful, full of relief to be out of the clutches of the pond. He lifted her and staggered on to the bank, out of the horror of wet, grey clay.

He laid her down on the bank. She was quite unconscious and running with water. He made the water come from her mouth, he worked to restore her. He did not have to work very long before he could feel the breathing begin again in her; she was breathing naturally. He worked a little longer. He could feel her live beneath his hands; she was coming back. He wiped her face, wrapped her in his overcoat, looked round into the dim, dark grey world, then lifted her and staggered down the bank and across the fields.

It seemed an unthinkably long way, and his burden so heavy he felt he would never get to the house. But at last he was in the stable-yard, and then in the house-yard. He opened the door and went into the house. In the kitchen he laid her down on the hearthrug, and called. The house was empty. But the fire was burning in the grate.

Then again he kneeled to attend to her. She was breathing regularly, her eyes were wide open and as if conscious, but there seemed something missing in her look. She was conscious in herself, but unconscious of her surroundings.

He ran upstairs, took blankets from a bed, and put them before the fire to warm. Then he removed her saturated, earthy-smelling clothing, rubbed her dry with a towel, and wrapped her naked in the blankets. Then he went into the dining-room, to look for spirits. There was a little whisky. He drank a gulp himself, and put some into her mouth.

The effect was instantaneous. She looked full into his face, as if she had been seeing him for some time, and yet had only just become conscious of him.

"Dr. Fergusson?" she said.

"What?" he answered.

He was divesting himself of his coat, intending to find some dry clothing upstairs. He could not bear the smell of the dead, clayey water, and he was mortally afraid for his own health.

"What did I do?" she asked.

"Walked into the pond," he replied. He had begun to shudder like one sick, and could hardly attend to her. Her eyes remained full on him, he seemed to be going dark in his mind, looking back at her helplessly. The shuddering became quieter in him, his life came back in him, dark and unknowing, but strong again.

"Was I out of my mind?" she asked, while her eyes were fixed on him all the time.

"Maybe, for the moment," he replied. He felt quiet, because his strength had come back. The strange fretful strain had left him.

"Am I out of my mind now?" she asked.

"Are you?" he reflected a moment. "No," he answered truthfully, "I don't see that you are." He turned his face aside. He was afraid now, because he felt dazed, and felt dimly that her power was stronger than his, in this issue. And she continued to look at him fixedly all the time. "Can you tell me where I shall find some dry things to put on?" he asked.

"Did you dive into the pond for me?" she asked.

"No," he answered. "I walked in. But I went in overhead as well."

There was silence for a moment. He hesitated. He very much wanted to go upstairs to get into dry clothing. But there was another desire in him. And she seemed to hold him. His will seemed to have gone to sleep, and left him, standing there slack before her. But he felt warm inside himself. He did not shudder at all, though his clothes were sodden on him.

"Why did you?" she asked.

"Because I didn't want you to do such a foolish thing," he said.

"It wasn't foolish," she said, still gazing at him as she lay on the floor, with a sofa cushion under her head. "It was the right thing to do. *I* knew best, then."

"I'll go and shift these wet things," he said. But still he had not the power to move out of her presence, until she sent him. It was as if she had the life of his body in her hands, and he could not extricate himself. Or perhaps he did not want to.

Suddenly she sat up. Then she became aware of her own immediate condition. She felt the blankets about her, she knew her own limbs. For a moment it seemed as if her reason were going. She looked round, with wild eye, as if seeking something. He stood still with fear. She saw her clothing lying scattered.

"Who undressed me?" she asked, her eyes resting full and inevitable on his face.

"I did," he replied, "to bring you round."

For some moments she sat and gazed at him awfully, her lips parted.

"Do you love me, then?" she asked.

He only stood and stared at her, fascinated. His soul seemed to melt. She shuffled forward on her knees, and put her arms round him, round his legs, as he stood there, pressing her breasts against his knees and thighs, clutching him with strange, convulsive certainty, pressing his thighs against her, drawing him to her face, her throat, as she looked up at him with flaring, humble eyes of transfiguration, triumphant in first possession. "You love me," she murmured, in strange transport, yearning and triumphant and confident. "You love me. I know you love me, I know."

And she was passionately kissing his knees, through the wet clothing, passionately and indiscriminately kissing his knees, his legs, as if unaware of everything.

He looked down at the tangled wet hair, the wild, bare, animal shoulders. He was amazed, bewildered, and afraid. He had never thought of loving her. He had never wanted to love her. When he rescued her and restored her, he was a doctor, and she was a patient. He had had no single personal thought of her. Nay, this introduction of the personal element was very distasteful to him, a violation of his professional honour. It was horrible to have her there embracing his knees. It was horrible. He revolted from it, violently. And yet—and yet—he had not the power to break away.

She looked at him again, with the same supplication of powerful love, and that same transcendent, frightening light of triumph. In view of the delicate flame which seemed to come from her face like a light, he was powerless. And yet he had never intended to love her. He had never intended. And something stubborn in him could not give way.

"You love me," she repeated, in a murmur of deep, rhapsodic assurance. "You love me."

Her hands were drawing him, drawing him down to her. He was afraid, even a little horrified. For he had, really, no intention of loving her. Yet her hands were drawing him towards her. He put out his hand quickly to steady himself, and grasped her bare shoulder. A flame seemed to burn the hand that grasped her soft shoulder. He had no intention of loving her: his whole will was against his yielding. It was horrible. And yet wonderful was the touch of her shoulders, beautiful the shining of her face. Was she perhaps mad? He had a horror of yielding to her. Yet something in him ached also.

He had been staring away at the door, away from her. But his hand remained on her shoulder. She had gone suddenly very still. He looked down at her. Her eyes were now wide with fear, with doubt, the light was dying from her face, a shadow of terrible greyness was returning. He could not bear the touch of her eyes' question upon him, and the look of death behind the question.

With an inward groan he gave way, and let his heart yield towards her. A sudden gentle smile came on his face. And her eyes, which never left his face, slowly, slowly filled with tears. He watched the strange water rise in her eyes, like some slow fountain coming up. And his heart seemed to burn and melt away in his breast.

He could not bear to look at her any more. He dropped on his knees and caught her head with his arms and pressed her face against his throat. She was very still. His heart, which seemed to have broken, was burning with a kind of agony in his breast. And he felt her slow, hot tears wetting his throat. But he could not move.

He felt the hot tears wet his neck and the hollows of his neck, and he remained motionless, suspended through one of man's eternities. Only now it had become indispensable to him to have her face pressed close to him; he could never let her go again. He could never let her head go away from the close clutch of his arm. He wanted to remain like that for ever, with his heart hurting him in a pain that was also life to him. Without knowing, he was looking down on her damp, soft brown hair.

Then, as it were suddenly, he smelt the horrid stagnant smell of that water. And at the same moment she drew away from him and looked at him. Her eyes were wistful and unfathomable. He was afraid of them, and he fell to kissing her, not knowing what he was doing. He wanted her eyes not to have that terrible, wistful, unfathomable look.

When she turned her face to him again, a faint delicate flush was glowing, and there was again dawning that terrible shining of joy in her eyes, which really terrified him, and yet which he now wanted to see, because he feared the look of doubt still more.

"You love me?" she said, rather faltering.

"Yes." The word cost him a painful effort. Not because it wasn't true. But because it was too newly true, the *saying* seemed to tear open again his newly-torn heart. And he hardly wanted it to be true, even now.

She lifted her face to him, and he bent forward and kissed her on the mouth, gently, with the one kiss that is an eternal pledge. And as he kissed her his heart strained again in his breast. He never intended to love her.

But now it was over. He had crossed over the gulf to her, and all that he had left behind had shrivelled and become void.

After the kiss, her eyes again slowly filled with tears. She sat still, away from him, with her face drooped aside, and her hands folded in her lap. The tears fell very slowly. There was complete silence. He too sat there motionless and silent on the hearthrug. The strange pain of his heart that was broken seemed to consume him. That he should love her? That this was love! That he should be ripped open in this way! Him, a doctor! How they would all jeer if they knew! It was agony to him to think they might know.

In the curious naked pain of the thought he looked again to her. She was sitting there drooped into a muse. He saw a tear fall, and his heart flared hot. He saw for the first time that one of her shoulders was quite uncovered, one arm bare, he could see one of her small breasts; dimly, because it had become almost dark in the room.

"Why are you crying?" he asked, in an altered voice.

She looked up at him, and behind her tears the consciousness of her situation for the first time brought a dark look of shame to her eyes.

"I'm not crying, really," she said, watching him half frightened.

He reached his hand, and softly closed it on her bare arm.

"I love you! I love you!" he said in a soft, low vibrating voice, unlike himself.

She shrank, and dropped her head. The soft, penetrating grip of his hand on her arm distressed her. She looked up at him.

"I want to go," she said. "I want to go and get you some dry things."

"Why?" he said. "I'm all right."

"But I want to go," she said. "And I want you to change your things."

He released her arm, and she wrapped herself in the blanket, looking at him rather frightened. And still she did not rise.

"Kiss me," she said wistfully.

He kissed her, but briefly, half in anger.

Then, after a second, she rose nervously, all mixed up in the blanket. He watched her in her confusion, as she tried to extricate herself and wrap herself up so that she could walk. He watched her relentlessly, as she knew. And as she went, the blanket trailing, and as he saw a glimpse of her feet and her white leg, he tried to remember her as she was when he had wrapped her in the blanket. But then he didn't want to remember, because she had been nothing to him then, and his nature revolted from remembering her as she was when she was nothing to him.

A tumbling, muffled noise from within the dark house startled him. Then he heard her voice:—"There are clothes." He rose and went to the foot of the stairs, and gathered up the garments she had thrown down. Then he came back to the fire, to rub himself down and dress. He grinned at his own appearance when he had finished.

The fire was sinking, so he put on coal. The house was now quite dark, save for the light of a street-lamp that shone in faintly from beyond the holly trees. He lit the gas with matches he found on the mantelpiece. Then he emptied the pockets of his own clothes, and threw all his wet things in a heap into the scullery. After which he gathered up her sodden clothes, gently, and put them in a separate heap on the copper-top in the scullery.

It was six o'clock on the clock. His own watch had stopped. He ought to go back to the surgery. He waited, and still she did not come down. So he went to the foot of the stairs and called:

"I shall have to go."

Almost immediately he heard her coming down. She had on her best dress of black voile, and her hair was tidy, but still damp. She looked at him—and in spite of herself, smiled.

"I don't like you in those clothes," she said.

"Do I look a sight?" he answered.

They were shy of one another.

"I'll make you some tea," she said.

"No, I must go."

"Must you?" And she looked at him again with the wide, strained, doubtful eyes. And again, from the pain of his breast, he knew how he loved her. He went and bent to kiss her, gently, passionately, with his heart's painful kiss.

"And my hair smells so horrible," she murmured in distraction. "And I'm so awful, I'm so awful! Oh, no, I'm too awful." And she broke into bitter, heart-broken sobbing. "You can't want to love me, I'm horrible."

"Don't be silly, don't be silly," he said, trying to comfort her, kissing her, holding her in his arms. "I want you, I want to marry you, we're going to be married, quickly, quickly—to-morrow if I can."

But she only sobbed terribly, and cried:

"I feel awful. I feel awful. I feel I'm horrible to you."

"No, I want you, I want you," was all he answered, blindly, with that terrible intonation which frightened her almost more than her horror lest he should *not* want her.

QUESTIONS AND TOPICS

1. Analyze Mabel—her appearance, her character, her actions. What kind of men are her brothers? How do they set off her character? Analyze the doctor also.
2. What is the significance of death in the story? Of the pond? Why is Mabel frightened at the end of the story, and what is the significance of the doctor's "terrible intonation"?
3. What is Lawrence saying about sex and the relationship between man and woman? Do you agree? Compare Lawrence's philosophy of sex with that of Dr. Clendening. How would Lawrence analyze Maugham's short story?
4. What might Lawrence say about the treatment of sex on television? In the movies or in recent fiction?
5. Write a sketch or short story describing Jack and Mabel the next day, or shortly after their marriage, or five years thereafter.
6. You might read Lawrence's essay, "Benjamin Franklin," in *Studies in Classic American Literature* and compare the theme of "The Horse-Dealer's Daughter" with the philosophy expressed in the essay.

7

ALTERNATE SOCIETIES

FROM EARLIEST TIMES men have envisioned societies radically different from their own. Mythologies often have their foundations in man's dream of a better world. Places such as the Garden of Eden and Paradise are important in religions both inside and outside the Judaeo-Christian heritage. Even Homer's Olympians, though they quarrel like mortals, exist in a kind of paradise: their passions are real, but they have escaped mortality and its inevitable sadness.

The science of anthropology, though designed to produce no such result, revitalized man's capacity for dreaming. Anthropologists did not speculate, like Swift, about possible Houyhnhnmlands; they described actual societies very different from those of Western civilization, and they described them without condescension. Their work led men to wonder what life is like in Tahiti, where sexual mores are different from ours. Or among the Arapesh of New Guinea, who have practiced communism for centuries without having heard of Marx.

Many authors have written works on what they suppose would be an ideal community. The nature of each man's utopia tells us a great deal about his convictions and commitments. Some feel that in order to create an ideal society in the United States, the historical clock would have to be turned back. Albert Jay Nock, for instance, leaves us with the impression that a simple, agrarian society, based on strong religious conviction, will most satisfy man's desire for happiness. Others, like B. F. Skinner, dream of creating communities in which all traditional ties are broken, even the institution of the family. Some men's utopias are anarchistic: in such societies pleasure and freedom replace duty and loyalty as primary values. Other utopias are socialist in nature: the absence of private property is their most distinguishing feature.

In other words, almost everyone wants a perfectly happy society. But few can agree on the means to achieve happiness.

Ruth Benedict

THE DIVERSITY OF CULTURES

The following essay is taken from Ruth Benedict's famous book Patterns of Culture, 1934. *Miss Benedict, 1887–1948, sought to bring to the layman the basic concepts of anthropology. According to Miss Benedict, no two cultures are alike or should be. She de-emphasizes the force of "human nature," and feels that most societies, through custom and tradition, shape the type of "human nature" they wish to see perpetuated.*

A chief of the Digger Indians, as the Californians call them, talked to me a great deal about the ways of his people in the old days. He was a Christian and a leader among his people in the planting of peaches and apricots on irrigated land, but when he talked of the shamans who had transformed themselves into bears before his eyes in the bear dance, his hands trembled and his voice broke with excitement. It was an incomparable thing, the power his people had had in the old days. He liked best to talk of the desert foods they had eaten. He brought each uprooted plant lovingly and with an unfailing sense of its importance. In those days his people had eaten 'the health of the desert,' he said, and knew nothing of the insides of tin cans and the things for sale at butcher shops. It was such innovations that had degraded them in these latter days.

One day, without transition, Ramon broke in upon his descriptions of grinding mesquite and preparing acorn soup. 'In the beginning,' he said, 'God gave to every people a cup, a cup of clay, and from this cup they drank their life.' I do not know whether the figure occurred in some traditional ritual of his people that I never found, or whether it was his own imagery. It is hard to imagine that he had heard it from the whites he had known at Banning; they were not given to discussing the ethos of different peoples. At any rate, in the mind of this humble Indian the figure of speech was clear and full of meaning. 'They all dipped in the water,' he continued, 'but their cups were different. Our cup is broken now. It has passed away.'

Our cup is broken. Those things that had given significance to the life of his people, the domestic rituals of eating, the obligations of the economic system, the succession of ceremonials in the villages, possession in the bear dance, their standards of right and wrong—these were gone, and with them the shape and meaning of their life. The old man was still vigorous and a leader in relationships with the whites. He did not mean that there was any question of the extinction of his people. But he had in mind the loss of something that had value equal to that of life itself, the whole fabric of his people's standards and beliefs. There were other cups of living left, and they held perhaps the same water, but the loss was irreparable. It was no matter of tinkering with an addition here, lopping off something there. The modelling had been fundamental, it was somehow all of a piece. It had been their own.

Ramon had had personal experience of the matter of which he spoke. He straddled two cultures whose values and ways of thought were incommensurable. It is a hard fate. In Western civilization our experiences have been different. We are bred to one cosmopolitan culture, and our social sciences, our psychology, and our theology persistently ignore the truth expressed in Ramon's figure.

The course of life and the pressure of environment, not to speak of the fertility of human imagination, provide an incredible number of possible leads, all of which, it appears, may serve a society to live by. There are the schemes of ownership, with the social hierarchy that may be associated with possessions; there are material things and their elaborate technology; there are all the facets of sex life, parenthood and post-parenthood; there are the guilds or cults which may give structure to the society; there is economic exchange; there are the gods and supernatural sanctions. Each one of these and many more may be followed out with a cultural and ceremonial elaboration which monopolizes the cultural energy and leaves small surplus for the building of other traits. Aspects of life that seem to us most important have been passed over with small regard by peoples whose culture, oriented in another direction, has been far from poor. Or the same trait may be so greatly elaborated that we reckon it as fantastic. It is in cultural life as it is in speech; selection is the prime necessity. The numbers of sounds that can be produced by our vocal cords and our oral and nasal cavities are practically unlimited. The three or four dozen of the English language are a selection which coincides not even with those of such closely related dialects as German and French. The total that are used in different languages of the world no one has even dared to estimate. But each language must make its selection and abide by it on pain of not being intelligible at all. A language that used even a few hundreds of the possible—and actually recorded—phonetic elements could not be used for communication. On the other hand a great deal of our misunderstanding of languages unrelated to our own has arisen from our attempts to refer alien phonetic systems back to ours as a point of reference. We recognize only one *k*. If other people have five *k* sounds placed in different positions in the throat and mouth, distinctions of vocabulary and of syntax that depend on these differences are impossible to us until we master them. We have a *d* and an *n*. They may have an intermediate sound which, if we fail to identify it, we write now *d* and now *n,* introducing distinctions which do not exist. The elementary prerequisite of linguistic analysis is a consciousness of these incredibly numerous available sounds from which each language makes its own selections.

In culture too we must imagine a great arc on which are ranged the possible interests provided either by the human age-cycle or by the environment or by man's various activities. A culture that capitalized even a considerable proportion of these would be as unintelligible as a language that used all the clicks, all the glottal stops, all the labials, dentals, sibilants, and gutturals from voiceless to voiced and from oral to nasal. Its identity as a culture depends upon the selection of some segments of this arc. Every human society everywhere has made such selection in its cultural institutions. Each from the point of view of another ignores fundamentals and exploits irrelevancies. One culture hardly recognizes monetary values; another has made them fundamental in every field of behaviour. In one society technology is unbelievably slighted even in those aspects of life which seem necessary to ensure survival; in another, equally simple, technological achievements are complex and fitted with admirable nicety to the situation. One builds an enormous cultural superstructure upon adolescence, one upon death, one upon after-life.

The case of adolescence is particularly interesting, because it is in the limelight in our own civilization and because we have plentiful information from other cultures. In our own civilization a whole library of psychological studies has emphasized the inevitable unrest of the period of puberty. It is in our tradition a physiological state as definitely characterized by domestic explosions and rebellion as typhoid is marked by fever. There is no question of the facts. They are common in America. The question is rather of their inevitability.

The most casual survey of the ways in which different societies have handled adolescence makes one fact inescapable: even in those cultures which have made most of the trait, the age upon which they focus their attention varies over a great range of years. At the outset, therefore, it is clear that the so-called puberty institutions are a misnomer if we continue to think of biological puberty. The puberty they recognize is social, and the ceremonies are a recognition in some fashion or other of the child's new status of adulthood. This investiture with new occupations and obligations is in consequence as various and as culturally conditioned as the occupations and obligations themselves. If the sole honourable duty of manhood is conceived to be deeds of war, the investiture of the warrior is later and of a different sort from that in a society where adulthood gives chiefly the privilege of dancing in a representation of masked gods. In order to understand puberty institutions, we do not most need analyses of the necessary nature of *rites de passage;* we need rather to know what is identified in different cultures with the beginning of adulthood and their methods of admitting to the new status. Not biological puberty, but what adulthood means in that culture conditions the puberty ceremony.

Adulthood in central North America means warfare. Honour in it is the great goal of all men. The constantly recurring theme of the youth's coming-of-age, as also of preparation for the warpath at any age, is a magic ritual for success in war. They torture not one another, but themselves: they cut strips of skin from their arms and legs, they strike off their fingers, they drag heavy weights pinned to their chest or leg muscles. Their reward is enhanced prowess in deeds of warfare.

In Australia, on the other hand, adulthood means participation in an exclusively male cult whose fundamental trait is the exclusion of women.

Any woman is put to death if she so much as hears the sound of the bull-roarer at the ceremonies, and she must never know of the rites. Puberty ceremonies are elaborate and symbolic repudiations of the bonds with the female sex; the men are symbolically made self-sufficient and the wholly responsible element of the community. To attain this end they use drastic sexual rites and bestow supernatural guaranties.

The clear physiological facts of adolescence, therefore, are first socially interpreted even where they are stressed. But a survey of puberty institutions makes clear a further fact: puberty is physiologically a different matter in the life-cycle of the male and the female. If cultural emphasis followed the physiological emphasis, girls' ceremonies would be more marked than boys'; but it is not so. The ceremonies emphasize a social fact: the adult prerogatives of men are more far-reaching in every culture than women's, and consequently, as in the above instances, it is more common for societies to take note of this period in boys than in girls.

Girls' and boys' puberty, however, may be socially celebrated in the same tribe in identical ways. Where, as in the interior of British Columbia, adolescent rites are a magical training for all occupations, girls are included on the same terms as boys. Boys roll stones down mountains and beat them to the bottom to be swift of foot, or throw gambling-sticks to be lucky in gambling; girls carry water from distant springs, or drop stones down inside their dresses that their children may be born as easily as the pebble drops to the ground.

In such a tribe as the Nandi of the lake region of East Africa, also, girls and boys share an even-handed puberty rite, though, because of the man's dominant rôle in the culture, his boyhood training period is more stressed than the woman's. Here adolescent rites are an ordeal inflicted by those already admitted to adult status upon those they are now forced to admit. They require of them the most complete stoicism in the face of ingenious tortures associated with circumcision. The rites for the two sexes are separate, but they follow the same pattern. In both the novices wear for the ceremony the clothing of their sweethearts. During the operation their faces are watched for any twinge of pain, and the reward of bravery is given with great rejoicing by the lover, who runs forward to receive back some of his adornments. For both the girl and the boy the rites mark their *entrée* into a new sex status: the boy is now a warrior and may take a sweetheart, the girl is marriageable. The adolescent tests are for both a pre-marital ordeal in which the palm is awarded by their lovers.

Puberty rites may also be built upon the facts of girls' puberty and admit of no extension to boys. One of the most naïve of these is the institution of the fatting-house for girls in central Africa. In the region where feminine beauty is all but identified with obesity, the girl at puberty is segregated, sometimes for years, fed with sweet and fatty foods, allowed no activity, and her body rubbed assiduously with oils. She is taught during this time her future duties, and her seclusion ends with a parade of her corpulence that is followed by her marriage to her proud bridegroom. It is not regarded as necessary for the man to achieve pulchritude before marriage in a similar fashion.

The usual ideas around which girls' puberty institutions are centred, and which are not readily extended to boys', are those concerned with menstruation. The uncleanness of the menstruating woman is a very widespread idea, and in a few regions first menstruation has been made the focus of all the associated attitudes. Puberty rites in these cases are of a thoroughly different character from any of which we have spoken. Among the Carrier Indians of British Columbia, the fear and horror of a girl's puberty was at its height. Her three or four years of seclusion was called 'the burying alive,' and she lived for all that time alone in the wilderness, in a hut of branches far from all beaten trails. She was a threat to any person who might so much as catch a glimpse of her, and her mere footstep defiled a path or a river. She was covered with a great headdress of tanned skin that shrouded her face and breasts and fell to the ground behind. Her arms and legs were loaded with sinew bands to protect her from the evil spirit with which she was filled. She was herself in danger and she was a source of danger to everybody else.

Girls' puberty ceremonies built upon ideas associated with the menses are readily convertible into what is, from the point of view of the individual concerned, exactly opposite behaviour. There are always two possible aspects to the sacred: it may be a source of peril or it may be a source of blessing. In some tribes the first menses of girls are a potent supernatural blessing. Among the Apaches I have seen the priests themselves pass on their knees before the row of solemn little girls to receive from them the blessing of their touch. All the babies and the old people come also of necessity to have illness removed from them. The adolescent girls are not segregated as sources of danger, but court is paid to them as to direct sources of supernatural blessing. Since the ideas that underlie puberty rites for girls, both among the Carrier and among the Apache, are founded on beliefs concerning menstruation, they are not extended to boys, and boys' puberty is marked instead, and lightly, with simple tests and proofs of manhood.

The adolescent behaviour, therefore, even of girls was not dictated by some physiological characteristic of the period itself, but rather by marital or magic requirements socially connected with it. These beliefs made adolescence in one tribe serenely religious and beneficent, and in another so dangerously unclean that the child had to cry out in warning that others might avoid her in the woods. The adolescence of girls may equally, as we have seen, be a theme which a culture does not institutionalize. Even where, as in most of Australia, boys' adolescence is given elaborate treatment, it may be that the rites are an induction into the status of manhood and male participation in tribal matters, and female adolescence passes without any kind of formal recognition.

These facts, however, still leave the fundamental question unanswered. Do not all cultures have to cope with the natural turbulence of this period, even though it may not be given institutional expression? Dr. Mead has studied this question in Samoa. There the girl's life passes through well-marked periods. Her first years out of babyhood are passed in small neighbourhood gangs of age mates from which the little boys are strictly excluded. The corner of the village to which she belongs is all-important, and the little boys are traditional enemies. She has one duty, that of baby-tending, but she takes the baby with her rather than stays home to mind it, and her play is not seriously hampered. A couple of years before puberty, when she grows strong enough to have more difficult tasks required of her and old enough to learn more skilled techniques, the little girls' play group in which she grew up ceases to exist. She assumes woman's dress and must contribute to the work of the household. It is an uninteresting period of life to her and quite without turmoil. Puberty brings no change at all.

A few years after she has come of age, she will begin the pleasant years of casual and irresponsible love affairs that she will prolong as far as possible into the period when marriage is already considered fitting. Puberty itself is marked by no social recognition, no change of attitude or of expectancy. Her pre-adolescent shyness is supposed to remain unchanged for a couple of years. The girl's life in Samoa is blocked out by other considerations than those of physiological sex maturity, and puberty falls in a particularly unstressed and peaceful period during which no adolescent conflicts manifest themselves. Adolescence, therefore, may not only be culturally passed over without ceremonial; it may also be without importance in the emotional life of the child and in the attitude of the village toward her.

Warfare is another social theme that may or may not be used in any culture. Where war is made much of, it may be with contrasting objectives, with contrasting organization in relation to the state, and with contrasting sanctions. War may be, as it was among the Aztecs, a way of getting captives for the religious sacrifices. Since the Spaniards fought to kill, according to Aztec standards they broke the rules of the game. The Aztecs fell back in dismay and Cortez walked as victor into the capital.

There are even quainter notions, from our standpoint, associated with warfare in different parts of the world. For our purposes it is sufficient to notice those regions where organized resort to mutual slaughter never occurs between social groups. Only our familiarity with war makes it intelligible that a state of warfare should alternate with a state of peace in one tribe's dealings with another. The idea is quite common over the world, of course. But on the one hand it is impossible for certain peoples to conceive the possibility of a state of peace, which in their notion would be equivalent to admitting enemy tribes to the category of human beings, which by definition they are not even though the excluded tribe may be of their own race and culture.

On the other hand, it may be just as impossible for a people to conceive of the possibility of a state of war. Rasmussen tells of the blankness with which the Eskimo met his exposition of our custom. Eskimos very well understand the act of killing a man. If he is in your way, you cast up your estimate of your own strength, and if you are ready to take it upon yourself, you kill him. If you are strong, there is no social retribution. But the idea of an Eskimo village going out against another Eskimo village in battle array or a tribe against a tribe, or even of another village being fair game in ambush warfare, is alien to them. All killing comes under one head, and is not separated, as ours is, into categories, the one meritorious, the other a capital offence.

I myself tried to talk of warfare to the Mission Indian of California, but it was impossible. Their misunderstanding of warfare was abysmal. They did not have the basis in their own culture upon which the idea could exist, and their attempts to reason it out reduced the great wars to which we are able to dedicate ourselves with moral fervour to the level of alley brawls. They did not happen to have a cultural pattern that distinguished between them.

War is, we have been forced to admit even in the face of its huge place in our own civilization, an asocial trait. In the chaos following the World War all the wartime arguments that expounded its fostering of courage, of altruism, of spiritual values, give out a false and offensive ring. War in our own civilization is as good an illustration as one can take of the destructive lengths to which the development of a culturally selected trait may go. If we justify war, it is because all peoples always justify the traits of which they find themselves possessed, not because war will bear an objective examination of its merits.

Warfare is not an isolated case. From every part of the world and from all levels of cultural complexity it is possible to illustrate the overweening and finally often the asocial elaboration of a cultural trait. Those cases are clearest where, as in dietary or mating regulations, for example, traditional usage runs counter to biological drives. Social organization, in anthropology, has a quite specialized meaning owing to the unanimity of all human societies in stressing relationship groups within which marriage is forbidden. No known people regard all women as possible mates. This is not in an effort, as is so often supposed, to prevent inbreeding in our sense, for over great parts of the world it is an own cousin, often the daughter of one's mother's brother, who is the predestined spouse. The relatives to whom the prohibition refers differ utterly among different peoples, but all human societies are alike in placing a restriction. No human idea has received more constant and complex elaboration in culture than this of incest. The incest groups are often the most important functioning units of the tribe, and the duties of every individual in relation to any other are defined by their relative positions in these groups. These groups function as units in religious ceremonials and in cycles of economic exchange, and it is impossible to exaggerate the importance of the rôle they have played in social history.

Some areas handle the incest tabu with moderation. In spite of the restrictions there may be a considerable number of women available for a man to marry. In others the group that is tabu has been extended by a social fiction to include vast numbers of individuals who have no traceable ancestors in common, and choice of a mate is in consequence excessively limited. This social fiction receives unequivocal expression in the terms of relationship which are used. Instead of distinguishing lineal from collateral kin as we do in the distinction between father and uncle, brother and cousin, one term means literally 'man of my father's group (relationship, locality, etc.) of his generation,' not distinguishing between direct and collateral lines, but making other distinctions that are foreign to us. Certain tribes of eastern Australia use an extreme form of this so-called classificatory kinship system. Those whom they call brothers and sisters are all those of their generation with whom they recognize any relationship. There is no cousin category or anything that corresponds to it; all relatives of one's own generation are one's brothers and sisters.

This manner of reckoning relationship is not uncommon in the world, but Australia has in addition an unparalleled horror of sister marriage and an unparalleled development of exogamous restrictions. So the Kurnai, with their extreme classificatory relationship system, feel the Australian horror of sex relationship with all their 'sisters,' that is, women of their own generation who are in any way related to them. Besides this, the Kurnai have strict locality rules in the choice of a mate. Sometimes two localities, out of the fifteen or sixteen of which the tribe is composed, must exchange women, and can have no mates in any other group. Sometimes there is a group of two or three localities that may exchange with two or three others. Still further, as in all Australia, the old men are a privileged group, and their prerogatives extend to marrying the young and attractive girls. The consequence of these rules is, of course, that in all the local group which must by absolute prescription furnish a young man with his wife, there is no girl who is not touched by one of these tabus. Either she is one of those who through relationship with his mother is his 'sister,' or she is already bargained for by an old man, or for some lesser reason she is forbidden to him.

That does not bring the Kurnai to reformulate their exogamous rules. They insist upon them with every show of violence. Therefore, the only way they are usually able to marry is by flying violently in the face of the regulations. They elope. As soon as the village knows that an elopement has occurred, it sets out in pursuit, and if the couple are caught the two are killed. It does not matter that possibly all of the pursuers were married by elopement in the same fashion. Moral indignation runs high. There is, however, an island traditionally recognized as a safe haven, and if the couple can reach it and remain away till the birth of a child, they are received again with blows, it is true, but they may defend themselves. After they have run the gauntlet and been given their drubbing, they take up the status of married people in the tribe.

The Kurnai meet their cultural dilemma typically enough. They have extended and complicated a particular aspect of behaviour until it is a social liability. They must either modify it, or get by with a subterfuge. And they use the subterfuge. They avoid extinction, and they maintain their ethics without acknowledged revision. This manner of dealing with the *mores* has lost nothing in the progress of civilization. The older generation of our own civilization similarly maintained monogamy and supported prostitution, and the panegyrics of monogamy were never so fervent as in the great days of the red-light districts. Societies have always justified favourite traditional forms. When these traits get out of hand and some form of supplementary behaviour is called in, lip service is given as readily to the traditional form as if the supplementary behaviour did not exist.

Such a bird's-eye survey of human cultural forms makes clear several common misconceptions. In the first place, the institutions that human cultures build up upon the hints presented by the environment or by man's physical necessities do not keep as close to the original impulse as we easily imagine. These hints are, in reality, mere rough sketches, a list of bare facts. They are pin-point potentialities, and the elaboration that takes place around them is dictated by many alien considerations. Warfare is not the expression of the instinct of pugnacity. Man's pugnacity is so small a hint in the human equipment that it may not be given any expression in inter-tribal relations. When it is institutionalized, the form it takes follows other grooves of thought than those implied in the original impulse. Pugnacity is no more than the touch to the ball of custom, a touch also that may be withheld.

Such a view of cultural processes calls for a recasting of many of our current arguments upholding our traditional institutions. These arguments are usually based on the impossibility of man's functioning without these particular traditional forms. Even very special traits come in for this kind of validation, such as the particular form of economic drive that arises under our particular system of property ownership. This is a remarkably special motivation and there are evidences that even in our generation it is being strongly modified. At any rate, we do not have to confuse the issue by discussing it as if it were a matter of biological survival values. Self-support is a motive our civilization has capitalized. If our economic structure changes so that this motive is no longer so potent a drive as it was in the era of the great frontier and expanding industrialism, there are many other motives that would be appropriate to a changed economic organization. Every culture, every era, exploits some few out of a great number of possibilities. Changes may be very disquieting, and involve great losses, but this is due to the difficulty of change itself, not to the fact that our age and country has hit upon the one possible motivation under which human life can be conducted. Change, we must remember, with all its difficulties, is inescapable. Our fears over even very minor shifts in custom are usually quite beside the point. Civilizations might change far more radically than any human authority has ever had the will or the imagination to change them, and still be completely workable. The minor changes that occasion so much denunciation today, such as the increase of divorce, the growing secularization in our cities, the prevalence of the petting party, and many more, could be taken up quite readily into a slightly different pattern of culture. Becoming traditional, they would be given the same richness of content, the same importance and value, that the older patterns had in other generations.

The truth of the matter is rather that the possible human institutions and motives are legion, on every plane of cultural simplicity or complexity, and that wisdom consists in a greatly increased tolerance toward their divergencies. No man can thoroughly participate in any culture unless he has been brought up and has lived according to its forms, but he can grant to other cultures the same significance to their participants which he recognizes in his own.

II

The diversity of culture results not only from the ease with which societies elaborate or reject possible aspects of existence. It is due even more to a complex interweaving of cultural traits. The final form of any traditional institution, as we have just said, goes far beyond the original human impulse. In great measure this final form depends upon the way in which the trait has merged with other traits from different fields of experience.

A widespread trait may be saturated with religious beliefs among one people and function as an important aspect of their religion. In another area it may be wholly a matter of economic transfer and be therefore an aspect of their monetary arrangements. The possibilities are endless and the adjustments are often bizarre. The nature of the trait will be quite different in the different areas according to the elements with which it has combined.

It is important to make this process clear to ourselves because otherwise we fall easily into the temptation to generalize into a sociological law the results of a local merging of traits, or we assume their union to be a universal phenomenon. The great period of European plastic art was religiously motivated. Art pictured and made common property the religious scenes and dogmas which were fundamental in the outlook of that period. Modern European æsthetics would have been quite different if mediæval art had been purely decorative and had not made common cause with religion.

As a matter of history great developments in art have often been re-markably separate from religious motivation and use. Art may be kept definitely apart from religion even where both are highly developed. In the pueblos of the Southwest of the United States, art-forms in pottery and textiles command the respect of the artist in any culture, but their sacred bowls carried by the priests or set out on the altars are shoddy and the decorations crude and unstylized. Museums have been known to throw out Southwest religious objects because they were so far below the traditional standard of workmanship. 'We have to put a frog there,' the Zuñi Indians say, meaning that the religious exigencies eliminate any need of artistry. This separation between art and religion is not a unique trait of the Pueblos. Tribes of South America and of Siberia make the same distinction, though they motivate it in various ways. They do not use their artistic skill in the service of religion. Instead, therefore, of finding the sources of art in a locally important subject matter, religion, as older critics of art have sometimes done, we need rather to explore the extent to which these two can mutually interpenetrate, and the consequences of such merging for both art and religion.

The interpenetration of different fields of experience, and the consequent modification of both of them, can be shown from all phases of existence: economics, sex relations, folklore, material culture, and religion. The process can be illustrated in one of the widespread religious traits of the North American Indians. Up and down the continent, in every culture area except that of the pueblos of the Southwest, supernatural power was obtained in a dream or vision. Success in life, according to their beliefs, was due to personal contact with the supernatural. Each man's vision gave him power for his lifetime, and in some tribes he was constantly renewing his personal relationship with the spirits by seeking further visions. Whatever he saw, an animal or a star, a plant or a supernatural being, adopted him as a personal protégé, and he could call upon him in need. He had duties to perform for his visionary patron, gifts to give him and obligations of all kinds. In return the spirit gave him the specific powers he promised him in his vision.

In every great region of North America this guardian spirit complex took different form according to the other traits of the culture with which it was most closely associated. In the plateaus of British Columbia it merged with the adolescent ceremonies we have just spoken of. Both boys and girls, among these tribes, went out into the mountains at adolescence for a magic training. Puberty ceremonies have a wide distribution up and down the Pacific Coast, and over most of this region they are quite distinct from the guardian spirit practices. But in British Columbia they were merged. The climax of the magic adolescent training for boys was the acquisition of a guardian spirit who by its gifts dictated the lifetime profession of the young man. He became a warrior, a shaman, a hunter, or a gambler according to the supernatural visitant. Girls also received guardian spirits representing their domestic duties. So strongly is the guardian spirit experience among these peoples moulded by its association with the ceremonial of adolescence that anthropologists who know this region have argued that the entire vision complex of the American Indians had its origin in puberty rites. But the two are not genetically connected. They are locally merged, and in the merging both traits have taken special and characteristic forms.

In other parts of the continent, the guardian spirit is not sought at puberty, nor by all the youths of the tribe. Consequently the complex has in these cultures no kind of relationship with puberty rites even when any such exist. On the southern plains it is adult men who must acquire mystic sanctions. The vision complex merged with a trait very different from puberty rites. The Osage are organized in kinship groups in which descent is traced through the father and disregards the mother's line. These clan groups have a common inheritance of supernatural blessing. The legend of each clan tells how its ancestor sought a vision, and was blessed by the animal whose name the clan has inherited. The ancestor of the mussel clan sought seven times, with the tears running down his face, a supernatural blessing. At last he met the mussel and spoke to it, saying:

O grandfather,
The little ones have nothing of which to make their bodies.

Thereupon the mussel answered him:

You say the little ones have nothing of which to make their bodies.
Let the little ones make of me their bodies.
When the little ones make of me their bodies,
They shall always live to see old age.
Behold the wrinkles upon my skin [shell]
Which I have made to be the means of reaching old age.
When the little ones make of me their bodies
They shall always live to see the signs of old age upon their skins
The seven bends of the river [of life]
I pass successfully.
And in my travels the gods themselves have not the power to see the trail
that I make.
When the little ones make of me their bodies
No one, not even the gods, shall be able to see the trail they make.

Among these people all the familiar elements of the vision quest are
present, but it was attained by a first ancestor of the clan, and its blessings
are inherited by a blood-relationship group.

This situation among the Osage presents one of the fullest pictures in
the world of totemism, that close mingling of social organization and of
religious veneration for the ancestor. Totemism is described from all parts
of the world, and anthropologists have argued that the clan totem originated in the 'personal totem,' or guardian spirit. But the situation is
exactly analogous to that of the plateaus of British Columbia where the
vision quest merged with the adolescent rites, only that here it has merged
with hereditary privileges of the clan. So strong has this new association
become that a vision is no longer thought to give a man power auto-
matically. The blessings of the vision are attained only by inheritance, and
among the Osage long chants have grown up describing the ancestor's
encounters, and detailing the blessings which his descendants may claim
in consequence.

In both these cases it is not only the vision complex which receives a
different character in different regions as it merges with puberty rites or
clan organization. The adolescence ceremonies and the social organization
are equally coloured by the interweaving of the vision quest. The inter-

action is mutual. The vision complex, the puberty rites, the clan organization, and many other traits that enter also into close relationship with the vision, are strands which are braided in many combinations. The consequences of the different combinations that result from this intermingling of traits cannot be exaggerated. In both the regions of which we have just spoken, both where the religious experience was merged with puberty rites and where it was merged with clan organization, as a natural corollary of the associated practices all individuals of the tribe could receive power from the vision for success in any undertaking. Achievement in any occupation was credited to the individual's claim upon a vision experience. A successful gambler or a successful hunter drew his power from it just as a successful shaman did. According to their dogma all avenues of advancement were closed to those who had failed to obtain a supernatural patron.

In California, however, the vision was the professional warrant of the shaman. It marked him as a person apart. It was just in this region, therefore, that the most aberrant aspects of this experience were developed. The vision was no longer a slight hallucination for which the stage could be set by fasting and torture and isolation. It was a trance experience which overtook the exceptionally unstable members of the community and especially the women. Among the Shasta it was the convention that only women were so blessed. The required experience was definitely cataleptic and came upon the novice after a preliminary dreaming had prepared the way. She fell senseless and rigid to the ground. When she came to herself, blood oozed from her mouth. All the ceremonies by which for years after she validated her call to be a shaman were further demonstrations of her liability to cataleptic seizures and were regarded as the cure by which her life was saved. In tribes like the Shasta not only the vision experience had changed its character to a violent seizure which differentiated religious practitioners from all others, but the character of the shamans was equally modified by the nature of the trance experience. They were definitely the unstable members of the community. In this region contests between shamans took the form of dancing each other down, that is, of seeing which one could withstand longest in a dance the cataleptic seizure which would inevitably overtake them. Both the vision experience and shamanism had been profoundly affected by the close relationship into which they had entered. The merging of the two traits, no less than the merging of the vision experience and puberty rites or clan organization, had drastically modified both fields of behaviour.

In the same way in our own civilization the separateness of the church and of the marriage sanction is historically clear, yet the religious sacrament of wedlock for centuries dictated developments both in sex behaviour and in the church. The peculiar character of marriage during those centuries was due to the merging of two essentially unrelated cultural traits. On the other hand, marriage has often been the means by which wealth was traditionally transferred. In cultures where this is true, the close association of marriage with economic transfer may quite obliterate the fact that marriage is fundamentally a matter of sexual and child-rearing adjustments. Marriage in each case must be understood in relation to other traits to which it has become assimilated, and we should not run into the mistake of thinking that 'marriage' can be understood in the two cases by the same set of ideas. We must allow for the different components which have been built up into the resulting trait.

We greatly need the ability to analyze traits of our own cultural heritage into their several parts. Our discussions of the social order would gain in clarity if we learned to understand in this way the complexity of even our simplest behaviour. Racial differences and prestige prerogatives have so merged among Anglo-Saxon peoples that we fail to separate biological racial matters from our most socially conditioned prejudices. Even among nations as nearly related to the Anglo-Saxons as the Latin peoples, such prejudices take different forms, so that, in Spanish-colonized countries and in British colonies racial differences have not the same social significance. Christianity and the position of women, similarly, are historically interrelated traits, and they have at different times interacted very differently. The present high position of women in Christian countries is no more a 'result' of Christianity than was Origen's coupling of woman with the deadly temptations. These interpenetrations of traits occur and disappear, and the history of culture is in considerable degree a history of their nature and fates and associations. But the genetic connection we so easily see in a complex trait and our horror at any disturbance of its interrelationships is largely illusory. The diversity of the possible combinations is endless, and adequate social orders can be built indiscriminately upon a great variety of these foundations.

QUESTIONS AND TOPICS

1. Do you agree with Miss Benedict that the loss of one's native culture is a gravely serious matter? Do you think Americans assume too easily that other peoples can discard their customs and "become like us"?
2. How are adolescents treated in America? Compare this treatment with those in the cultures Miss Benedict discusses. Is the American pattern preferable?
3. Miss Benedict tells us that the Kurnai "have extended and complicated a particular aspect of behavior [the incest taboo] until it is a social liability." Describe an aspect of our culture which has become a social liability.
4. Do we endow customs that are social liabilities with religious sanctity?
5. Is Miss Benedict correct in thinking that wisdom lies in greatly increased tolerance toward cultural divergencies?

Margaret Mead

A
COOPERATIVE
SOCIETY

In the following essay by Margaret Mead, 1901–, taken from her Sex and Temperament in Three Primitive Societies, *1935, we are given a full-length portrait of the Arapesh of New Guinea, a primitive tribe whose mores differ radically from those of Western society.*

Arapesh life is organized about this central plot of the way men and women, physiologically different and possessed of differing potencies, unite in a common adventure that is primarily maternal, cherishing, and oriented away from the self towards the needs of the next generation. It is a culture in which men and women do different things for the same reasons, in which men are not expected to respond to one set of motivations and women to another, in which if men are given more authority it is because authority is a necessary evil that someone, and that one the freer partner, must carry. It is a culture in which if women are excluded from ceremonies, it is for the sake of the women themselves, not as a device to bolster up the pride of the men, who work desperately hard to keep the dangerous secrets that would make their wives ill and deform their unborn children. It is a society where a man conceives responsibility, leadership, public appearance, and the assumption of arrogance as onerous duties that are forced upon him, and from which he is only too glad to escape in middle years, as soon as his eldest child attains puberty. In order to understand a social order that substitutes responsiveness to the concerns of others, and attentiveness to the needs of others, for aggressiveness, initiative, competitiveness, and possessiveness—the familiar motivations upon which our culture depends—it is necessary to discuss in some detail the way in which Arapesh society is organized.

There are no political units. Clusters of villages are grouped into localities, and each locality and its inhabitants have names. These names
are sometimes used rhetorically at feasts, or to refer to the region, but the
localities themselves have no political organization. Marriages, feasting
organizations, and occasional semi-hostile clashes between neighbouring
groups take place between hamlets or clusters of hamlets across locality
lines. Each hamlet belongs theoretically to one patrilineal family line,
which again has a name to distinguish it. The patrilineal families, or small
localized clans, also possess hunting and gardening land, and located somewhere on their hunting-land is a water-hole or a quicksand or a steep
waterfall that is inhabited by their *marsalai,* a supernatural who appears
in the form of a mythical and bizarrely coloured snake or lizard, or occasionally as a larger animal. In the abode of the *marsalai* and along the
borders of the ancestral lands live the ghosts of the clan dead, including
the wives of the men of the clan, who after death continue to live with
their husbands instead of returning to their own clan-lands.

The Arapesh do not conceive of themselves as owning these ancestral
lands, but rather as belonging to the lands; in their attitude there is none
of the proud possessiveness of the landowner who vigorously defends his
rights against all comers. The land itself, the game animals, the timber
trees, the sago, and especially the bread-fruit-trees, which are thought of
as very old and dear to the ghosts—these all belong to the ghosts. For the
feelings and attitudes of the ghosts the *marsalai* is a focusing-point. This
being is not exactly an ancestor and not exactly not an ancestor—Arapesh
casualness does not attempt to answer the question. The *marsalai* has a
special touchiness about a few ritual points; he dislikes menstruating
women, pregnant women, and men who come directly from intercourse
with their wives. Such trespass he punishes with illness and death to the
women or unborn children, unless he is especially placated by a mimic
offering of a pig's tusk, an empty betel-sheath, a sago-container, and a
taro-leaf, on which one of the ancestor souls will alight as a bird or a
butterfly and absorb the spirit of the offering. The ghosts themselves are
the residents of the lands, and a man going upon his own inherited land
will announce himself, his name and relationship to them, remarking: "It
is I, your grandson, of Kanehoibis. I have come to cut some posts for my
house. Do not object to my presence, nor to my timber-cutting. As I return
pluck back the brambles from my path, and bend back the branches so
that I walk easily." This he must do even if he goes alone on the land

that he has inherited from his forefathers. More often he has with him someone less directly connected, a relative or a brother-in-law, who is hunting with him or plans to make a garden on his land. Then introductions are in order. "See, my grandfathers, this is my brother-in-law, the husband of my sister. He comes to garden here with me. Treat him as your grandson, do not object to his being here. He is good." If these precautions are neglected, a hurricane will knock down the careless man's house or a landslip destroy his garden. Wind and rain and landslips are sent by the *marsalais*, who employ these means to discipline those who are careless about expressing the proper attitudes towards the land. In all of this there is none of the sense of ownership with which a man bids a stranger welcome to his land or proudly chops down a tree because it is his.

On a neighbouring hilltop, the village of Alipinagle was sadly depleted. In the next generation there would not be enough people to occupy the land. The people of Alitoa sighed: "Alas, poor Alipinagle, after the present people are gone, who will care for the land, who will there be beneath the trees? We must give them some children to adopt, that the land and the trees may have people when we are gone." Such generosity had, of course, the practical consequences of placing a child or so in a more advantageous position, but it was never phrased in this way, nor did the people recognize any formulations based upon possessiveness about land. There was just one family in the locality that was possessive, and its attitude was incomprehensible to everyone else. Gerud, a popular young diviner and the eldest son of this family, once in a *séance* suggested as a motive for an alleged theft of dirt that the accused grudged to the children of a newcomer in the village a future share in the hunting-grounds. The rest of the community regarded his reasoning as little short of mad. Surely, people belonged to the land, not land to the people. As a correlate of this point of view, no one is at all particular as to where he lives, and as often as not members of a clan live not in their ancestral hamlets, but in the hamlets of cousins or brothers-in-law. Without political organization, without any fixed and arbitrary social rules, it is easy enough for people to do this.

As with residence sites, so with gardens. The Arapesh gardening is of two types: taro-gardens and banana-gardens, in which the men do the initial clearing, tree-lopping, and fencing, and the women do the planting, weeding, and harvesting; and yam-gardens, which with the exception of a little help rendered by women in weeding and in carrying the harvest are entirely men's work. Among many New Guinea tribes each married pair clears and fences a patch of land in their own inherited gardening-bush, and cultivates it more or less alone, with the help of their immature children, perhaps calling in other relatives at the harvest. In this way a New Guinea garden becomes a private place, almost as private as a house, and is frequently used for copulation; it is their own place. A man or his wife can go to the garden every day, repair any gaps in the fencing, and so protect the garden from the inroads of bush animals. All the external circumstances of the Arapesh environment would suggest such a gardening method as exceedingly practical. The distances are long and the roads difficult. People often have to sleep in their gardens because they are too far from other shelter, so they build small, badly thatched, uncomfortable huts on the ground, as it is not worth while to build a house on piles for one year's use. The steep slopes make fencing unsatisfactory and the pigs are always breaking in. Food is scarce and poor and it would seem likely that under these conditions of hardship and poverty people would be very possessive of and attentive to their own gardens. Instead the Arapesh have evolved a different and most extraordinary system, expensive in time and human effort, but conducive to the warm co-operation and sociability that they consider to be much more important.

Each man plants not one garden, but several, each one in co-operation with a different group of his relatives. In one of these gardens he is host, in the others he is guest. In each of these gardens three to six men, with one or two wives each, and sometimes a grown daughter or so, work together, fence together, clear together, weed together, harvest together, and while engaged in any large piece of work, sleep together, crowded up in the little inadequate shelter, with the rain dripping down the necks of more than half of the sleepers. These gardening groups are unstable— some individuals are unable to stand the strain of a bad crop; they tend to blame their gardening partners for it, and to seek new alliances the following year. Choice, now of one piece of long-fallow ground, now of another, sometimes makes next year's gardening-plot too far away for some of those who planted together last year. But each year a man's food-stakes lie not in one plot directly under his control, but scattered about, beneath the ghosts and on the land of his relatives, three miles in one direction, five miles in another.

This arrangement of work has several results. No two gardens are planted at the same time and therefore the Arapesh lack the "time hungry" so characteristic of yam-raising peoples where all the yam-gardens are planted simultaneously. Where several men work together to clear and fence one plot before scattering to co-operate in clearing and fencing other plots, the harvests succeed each other. This method of gardening is not based upon the slightest physical need for co-operative labour. Tall trees are simply ringed, not felled, and the branches are cut off to let in light, so that a garden looks like an army of ghosts, white against the surrounding deep-green of the bush. The fencing is done with saplings that an adolescent boy could cut. But the preference is strong for working in small happy groups in which one man is host and may feast his guest workers with a little meat—if he finds it. And so the people go up and down the mountain sides, from one plot to another, weeding here, staking vines there, harvesting in another spot, called hither and thither by the demands of gardens in different states of maturity.

This same lack of individualism obtains in the planting of coconut-trees. A man plants such trees for his young sons, but not upon his own land. Instead, he will walk four or five miles carrying a sprouting coconut in order to plant it by the door-step of his uncle, or of his brother-in-law. A census of the palm-trees in any village reveals a bewildering number of distantly residing owners and bears no relation to the actual residents. In the same way, men who are friends will plant new sago-palms together, and in the next generation their sons become a working unit.

In hunting, too, a man does not hunt alone, but with a companion, sometimes a brother, as often a cousin or a brother-in-law; the bush, the ghosts, and the *marsalai* belong to one of the pair or trio. The man, be he host or guest, who sees the game first claims it, and the only tact that is necessary here is the tact of not seeing game very much more often than other people do. Men who make a practice of always claiming first sight are left to hunt by themselves, and may develop into far better hunters, with increasingly unsocial characters. Such a man was Sumali, my self-nominated father, who in spite of his skill was little esteemed in co-operative enterprises. It was his son who divined stinginess about hunting-lands as a motive for imputed sorcery; and when Sumali's house burned accidentally to the ground, Sumali attributed the accident to jealousy over land. His traps yielded more than the traps of anyone else in the region, his tracking skill was greatest and his aim most accurate, but he hunted alone, or with his young sons, and presented his game to his relatives almost as formally as he might have presented it to strangers.

It is the same also with house-building. The houses are so small that they actually require very little communal labour. Materials from one house or several dilapidated houses are reassembled into another house; people take their houses down and rebuild them in another orientation; there is no attempt made to cut the rafters the same length or to saw off the ridge-pole if it is too long for the projected house—if it does not fit this house it will undoubtedly fit the next one. But no man, except one who has failed to help with the house-building of others, builds alone. A man announces his intention of building a house, and perhaps makes a small feast for raising the ridge-pole. Then his brothers and his cousins and his uncles, as they go about the bush upon their several errands, bear his partly completed house in mind, and stop to gather a bundle of creeper to bind the roof, or a bunch of sago-leaves for the thatching. These contributions they bring to the new houses when they pass that way, and gradually, casually, a little at a time, the house is built, out of the uncounted labour of many.

But this loosely co-operative fashion in which all work, even the routine of everyday gardening and hunting, is organized means that no man is master of his own plans for many hours together. If anything, he is less able to plan and carry through any consecutive activities than are the women, who at least know that meals and firewood and water must be provided each day. The men spend over nine-tenths of their time responding to other people's plans, digging in other people's gardens, going on hunting-parties initiated by others. The whole emphasis of their economic lives is that of participation in activities others have initiated, and only rarely and shyly does anyone tentatively suggest a plan of his own.

This emphasis is one factor in the lack of political organization. Where all are trained to a quick responsiveness to any plan, and mild ostracism is sufficient to prod the laggard into co-operation, leadership presents a different problem from that in a society where each man pits his own aggressiveness against that of another. If there is a weighty matter to be decided, one that may involve the hamlet or a cluster of hamlets in a brawl or accusations of sorcery, then the decision is arrived at in a quiet, roundabout, and wholly characteristic fashion. Suppose for instance that a young man finds that a pig belonging to a distant village has strayed into his garden. The pig is a trespasser, meat is scarce, he would like to kill it. But would it be wise to do so? Judgment must be made in terms of all kinds of relationships with the pig's owners. Is a feast pending? Or is a betrothal still unsettled? Does some member of his own group depend upon the pig's owner for assistance in some ceremonial plan? All these things the young man has not the judgment to decide. He goes to his elder brother. If his elder brother sees no objection to killing the pig, the two will take counsel with other elder male relatives, until finally one of the oldest and most respected men of the community is consulted. Of such men every locality with a population of one hundred and fifty to two hundred has one or two. If the big man gives his approval, the pig is killed and eaten and no censure will fall upon the young man from his elders; everyone will stand together to defend their bit of legal piracy.

Warfare is practically unknown among the Arapesh. There is no head-hunting tradition, no feeling that to be brave or manly one must kill. Indeed, those who have killed men are looked upon with a certain amount of discomfort, as men slightly apart. It is they who must perform the purificatory ceremonies over a new killer. The feeling towards a murderer and that towards a man who kills in battle are not essentially different. There are no insignia of any sort for the brave. There is only a modicum of protective magic which can be used by those who are going into a fight: they may scrape a little dust from their fathers' bones and eat it with areca-nut and magic herbs. But although actual warfare—organized expeditions to plunder, conquer, kill, or attain glory—is absent, brawls and clashes between villages do occur, mainly over women. The marriage system is such that even the most barefaced elopement of a betrothed or married woman must be phrased as an abduction and, since an abduction is an unfriendly act on the part of another group, must be avenged. This feeling for righting the balance, for paying back evil for evil, not in greater measure, but in exact measure, is very strong among the Arapesh. The beginning of hostilities they regard as an unfortunate accident; abductions of women are really the result of marital disagreements and the formation of new personal attachments, and are not unfriendly acts on the part of the next community. So also with pigs, since people attempt to keep their pigs at home. If the pigs stray, it is a bad accident, but if a pig is killed, it should be avenged.

All such clashes between hamlets start in angry conversation, the aggrieved party coming, armed but not committed to fighting, into the village of the offenders. An altercation follows; the offenders may justify or excuse their conduct, disclaim any knowledge of the elopement, or deny having known the ownership of the pig—it had not had its tail cut yet, how could they know it was not a bush pig? and so on. If the aggrieved party is protesting more as a matter of form than from real anger, the meeting may end in a few harsh words. Alternatively, it may progress from reproach to insult, until the most volatile and easily angered person hurls a spear. This is not a signal for a general fracas; instead everyone notes carefully where the spear—which is never thrown to kill—hits, and the next most volatile person of the opposite party throws a spear back at the man who hurled the first one. This in turn is recorded during a moment of attention, and a return spear thrown. Each reprisal is phrased as a matter of definite choice: "Then Yabinigi threw a spear. He hit my cross-cousin in the wrist. I was angry because my cross-cousin was hit and I threw a spear back and hit Yabinigi in the ankle. Then the mother's brother of Yabinigi, enraged that his sister's son had been wounded, drew back his arm and hurled a spear at me which missed," and so on. This serial and carefully recorded exchange of spears in which the aim is to wound lightly, not to kill, goes on until someone is rather badly wounded, when the members of the attacking party immediately take to their heels. Later, peace is made by an interchange of rings, each man giving a ring to the man whom he has wounded.

If, as occasionally happens, someone is killed in one of these clashes, every attempt is made to disavow any intention to kill: the killer's hand slipped; it was because of the sorcery of the Plainsmen. Almost always those on the other side are called by kinship terms, and surely no man would willingly have killed a relative. If the relative killed is a near one, an uncle or a first cousin, the assumption that it was unintentional and due to sorcery is regarded as established, and the killer is commiserated with and permitted to mourn whole-heartedly with the rest. If the relative is more distant, and the possibility of genuine intent more open, the killer may flee to another community. No blood feud will follow, although there may be an attempt to subsidize the sorcery of the Plainsmen against him. But in general sorcery deaths are avenged with sorcery deaths, and all killings within the locality or within avenging distance are regarded as too aberrant, too unexpected and inexplicable, for the community to deal with them. And each man who is wounded in a fight has a further penalty to pay, for he must reimburse his mother's brothers, and his mother's brothers' sons, for his own shed blood. All blood comes to the child from its mother; it is therefore the property of the mother's group. The mother's brother has the right to shed a sister's son's blood; it is he who must open a boil, he who scarifies the adolescent girl. So the man who is injured in any way suffers not only in his person but in his supply of valuables: he must pay for having been in any scene in which he is injured. This sanction is extended to cover injuries in hunting, and involvement in a shameful situation.

The general policy of Arapesh society is to punish those who are indiscreet enough to get involved in any kind of violent or disreputable scene, those who are careless enough to get hurt in hunting, or stupid enough to let themselves become the butt of public vituperation from their wives. In this society unaccustomed to violence, which assumes that all men are mild and co-operative and is always surprised by the individuals who fail to be so, there are no sanctions to deal with the violent man. But it is felt that those who stupidly and carelessly provoke violence can be kept in order. In mild cases of offence, as when a man has been one member of a fighting group, his individual mother's brother calls out for payment. After all, the poor sister's son has already suffered a wound and loss of blood. But if instead he has got himself involved in an undignified public disputation with a wife, or with a young relative who has been overheard by others to insult him, then the whole men's group of the hamlet or cluster of hamlets may act, still instigated by the mother's brothers, who are the official executors of the punishment. The men's group will take the sacred flutes, the voice of the *tamberan*—the supernatural monster who is the patron of the men's cult—and going by night to the house of the offender, play his wife and himself off the premises, break into his house, litter his house-floor with leaves and rubbish, cut down an areca-palm or so, and depart. If the man has been steadily falling in the esteem of the community, if he has been unco-operative, given to sorcery, bad-tempered, they may take up his fire-place and dump it out, which is practically equivalent to saying that they can dispense with his presence—for a month at least. The victim, deeply shamed by this procedure, flees to distant relatives and does not return until he has obtained a pig with which to feast the community, and so wipe out his offence.

But against the really violent man the community has no redress. Such men fill their fellows with a kind of amazed awe; if crossed they threaten to burn down their own houses, break all their pots and rings, and leave that part of the country for ever. Their relatives and neighbours, aghast at the prospect of being deserted in this way, beseech the violent man not to leave them, not to desert them, not to destroy his own property, and placate him by giving him what he wishes. It is only because the whole education of the Arapesh tends to minimize violence and confuse the motivations of the violent that the society is able to operate by disciplining those who provoke and suffer from violence rather than those who actually perpetrate it.

With work a matter of amiable co-operation, and the slight warfare so slenderly organized, the only other need that the community has for leadership is for carrying out large-scale ceremonial operations. Without any leadership whatsoever, with no rewards beyond the daily pleasure of eating a little food and singing a few songs with one's fellows, the society could get along very comfortably, but there would be no ceremonial occasions. And the problem of social engineering is conceived by the Arapesh not as the need to limit aggression and curb acquisitiveness, but as the need to force a few of the more capable and gifted men into taking, against their will, enough responsibility and leadership so that occasionally, every three or four years or at even rarer intervals, a really exciting ceremonial may be organized. No one, it is assumed, really wants to be a leader, a "big man." "Big men" have to plan, have to initiate exchanges, have to strut and swagger and talk in loud voices, have to boast of what they have done in the past and are going to do in the future. All of this the Arapesh regard as most uncongenial, difficult behaviour, the kind of behaviour in which no normal man would indulge if he could possibly avoid it. It is a rôle that the society forces upon a few men in certain recognized ways.

While boys are in their early teens, their elders tend to classify their potentialities to become "big men." Native capacity is roughly divided into three categories: "those whose ears are open and whose throats are open," who are the most gifted, the men who understand the culture and are able to make their understanding articulate: "those whose ears are open and whose throats are shut," useful quiet men who are wise but shy and inarticulate: and a group of the two least useful kinds of people, "those whose ears are closed but whose throats are open" and "those whose ears and throats are both shut." A boy of the first class is specially trained by being assigned in early adolescence a *buanyin,* or exchange partner,

from among the young males of a clan in which one of his elder male relatives has a *buanyin*. This *buanyin* relationship is a reciprocal feast-giving
relationship between pairs of males, members of different clans, and prefer-
ably of opposite dual organization membership—which is loosely hereditary. It is a social institution that develops aggressiveness and encourages
the rare competitive spirit. It is the duty of *buanyins* to insult each other
whenever they meet, to inquire sneeringly whether the other *buanyin*
ever means to make anything of his life—has he no pigs, no yams, has he
no luck in hunting, has he no trade-friends and no relatives, that he never
gives feasts or organizes a ceremony? Was he born head first like a normal
human being, or perhaps he came feet first from his mother's womb? The
buanyin relationship is also a training-ground in the kind of hardness
that a big man must have, which in an ordinary Arapesh is regarded as
undesirable.

The functioning of this *buanyin* relationship must be understood against
Arapesh attitudes about the exchange of food. To a people who disguise
all their trading as voluntary and casual gift-giving, any rigid accounting
is uncongenial. As with trading from village to village, so it is in all exchange between relatives. The ideal distribution of food is for each person
to eat food grown by another, eat game killed by another, eat pork from
pigs that not only are not his own but have been fed by people at such
a distance that their very names are unknown. Under the guidance of
this ideal, an Arapesh man hunts only to send most of his kill to his
mother's brother, his cousin, or his father-in-law. The lowest man in the
community, the man who is believed to be so far outside the moral pale
that there is no use reasoning with him, is the man who eats his own kill—
even though that kill be a tiny bird, hardly a mouthful in all.

There is no encouragement given to any individual to build up a surplus
of yams, the strong reliable crop that can be stored and the increase of
which depends upon the conservation of seed. Anyone whose yam crop is
conspicuously larger than his neighbour's is graciously permitted to give
an *abūllū*, a special feast at which, having painted his yams in bright
colours and having laid them out on a ratan measuring-tape, which he may
keep as a trophy, all of his yams are given away for seed. His relatives and
neighbours come bringing a return gift of their own selection, and carry
away a bag of seed. Of this seed he may never eat; even when it has
multiplied in the fourth or fifth generation, a careful record is kept. In this
way, the good luck or the better gardening of one man does not redound

to his personal gain, but is socialized, and the store of seed-yams of the entire community is increased.

From all of this socialized treatment of food and property, this non-competitive, unaccounted, easy give and take, the *huanyin* partnership pattern stands out. Within it are definitely encouraged all the virtues of a competitive, cost-accounting system. A *huanyin* does not wait for the stimulus of an insult given in anger; he insults his *huanyin* as a matter of course. He does not merely share with him of his abundance, but he definitely raises pigs or hunts game in order to give it publicly and ostentatiously to his *huanyin,* accompanied by a few well-chosen insults as to his *huanyin's* inability to repay the gift. Careful accounting is kept of every piece of pig or haunch of kangaroo, and a bundle of coconut-leaf rib is used to denote these in the public altercation during which *huanyins* dun each other. Most astonishing of all is the definite convention of stinginess between *huanyins.* A generous *huanyin* will set aside a special basket of choice entrails and his wife will give it secretly to his *huanyin's* wife, after a feast. For this there need be no return. But while good behaviour is expected everywhere else in social life, people are reconciled to their *huanyins'* neglecting to make this generous gesture.

Thus in a society where the norm for men is to be gentle, unacquisitive, and co-operative, where no man reckons up the debts that another owes him, and each man hunts that others may eat, there is a definite training for the special contrasting behaviour that "big men" must display. The young men on the way to become big men suffer continual pressure from their elders, as well as from their *huanyins.* They are urged to assume the responsibility of organizing the preliminary feasts that will finally culminate in a big initiation ceremony or the purchase of a new dance-complex from the beach. And a few of them yield to all this pressure, learn to stamp their feet and count their pigs, to plant special gardens and organize hunting-parties, and to maintain the long-time planning over several years that is necessary in order to give a ceremony which lasts no longer than a day or so. But when his eldest child reaches puberty, the big man can retire; he need no longer stamp and shout, he need no longer go about to feasts looking for opportunities to insult his *huanyin;* he can stay quietly at home, guiding and educating his children, gardening, and arranging his children's marriages. He can retire from the active competitive life that his society assumes, usually correctly, to be eminently uncongenial and distasteful to him.

QUESTIONS AND TOPICS

1. Contrast the big man among the Arapesh with his counterpart in America. How is each viewed by his society?
2. Would you like to live in a society like that of the Arapesh?
3. Could a society fundamentally like that of the Arapesh conduct a modern industrial civilization?
4. Could a society such as the Arapesh survive external aggression?
5. Should American society become more like that of the Arapesh, or has it already moved too far in that direction?

B. F. Skinner

LOVE AND
MARRIAGE IN
WALDEN TWO

The following is a selection from a novel, Walden Two, *1948, by B. F. Skinner, 1914–. Its scientific approach to Utopia aroused great interest. The community invented by Dr. Skinner resembles Arapesh society economically, though experimentation, not tradition, is the basis of order and values. (Note: Frazier is the founder of the community; the other characters are visitors from the outside world.)*

Just south of the flower gardens, on a blanket spread out upon the warm grass, lay a naked baby nine or ten months old. A boy and girl were trying to make her crawl toward a rubber doll. We stopped for a moment on our way to the common rooms to enjoy her grotesquely unavailing efforts.

When we resumed our walk, Frazier said casually, "Their first child."

"Good heavens!" I cried. "Do you mean to say those children are the parents of that baby?"

"Why, of course. And a very fine baby it is, too."

"But they can't be more than sixteen or seventeen years old!"

"Probably not."

"But isn't that rather remarkable? It's not the usual thing, I hope." My voice trailed off doubtfully.

"It's not at all unusual with us," Frazier said. "The average age of the Walden Two mother is eighteen at the birth of her first child, and we hope to bring the figure down still further. The war interfered a bit there. I believe the girl you saw was sixteen when her baby was born."

"But why do you encourage *that?*" Barbara said.

"There are a dozen good reasons. There is no excuse for the usual delay in getting married or the still greater delay in bearing children— But shall we save this for luncheon? How about one o'clock in the serving room?"

We reached our quarters, and Frazier took leave of us abruptly. We washed up and met again in front of the building, sitting in a row on a long bench against the wall, partially shaded by the overhanging roof. We were exhausted.

"I want labor-credits for that kind of thing," said Castle, as he dropped onto the bench, "and it will have to be about two point zero zero or I won't play."

"What do you think of what Mr. Frazier said this morning?" Rodge said.

"Well, I can tell you this," Castle said, "I wouldn't sign on the dotted line!"

Rodge, in obvious disappointment, glanced uneasily at Barbara.

"Why not?" I asked, offering whatever support I could.

"Would you?" Castle said.

"Well, I don't know about that. But what Frazier said this morning seemed sound enough. He admitted it was all experimental. If he can really keep himself free to change practices—if he can avoid committing himself stubbornly to some theory—I think he'll come through."

"It's a handy thing, this experimental attitude," said Castle. "The scientist can be sure of himself before he knows anything. We philosophers should have thought of that."

"I suppose you're right," I said. "The scientist may not be sure of the answer, but he's often sure he can find one. And that's a condition which is clearly not enjoyed by philosophy."

"I want to see a few answers—not just the assurance of answers."

"Don't you believe your own eyes?" I said. I was still trying to bolster Rodge's enthusiasm.

"My eyes tell me nothing. Ventures of this sort have often run along very well for a while. What we want to know is whether the thing carries the potentialities of permanence. I want to see more of this wonderful second generation."

"That's curious," I said. "I worry more about the first. I think Frazier is perfectly right about educating people for cooperative living. What bothers me is how to get the first generation safely into their graves, or at least their rocking chairs, when the second are ready to take over. Frazier has promised us more about that this evening."

"There had better be more," said Castle petulantly. "A great deal more."

"Isn't it time to start for lunch?" said Barbara brightly. "Can you imagine having a baby at sixteen?"

We found the dining rooms rather crowded, and we chose a small table in the English inn. Frazier was waiting for us, and we had scarcely picked up our forks before he began to speak, as if he had just broken off.

"No doubt the thought of a girl getting married a year or two after she is ready for childbearing strikes you as something characteristic of primitive cultures or worse still, backward communities in our own country," he said. "Early marriages are regarded as inadvisable. The figures show they tend to be less successful in the long run, and they are often plainly impossible from an economic point of view. I need scarcely point out, however, that there's no economic obstacle to marriage at any age in Walden Two. The young couple will live quite as well whether married or unmarried. Children are cared for in the same way regardless of the age, experience, or earning power of their parents.

"Certainly most girls are ready for childbearing at fifteen or sixteen. We like to ridicule 'puppy love.' We say it won't last, and judge its depth accordingly. Well, of course it doesn't last! A thousand forces conspire against it. And they are not the forces of nature, either, but of a badly organized society. The boy and girl are ready for love. They will never have the same capacity for love again. And they are ready for marriage and childbearing. It's all part of the same thing. But society never lets them prove it."

"Instead, society makes it into a sex problem," I said.

"Of course!" said Frazier. "Sex is no problem in itself. Here the adolescent finds an immediate and satisfactory expression of his natural impulses. It's a solution which is productive, honorable, and viewed by the community with admiration and pride. How very different from the secrecy and shame which most of us recall in connection with sex at some time or other! Adolescence is seldom pleasant to remember, it's full of unnecessary problems, unnecessary delays. It should be brief and painless, and we make it so in Walden Two.

"All your schemes to keep the adolescent out of trouble—your 'wholesome' substitutes for sex!" Frazier continued. "What is unwholesome about sex? Why must there be a substitute? What's wrong with love, or marriage, or parenthood? You don't solve anything by delay—you make things worse. The more or less pathological aberrations which follow are easily recognized, but there is a great deal more. A normal sexual adjustment is often prevented. And the sportive element in sex is played up—every person of the opposite sex becomes a challenge to seduction. That's a bothersome cultural trait that we're glad to avoid. Promiscuous aggression is no more natural than quarrelsomeness, or an inclination to tease, or jovial backslapping. But if you insist on making sex into a game or hunt before you let it become serious, how can you expect a sane attitude later on?"

"Do girls have babies as easily when they are so young, though?" said Barbara.

"Easier," said Frazier flatly, as if he himself had had several at a tender age. "We make sure, of course, that the girl is capable of normal child-bearing, but we should do that at any age."

"How long does she go on having babies?"

"As long as she likes, but generally no longer than usual. If she wants four children, say, she will be finished with childbearing by the time she's twenty-two or -three. That's not too fast, because she is freed of the heavy labor of child care, even though she will probably work in the nursery for her daily stint, and because she gets top medical attention. At twenty-three she will find herself as young in body and spirit as if she had spent the same years unmarried. Her adult life opens up to her with many interesting prospects. For one thing, she is then quite on a par with men. She has made the special contribution which is either the duty or the privilege of woman, and can take her place without distinction of sex. You may have noticed the complete equality of men and women among us. There are scarcely any types of work which are not shared equally."

A remark suddenly struck me with such force that I was surprised to hear myself utter it:

"A 'generation' in Walden Two must mean about twenty years!"

"Instead of the usual thirty," said Frazier, laughing at my astonishment. "We get no end of amusement out of that, at the expense of the 'big litter' people. We don't sacrifice our women to a policy of maximal childbearing, but we equal or exceed their rate of propagation, and with healthy children, too, by the simple expedient of getting three generations for two."

"And a man can be a grandfather at thirty-five," I said, in growing amazement. "And reach three score and ten at about the time the fifth generation is born!"

"One of us may have as many great-grandchildren as one usually has grandchildren at the same age—with fewer children per couple," said Frazier. "And that should be a sufficient answer to the charge that we have somehow interfered with the joy of family or family ties. The average member of Walden Two will see more of his descendants than the very exceptional member of society at large. And every child will have many more living grandparents, great-grandparents, and other relatives, to take an interest in him."

"I should think there might be another advantage," I said. "Young parents should have a fresher memory and a better understanding of the problems of children. They must tend to be more sympathetic and helpful."

"If sympathy and help were needed," said Frazier rather irritably, as if I had suggested that the community was deficient in some respect.

"But isn't there one trouble?" said Barbara. "Do young people really know what kind of person they want to live with for the rest of their lives?"

"They seem to think so," said Frazier.

"But young people grow apart."

"Is that really true?"

"The figures," said Barbara, with obvious pride in talking in Frazier's terms, "show that early marriages tend to be unhappy."

"Because husband and wife grow apart, or because our economic system penalizes early marriage?"

"I don't know."

"Economic hardships could make people grow apart," said Frazier.

"All I know is, the boys I fell for when I was younger wouldn't interest me now," said Barbara, giving up the figures with relief. "I can't imagine what I saw in them."

"I wonder if that wouldn't be true at any age. We grow apart when we live apart."

"I think there may be something in what Miss Macklin says," said Castle. "We are less likely to have fallen into our final life pattern at that age. We're still trying to find ourselves."

"Very well, then. Let that point stand—though I can't see that it makes any difference, since people in Walden Two never stop changing. But at least we can offer some compensating advantages. We can be sure that husband and wife will come from the same economic level, from the same culture, and have the same sort of education. What do the figures show about that?"

Barbara tried to think. "As I remember it, those things are important, too," she said at last.

"Then we are even," said Frazier. "Our boys and girls know each other very well, too. There are no hasty marriages among us."

"The very fact of early marriage itself ought to prevent marriages due to sexual infatuation," I said, "unless you feel I'm spoiling your sympathetic picture of puppy love."

"You aren't spoiling it at all. Puppy love tends not to be overtly sexual at all. It's usually highly idealistic. I wasn't talking about the excitement which springs from the thwarting of natural impulses, but a love which arises spontaneously and with the least possible hindrance and which is therefore its own surest guarantee of success."

"Very romantic and unscientific," I said.

"Then let me add a scientific touch. When a young couple become engaged, they go to our Manager of Marriages. Their interests, school records, and health are examined. If there's any great discrepancy in intellectual ability or temperament they are advised against marrying. The marriage is at least postponed, and that usually means it's abandoned."

"As easy as all that?" I said.

"Usually so. The opportunities for other associations are a great help, just as in the case of personal jealousy."

"But aren't you spoiling some of the best years of a girl's life when you make her marry so young?" said Barbara.

"She is not 'made to marry.' It's all a matter of choice. She skips some of the years in the late teens and early twenties which are romantically painted in our literature. But she gets them back very soon, when her childbearing is over. And they are really better than the years she gave up. For most girls, adolescence is a period of concern over personal success and marriage. For the few happy ones, it's a spurious excitement. The glowing young debutante with a string of devoted swains is an artificial bit of trumpery that civilization can well do without."

"I wonder why your disclosure has been so disconcerting," I said. "Marriage at sixteen or seventeen was not at all uncommon in other times and other cultures. Yet in a way it strikes me as the most radical feature of life at Walden Two."

"I don't think I'd like it," said Barbara.

Frazier gave her a cold glance. "You have made it hard for me to answer Mr. Burris," he said. "I was going to point out that in other times and other cultures there was a much more rapid maturation. One could be an adult at sixteen. I am sure that Miss Macklin has made good use of the years which she values so highly, but that's not the universal case. At least half of the high-school years are a total waste—and half of college, too, as our more emancipated educators are beginning to discover. Whatever their age, young members of Walden Two don't marry before they are mature. They have much better control of themselves than youngsters of the same age elsewhere, and they are much less likely to misunderstand their own emotions or the motives of others. The 'best years of one's life,' Miss Macklin, are reached after the problems of adolescence have been solved or passed by. We multiply them many fold."

"I'm afraid the birth control people aren't going to thank you for your early marriages," I said. "Malthus must have taken an extra turn in his grave."

"It's no solution of the Malthusian problem to lower the birth rate of those who understand it. On the contrary, we need to expand the culture which recognizes the need for birth control. If you argue that we should set an example, you must prove to me that we shall not all be extinguished before the example is followed. No, our genetic program is a vital one. We don't worry about our birth rate, or its consequences."

"Are you conducting any genetic experiments?" I said.

"No," said Frazier, but he sat straight up as if the subject were especially interesting. "We discourage childbearing by the unfit, of course, but that's all. You must remember that we've only recently reached our present size, and even so, we aren't large enough for serious experimentation. Later, perhaps, something can be done. The weakening of the family structure will make experimental breeding possible."

Frazier smiled quietly.

"I have been waiting for that one!" said Castle explosively. "What about the 'weakening of the family structure,' Mr. Frazier?"

"The all-absorbing concern of the outside world," he said, "is what happens to the family in Walden Two. The family is the frailest of modern institutions. Its weakness is evident to everyone. Will it survive as the culture changes? We watch it with all the panic which besets a mother as her backward child steps to the platform and begins to speak a piece. Well, a great deal happens to the family in Walden Two, Mr. Castle, I can tell you that."

We had finished our lunch, but the dining rooms had become less crowded and we had therefore kept our table. Frazier, with a demonstrative gesture of discomfort, suggested that we find a more comfortable spot for a few minutes before getting our work assignments. The nearer lounges were occupied, but we found an empty studio. A number of leather cushions were scattered on the floor, and we arranged ourselves on them, feeling very Bohemian and therefore very objective with respect to the subject under discussion.

"The significant history of our times," Frazier began, "is the story of the growing weakness of the family. The decline of the home as a medium for perpetuating a culture, the struggle for equality for women, including their right to select professions other than housewife or nursemaid, the extraordinary consequences of birth control and the practical separation of sex and parenthood, the social recognition of divorce, the critical issue of blood relationship or race—all these are parts of the same field. And you can hardly call it quiescent.

"A community must solve the problem of the family by revising certain established practices. That's absolutely inevitable. The family is an ancient form of community, and the customs and habits which have been set up to perpetuate it are out of place in a society which isn't based on blood ties. Walden Two replaces the family, not only as an economic unit, but to some extent as a social and psychological unit as well. What survives is an experimental question."

"What answer have you reached?" said Castle.

"No definite answer yet. But I can describe some of the family practices which were part of the plan of Walden Two and tell you the consequences to date. A few experimental questions have been answered to our satisfaction."

"Such as?"

"Oh, the advisability of separate rooms for husband and wife, for example. We don't insist on it, but in the long run there's a more satisfactory relation when a single room isn't shared. Many of our visitors suppose that a community means a sacrifice of privacy. On the contrary, we've carefully provided for much more personal privacy than is likely to be found in the world at large. You may be alone here whenever you wish. A man's room is his castle. And a woman's, too."

"But how could you *prove* that separate rooms were advisable?" said Castle.

"Very simply. We asked all husbands and wives who were willing to do so to accept separate or common rooms on the basis of a drawing of lots. That was in the early days. We did the same thing with new members. Our psychologists kept in close touch with all personal problems and at the end of eight years the troubles and satisfactions of our members were analyzed with respect to the factor of separate or common rooms. It's the sort of experiment that would be impossible, or next to impossible, anywhere except in Walden Two. The result was clear-cut. Living in a separate room not only made the individual happier and better adjusted, it tended to strengthen the love and affection of husband and wife. Most of our married couples have now changed to separate rooms. It's difficult to explain the advantages to the newly married, and I suspect it will become a sort of tradition to room together until the period of childbearing is over. But the later advantages in point of health, convenience, and personal freedom are too great to be overlooked."

"But aren't you leaving the door wide open to promiscuity?" said Castle.

"On the contrary, we are perpetuating loyalty and affection. We can be sure that any continuing affection is genuine, and not the result of a police system, and hence it's something in which we take pride. We place abiding affection on a very high plane.

"The simple fact is, there's no more promiscuity in Walden Two than in society at large. There's probably less. For one thing, we encourage simple friendship between the sexes. The world at large all but forbids it. What might have been a satisfying friendship must become a clandestine affair. Here we give friendship every support. We don't practice 'free love,' but we have a great deal of 'free affection.' And that goes a long way toward satisfying the needs which lead to promiscuity elsewhere. We have successfully established the principle of 'Seduction not expected.' When a man strikes up an acquaintanceship with a woman, he does not worry about failing to make advances, and the woman isn't hurt if advances aren't made. We recognize that sort of sexual play for what it is— a sign, not of potency, but of malaise or instability.

"I don't mean that no one in Walden Two has fallen in love 'illicitly,' "

Frazier continued, "but I'm sure there has been a minimum of mere sex without love. We don't regard extramarital love as wholly justifiable or without its difficulties. The problem of the deserted mate always remains. But we've done all we can to avoid unhappiness. It's part of the Walden Two Code to avoid gossip about personal ties, and a slight disturbance often works itself out quietly. Our vastly extended opportunities for affection also help. No one really feels very much deserted. There's not much wounded pride.

"At the moment that's the best we can do. It's not a final solution, but it's an improvement. Remember that many cultures condone the occasional reassortment of mates—look at the frequent divorces among those who can afford them. We haven't gone that far here and we shan't. Economically we could dispense with permanent marriage altogether, but we don't. Abiding personal affection is more than a romantic rationalization of a crude economic unit."

"Have you found it necessary," I said, "to conceal or misrepresent your practices to avoid unfavorable gossip or even legal action?"

"Not at all. We follow the legal practices of the state. But these are always subject to local interpretation, and Walden Two is no exception. We make a great deal of the 'engagement.' In the world at large this is a statement of intention and a period of trial. It's that with us. The young couple receive medical and psychological counsel during this period. Long engagements are not encouraged and, of course, are unnecessary for economic reasons. Our marriage ceremony is unambiguous, and I'm sure its entered into in good faith. If in the course of time extramarital friendships weaken the original tie, we try to avoid an open break. A disinterested person, usually one of our psychologists, gives immediate counsel and guidance. Frequently the matter straightens itself out, and the original tie is preserved. But if the old affection is quite dead and the new one genuine, a divorce is carried through.

"It will be hard for you to understand how simple this is, because you can't quite appreciate our triumph over emotions like jealousy or wounded pride. Here the whole community works toward making a personal readjustment as easy as possible, instead of converting it into stock for the scandalmonger."

There was a slight flash of anger in Frazier's eyes as he said this, and he shifted his position on his cushion impatiently. I suddenly realized that he had been exceptionally unemotional up to this point. There had been no sign of his usual aggression. He was showing a beneficent, almost fatherly concern for the problem of marriage. I was inclined to interpret this again as merely a sign of confidence, but there was a suggestion of tenderness—of sentimentality—which almost astonished me. His manner became even softer as the conversation proceeded.

"What about the children?" I said. "The group care we saw this morning must also weaken the relation between parent and child."

"It does. By design. We have to attenuate the child-parent relation for several reasons. Group care is better than parental care. In the old pre-scientific days the early education of the child could be left to the parents, and indeed almost certainly had to be left to them. But with the rise of a science of behavior all is changed. The bad repute into which scientific child care has fallen is no reflection upon our technical knowledge of what should be done. The requirements of good child care are well established. Where we have failed is in getting good care in the average home. We have failed to teach the average parent even the simplest scientific principles. And that's not surprising. The control of behavior is an intricate science, into which the average mother could not be initiated without years of training. But the fact that most children today are badly raised isn't all the fault of a lack of technical skill, either. Even when the mother knows the right thing to do, she often can't do it in a household which is busy with other affairs. Home is not the place to raise children.

"Even when our young mothers and fathers become skilled nursery-school workers, we avoid a strong personal dependency. Our goal is to have every adult member of Walden Two regard all our children as his own, and to have every child think of every adult as his parent. To this end we have made it bad taste to single out one's own child for special favors. If you want to take your child on a picnic, the correct thing is to take several of his friends as well. If you want to give him a little present for his birthday, you are expected to give similar presents to the guests at his party. You may spend as much time as you like with your children, but to do so exclusively is taboo. The result is that a child never gets from its parents any services or favors which it does not also frequently get from others. We have untied the apron strings."

Frazier was still having trouble with his cushion. He tried several positions and eventually assumed a Buddha-like posture from which he seemed to speak with even greater oracular authority.

"Think what this means to the child who has no mother or father!

There is no occasion to envy companions who are not so deprived, because there is little or no practical difference. It's true he may not call any one 'Mother' or 'Father,' but we discourage this anyway, in favor of given names. And he frequently receives presents and attentions from many adults and may find among them one or more for whom he will develop deep affection.

"And think what it means, too, for the childless! They can express their natural affection toward children in spite of the biological or social accident which deprived them of parenthood. No sensible person will suppose that love or affection has anything to do with blood. One's love for one's wife is required by law to be free of a close blood connection. Foster children and stepchildren are loved as dearly as one's own. Love and affection are psychological and cultural, and blood relationships can be happily forgotten."

"Don't many parents resent sharing their children?" I said.

"Why should they? What are they actually sharing? They see more of their children than the typical mother in most upper-class households—where the arrangement is also, by the way, from choice. And much more than the average father. Many parents are glad to be relieved of the awful responsibility of being a child's only source of affection and help. Here it's impossible to be an inadequate or unskillful parent, and the vigorous, happy growth of our children is enough to remove any last suspicion that we have been deprived of anything.

"The weakening of the relation between parent and child is valuable in other ways," Frazier continued, with sustained gentleness. "When divorce cannot be avoided, the children are not embarrassed by severe changes in their way of life or their behavior toward their parents. It's also easy to induce the unfit or unwell to forego parenthood. No stigma attaches to being childless, and no lack of affection. That's what I meant when I said that experments in selective breeding would eventually be possible in Walden Two. The hereditary connection will be minimized to the point of being forgotten. Long before that, it will be possible to breed through artificial insemination without altering the personal relation of husband and wife. Our people will marry as they wish, but have children according to a genetic plan."

"It seems to me," said Castle, "that you're flying in the face of strong natural forces, just the same."

"What would you have said if I had proposed killing unwanted female babies?" said Frazier. "Yet that practice is condoned in some cultures. What do we really know about the *nature* of the parental relations? Anything? I doubt it."

"I'm reminded," I said, "of an earlier question of Mr. Castle's. What happens to 'identification'? Have you any substitute for the parent as a pattern for the child? If your boys don't want to 'be like Daddy' or, less happily, 'like Mama,' how are their personalities built up?"

"We know very little about what happens in identification," Frazier said. "No one has ever made a careful scientific analysis. The evidence isn't truly experimental. We have seen the process at work only in our standard family structure. The Freudian pattern may be due to the peculiarities of that structure or even the eccentricities of the members of the family. All we really know is that children tend to imitate adults, in gestures and mannerisms, and in personal attitudes and relations. They do that here, too, but since the family structure is changed, the effect is very different.

"Our children are cared for by many different people. It isn't institutional care, but genuine affection. Our members aren't overworked, and they haven't been forced into a job for which they have no talent or inclination. What the child imitates is a sort of essential happy adult. He can avoid the idiosyncrasies of a single parent. Identification is easy and valuable.

"Remember that the adults who care for our children are of both sexes. We have broken down prejudices regarding the occupations of the sexes, and we have worked particularly hard to keep a balance in the nursery and school system. There's no stigma attached to such work, and many men find it satisfying. The work in the nursery is very close to that of a highly skilled laboratory technician. By balancing the sexes we eliminate all the Freudian problems which arise from the asymmetrical relations to the female parent. But that's a technical problem which you and I can discuss some other time."

"But as the child grows older," I said, "doesn't he naturally single out particular individuals as objects of interest and affection?"

"That's exactly what we intend," said Frazier. "It may happen because of common interests: the artistically inclined will naturally be attracted to artists, the potential farmer will like to hang around the dairy. Or it may arise from a similarity of character or personality. In the family, identification is usually confined to one parent or the other, but neither one may have characteristics suitable to the child's developing personality. It's a sort of coerced identification, which we are glad to avoid."

"Don't these attenuated personal ties lead to feelings of insecurity?" said Castle.

"Who is insecure? And about what? Not our children, certainly. They have every chance in the world of getting affection and help from hundreds of adults. You will find your insecure child in the care of an overworked or emotional mother, or living with quarrelsome parents, or sent to school unprepared for needed adjustments, or left to get along with children from different cultural levels. We have *increased* the feeling of security of our children."

"I was thinking more of the women," Castle said, "the wives and mothers. Don't they feel that they are less necessary to their families?"

"Of course they do, and they ought to. You are talking about a tradition of slavery, and of the sentiments which have preserved it for thousands of years. The world has made some progress in the emancipation of women, but equality is still a long way off. There are few cultures today in which the rights of women are respected at all. America is one of perhaps three or four nations in which some progress has been made. Yet very few American women have the economic independence and cultural freedom of American men.

"Feelings of insecurity!" Frazier continued with increasing warmth. "The marriage system trades on them! What does the ordinary middle-class marriage amount to? Well, it's agreed that the husband will provide shelter, clothing, food, and perhaps some amusement, while the wife will work as a cook and cleaning woman and bear and raise children. The man is reasonably free to select or change his work; the woman has no choice, except between accepting and neglecting her lot. She has a legal claim for support, he has a claim for a certain type of labor.

"To make matters worse, we educate our women as if they were equal, and promise them equality. Is it any wonder they are soon disillusioned? The current remedy is to revive the slogans and sentiments which have made the system work in the past. The good wife is told to consider it an honor and a privilege to work in the kitchen, to make the beds every day, to watch the children. She is made to believe that she is *necessary,* that she has the care of her husband's happiness and health and also her children's. That's the stock treatment of the neurotic housewife: reconcile her to her lot! But the intelligent woman sees through it at once, no matter how hard she wants to believe. She knows very well that someone else could make the beds and get the meals and wash the clothes, and her family wouldn't know the difference. The role of mother she wants to play herself, but that has no more connection with her daily work than the role of father with his work in the office or factory or field.

"Here, there's no reason to feel that anyone is necessary to anyone else. Each of us is necessary in the same amount, which is very little. The community would go on just as smoothly tomorrow if any one of us died tonight. We cannot, therefore, get much satisfaction out of feeling important. But there are compensating satisfactions. Each of us is necessary as a person to the extent that he is loved as a person. No woman gets much satisfaction out of feeling that she will be missed as one misses a departed cook or scrub woman; she wants to be missed as a wife and mother. By providing good care for everyone as a matter of course, we emphasize the personal need. When a mother feels she is losing the affection of her child, she is more likely to discover the true reason. She will not try to make herself necessary by making her child more helpless. That's impossible. Her only recourse is to win back the affection of her child, and she is likely to do it if she understands the problem.

"The community, as a revised family, has changed the place of women more radically than that of men. Some women feel momentarily insecure for that reason. But their new position is more dignified, more enjoyable, and more healthful, and the whole question of security eventually vanishes. In a world of complete economic equality, you get and keep the affections you deserve. You can't buy love with gifts or favors, you can't hold love by raising an inadequate child, and you can't be secure in love by serving as a good scrub woman or a good provider."

"But I suspect you find it hardest to convince women of the advantages of community life," I said.

"Naturally! Those who stand to gain most are always the hardest to convince. That 's true of the exploited worker, too—and for the same reason. They have both been kept in their places, not by external force, but much more subtly by a system of beliefs implanted within their skins. It's sometimes an almost hopeless task to take the shackles off their souls, but it can be done. But, speaking of shackles, I mustn't keep you any longer from your work."

QUESTIONS AND TOPICS

1. Do you like the institution of early marriage advocated by Frazier? Can it work in an actual society? Could it be made to work in America?
2. Are Frazier's ideas about the rearing of children realistic? Can children be happy without strong family ties?
3. Frazier seems to favor the breakdown of the family unit. Do you think this breakdown is desirable?
4. In Walden Two women are treated equally once their biological function has been fulfilled. Is this desirable? Would most wives be happier not tied down to a household and its daily chores?

Albert Jay Nock

UTOPIA IN PENNSYLVANIA: THE AMISH

Though the Amish are an actual group of people, Albert Jay Nock, 1872?–1945, feels that they have achieved a utopia. It is the utopia of the conservative, a place where strong religious principle, sterling character, and hard work comprise the good life. Though some of these virtues may be fostered in Walden Two, Mr. Nock, in this 1941 essay, seems to favor the old-fashioned and reliable, rather than the new and experimental.

I

A long time ago, "when I was still a prince in Arcadia," I became interested in the language and literature of the Pennsylvania Germans. I had been rather astonished—I don't know why—at discovering accidentally that they had not only a literature of their own, but a good one, and that a thriving organization called the Pennsylvania German Society was busy fostering and preserving it. This was a pleasant surprise; and at odd times during two or three years I dipped at random into this literature, thus finally getting a fair-to-middling acquaintance with it, especially with its religious and pastoral poetry, the side by which it is seen in perhaps its most amiable and attractive aspect.

By origin, the Pennsylvania Germans spoke the dialect of the Pfalz; but in the course of a couple of centuries a good many English words have crept into their vocabulary to make everlasting sorrow and vexation for the outsider. A macaronic speech is easy enough to read when printed, but hardest of all (for me, at least) to understand when spoken. The

Italian which one hears down Greenwich Village way in New York, for instance, is very difficult on this account, even when it is otherwise pretty good Italian. The Pfälzer dialect is not troublesome if you take it straight, but by the time you have shifted gears to accommodate two or three English words in the course of a long sentence, your interlocutor is away out of sight down the homestretch, leaving you in an exhausted and ignorant state; especially since the English words come out so heavily coated with a foreign inflection that it takes a minute or so to penetrate their disguise and recognize them. In dealing with the printed word, however, one escapes these tribulations. Here, for example, is the first stanza of a poem from Harbaugh's *Harfe*. Read it aloud at ordinary conversational speed to someone who knows German well, and see what he makes of it; then let him look at it as printed, and see what he makes of that:—

> *Heit is 's 'xäctly zwansig Johr,*
> *Dass ich bin owwe naus;*
> *Nau bin ich widder lewig z'rick*
> *Un schteh am Schulhaus an d'r Krick,*
> *Juscht neekscht an's Dady's Haus.**

The second verse is still more distressing. Here you have a colloquial English verb—slang, to the purist—handsomely tailored up with a good German prefix; and you have also an exact German rendering of an English idiomatic expression. These are heartbreakers; to the ear they carry nothing but grief and woe, yet see how familiar and domestic is their look in print:—

> *Ich bin in hunnert Heiser g'west,*
> *Vun Märbelstee' un Brick,*
> *Un alles was sie hen, die Leit,*
> *Dhet ich verschwappe eenig Zeit*
> *For's Schulhaus an der Krick.†*

* It's exactly twenty years today
  That I've been out of the house;
  And now I'm back, feeling alive again
  By the schoolhouse on the creek,
  Right next to Daddy's house. [Ed.]
† I've stayed at a hundred houses,
  Of marble and of brick;
  And all the riches those people have
  I'd be willing to swap any time
  For the schoolhouse on the creek. [Ed.]

But I must stop rambling around in this peculiar philology, and get on with my story. Some years later, when the first bloom of my interest in the Pennsylvania Germans had been rubbed off under pressure of more immediate concerns, I noticed that they were being visited with the curse of publicity. Fictioneers, mostly of the female persuasion, *Gott soll hüten,** were exploiting them in popular magazinedom. Reporters played them up by the side of their prowess in eating and their alleged prowess in witch-craft, the two accomplishments most likely to strike fire with the great American public. One or two cookbooks of dubious authenticity appeared. Then when lately the inhabitants of a certain district were had up in court for refusing to send their children to a State central school, I perceived that the Pennsylvania Germans were really in the news.

I did not read any of the fiction, nor did I care about the *Hexerei,* but the two items about food and schools attracted me. The mention of food set up a nagging persistent hankering for a certain native country-made product which I had sampled many years before. I am not naming it because it seems to be scarce as hens' teeth, and having at last found it I am happily on the inside track and propose to stay there; so any inquiry about it will merely waste postage.

Thus my interest in the Pennsylvania Germans livened up again. My hankering for the food product would not subside, so I began to take measures. I wrote to the publisher of a book dealing largely with the region's cookery, asking him to sound out the young woman who wrote it; which he did, with no result. I wrote the chambers of commerce in the principal towns; the executive secretaries gave me names of some producers, to whom in turn I wrote without result. I then bethought me of my old friend Jeff Jones, who maintains a sales force in those parts; so I wrote him, suggesting that he turn his hellhounds loose to harry the whole countryside without respite, which I don't doubt he did, but they brought down no prey. At last I perceived that the matter required my personal attention. I determined to set forth in person and explore the counties of Lebanon and Lancaster with two objects in view. First, I would see what account of themselves the Pennsylvania Germans were actually giving. Second, I would find that food product if it existed, whether in the heavens above those two counties, or on the earth beneath, or in the waters under the earth. The opportunity presenting itself, I went and was successful. I found the food product, as I have already said,

* God help us! [Ed.]

and bore it away in a burst of glory. I also found that the Pennsylvania Germans have a vast deal to say for themselves. One group especially excited my interest, and it is of them that I propose now to speak.

II

They are known as the Old Amish or House Amish. They are a split-off from the Mennonites, a religious body formed at Zurich early in the sixteenth century. In number, the Old Amish run to something between 8500 and 9000, and of these some 1500 are settled in the county of Lancaster, mostly on a stretch of rich farmland bordered by the Conestoga. They have been there since 1720, and their small rural communities grew up under odd names like Smoketown, Bird-in-hand, Blue Ball. I could get no reliable account of the origin of these names.

The Old Amish are reputed to be the best farmers in America, and a glance at their territory sets up a strong conviction that this is so. The Amishman is actually a farmer, not a manufacturer, like our large-scale single-crop producers. Nor is he a political farmer, of the kind whose perennial sorrows lie so close to the heart of Mr. Wallace.* He cares nothing whatever for Mr. Wallace, and asks no political favors from anybody. His produce goes first to feed his family and his livestock. If any be left over, he takes it to the public markets at Lancaster; and by the way, if you want to see something which you could really call a public market, go to Lancaster. I never in my life saw so much superexcellent superelegant produce of all kinds clustered together as I saw there, and practically all of it was Amish produce. But speaking commercially, the Amishman's market trade is on the side; what he gets out of it is loose change—lagniappe. He is not a truck-gardener. After the needs of his family are provided for, after he has put down great store and abundance of beef products, pork products, dairy products, vegetable and cereal products, all of his own raising—then if he can pick up an odd dollar or two in the markets, well and good; but not before.

Judged by current standards, the Amishman has an unorthodox view of his mission in life. His one cash crop is tobacco. If he were a right-minded man, he would put down all the land he could get hold of in tobacco, and let his family eat out of tin cans. But in the first place, he does not want any more land than he and his family can work properly

* Henry Wallace, Secretary of Agriculture under Franklin D. Roosevelt.

under their own steam. He is not keen on hired help, and sees nothing in share-cropping. Then further, he has only very vague and uncertain notions about tin cans; I suspect you might have to go quite a way to find a can opener in an Amish household, or to find anybody who has ever seen one. For the Amishman, the idea of paying out good money for canned foodstuffs far inferior to what one can raise for oneself is one of those things that simply will not bear thinking about. Hence he limits his cash crop rigorously; it is strictly a side line, like his other market trade. It yields him plenty of money to go on with, for he needs hardly any, and he lets it go at that.

By sticking to this general policy for a couple of centuries, the Amish have worked themselves into an economic position that is pretty nearly impregnable. They have the real thing in "social security." Ten years ago, one of my town-dwelling friends wrote to a correspondent asking how Lancaster was doing under the depression. The correspondent telegraphed back, "What depression? There is no depression here." The Amish, putting it mildly, are exceeding well-to-do; or as the sinful would phrase it, they are rich as soap grease. I have heard say that Lancaster County is the richest agricultural region in the world, and I believe it; richest, that is, in good hard available cash money that can be dug up on demand at any moment, out of the Amishman's pants pocket.

The Amish beat the New Deal's whole program of social security, hands down. They have the best form of old-age pension that can be devised; when you grow old you simply take things easy, and live *wie Gott in Frankreich* * while your family carries on. No need for some officious nincompoop to come down from Washington and tell you how to do that. So also with "relief." No Amishman's name was ever yet on the relief roll of Lancaster County, and none ever will be. The Amishman does not waste a single bawbee on insurance, for he already has the best kind of insurance, on which he pays no premiums and his policy never expires. If lightning strikes his barn, his coreligionists in that district build him a new one; if he is ill, they help out with his work; if he dies untimely, they make arrangements to have things go on. No insurance company can compete with that.

He takes no oaths and signs no contracts or any form of written agreement, nor will he serve on juries or have anything to do with litigation;

* As God lives in France. Metaphorically, living on the fat of the land. [Ed.]

his religion forbids him all such. He lets his yea be yea and his nay nay, as the Bible commands, and he always keeps his given word. He is not a speculator or a borrower, and he does not hold public office. He is punctilious about taxes, paying the State's blackmail in full, and asking nothing in return but to be let alone—poor soul, as if that were not the very last thing the State would ever consent to do for anybody! The State lately foisted a grant of some $56,000 on the Old Amish for a PWA project in one of their townships, and they not only refused to accept it but appealed to the courts to have the noisome proposal nullified. It is no wonder that when this incredible miracle was reported at Washington the effect on the PWA personnel was devastating; fifteen fainted away, eleven went into convulsions, and three of them died. I have this on good authority.

III

The visitor does not have to look too closely to see what principle, what general theory of life, is at work here to bring this exemplary state of things about. It is religion. The Old Amish have the record of sticking longer and more faithfully to the original tenets, customs, and practices of their religion than any other Christian body in America; and it is this fidelity which has brought them where they are. This obviously says something for the Old Amish themselves, individually and collectively; but it also says something rather handsome for their religion. In the matter of getting results—and this is what all variants of religion presumably aim at—the Old Amish variant seems valid enough to stand up under the fire of criticism's most heftiest *Blitzkrieg*. Like the provisions of the Levitical law, its tenets, apparently arbitrary as many of them are, turn out to have a surprising deal of sound science and sound common sense behind them. In this they furnish material for advantageous comparison with the tenets and practices of other religious bodies. They will not, and should not, suggest to these bodies a wholesale taking over and substitution of Old Amish tenets and practices to displace their own. They do suggest, however, that if the other bodies want results comparable with those the Old Amish get under their conditions, they should make whatever modifications and displacements are appropriate to bringing them about under their own conditions.

The Old Amish believe that the agrarian life is the one most in accord with the Scriptures. This is their fundamental tenet; it merely puts a religious sanction on the agrarian doctrine held by Turgot, Benjamin Franklin, and above all by Mr. Jefferson. The Amishman's logic of it is that man is a land-animal; God made him so. He derives his sustenance wholly from the land, and every kind and form of wealth that exists or can exist is producible only by the application of labor and capital to land; God made this arrangement. Therefore the more direct the mode of this application, the better and simpler becomes the fulfillment of God's will.

Now, whatever one may think of the theological side of this reasoning, the economic side of it is sound to the core. It is the basic position of fundamental economics, and there is no sophistry by which one can squirm away from it. But for the Amish the theological side is also sound, and they are strong on it; it sums up pretty much all the dogmatic theology the Amish have. They are probably a little weak on economic theory, but they are strong on the theological rationale of their agrarianism. It is the controlling principle of their lives. The result is that under this control their practice of sound agrarian economics has made them a solvent, stable, self-respecting people, as prosperous as any in the land and certainly the most independent; and it has also confirmed in them the sterling character and sterling moral qualities to which I have alluded.

Perhaps—I put it tentatively—perhaps this is about all that should be expected from this combination of forces. It is a highly respectable showing, to say the very least of it. I am told there is complaint against organized Christianity as being "out of touch with practical life" and therefore so dissatisfying that the churches are losing ground—well, here is one variant of organized Christianity, at any rate, which surely does not come under that censure.

Artemus Ward said the trouble with Napoleon was that he tried to do too much, and did it. Something like this may be the trouble with organized Christianity at large. The expectations it puts upon human nature may be a little excessive. The ultimate secular aim it proposes for the individual may not be quite simple and definite enough, and its confessional constructions may involve more metaphysics than the average mind can comfortably take in. I feel free to suggest this because I myself am far too simple-minded to get the drift of such apologetic literature, even of the most modern type, as has come my way. When I ask myself just what it is driving at, and what it proposes for me to drive at, I am wholly at a loss for an answer.

In these respects the Old Amish variant is exceptional. On its confessional side it has next to nothing, no formal creed, no metaphysical formulas, no elaborate theology. On its secular side, its aim for the individual is simple, clear, and moderate. Its counsels and assistances are all directed towards the twofold end of making him an upright man and a first-class farmer. Beyond this they seem not to go. Judging by results, one would think that the rest of organized Christianity might profit by analogous— not the same, or similar, but analogous—simplifications, both of confessional content and practical intention.

All the prescriptions, customs, and practices which the Old Amish variant enforces tend towards the same end, even those which, as I have said, seem petty and arbitrary. They have actually the character and sanction of religious ritual, and there is no trouble about understanding their full and exact import. With the best will in the world, one can hardly say so much for such other variants of organized Christianity as I am acquainted with. For instance, in the November *Atlantic* Dr. Bell cites "one of the world's most harassed statesmen" as saying, "I could not live, I think . . . if I could not go to Mass. I assist several times a week." This devotion is all very well and highly commendable, but when this harassed statesman goes on to account for his devotion to this ritual practice in terms of what accrues from it (*mea culpa,* maybe *maxima culpa; prava et turpissima culpa,** if you like—however, there it is) I don't understand one single word of what he is talking about.

On the other hand, I get the bearing of the Amishman's ritual prescriptions instantly and with no trouble at all. They all aim, as I have said, at making him an upright man and a good farmer; and anybody knows sufficiently well what a good farmer is and what an upright man is, and what qualities go into their making. Moreover, one can hardly fail to see that if conduct be three-fourths of life, and if religion be supposed to bear at all on conduct, the very simplicity, clearness, and directness of the Amishman's prescriptions, their strict avoidance of trying to do too much, are decidedly advantageous in respect of conduct, by comparison with the more indeterminate and apparently unrelated prescriptions laid down by other variants of organized Christianity. For instance, while Dr. Bell's harassed statesman may be an exception, I never knew or heard of a modern statesman, harassed or otherwise, who would boggle for an instant at

---

* I am guilty, I am most guilty; I am wrongly and most repulsively guilty. [Ed.]

lying like a hundred devils, if some political exigency required it of him; nor one who would not on like occasion break his word at a moment's notice, connive at any form of violence and crime, or act the part of an arrant swindler. The Amishman will do none of these things under any circumstances. Thus while religion's higher satisfactions such as the harassed statesman speaks of, whatever those are, may be inaccessible to the Amishman, he plods his way throughout the whole broad area of conduct with the firm step of a pretty tolerably well accredited citizen; and this, I repeat, no modern statesman that I know or ever heard of seems either able to do or even notably desirous of doing. The Amishman quite literally "lives by his religion," and his religion seems to be a workable one to live by. At any rate, he does not turn to it, or return to it, from motives of weakness, disillusionment, or fear. In this respect he appears to have a decided advantage over the reclaimed brethren Dr. Bell cites in his admirable article.

Coming now to less recondite matters, the Old Amish get a little "edge" even on the Quakers, in not having any churches. They meet for worship in their houses, taking them in turn throughout the district. They have no stated ministry. Each district chooses its minister by lot from among its own number, to serve for a year. He has no special training; every Amishman is presumed to be qualified for a job of such simplicity, and no doubt is. He is not paid one single picayune. These economical arrangements keep down the overhead, thereby wholly doing away with the need for ministerial salesmanship, advertising, canvassing for new members, and all other money-raising devices—a need which appears most seriously, often exclusively, to preoccupy other Christian communities.

There is a sound idea here. If you want to "purify politics," whether Church politics or secular politics, begin by taking the money out of it. You won't have to do much else; human nature will do the rest. It is exactly Lincoln Steffens's idea of fixing the responsibility for the Fall of Man. Some blame Adam, while others put the blame on Eve; Steffens put it on the apple. If the apple had not been there everything would have gone smoothly. Obviously, then, the thing to do in like circumstances is to take away the apple. If you do this you can't have any trouble, and this is what the Old Amish have done, thereby giving evidence of a great brain and a level head.

By this device they have closed up every loophole against professionalism. Rapid rotation in unpaid office, combined with absence of all special training, is death on the development of a priestly class. Sacerdotalism does not stand a dog's chance with the Old Amish; and the elaborate metaphysical *Aberglaube* * of its associated sacramentalism stands no better chance. All this seems to suggest an opportunity for further simplification on the part of other Christian bodies. It is surely a fair question whether a competent practice of religion calls for quite as much apparatus, metaphysical and physical, as the main body of organized Christianity has constructed and is trying, none too successfully, to keep in running order. There need be, and should be, no thought of taking over the Old Amish pattern as it stands; yet no well-ordered mind should be above looking it over, on the chance of finding food for profitable thought.

Like orthodox Jews and Roman Catholics, the Old Amish send their children to schools of their own, to avoid contaminating contacts. They do not educate their children beyond the eighth grade, in the belief that this comprises all the book learning that a good farmer needs. There is much to be said for this view, and everything to be said for Mr. Jefferson's further view that this is as much as any but the very rarely exceptional child can use to any good purpose. America is now paying enormous amounts of margin on its cat-and-dog investments in a type of citizen "whose education is far too much for his abilities," as the Duke of Wellington said. Amish children may not enter the professions or the white-collar vocations, and this without prejudice to either; if, for instance, the Amishman has occasion to employ a physician, he gets the best one he can find and ungrudgingly pays him top prices. The only point is that in pursuance of the will of God those children are to stay on the land, and should be learning how to work the paternal acreage with love and reverence as well as skill. An Amish boy who wants to go to college and then take up a profession may of course do so, but not by easy gravitation. He must break with his religion, tradition, and family; and if his call is loud enough, and if he has grit enough to scrabble over this three-barred obstruction, the chances are that he is the sort to succeed. One cannot be sure but that this is as it should be, for we are discovering that the way to a desirable thing can be made altogether too easy. I am told, however, that the Amish children very seldom break over the traces, and one can easily see good reason why this should be so. They are already booked at birth for inheritance in about the soundest going

* Superstition. [Ed.]

concern in the United States, so why leave a bone for a shadow? They will always eat, and eat mighty well, always be well-clad, well-housed. They will never lose their jobs, never worry about their wives and children wanting bread, never punch a clock, truckle to a gang-boss, or scuffle for a living against cutthroat competition. They will always be able to look the world in the face and think and say exactly what they dam' well please about anything and anybody. Isn't that pretty much the old-time American ideal?

The Old Amish house themselves well, and keep their houses with the most painstaking neatness, but they have no central heating, their furniture is sparse and simple, and they have no ornaments. They use no electricity, thus escaping the distractions of the telephone, radio, telegraph, and motion picture. They do not use automobiles, but are finished experts with the horse and buggy; many, probably most of them, have never been farther away from home than the county town. They wear always the same cut of clothes, as distinctive as a uniform, with no adornment of any kind, not even buttons; their coats are fastened with hooks and eyes. If someone appears in their midst wearing buttoned garments, he is known at once as a "stylisher," and is given more or less of a wide berth. All these are religious observances. As can be easily seen, their aim is to encourage thrift and a wholesome simplicity of living, to promote domestic and communal solidarity, and to hit the golden mean between too much ease and comfort and too little. However rigorous and niggling such regulations may appear to us, it is a mistake to regard them as bearing heavily on their votaries, or to regard the Amish as a "stubborn, fierce and isolated people," as Matthew Arnold describes the Jews of early days. On the contrary, they have excellent humor, are fond of fun, and are extremely sociable and jolly among themselves; not, however, with strangers. They amuse themselves, as they do all things, simply and heartily; the lighter side of their life seems to be about what it was with their progenitors living in the Pfalz; or indeed, pretty much what it was with our own progenitors living in America not so many years ago.

IV

In studying any order of fauna one gets some impressions less agreeable than others. I got a few from the Amish that I thought were hardly worth carrying away with me, so I was glad to forget them. What did me a great and lasting good was to see what I had come to think existed no-

where in America, a people with clear strong sense of the *ne quid nimis,* *
and resolute determination to live by that sense. I was among them for
only a short time, and saw their life only from outside; they are not
partial to strangers. But even so, it was a cheering and hope-inspiring
experience to touch the fringes of a well-to-do, prosperous, hard-working
society which does not believe in too much money, too much land, too
much impedimenta, too much ease, comfort, schooling, mechanization,
aimless movement, idle curiosity; which does not believe in too many
labor-saving devices, gadgets, gimcracks; and which has the force of character—fed and sustained by a type of religion which seems really designed
to get results—the force of sterling character, I say, to keep itself well on
the safe lee side of all such excesses.

QUESTIONS AND TOPICS

1. Would you like to live among the Amish? What would you find congenial
   in their society? What would you dislike?
2. Mr. Nock's conservatism is revealed by his strong dislike of federal inter-
   ference and his stress on religion and character. Do you think that old-
   fashioned religion is a virtue? Do you think that "character" can win out in
   the modern world?
3. Lately there have been reports that many Amish and Mennonite children
   have become dissatisfied with their traditional way of life. They are lured by
   television, central heating, and automobiles. Do you sympathize with their
   parents, who lament the destruction of the old way of life, or with the children, who wish to share in the bounties of modern civilization?

* Nothing too much. [Ed.]

Alfred, Lord Tennyson

THE
LOTOS-EATERS

*Alfred, Lord Tennyson, 1809–
1892, was an English poet fascinated by ancient fable and romance.
One of his most famous poems is a
dramatic monologue concerning the
spiritual seduction of some of Odys-
seus' sailors. They choose to stay in
a land of languor and forgetfulness
rather than return home. According
to many critics, Tennyson finds
fault with these men for having
given up family, ambition, and responsibility.*

"Courage!" he said, and pointed toward the land,
"This mounting wave will roll us shoreward soon."
In the afternoon they came unto a land
In which it seemed always afternoon.
All round the coast the languid air did swoon,
Breathing like one that hath a weary dream.
Full-faced above the valley stood the moon;
And, like a downward smoke, the slender stream
Along the cliff to fall and pause and fall did seem.

A land of streams! some, like a downward smoke,
Slow-dropping veils of thinnest lawn, did go;
And some thro' wavering lights and shadows broke,
Rolling a slumbrous sheet of foam below.
They saw the gleaming river seaward flow
From the inner land; far off, three mountain-tops,
Three silent pinnacles of aged snow,

Stood sunset-flush'd; and, dew'd with showery drops,
Up-clomb the shadowy pine above the woven copse.

The charmed sunset linger'd low adown
In the red West; thro' mountain clefts the dale
Was seen far inland, and the yellow down
Border'd with palm, and many a winding vale
And meadow, set with slender galingale;
A land where all things always seem'd the same!
And round about the keel with faces pale,
Dark faces pale against that rosy flame,
The mild-eyed melancholy Lotos-eaters came.

Branches they bore of that enchanted stem,
Laden with flower and fruit, whereof they gave
To each, but whoso did receive of them
And taste, to him the gushing of the wave
Far far away did seem to mourn and rave
On alien shores; and if his fellow spake,
His voice was thin, as voices from the grave;
And deep-asleep he seem'd, yet all awake,
And music in his ears his beating heart did make.

They sat them down upon the yellow sand,
Between the sun and moon upon the shore;
And sweet it was to dream of Fatherland,
Of child, and wife, and slave; but evermore
Most weary seem'd the sea, weary the oar,
Weary the wandering fields of barren foam.
Then some one said, "We will return no more";
And all at once they sang, "Our island home
Is far beyond the wave; we will no longer roam."

CHORIC SONG

There is sweet music here that softer falls
Than petals from blown roses on the grass,

Or night-dews on still waters between walls
Of shadowy granite, in a gleaming pass;
Music that gentlier on the spirit lies,
Than tired eyelids upon tired eyes;
Music that brings sweet sleep down from the blissful skies.
Here are cool mosses deep,
And through the moss the ivies creep,
And in the stream the long-leaved flowers weep,
And from the craggy ledge the poppy hangs in sleep.

Why are we weighed upon with heaviness,
And utterly consumed with sharp distress,
While all things else have rest from weariness?
All things have rest: why should we toil alone,
We only toil, who are the first of things,
And make perpetual moan,
Still from one sorrow to another thrown;
Nor ever fold our wings,
And cease from wanderings,
Nor steep our brows in slumber's holy balm;
Nor hearken what the inner spirit sings,
"There is no joy but calm!"—
Why should we only toil, the roof and crown of things?

Lo! in the middle of the wood,
The folded leaf is wooed from out the bud
With winds upon the branch, and there
Grows green and broad, and takes no care,
Sun-steeped at noon, and in the moon
Nightly dew-fed; and turning yellow
Falls, and floats adown the air.
Lo! sweetened with the summer light,
The full-juiced apple, waxing over-mellow,
Drops in a silent autumn night.
All its allotted length of days
The flower ripens in its place,
Ripens and fades, and falls, and hath no toil,
Fast-rooted in the fruitful soil.

Hateful is the dark-blue sky,
Vaulted o'er the dark-blue sea.
Death is the end of life; ah, why
Should life all labour be?
Let us alone. Time driveth onward fast,
And in a little while our lips are dumb.
Let us alone. What is it that will last?
All things are taken from us, and become
Portions and parcels of the dreadful past.
Let us alone. What pleasure can we have
To war with evil? Is there any peace
In ever climbing up the climbing wave?
All things have rest, and ripen toward the grave
In silence—ripen, fall, and cease:
Give us long rest or death, dark death, or dreamful ease.

How sweet it were, hearing the downward stream,
With half-shut eyes ever to seem
Falling asleep in a half-dream!
To dream and dream, like yonder amber light,
Which will not leave the myrrh-bush on the height;
To hear each other's whispered speech;
Eating the Lotos day by day,
To watch the crisping ripples on the beach,
And tender curving lines of creamy spray;
To lend our hearts and spirits wholly
To the influence of mild-minded melancholy;
To muse and brood and live again in memory,
With those old faces of our infancy
Heaped over with a mound of grass,
Two handfuls of white dust, shut in an urn of brass!

Dear is the memory of our wedded lives,
And dear the last embraces of our wives
And their warm tears; but all hath suffered change;
For surely now our household hearths are cold,
Our sons inherit us, our looks are strange,
And we should come like ghosts to trouble joy.

Or else the island princes over-bold
Have eat our substance, and the minstrel sings
Before them of the ten years' war in Troy,
And our great deeds, as half-forgotten things.
Is there confusion in the little isle?
Let what is broken so remain.
The Gods are hard to reconcile;
'Tis hard to settle order once again.
There *is* confusion worse than death,
Trouble on trouble, pain on pain,
Long labour unto aged breath,
Sore task to hearts worn out by many wars
And eyes grown dim with gazing on the pilot-stars.

But, propt on beds of amaranth and moly,
How sweet—while warm airs lull us, blowing lowly—
With half-dropt eyelid still,
Beneath a heaven dark and holy,
To watch the long bright river drawing slowly
His waters from the purple hill—
To hear the dewy echoes calling
From cave to cave through the thick-twined vine—
To watch the emerald-coloured water falling
Through many a woven acanthus-wreath divine!
Only to hear and see the far-off sparkling brine,
Only to hear were sweet, stretched out beneath the pine.

The Lotos blooms below the barren peak,
The Lotos blows by every winding creek;
All day the wind breathes low with mellower tone;
Through every hollow cave and alley lone
Round and round the spicy downs the yellow Lotos-dust is blown.
We have had enough of action, and of motion we,
Rolled to starboard, rolled to larboard, when the surge was seething free,
Where the wallowing monster spouted his foam-fountains in the sea.

Let us swear an oath, and keep it with an equal mind,
In the hollow Lotos-land to live and lie reclined

On the hills like Gods together, careless of mankind.
For they lie beside their nectar, and the bolts are hurled
Far below them in the valleys, and the clouds are lightly curled
Round their golden houses, girdled with the gleaming world;
Where they smile in secret, looking over wasted lands,
Blight and famine, plague and earthquake, roaring deeps and fiery sands,
Clanging fights, and flaming towns, and sinking ships and praying hands.
But they smile, they find a music centred in a doleful song
Steaming up, a lamentation and an ancient tale of wrong,
Like a tale of little meaning though the words are strong;
Chanted from an ill-used race of men that cleave the soil,
Sow the seed, and reap the harvest with enduring toil,
Storing yearly little dues of wheat, and wine and oil;
Till they perish and they suffer—some, 'tis whispered—down in hell
Suffer endless anguish, others in Elysian valleys dwell,
Resting weary limbs at last on beds of asphodel.
Surely, surely, slumber is more sweet than toil, the shore
Than labour in the deep mid-ocean, wind and wave and oar;
O, rest, brother mariners, we will not wander more.

QUESTIONS AND TOPICS

1. How would you describe Tennyson's attitude toward the lotos-eaters?
2. Does the lotos-eater's "paradise" resemble the world of the hippies? What do you think of the hippies' world?
3. Would you like to live with the lotos-eaters? Temporarily or permanently?

8

THE
LIMITATIONS
OF
MAN

DESPITE THE FACT that men long for utopias, they have never achieved one. Perhaps it would be contrary to their nature for them to do so. Though Shakespeare's Hamlet remarked: "What a piece of work is a man! How noble in reason! how infinite in faculty! in form, in moving, how express and admirable!" he also saw man as a "quintessence of dust." In fact, much of the world's great writing concerns itself, not with dreams, but with realities, not with wish fulfillment, but with a sober assessment of man's limitations.

Many students decry man's propensity for war. Though Marxists have blamed warfare on capitalism, the Soviet Union has not hesitated to use armed force, or the threat of it, to keep its smaller neighbors in line. It would appear that, whatever his political institutions, man's natural inclinations sometimes lead him toward agression.

Man is also attacked for his deficiency in the values he preaches. Both Tolstoy's Ivan Ilyich and Dostoevsky's ridiculous man contain within themselves the forces that destroy the goodness they crave. Apart from man's ambivalence, other internal troubles plague him: the despair expressed so vividly by Emily Dickinson is a human emotion all of us have felt.

Yet man cannot be held accountable for all his suffering. He is subject to the forces of nature and chance. Old age and death await him. Moved by man's helplessness in an alien universe, Theodore Roethke in "The Meadow Mouse" expresses compassion for all who suffer without cause.

Ultimately the student will decide for himself whether to be optimistic or pessimistic about life. If he chooses the pessimistic position, some day, like Ivan Ilyich and the ridiculous man, he may discover several good reasons why life is worth living, in spite of man's limitations.

William Butler Yeats

LAMENTATION
OF THE
OLD PENSIONER

*William Butler Yeats, 1895–1939,
a significant force in Ireland's literary revival and one of the greatest
modern poets, often treated old age
in an immediate and dramatic
manner. In the following poem his
old pensioner confronts what has
been one of man's greatest limitations.*

Although I shelter from the rain
Under a broken tree
My chair was nearest to the fire
In every company
That talked of love or politics,
Ere Time transfigured me.

Though lads are making pikes again
For some conspiracy,
And crazy rascals rage their fill
At human tyranny,
My contemplations are of Time
That has transfigured me.

There's not a woman turns her face
Upon a broken tree,
And yet the beauties that I loved
Are in my memory;
I spit into the face of Time
That has transfigured me.

QUESTIONS AND TOPICS

1. Do you find the old pensioner's attitude towards time admirable or offensive?
2. What negative effects must old age have on a person's private and professional life? What compensations does old age bring?
3. With modern improvements in medicine and increased pensions, elderly people now are faced with many years of life after retirement. What kind of life awaits them?
4. Write a character sketch of an elderly person whom you know.

Dylan Thomas

DO NOT GO
GENTLE INTO
THAT GOOD NIGHT

*The Welsh poet, Dylan Thomas,
1914–1953, was a man with an
immense passion for life and a
writer with an enormous gift for
language. Here he manifests both
qualities in an eloquent attack
against mortality.*

Do not go gentle into that good night,
Old age should burn and rave at close of day;
Rage, rage against the dying of the light.

Though wise men at their end know dark is right,
Because their words had forked no lightning they
Do not go gentle into that good night.

Good men, the last wave by, crying how bright
Their frail deeds might have danced in a green bay
Rage, rage against the dying of the light.

Wild men who caught and sang the sun in flight,
And learn, too late, they grieved it on its way,
Do not go gentle into that good night.

Grave men, near death, who see with blinding sight
Blind eyes could blaze like meteors and be gay,
Rage, rage against the dying of the light.

And you, my father, there on the sad height,
Curse, bless, me now with your fierce tears, I pray.
Do not go gentle into that good night.
Rage, rage against the dying of the light.

QUESTIONS AND TOPICS

1. The four kinds of men described in the middle stanzas rage at death for different reasons. What are these reasons?
2. Do you find the poem a proper response to death?
3. Read Swift's account of the Struldbrugs, or immortals, in Book III of *Gulliver's Travels*. Why does Swift feel that death is necessary? Do you agree? Write your own account of a world without death.

Carl Sandburg

FOUR PRELUDES
ON PLAYTHINGS
OF THE WIND

Carl Sandburg, 1878–1967, was a poet who saw the glories and deficiencies of America's great cities. In this poem from Smoke and Steel, *1920, he offers a commentary on the vanity of man's achievements.*

"The past is a bucket of ashes."

I

The woman named To-morrow
sits with a hairpin in her teeth
and takes her time
and does her hair the way she wants it
and fastens at last the last braid and coil
and puts the hairpin where it belongs
and turns and drawls: Well, what of it?
My grandmother, Yesterday, is gone.
What of it? Let the dead be dead.

II

The doors were cedar
and the panels strips of gold
and the girls were golden girls
and the panels read and the girls chanted:
   We are the greatest city,
   the greatest nation:
   nothing like us ever was.

The doors are twisted on broken hinges.
Sheets of rain swish through on the wind
  where the golden girls ran and the panels read:
  We are the greatest city,
  the greatest nation:
  nothing like us ever was.

III

It has happened before.
Strong men put up a city and got
  a nation together,
And paid singers to sing and women
  to warble: We are the greatest city,
  the greatest nation:
  nothing like us ever was.

And while the singers sang
and the strong men listened
and paid the singers well
and felt good about it all,
  there were rats and lizards who listened
  . . . and the only listeners left now
  . . . are . . . the rats . . . and the lizards.

And there are black crows
crying, "Caw, caw,"
bringing mud and sticks
building a nest
  over the words carved
  on the doors where the panels were cedar
  and the strips on the panels were gold
  and the golden girls came singing:
  We are the greatest city,
  the greatest nation:
  nothing like us ever was.

The only singers now are crows crying, "Caw,
  caw,"

And the sheets of rain whine in the wind and
    doorways.
And the only listeners now are . . . the rats . . .
    and the lizards.

IV

The feet of the rats
scribble on the doorsills;
the hieroglyphs of the rat footprints
chatter the pedigrees of the rats
and babble of the blood
and gabble of the breed
of the grandfathers and the great-grandfathers
of the rats.

And the wind shifts
and the dust on a doorsill shifts
and even the writing of the rat footprints
tells us nothing, nothing at all
about the greatest city, the greatest nation
where the strong men listened
and the women warbled: Nothing like us ever was.

QUESTIONS AND TOPICS

1. What meaning does the figure "To-morrow" have in the context of the poem? What is the significance of the singing girls? Why do the hieroglyphs of the rats' footprints chatter about pedigrees?
2. Is the poet's commentary applicable to our present great cities—to New York, Chicago or Los Angeles? Will it be?
3. Is Sandburg also attacking nationalism? How does this theme relate to the decay of cities?
4. Do you think American civilization will ultimately decay?
5. Write a fable of your own about the destruction of a city or civilization.

Wilfred Owen

DULCE ET DECORUM EST

Although death must come to everyone, man has consistently assisted the process through what some have called legalized murder. Wilfred Owen, 1893–1918, one of the best war poets of our century, was himself killed in battle one week before the end of World War I.

Bent double, like old beggars under sacks,
Knock-kneed, coughing like hags, we cursed through sludge
Till on the haunting flares we turned our backs,
And towards our distant rest began to trudge.
Men marched asleep. Many had lost their boots,
But limped on, blood-shod. All went lame, all blind;
Drunk with fatigue; deaf even to the hoots
Of gas-shells dropping softly behind.

Gas! Gas! Quick, boys!—An ecstasy of fumbling,
Fitting the clumsy helmets just in time,
But someone still was yelling out and stumbling
And floundering like a man in fire or lime.—
Dim through the misty panes and thick green light,
As under a green sea, I saw him drowning.

In all my dreams before my helpless sight
He plunges at me, guttering, choking, drowning.

If in some smothering dreams, you too could pace
Behind the wagon that we flung him in,

And watch the white eyes writhing in his face,
His hanging face, like a devil's sick of sin;
If you could hear, at every jolt, the blood
Come gargling from the froth-corrupted lungs,
Bitter as the cud
Of vile, incurable sores on innocent tongues,—
My friend, you would not tell with such high zest
To children ardent for some desperate glory,
The old Lie: Dulce et decorum est
Pro patria mori.*

QUESTIONS AND TOPICS

1. Why does the poet use "Dulce et Decorum Est" for the title?
2. Do you think that it is right that a country ask its young men to go through the experience described in the poem?
3. What do you think of John F. Kennedy's statement, "Ask not what your country can do for you—ask what you can do for your country"?
4. Is war a necessary result of Western man's political structure? Do you think it is possible to have a world without war?
5. Recently a social scientist claimed that wars are caused by man's inherent aggression. Do you agree? Are men and women different in this respect?

* "Dulce et decorum est pro patria mori" means "It is sweet and fitting to die for one's country" (Horace's *Odes,* Book III, Poem ii). [Ed.]

Emily Dickinson

THERE'S A CERTAIN SLANT OF LIGHT

Unrecognized and almost unpublished during her lifetime, Emily Dickinson, 1830–1886, today is considered one of America's greatest poets. During her quiet life she wrote some eight hundred short poems which present in a remarkably concentrated way the history of an intense and complex woman. Despair was one of her themes, a despair deeply poignant in its expression, and universal in its implications.

There's a certain Slant of light,
Winter Afternoons—
That oppresses, like the Heft
Of Cathedral Tunes—

Heavenly Hurt, it gives us—
We can find no scar,
But internal difference,
Where the Meanings, are—

None may teach it— Any—
'Tis the Seal Despair—
An imperial affliction
Sent us of the Air—

When it comes, the Landscape listens—
Shadows—hold their breath—

When it goes, 'tis like the Distance
On the look of Death—

QUESTIONS AND TOPICS

1. Why does the poet use religious imagery?
2. Have you ever had an experience similar to the poet's? Describe it in your own language.
3. Why does man fall to victim to despair in spite of his achievements?

Theodore Roethke

THE
MEADOW
MOUSE

A victim of despair, Theodore Roethke, 1908–1963, apparently took his own life when he was beginning to achieve great fame as a poet. In an informal way "The Meadow Mouse" makes a relatively unimportant experience into a significant commentary on human fragility.

1

In a shoe box stuffed in an old nylon stocking
Sleeps the baby mouse I found in the meadow,
Where he trembled and shook beneath a stick
Till I caught him up by the tail and brought him in,
Cradled in my hand,
A little quaker, the whole body of him trembling,
His absurd whiskers sticking out like a cartoon-mouse,
His feet like small leaves,
Little lizard-feet,
Whitish and spread wide when he tried to struggle away,
Wriggling like a miniscule puppy.

Now he's eaten his three kinds of cheese and drunk from his bottle-cap
    watering-trough—
So much he just lies in one corner,
His tail curled under him, his belly big
As his head; his bat-like ears
Twitching, tilting toward the least sound.

Do I imagine he no longer trembles
When I come close to him?
He seems no longer to tremble.

2

But this morning the shoe-box house on the back porch is empty
Where has he gone, my meadow mouse,
My thumb of a child that nuzzled in my palm?—
To run under the hawk's wing,
Under the eye of the great owl watching from the elm-tree,
To live by courtesy of the shrike, the snake, the tom-cat.

I think of the nestling fallen into the deep grass,
The turtle gasping in the dusty rubble of the highway,
The paralytic stunned in the tub, and the water rising,—
All things innocent, hapless, forsaken.

QUESTIONS AND TOPICS

1. Discuss the meaning of the last stanza. How does the poet involve mankind
   in the meaning of the poem?
2. Can you relate the poem to Emily Dickinson's?
3. Are there people born to be life's victims or is the role self-made? Is it possible to have a world without such victims? Are we all, in a sense, "The
   paralytic stunned in the tub"?

Leo Tolstoy

THE DEATH
OF
IVAN ILYICH

Deeply concerned with spiritual values, the great Russian novelist, Leo Tolstoy, 1828–1910, examined the everyday existence of his characters with extraordinary realism. The Death of Ivan Ilyich, one of the most famous nineteenth-century novellas, expresses man's limitations and his triumphs with extraordinary accuracy and insight.

I

Inside the great building of the Law Courts, during the interval in the hearing of the Melvinski case, the members of the judicial council and the public prosecutor were gathered together in the private room of Ivan Yegorovich Shebek, and the conversation turned upon the celebrated Krasovski case. Fyodor Vassilyevich hotly maintained that the case was not in the jurisdiction of the court. Yegor Ivanovich stood up for his own view; but from the first Pyotr Ivanovich, who had not entered into the discussion, took no interest in it, but was looking through the newspapers which had just been brought in.

"Gentlemen!" he said, "Ivan Ilyich is dead!"

"You don't say so!"

"Here, read it," he said to Fyodor Vassilyevich, handing him the fresh still damp smelling paper.

Within a black margin was printed: "Praskovya Fyodorovna Golovin with heartfelt affliction informs friends and relatives of the decease of her beloved husband, member of the Court of Justice, Ivan Ilyich Golovin, who passed away on the 4th of February. The funeral will take place on Thursday at one o'clock."

Ivan Ilyich was a colleague of the gentlemen present, and all liked him. It was some weeks now since he had been taken ill; his illness had been said to be incurable. His post had been kept open for him, but it had been thought that in case of his death Alexeyev might receive his appointment, and either Vinnikov or Shtabel would succeed to Alexeyev's. So that on hearing of Ivan Ilyich's death, the first thought of each of the gentlemen in the room was of the effect this death might have on the transfer or promotion of themselves or their friends.

"Now I am sure of getting Shtabel's place or Vinnikov's," thought Fyodor Vassilyevich. "It was promised me long ago, and the promotion means eight hundred rubles additional income, besides the grants for office expenses."

"Now I shall have to petition for my brother-in-law to be transferred from Kaluga," thought Pyotr Ivanovich. "My wife will be very glad. She won't be able to say now that I've never done anything for her family."

"I thought somehow that he'd never get up from his bed again," Pyotr Ivanovich said aloud. "I'm sorry!"

"But what was it exactly was wrong with him?"

"The doctors could not decide. That's to say, they did decide, but differently. When I saw him last, I thought he would get over it."

"Well, I positively haven't called there ever since the holidays. I've kept meaning to go."

"Had he any property?"

"I think there's something, very small, of his wife's. But something quite trifling."

"Yes, one will have to go and call. They live such a terribly long way off."

"A long way from you, you mean. Everything's a long way from your place."

"There, he can never forgive me for living the other side of the river," said Pyotr Ivanovich, smiling at Shebek. And they began to talk of the great distances between different parts of the town, and went back into the court.

Besides the reflections upon the changes and promotions in the service likely to ensue from this death, the very fact of the death of an intimate acquaintance excited in every one who heard of it, as such a fact always does, a feeling of relief that "it is he that is dead, and not I."

"Only think! he is dead, but here am I all right," each one thought or felt. The more intimate acquaintances, the so-called friends of Ivan Ilyich, could not help thinking too that now they had the exceedingly tiresome social duties to perform of going to the funeral service and paying the widow a visit of condolence.

The most intimately acquainted with their late colleague were Fyodor Vassilyevich and Pyotr Ivanovich.

Pyotr Ivanovich had been a comrade of his at the school of jurisprudence, and considered himself under obligations to Ivan Ilyich.

Telling his wife at dinner of the news of Ivan Ilyich's death and his reflections as to the possibility of getting her brother transferred into their circuit, Pyotr Ivanovich, without lying down for his usual nap, put on his frock coat and drove to Ivan Ilyich's.

At the entrance before Ivan Ilyich's flat stood a carriage and two hired hacks. Downstairs in the entry near the hatstand there was leaning against the wall a coffin lid with tassels and braiding freshly rubbed up with pipe clay. Two ladies were taking off their cloaks. One of them he knew, the sister of Ivan Ilyich; the other was a lady he did not know. Pyotr Ivanovich's colleague, Shvarts, was coming down; and from the top stair, seeing who it was coming in, he stopped and winked at him, as though to say: "Ivan Ilyich has made a mess of it; it's a very different matter with you and me."

Shvarts's face, with his English whiskers and all his thin figure in his frock coat, had, as it always had, an air of elegant solemnity; and this solemnity, always such a contrast to Shvarts's playful character, had a special piquancy here. So thought Pyotr Ivanovich.

Pyotr Ivanovich let the ladies pass on in front of him, and walked slowly up the stairs after them. Shvarts had not come down, but was waiting at the top. Pyotr Ivanovich knew what for; he wanted obviously to settle with him where their game of "screw" was to be that evening. The ladies went up to the widow's room; while Shvarts, with his lips tightly and gravely shut, and amusement in his eyes, with a twitch of his eyebrows motioned Pyotr Ivanovich to the right, to the room where the dead man was.

Pyotr Ivanovich went in, as people always do on such occasions, in uncertainty as to what he would have to do there. One thing he felt sure of —that crossing oneself never comes amiss on such occasions. As to whether it was necessary to bow down while doing so, he did not feel quite sure, and so chose a middle course. On entering the room he began crossing himself, and made a slight sort of bow. So far as the movements of his hands and head permitted him, he glanced while doing so about the room. Two young men, one a high school boy, nephews probably, were going out of the room, crossing themselves. An old lady was standing motionless; and a lady, with her eyebrows queerly lifted, was saying something to her in a whisper. A deacon in a frock coat, resolute and hearty, was reading something aloud with an expression that precluded all possibility of contradiction. A young peasant who used to wait at table, Gerasim, walking with light footsteps in front of Pyotr Ivanovich, was sprinkling something on the floor. Seeing this, Pyotr Ivanovich was at once aware of the faint odor of the decomposing corpse. On his last visit to Ivan Ilyich Pyotr Ivanovich had seen this peasant in his room; he was performing the duties of a sicknurse, and Ivan Ilyich liked him particularly. Pyotr Ivanovich continued crossing himself and bowing in a direction intermediate between the coffin, the deacon, and the holy pictures on the table in the corner. Then when this action of making the sign of the cross with his hand seemed to him to have been unduly prolonged, he stood still and began to scrutinize the dead man.

The dead man lay, as dead men always do lie, in a peculiarly heavy dead way, his stiffened limbs sunk in the cushions of the coffin, and his head bent back for ever on the pillow, and thrust up, as dead men always do, his yellow waxen forehead with bald spots on the sunken temples, and his nose that stood out sharply and, as it were, squeezed on the upper lip. He was much changed, even thinner since Pyotr Ivanovich had seen him, but his face—as always with the dead—was more handsome, and, above all, more impressive than it had been when he was alive. On the face was an expression what had to be done having been done, and rightly done. Besides this, there was too in that expression a reproach or reminder for the living. This reminder seemed to Pyotr Ivanovich uncalled for, or, at least, to have nothing to do with him. He felt something unpleasant; and so Pyotr Ivanovich once more crossed himself hurriedly, and, as it struck him, too hurriedly, not quite in accordance with the proprieties, turned and went to the door. Shvarts was waiting for him in the adjoining room, standing with his legs apart and both hands behind his back playing with his top hat. A single glance at the playful, sleek, and elegant figure of Shvarts revived Pyotr Ivanovich. He felt that he, Shvarts, was above it, and would not give way to depressing impressions. The mere sight of him said plainly: the incident of the service over the body of Ivan Ilyich cannot possibly constitute a sufficient ground for recognizing the business of the session suspended,—in other words, in no way can it hinder us from shuffling and cutting a pack of cards this evening, while the footman sets four unsanctified candles on the table for us; in fact, there is no ground for supposing that this incident could prevent us from spending the evening agreeably. He said as much indeed to Pyotr Ivanovich as he came out, proposing that the party should meet at Fyodor Vassilyevich's. But apparently it was Pyotr Ivanovich's destiny not to play "screw" that evening. Praskovya Fyodorovna, a short, fat woman who, in spite of all efforts in a contrary direction, was steadily broader from her shoulders downwards, all in black, with lace on her head and her eyebrows as queerly arched as those of the lady standing beside the coffin, came out of her own apartments with some other ladies, and conducting them to the dead man's room, said: "The service will take place immediately; come in."

Shvarts, making an indefinite bow, stood still, obviously neither accepting or declining this invitation. Praskovya Fyodorovna, recognising Pyotr Ivanovich, sighed, went right up to him, took his hand, and said, "I know that you were a true friend of Ivan Ilyich's . . ." and looked at him, expecting from him the suitable action in response to these words. Pyotr Ivanovich knew that, just as before he had to cross himself, now what he had to do was to press her hand, to sigh and to say, "Ah, I was indeed!" And he did so. And as he did so, he felt that the desired result had been attained; that he was touched, and she was touched.

"Come, since it's not begun yet, I have something I want to say to you," said the widow. "Give me your arm."

Pyotr Ivanovich gave her his arm, and they moved towards the inner rooms, passing Shvarts, who winked gloomily at Pyotr Ivanovich.

"So much for our 'screw'! Don't complain if we find another partner. You can make a fifth when you do get away," said his humorous glance.

Pyotr Ivanovich sighed still more deeply and despondently, and Praskovya Fyodorovna pressed his hand gratefully. Going into her drawing room, which was upholstered with pink cretonne and lighted by a dismal looking lamp, they sat down at the table, she on a sofa and Pyotr Ivanovich on a low ottoman with deranged springs which yielded spasmodically under his weight. Praskovya Fyodorovna was about to warn him to sit on another seat, but felt such a recommendation out of keeping with her position, and changed her mind. Sitting down on the ottoman, Pyotr Ivanovich remembered how Ivan Ilyich had arranged this drawing room, and had consulted him about this very pink cretonne with green leaves. Seating herself on the sofa, and pushing by the table (the whole drawing room was crowded with furniture and things), the widow caught the lace of her black fichu in the carving of the table. Pyotr Ivanovich got up to disentangle it for her; and the ottoman, freed from his weight, began bobbing up spasmodically under him. The widow began unhooking her lace herself, and Pyotr Ivanovich again sat down, suppressing the mutinous ottoman springs under him. But the widow could not quite free herself, and Pyotr Ivanovich rose again, and again the ottoman became mutinous and popped up with a positive snap. When this was all over, she took out a clean cambric handkerchief and began weeping. Pyotr Ivanovich had been chilled off by the incident with the lace and the struggle with the ottoman springs, and he sat looking sullen. This awkward position was cut short by the entrance of Sokolov, Ivan Ilyich's butler, who came in to announce that the place in the cemetery fixed on by Praskovya Fyodorovna would cost two hundred rubles. She left off weeping, and with the air of a victim glancing at Pyotr Ivanovich, said in French that it was very terrible for her. Pyotr Ivanovich made a silent gesture signifying his unhesitating conviction that it must indeed be so.

"Please, smoke," she said in a magnanimous, and at the same time, crushed voice, and she began discussing with Sokolov the question of the price of the site for the grave.

Pyotr Ivanovich, lighting a cigarette, listened to her very circumstantial inquiries as to the various prices of sites and her decision as to the one to be selected. Having settled on the site for the grave, she made arrangements also about the choristers. Sokolov went away.

"I see to everything myself," she said to Pyotr Ivanovich, moving on one side the albums that lay on the table; and noticing that the table was in danger from the cigarette ash, she promptly passed an ash tray to Pyotr Ivanovich, and said: "I consider it affectation to pretend that my grief prevents me from looking after practical matters. On the contrary, if anything could—not console me . . . but distract me, it is seeing after everything for him." She took out her handkerchief again, as though preparing to weep again; and suddenly, as though struggling with herself, she shook herself, and began speaking calmly: "But I've business to talk about with you."

Pyotr Ivanovich bowed, carefully keeping in check the springs of the ottoman, which had at once begun quivering under him.

"The last few days his sufferings were awful."

"Did he suffer very much?" asked Pyotr Ivanovich.

"Oh, awfully! For the last moments, hours indeed, he never left off screaming. For three days and nights in succession he screamed incessantly. It was insufferable. I can't understand how I bore it; one could hear it through three closed doors. Ah, what I suffered!"

"And was he really conscious?" asked Pyotr Ivanovich.

"Yes," she whispered, "up to the last minute. He said good-by to us a quarter of an hour before his death, and asked Volodya to be taken away too."

The thought of the sufferings of a man he had known so intimately, at first as a light-hearted boy, a schoolboy, then grown up as a partner at whist, in spite of the unpleasant consciousness of his own and this woman's hypocrisy, suddenly horrified Pyotr Ivanovich. He saw again that forehead, the nose that seemed squeezing the lip, and he felt frightened for himself. "Three days and nights of awful suffering and death. Why, that may at once, any minute, come upon me too," he thought, and he felt for an instant terrified. But immediately, he could not himself have said how, there came to his support the customary reflection that this had happened to Ivan Ilyich and not to him, and that to him this must not and could not happen; that in thinking thus he was giving way to depression, which was not the right thing to do, as was evident from Shvarts's expression of face. And making these reflections, Pyotr Ivanovich felt reassured, and began with interest inquiring details about Ivan Ilyich's end, as though death were a mischance peculiar to Ivan Ilyich, but not at all incidental to himself.

After various observations about the details of the truly awful physical sufferings endured by Ivan Ilyich (these details Pyotr Ivanovich learned only through the effect Ivan Ilyich's agonies had had on the nerves of Praskovya Fyodorovna), the widow apparently thought it time to get to business.

"Ah, Pyotr Ivanovich, how hard it is, how awfully, awfully hard!" and she began to cry again.

Pyotr Ivanovich sighed, and waited for her to blow her nose. When she had done so, he said, "Indeed it is," and again she began to talk, and brought out what was evidently the business she wished to discuss with him; that business consisted in the inquiry as to how on the occasion of her husband's death she was to obtain a grant from the government. She made a show of asking Pyotr Ivanovich's advice about a pension. But he perceived that she knew already to the minutest details, what he did not know himself indeed, everything that could be got out of the government on the ground of this death; but that what she wanted to find out was, whether there were not any means of obtaining a little more? Pyotr Ivanovich tried to imagine such means; but after pondering a little, and out of politeness abusing the government for its stinginess, he said that he believed that it was impossible to obtain more. Then she sighed and began unmistakably looking about for an excuse for getting rid of her visitor. He perceived this, put out his cigarette, got up, pressed her hand, and went out into the passage.

In the dining room, where was the bric-à-brac clock that Ivan Ilyich had been so delighted at buying, Pyotr Ivanovich met the priest and several people he knew who had come to the service for the dead, and saw too Ivan Ilyich's daughter, a handsome young lady. She was all in black. Her very slender figure looked even slenderer than usual. She had a gloomy, determined, almost wrathful expression. She bowed to Pyotr Ivanovich as though he were to blame in some way. Behind the daughter, with the same offended air on his face, stood a rich young man, whom Pyotr Ivanovich knew, too, an examining magistrate, the young lady's *fiancé,* as he had heard. He bowed dejectedly to him, and would have gone on into the dead man's room, when from the staircase there appeared the figure of the son, the high school boy, extraordinarily like Ivan Ilyich. He was the little Ivan Ilyich over again as Pyotr Ivanovich remembered him at school. His eyes were red with crying, and had that look often seen in unclean boys of thirteen or fourteen. The boy, seeing Pyotr Ivanovich, scowled morosely and bashfully. Pyotr Ivanovich nodded to him and went into the dead man's room. The service for the dead began—candles, groans, incense, tears, sobs. Pyotr Ivanovich stood frowning, staring at his feet in front of him. He did not once glance at the dead man, and right through to the end did not once give way to depressing influences, and was one of the first to walk out. In the hall there was no one. Gerasim, the young peasant, darted out of the dead man's room, tossed over with his strong hand all the fur cloaks to find Pyotr Ivanovich's, and gave it him.

"Well, Gerasim, my boy?" said Pyotr Ivanovich, so as to say something. "A sad business, isn't it?"

"It's God's will. We shall come to the same," said Gerasim, showing his white, even, peasant teeth in a smile, and, like a man in a rush of extra work, he briskly opened the door, called up the coachman, saw Pyotr Ivanovich into the carriage, and darted back to the steps as though bethinking himself of what he had to do next.

Pyotr Ivanovich had a special pleasure in the fresh air after the smell of incense, of the corpse, and of carbolic acid.

"Where to?" asked the coachman.

"It's not too late. I'll still go round to Fyodor Vassilyevich's."

And Pyotr Ivanovich drove there. And he did, in fact, find them just finishing the first rubber, so that he came just at the right time to take a hand.

II

The previous history of Ivan Ilyich was the simplest, the most ordinary, and the most awful.

Ivan Ilyich died at the age of forty-five, a member of the Judicial Council. He was the son of an official, whose career in Petersburg through various ministries and departments had been such as leads people into that position in which, though it is distinctly obvious that they are unfit to perform any kind of real duty, they yet cannot, owing to their long past service and their official rank, be dismissed; and they therefore receive a specially created fictitious post, and by no means fictitious thousands— from six to ten—on which they go on living till extreme old age. Such was the privy councillor, the superfluous member of various superfluous institutions, Ilya Efimovich Golovin.

He had three sons. Ivan Ilyich was the second son. The eldest son's career was exactly like his father's, only in a different department, and he was by now close to that stage in the service in which the same sinecure would be reached. The third son was the unsuccessful one. He had in various positions always made a mess of things, and was now employed in the railway department. And his father and his brothers, and still more their wives, did not merely dislike meeting him, but avoided, except in extreme necessity, recollecting his existence. His sister had married Baron Gref, a Petersburg official of the same stamp as his father-in-law. Ivan Ilyich was *le phénix de la famille,* as people said. He was not so frigid and precise as the eldest son, nor so wild as the youngest. He was the happy mean between them—a shrewd, lively, pleasant, and well-bred man. He had been educated with his younger brother at the school of jurisprudence. The younger brother had not finished the school course, but was expelled when in the fifth class. Ivan Ilyich completed the course successfully. At school he was just the same as he was later on all his life—an intelligent fellow, highly good-humored and sociable, but strict in doing what he considered to be his dtuy. His duty he considered whatever was so considered by those persons who were set in authority over him. He was not a toady as a boy, nor later on as a grownup person; but from his earliest years he was attracted, as a fly to the light, to persons of good standing in the world, assimilated their manners and their views of life, and established friendly relations with them. All the enthusiasms of childhood and youth passed, leaving no great traces in him; he gave way to sensuality and to vanity, and latterly when in the higher classes at school to liberalism, but always keeping within certain limits which were unfailingly marked out for him by his instincts.

At school he had committed actions which had struck him beforehand as great vileness, and gave him a feeling of loathing for himself at the very time he was committing them. But later on, perceiving that such actions were committed also by men of good position, and were not regarded by them as base, he was able, not to regard them as good, but to forget about them completely, and was never mortified by recollections of them.

Leaving the school of jurisprudence in the tenth class, and receiving from his father a sum of money for his outfit, Ivan Ilyich ordered his clothes at Sharmer's, hung on his watchchain a medallion inscribed *respice finem,* said good-by to the prince who was the principal of his school, had a farewell dinner with his comrades at Donon's, and with all his new fashionable belongings—travelling trunk, linen, suits of clothes, shaving and toilet appurtenances, and travelling rug, all ordered and purchased at the very best shops—set off to take the post of secretary on special commissions for the governor of a province, a post which had been obtained for him by his father.

In the province Ivan Ilyich without loss of time made himself a position as easy and agreeable as his position had been in the school of jurisprudence. He did his work, made his career, and at the same time led a life of well-bred social gaiety. Occasionally he visited various districts on official duty, behaved with dignity both with his superiors and his inferiors; and with exactitude and an incorruptible honesty of which he could not help feeling proud, performed the duties with which he was intrusted, principally having to do with the dissenters. When engaged in official work he was, in spite of his youth and taste for frivolous amusement, exceedingly reserved, official, and even severe. But in social life he was often amusing and witty, and always good-natured, well-bred, and *bon enfant*, as was said of him by his chief and his chief's wife, with whom he was like one of the family.

In the province there was, too, a connection with one of the ladies who obtruded their charms on the stylish young lawyer. There was a dressmaker, too, and there were drinking bouts with smart officers visiting the neighborhood, and visits to a certain outlying street after supper; there was a rather cringing obsequiousness in his behaviour, too, with his chief, and even his chief's wife. But all this was accompanied with such a tone of the highest breeding, that it could not be called by harsh names; it all came under the rubric of the French saying, *Il faut que la jeunesse se passe.* Everything was done with clean hands, in clean shirts, with French phrases, and, what was of most importance, in the highest society, and consequently with the approval of people of rank.

Such was Ivan Ilyich's career for five years, and then came a change in his official life. New methods of judicial procedure were established; new men were wanted to carry them out. And Ivan Ilyich became such a new man. Ivan Ilyich was offered the post of examining magistrate, and he accepted it in spite of the fact that this post was in another province, and he would have to break off all the ties he had formed and form new ones. Ivan Ilyich's friends met together to see him off, had their photographs taken in a group, presented him with a silver cigarette case, and he set off to his new post.

As an examining magistrate, Ivan Ilyich was as *comme il faut*, as well-bred, as adroit in keeping official duties apart from private life, and as successful in gaining universal respect, as he had been as secretary of private commissions. The duties of his new office were in themselves of far greater interest and attractiveness for Ivan Ilyich. In his former post it had been pleasant to pass in his smart uniform from Sharmer's through the crowd of petitioners and officials waiting timorously and envying him, and to march with his easy swagger straight into the governor's private room, there to sit down with him to tea and cigarettes. But the persons directly subject to his authority were few. The only such persons were the district police superintendents and the dissenters, when he was serving on special commissions. And he liked treating such persons affably, almost like comrades; liked to make them feel that he, able to annihilate them, was behaving in this simple, friendly way with them. But such people were then few in number. Now as an examining magistrate Ivan Ilyich felt that every one—every one without exception—the most dignified, the most self-satisfied people, all were in his hands, and that he had but to write certain words on a sheet of paper with a printed heading, and this dignified self-satisfied person would be brought before him in the capacity of a defendant or a witness; and if he did not care to make him sit down, he would have to stand up before him and answer his question. Ivan Ilyich never abused this authority of his; on the contrary, he tried to soften the expression of it. But the consciousness of this power and the possibility of softening its effect constituted for him the chief interest and attractiveness of his new position. In the work itself, in the preliminary inquiries, that is, Ivan Ilyich very rapidly acquired the art of setting aside every consideration irrelevant to the official aspect of the case, and of reducing every case, however complex, to that form in which it could in a purely external fashion be put on paper, completely excluding his personal view of the matter, and what was of paramount importance, observing all the necessary formalities. All this work was new. And he was one of the first men who put into practical working the reforms in judicial procedure enacted in 1864.

On settling in a new town in his position as examining magistrate, Ivan Ilyich made new acquaintances, formed new ties, took up a new line, and adopted a rather different attitude. He took up an attitude of somewhat dignified aloofness towards the provincial authorities, while he picked out the best circle among the legal gentlemen and wealthy gentry living in the town, and adopted a tone of slight dissatisfaction with the government, moderate liberalism, and lofty civic virtue. With this, while making no change in the elegance of his getup, Ivan Ilyich in his new office gave up shaving, and left his beard free to grow as it liked. Ivan Ilyich's existence in the new town proved to be very agreeable; the society which took the line of opposition to the governor was friendly and good; his income was larger, and he found a source of increased enjoyment in whist, at which he began to play at this time; and having a faculty for playing cards good-humoredly, and being rapid and exact in his calculations, he was as a rule on the winning side.

After living two years in the new town, Ivan Ilyich met his future wife. Praskovya Fyodorovna Mikhel was the most attractive, clever, and brilliant girl in the set in which Ivan Ilyich moved. Among other amusements and recreations after his labors as a magistrate, Ivan Ilyich started a light, playful flirtation with Praskovya Fyodorovna.

Ivan Ilyich when he was an assistant secretary had danced as a rule; as an examining magistrate he danced only as an exception. He danced now as it were under protest, as though to show "that though I am serving on the new reformed legal code, and am of the fifth class in official rank, still if it comes to a question of dancing, in that line, too, I can do better than others." In this spirit he danced now and then towards the end of the evening with Praskovya Fyodorovna, and it was principally during these dances that he won the heart of Praskovya Fyodorovna. She fell in love with him. Ivan Ilyich had no clearly defined intention of marrying; but when the girl fell in love with him, he put the question to himself: "After all, why not get married?"

The young lady, Praskovya Fyodorovna, was of good family, nice-looking. There was a little bit of property. Ivan Ilyich might have reckoned on a more brilliant match, but this was a good match. Ivan Ilyich had his salary; she, he hoped, would have as much of her own. It was a good family; she was a sweet, pretty, and perfectly *comme il faut* young woman. To say that Ivan Ilyich got married because he fell in love with his wife and found in her sympathy with his views of life, would be as untrue as to say that he got married because the people of his world approved of the match. Ivan Ilyich was influenced by both considerations; he was doing what was agreeable to himself in securing such a wife, and at the same time doing what persons of higher standing looked upon as the correct thing.

And Ivan Ilyich got married.

The process itself of getting married and the early period of married life, with the conjugal caresses, the new furniture, the new crockery, the new house linen, all up to the time of his wife's pregnancy, went off very well; so that Ivan Ilyich had already begun to think that so far from marriage breaking up that kind of frivolous, agreeable, light-hearted life, always decorous and always approved by society, which he regarded as the normal life, it would even increase its agreeableness. But at that point, in the early months of his wife's pregnancy, there came in a new element, unexpected, unpleasant, tiresome and unseemly, which could never have been anticipated, and from which there was no escape.

His wife, without any kind of reason, it seemed to Ivan Ilyich, *de gaîté de cœur,* as he expressed it, began to disturb the agreeableness and decorum of their life. She began without any sort of justification to be jealous, exacting in her demands on his attention, squabbled over everything, and treated him to the coarsest and most unpleasant scenes.

At first Ivan Ilyich hoped to escape from the unpleasantness of this position by taking up the same frivolous and well-bred line that had served him well on other occasions of difficulty. He endeavoured to ignore his wife's ill-humor, went on living light-heartedly and agreeably as before, invited friends to play cards, tried to get away himself to the club or to his friends. But his wife began on one occasion with such energy, abusing him in such coarse language, and so obstinately persisted in her abuse of him every time he failed in carrying out her demands, obviously having made up her mind firmly to persist till he gave way, that is, stayed at home and was as dull as she was, that Ivan Ilyich took alarm. He perceived that matrimony, at least with his wife, was not invariably conducive to the pleasures and proprieties of life; but, on the contrary, often destructive of them, and that it was therefore essential to erect some barrier to protect himself from these disturbances. And Ivan Ilyich began to look about for such means of protecting himself. His official duties were the only thing that impressed Praskovya Fyodorovna, and Ivan Ilyich began to use his official position and the duties arising from it in his struggle with his wife to fence off his own independent world apart.

With the birth of the baby, the attempts at nursing it, and the various unsuccessful experiments with foods, with the illnesses, real and imaginary, of the infant and its mother, in which Ivan Ilyich was expected to sympathize, though he never had the slightest idea about them, the need for him to fence off a world apart for himself outside his family life became still more imperative. As his wife grew more irritable and exacting, so did Ivan Ilyich more and more transfer the center of gravity of his life to his official work. He became fonder and fonder of official life, and more ambitious than he had been.

Very quickly, not more than a year after his wedding, Ivan Ilyich had become aware that conjugal life, though providing certain comforts, was in reality a very intricate and difficult business towards which one must, if one is to do one's duty, that is, lead the decorous life approved by society, work out for oneself a definite line, just as in the government service.

And such a line Ivan Ilyich did work out for himself in his married life. He expected from his home life only those comforts—of dinner at home, of housekeeper and bed which it could give him, and, above all, that perfect propriety in external observances required by public opinion. For the rest, he looked for good-humored pleasantness, and if he found it he was very thankful. If he met with antagonism and querulousness, he promptly retreated into the separate world he had shut off for himself in his official life, and there he found solace.

Ivan Ilyich was prized as a good official, and three years later he was made assistant public prosecutor. The new duties of this position, their dignity, the possibility of bringing any one to trial and putting any one in prison, the publicity of the speeches and the success Ivan Ilyich had in that part of his work,—all this made his official work still more attractive to him.

Children were born to him. His wife became steadily more querulous and ill-tempered, but the line Ivan Ilyich had taken up for himself in home life put him almost out of reach of her grumbling.

After seven years of service in the same town, Ivan Ilyich was transferred to another province with the post of public prosecutor. They moved, money was short, and his wife did not like the place they had moved to. The salary was indeed a little higher than before, but their expenses were larger. Besides, a couple of children died, and home life consequently became even less agreeable for Ivan Ilyich.

For every mischance that occurred in their new place of residence, Praskovya Fyodorovna blamed her husband. The greater number of subjects of conversation between husband and wife, especially the education of the children, led to questions which were associated with previous quarrels, and quarrels were ready to break out at every instant. There remained only those rare periods of being in love which did indeed come upon them, but never lasted long. These were the islands at which they put in for a time, but they soon set off again upon the ocean of concealed hostility, that was made manifest in their aloofness from one another. This aloofness might have distressed Ivan Ilyich if he had believed that this ought not to be so, but by now he regarded this position as perfectly normal, and it was indeed the goal towards which he worked in his home life. His aim was to make himself more and more free from the unpleasant aspects of domestic life and to render them harmless and decorous. And he attained this aim by spending less and less time with his family; and when he was forced to be at home, he endeavoured to secure his tranquillity by the presence of outsiders. The great thing for Ivan Ilyich was having his office. In the official world all the interest of life was concentrated for him. And this interest absorbed him. The sense of his own power, the consciousness of being able to ruin any one he wanted to ruin, even the external dignity of his office, when he made his entry into the court or met subordinate officials, his success in the eyes of his superiors and his subordinates, and, above all, his masterly handling of cases, of which he was conscious,—all this delighted him and, together with chats with his colleagues, dining out, and whist, filled his life. So that, on the whole, Ivan Ilyich's life still went on in the way he thought it should go—agreeably and decorously.

So he lived for another seven years. His eldest daughter was already sixteen, another child had died, and there was left only one other, a boy at the high school, a subject of dissension. Ivan Ilyich wanted to send him to the school of jurisprudence, while Praskovya Fyodorovna to spite him sent him to the high school. The daughter had been educated at home, and had turned out well; the boy too did fairly well at his lessons.

III

Such was Ivan Ilyich's life for seventeen years after his marriage. He had been by now a long while prosecutor, and had refused several appointments offered him, looking out for a more desirable post, when there occurred an unexpected incident which utterly destroyed his peace of mind. Ivan Ilyich had been expecting to be appointed presiding judge in a university town, but a certain Goppe somehow stole a march on him and secured the appointment. Ivan Ilyich took offence, began upbraiding him, and quarrelled with him and with his own superiors. A coolness was felt towards him, and on the next appointment that was made he was again passed over.

This was in the year 1880. That year was the most painful one in Ivan Ilyich's life. During that year it became evident on the one hand that his pay was insufficient for his expenses; on the other hand, that he had been forgotten by every one, and that what seemed to him the most monstrous, the cruelest injustice, appeared to other people as a quite commonplace fact. Even his father felt no obligation to assist him. He felt that every one had deserted him, and that every one regarded his position with an income of three thousand five hundred rubles as a quite normal and even fortunate one. He alone, with a sense of the injustice done him, and the everlasting nagging of his wife and the debts he had begun to accumulate, living beyond his means, knew that his position was far from being normal.

The summer of that year, to cut down his expenses, he took a holiday and went with his wife to spend the summer in the country at her brother's.

In the country, with no official duties to occupy him, Ivan Ilyich was for the first time a prey not to simple boredom, but to intolerable depression; and he made up his mind that things could not go on like that, and that it was absolutely necessary to take some decisive steps.

After a sleepless night spent by Ivan Ilyich walking up and down the terrace, he determined to go to Petersburg to take active steps and to get transferred to some other department, so as to revenge himself on *them,* the people, that is, who had not known how to appreciate him.

Next day, in spite of all the efforts of his wife and his mother-in-law to dissuade him, he set off to Petersburg.

He went with a single object before him—to obtain a post with an income of five thousand. He was ready now to be satisfied with a post in any department, of any tendency, with any kind of work. He must only have a post—a post with five thousand, in the executive department, the banks, the railways, the Empress Marya's institutions, even in the customs duties—what was essential was five thousand, and essential it was, too, to get out of the department in which they had failed to appreciate his value.

And, behold, this quest of Ivan Ilyich's was crowned with wonderful, unexpected success. At Kursk there got into the same first-class carriage F. S. Illyin, an acquaintance, who told him of a telegram just received by the governor of Kursk, announcing a change about to take place in the ministry—Pyotr Ivanovich was to be superseded by Ivan Semyonovich.

The proposed change, apart from its significance for Russia, had special significance for Ivan Ilyich from the fact that by bringing to the front a new person, Pyotr Petrovich, and obviously, therefore, his friend Zakhar Ivanovich, it was in the highest degree propitious to Ivan Ilyich's own plans. Zakhar Ivanovich was a friend and schoolfellow of Ivan Ilyich's.

At Moscow the news was confirmed. On arriving at Petersburg, Ivan Ilyich looked up Zakhar Ivanovich, and received a positive promise of an appointment in his former department—that of justice.

A week later he telegraphed to his wife: *"Zakhar Miller's place. At first report I receive appointment."*

Thanks to these changes, Ivan Ilyich unexpectedly obtained, in the same department as before, an appointment which placed him two stages higher than his former colleagues, and gave him an income of five thousand, together with the official allowance of three thousand five hundred for travelling expenses. All his ill-humor with his former enemies and the whole department was forgotten, and Ivan Ilyich was completely happy.

Ivan Ilyich went back to the country more light-hearted and good-tempered than he had been for a very long while. Praskovya Fyodorovna was in better spirits, too, and peace was patched up between them. Ivan Ilyich described what respect every one had shown him in Petersburg; how all those who had been his enemies had been put to shame, and were cringing now before him; how envious they were of his appointment, and still more of the high favor in which he stood at Petersburg.

Praskovya Fyodorovna listened to this, and pretended to believe it, and did not contradict him in anything, but confined herself to making plans for her new arrangements in the town to which they would be moving. And Ivan Ilyich saw with delight that these plans were his plans; that they were agreed; and that his life after this disturbing hitch in its progress was about to regain its true, normal character of light-hearted agreeableness and propriety.

Ivan Ilyich had come back to the country for a short stay only. He had to enter upon the duties of his new office on the 10th of September; and besides, he needed some time to settle in a new place, to move all his belongings from the other province, to purchase and order many things in addition; in short, to arrange things as settled in his own mind, and almost exactly as settled in the heart too of Praskovya Fyodorovna.

And now when everything was so successfully arranged, and when he and his wife were agreed in their aim, and were, besides, so little together, they got on with one another as they had not got on together since the early years of their married life. Ivan Ilyich had thought of taking his family away with him at once; but his sister and his brother-in-law, who had suddenly become extremely cordial and intimate with him and his family, were so pressing in urging them to stay that he set off alone.

Ivan Ilyich started off; and the light-hearted temper produced by his success, and his good understanding with his wife, one thing backing up another, did not desert him all the time. He found a charming set of apartments, the very thing both husband and wife had dreamed of. Spacious, lofty reception rooms in the old style, a comfortable, dignified looking study for him, rooms for his wife and daughter, a schoolroom for his son, everything as though planned on purpose for them. Ivan Ilyich himself looked after the furnishing of them, chose the wallpapers, bought furniture, by preference antique furniture, which had a peculiar *comme-il-faut* style to his mind, and it all grew up and grew up, and really attained the ideal he had set before himself. When he had half finished arranging the house, his arrangement surpassed his own expectations. He saw the *comme-il-faut* character, elegant and free from vulgarity, that the whole would have when it was all ready. As he fell asleep he pictured to himself the reception room as it would be. Looking at the drawing room, not yet finished, he could see the hearth, the screen, the *étagère,* and the little chairs dotted here and there, the plates and dishes on the wall, and the bronzes as they would be when they were all put in their places. He was delighted with the thought of how he would impress Praskovya and Lizanka, who had taste too in this line. They would never expect anything like it. He was particularly successful in coming across and buying cheap old pieces of furniture, which gave a peculiarly aristocratic air to the whole. In his letters he purposely disparaged everything so as to surprise them. All this so absorbed him that the duties of his new office, though he was so fond of his official work, interested him less than he had expected. During sittings of the court he had moments of inattention; he pondered the question which sort of cornices to have on the window blinds, straight or fluted. He was so interested in this business that he often set to work with his own hands, moved a piece of furniture, or hung up curtains himself. One day he went up a ladder to show a workman, who did not understand, how he wanted some hangings draped, made a false step and slipped; but, like a strong and nimble person, he clung on, and only knocked his side against the corner of a frame. The bruised place ached, but it soon passed off. Ivan Ilyich felt all this time particularly good-humored and well. He wrote: "I feel fifteen years younger." He thought his house furnishing would be finished in September, but it dragged on to the middle of October. But then the effect was charming; not he only said so, but every one who saw it told him so too.

In reality, it was all just what is commonly seen in the houses of people who are not exactly wealthy but want to look like wealthy people, and so succeed only in being like one another—hangings, dark wood, flowers, rugs and bronzes, everything dark and highly polished, everything that all people of a certain class have so as to be like all people of a certain class. And in his case it was all so like that it made no impression at all; but it all seemed to him somehow special. When he met his family at the railway station and brought them to his newly furnished rooms, all lighted up in readiness, and a footman in a white tie opened the door into an entry decorated with flowers, and then they walked into the drawing room and the study, uttering cries of delight, he was very happy, conducted them everywhere, eagerly drinking in their praises, and beaming with satisfaction. The same evening, while they talked about various things at tea, Praskovya Fyodorovna inquired about his fall, and he laughed and showed them how he had gone flying, and how he had frightened the upholsterer.

"It's as well I'm something of an athlete. Another man might have been killed, and I got nothing worse than a blow here; when it's touched it hurts, but it's going off already; nothing but a bruise."

And they began to live in their new abode, which, as is always the case, when they had got thoroughly settled in they found to be short of just one room, and with their new income, which, as always, was only a little— some five hundred rubles—too little, and everything went very well. Things went particularly well at first, before everything was quite finally arranged, and there was still something to do to the place—something to buy, something to order, something to move, something to make to fit. Though there were indeed several disputes between husband and wife, both were so well satisfied, and there was so much to do, that it all went off without serious quarrels. When there was nothing left to arrange, it became a little dull, and something seemed to be lacking, but by then they were making acquaintances and forming habits, and life was filled up again.

Ivan Ilyich, after spending the morning in the court, returned home to dinner, and at first he was generally in a good humor, although this was apt to be upset a little, and precisely on account of the new abode. Every spot on the tablecloth, on the hangings, the string of a window blind broken, irritated him. He had devoted so much trouble to the arrangement of the rooms that any disturbance of their order distressed him. But, on the whole, the life of Ivan Ilyich ran its course as, according to his conviction, life ought to do—easily, agreeably, and decorously. He got up at nine, drank his coffee, read the newspaper, then put on his official uniform and went to the court. There the routine of the daily work was ready mapped out for him, and he stepped into it at once. People with petitions, inquiries in the office, the office itself, the sittings—public and

preliminary. In all this the great thing necessary was to exclude everything with the sap of life in it, which always disturbs the regular course
of official business, not to admit any sort of relations with people except
the official relations; the motive of all intercourse had to be simply the
official motive, and the intercourse itself to be only official. A man would
come, for instance, anxious for certain information. Ivan Ilyich, not being
the functionary on duty, would have nothing whatever to do with such a
man. But if this man's relation to him as a member of the court is such
as can be formulated on official stamped paper—within the limits of such
a relation Ivan Ilyich would do everything, positively everything he could,
and in doing so would observe the semblance of human friendly relations,
that is, the courtesies of social life. But where the official relation ended,
there everything else stopped too. This art of keeping the official aspect
of things apart from his real life, Ivan Ilyich possessed in the highest
degree; and through long practice and natural aptitude, he had brought it
to such a pitch of perfection that he even permitted himself at times, like
a skilled specialist as it were in jest, to let the human and official relations
mingle. He allowed himself this liberty just because he felt he had the
power at any moment if he wished it to take up the purely official line
again and to drop the human relation. This thing was not simply easy,
agreeable, and decorous; in Ivan Ilyich's hands it attained a positively
artistic character. In the intervals of business he smoked, drank tea, chatted
a little about politics, a little about public affairs, a little about cards, but
most of all about appointments in the service. And tired, but feeling like
some artist who has skilfully played his part in the performance, one of
the first violins in the orchestra, he returned home. At home his daughter
and her mother had been paying calls somewhere, or else some one had
been calling on them; the son had been at school, had been preparing his
lessons with his teachers, and duly learning correctly what was taught at
the high school. Everything was as it should be. After dinner, if there were
no visitors, Ivan Ilyich sometimes read some book of which people were
talking, and in the evening sat down to work, that is, read official papers,
compared them with the laws, sorted depositions, and put them under the
laws. This he found neither tiresome nor entertaining. It was tiresome
when he might have been playing "screw"; but if there were no "screw"
going on, it was anyway better than sitting alone or with his wife. Ivan
Ilyich's pleasures were little dinners, to which he invited ladies and gentlemen of good social position, and such methods of passing the time with

them as were usual with such persons, so that his drawing room might be like all other drawing rooms.

Once they even gave a party—a dance. And Ivan Ilyich enjoyed it, and everything was very successful, except that it led to a violent quarrel with his wife over the tarts and sweetmeats. Praskovya Fyodorovna had her own plan; while Ivan Ilyich insisted on getting everything from an expensive pastry cook, and ordered a great many tarts, and the quarrel was because these tarts were left over and the pastry cook's bill came to forty-five rubles. The quarrel was a violent and unpleasant one, so much so that Praskovya Fyodorovna called him, "Fool, imbecile." And he clutched at his head, and in his anger made some allusion to a divorce. But the party itself was enjoyable. There were all the best people, and Ivan Ilyich danced with Princess Trufonov, the sister of the one so well known in connection with the charitable association called, "Bear my Burden." His official pleasures lay in the gratification of his pride; his social pleasures lay in the gratification of his vanity. But Ivan Ilyich's most real pleasure was the pleasure of playing "screw," the Russian equivalent for "poker." He admitted to himself that, after all, after whatever unpleasant incidents there had been in his life, the pleasure which burned like a candle before all others was sitting with good players, and not noisy partners, at "screw"; and, of course, a four-hand game (playing with five was never a success, though one pretends to like it particularly), and with good cards, to play a shrewd, serious game, then supper and a glass of wine. And after "screw," especially after winning some small stakes (winning large sums was unpleasant), Ivan Ilyich went to bed in a particularly happy frame of mind.

So they lived. They moved in the very best circle, and were visited by people of consequence and young people.

In their views of their circle of acquaintances, the husband, the wife, and the daughter were in complete accord; and without any expressed agreement on the subject, they all acted alike in dropping and shaking off various friends and relations, shabby persons who swooped down upon them in their drawing room with Japanese plates on the walls, and pressed their civilities on them. Soon these shabby persons ceased fluttering about them, and none but the very best society was seen at the Golovins. Young men began to pay attention to Lizanka; and Petrishchev, the son of Dimitri Ivanovich Petrishchev, and the sole heir of his fortune, an examining magistrate, began to be so attentive to Lizanka, that Ivan Ilyich had raised the question with his wife whether it would not be as well to arrange a sledge drive for them, or to get up some theatricals. So they lived. And everything went on in this way without change, and everything was very nice.

IV

All were in good health. One could not use the word ill health in connection with the symptoms Ivan Ilyich sometimes complained of, namely, a queer taste in his mouth and a sort of uncomfortable feeling on the left side of the stomach.

But it came to pass that this uncomfortable feeling kept increasing, and became not exactly a pain, but a continual sense of weight in his side and irritable temper. This irritable temper continually growing and growing, began at last to mar the agreeable easiness and decorum that had reigned in the Golovin household. Quarrels between the husband and wife became more and more frequent, and soon all the easiness and amenity of life had fallen away, and mere propriety was maintained with difficulty. Scenes became again more frequent. Again there were only islands in the sea of contention—and but few of these—at which the husband and wife could meet without an outbreak. And Praskovya Fyodorovna said now, not without grounds, that her husband had a trying temper. With her characteristic exaggeration, she said he had always had this awful temper, and she had needed all her sweetness to put up with it for twenty years. It was true that it was he now who began the quarrels. His gusts of temper always broke out just before dinner, and often just as he was beginning to eat, at the soup. He would notice that some piece of the crockery had been chipped, or that the food was not nice, or that his son put his elbow on the table, or his daughter's hair was not arranged as he liked it. And whatever it was, he laid the blame of it on Praskovya Fyodorovna. Praskovya Fyodorovna had at first retorted in the same strain, and said all sorts of horrid things to him; but on two occasions, just at the beginning of dinner, he had flown into such a frenzy that she perceived that it was due to physical derangement, and was brought on by taking food, and she controlled herself; she did not reply, but simply made haste to get dinner over. Praskovya Fyodorovna took great credit to herself for this exercise of self-control. Making up her mind that her husband had a fearful temper, and made her life miserable, she began to feel sorry for herself. And the more she felt for herself, the more she hated her husband. She began to wish he were dead; yet could not wish it, because then there would be no income. And this exasperated her against him even more. She considered herself dreadfully unfortunate, precisely because even his death could not save her, and she felt irritated and concealed it, and this hidden irritation on her side increased his irritability.

After one violent scene, in which Ivan Ilyich had been particularly unjust, and after which he had said in explanation that he certainly was irritable, but that it was due to illness, she said that if he were ill he ought to take steps, and insisted on his going to see a celebrated doctor.

He went. Everything was as he had expected; everything was as it always is. The waiting and the assumption of dignity, that professional dignity he knew so well, exactly as he assumed it himself in court, and the sounding and listening and questions that called for answers that were foregone conclusions and obviously superfluous, and the significant air that seemed to insinuate—you only leave it all to us, and we will arrange everything, for us it is certain and incontestable how to arrange everything, everything in one way for every man of every sort. It was all exactly as in his court of justice. Exactly the same air as he put on in dealing with a man brought up for judgment, the doctor put on for him.

The doctor said: This and that proves that you have such-and-such a thing wrong inside you; but if that is not confirmed by analysis of this and that, then we must assume this and that. If we assume this and that, then—and so on. To Ivan Ilyich there was only one question of consequence, Was his condition dangerous or not? But the doctor ignored that irrelevant inquiry. From the doctor's point of view this was a side issue, not the subject under consideration; the only real question was the balance of probabilities between a loose kidney, chronic catarrh, and appendicitis. It was not a question of the life of Ivan Ilyich, but the question between the loose kidney and the intestinal appendix. And this question, as it seemed to Ivan Ilyich, the doctor solved in a brilliant manner in favor of the appendix, with the reservation that analysis of the water might give a fresh clue, and that then the aspect of the case would be altered. All this was point for point identical with what Ivan Ilyich had himself done in brilliant fashion a thousand times over in dealing with some man on his trial. Just as brilliantly the doctor made his summing up, and triumphantly, gaily even, glanced over his spectacles at the prisoner in the dock. From the doctor's summing up Ivan Ilyich deduced the conclusion—that things looked bad, and that he, the doctor, and most likely every one else, did not care, but that things looked bad for him. And this conclusion impressed Ivan Ilyich morbidly, arousing in him a great feeling of pity for himself, of great anger against this doctor who could be unconcerned about a matter of such importance.

But he said nothing of that. He got up, and, laying the fee on the table, he said, with a sigh, "We sick people probably often ask inconvenient questions. Tell me, is this generally a dangerous illness or not?"

The doctor glanced severely at him with one eye through his spectacles, as though to say: "Prisoner at the bar, if you will not keep within the limits of the questions allowed you, I shall be compelled to take measures for your removal from the precincts of the court." "I have told you what I thought necessary and suitable already," said the doctor; "the analysis will show anything further." And the doctor bowed him out.

Ivan Ilyich went out slowly and dejectedly, got into his sledge, and drove home. All the way home he was incessantly going over all the doctor had said, trying to translate all these complicated, obscure, scientific phrases into simple language, and to read in them an answer to the question, Is it bad—is it very bad, or nothing much as yet? And it seemed to him that the upshot of all the doctor had said was that it was very bad. Everything seemed dismal to Ivan Ilyich in the streets. The sledge drivers were dismal, the houses were dismal, the people passing, and the shops were dismal. This ache, this dull gnawing ache, that never ceased for a second, seemed, when connected with the doctor's obscure utterances, to have gained a new, more serious significance. With a new sense of misery Ivan Ilyich kept watch on it now.

He reached home and began to tell his wife about it. His wife listened; but in the middle of his account his daughter came in with her hat on, ready to go out with her mother. Reluctantly she half sat down to listen to these tedious details, but she could not stand it for long, and her mother did not hear his story to the end.

"Well, I'm very glad," said his wife; "now you must be sure and take the medicine regularly. Give me the prescription; I'll send Gerasim to the chemist's!" And she went to get ready to go out.

He had not taken breath while she was in the room, and he heaved a deep sigh when she was gone.

"Well," he said, "may be it really is nothing as yet."

He began to take the medicine, to carry out the doctor's directions, which were changed after the analysis of the water. But it was just at this point that some confusion arose, either in the analysis or in what ought to have followed from it. The doctor himself, of course, could not be blamed for it, but it turned out that things had not gone as the doctor had told him. Either he had forgotten or told a lie, or was hiding something from him.

But Ivan Ilyich still went on just as exactly carrying out the doctor's direction, and in doing so he found comfort at first.

From the time of his visit to the doctor Ivan Ilyich's principal occupation became the exact observance of the doctor's prescriptions as regards hygiene and medicine and the careful observation of his ailment in all the functions of his organism. Ivan Ilyich's principal interest came to be people's ailments and people's health. When anything was said in his presence about sick people, about deaths and recoveries, especially in the case of an illness resembling his own, he listened, trying to conceal his excitement, asked questions, and applied what he heard to his own trouble.

The ache did not grow less; but Ivan Ilyich made great efforts to force himself to believe that he was better. And he succeeded in deceiving himself so long as nothing happened to disturb him. But as soon as he had a mischance, some unpleasant words with his wife, a failure in his official work, an unlucky hand at "screw," he was at once acutely sensible of his illness. In former days he had borne with such mishaps, hoping soon to retrieve the mistake, to make a struggle, to reach success later, to have a lucky hand. But now he was cast down by every mischance and reduced to despair. He would say to himself: "Here I'm only just beginning to get better, and the medicine has begun to take effect, and now this mischance or disappointment." And he was furious against the mischance or the people who were causing him the disappointment and killing him, and he felt that this fury was killing him, but could not check it. One would have thought that it should have been clear to him that this exasperation against circumstances and people was aggravating his disease, and that therefore he ought not to pay attention to the unpleasant incidents. But his reasoning took quite the opposite direction. He said that he needed peace, and was on the watch for everything that disturbed his peace, and at the slightest disturbance of it he flew into a rage. What made his position worse was that he read medical books and consulted doctors. He got worse so gradually that he might have deceived himself, comparing one day with another, the difference was so slight. But when he consulted the doctors, then it seemed to him that he was getting worse, and very rapidly so indeed. And in spite of this, he was continually consulting the doctors.

That month he called on another celebrated doctor. The second celebrity said almost the same as the first, but put his questions differently; and the interview with this celebrity only redoubled the doubts and terrors of Ivan Ilyich. A friend of a friend of his, a very good doctor, diagnosed the disease quite differently; and in spite of the fact that he guaranteed recovery, by his questions and his suppositions he confused Ivan Ilyich even more and strengthened his suspicions. A homeopath gave yet another diagnosis of the complaint, and prescribed medicine, which Ivan Ilyich took secretly for a week; but after a week of the homeopathic medicine he felt no relief, and losing faith both in the other doctor's treatment and in this, he fell into even deeper depression. One day a lady of his acquaintance talked to him of the healing wrought by the holy pictures. Ivan Ilyich caught himself listening attentively and believing in the reality of the facts alleged. This incident alarmed him. "Can I have degenerated to such a point of intellectual feebleness?" he said to himself. "Nonsense! it's all rubbish. I must not give way to nervous fears, but fixing on one doctor, adhere strictly to his treatment. That's what I will do. Now it's settled. I won't think about it, but till next summer I will stick to the treatment, and then I shall see. Now I'll put a stop to this wavering!" It was easy to say this, but impossible to carry it out. The pain in his side was always dragging at him, seeming to grow more acute and ever more incessant; it seemed to him that the taste in his mouth was queerer, and there was a loathsome smell even from his breath, and his appetite and strength kept dwindling. There was no deceiving himself; something terrible, new, and so important that nothing more important had ever been in Ivan Ilyich's life, was taking place in him, and he alone knew of it. All about him did not or would not understand, and believed that everything in the world was going on as before. This was what tortured Ivan Ilyich more than anything. Those of his own household, most of all his wife and daughter, who were absorbed in a perfect whirl of visits, did not, he saw, comprehend it at all, and were annoyed that he was so depressed and exacting, as though he were to blame for it. Though they tried indeed to disguise it, he saw he was a nuisance to them; but that his wife had taken up a definite line of her own in regard to his illness, and stuck to it regardless of what he might say and do. This line was expressed thus: "You know," she would say to acquaintances, "Ivan Ilyich cannot, like all other simple-hearted folks, keep to the treatment prescribed him. One day he'll take his drops and eat what he's ordered, and go to bed in good time; the next day, if I don't see to it, he'll suddenly forget to take his medicine, eat sturgeon (which is forbidden by the doctors), yes, and sit up at 'screw' till past midnight."

"Why, when did I do that?" Ivan Ilyich asked in vexation one day at Pyotr Ivanovich's.

"Why, yesterday, with Shebek."

"It makes no difference. I couldn't sleep for pain."

"Well, it doesn't matter what you do it for, only you'll never get well like that, and you make us wretched."

Praskovya Fyodorovna's external attitude to her husband's illness, openly expressed to others and to himself, was that Ivan Ilyich was to blame in the matter of his illness, and that the whole illness was another injury he was doing to his wife. Ivan Ilyich felt that the expression of this dropped from her unconsciously, but that made it no easier for him.

In his official life, too, Ivan Ilyich noticed, or fancied he noticed, a strange attitude to him. At one time it seemed to him that people were looking inquisitively at him, as a man who would shortly have to vacate his position; at another time his friends would suddenly begin chaffing him in a friendly way over his nervous fears, as though that awful and horrible, unheard-of thing that was going on within him, incessantly gnawing at him, and irresistibly dragging him away somewhere, were the most agreeable subject for joking. Shvarts especially, with his jocoseness, his liveliness, and his *comme-il-faut* tone, exasperated Ivan Ilyich by reminding him of himself ten years ago.

Friends came sometimes to play cards. They sat down to the card table; they shuffled and dealt the new cards. Diamonds were led and followed by diamonds, the seven. His partner said, "Can't trump," and played the two of diamonds. What then? Why, delightful, capital, it should have been—he had a trump hand. And suddenly Ivan Ilyich feels that gnawing ache, that taste in his mouth, and it strikes him as something grotesque that with that he could be glad of a trump hand.

He looks at Mikhail Mikhaylovich, his partner, how he taps on the table with his red hand, and affably and indulgently abstains from snatching up the trick, and pushes the cards towards Ivan Ilyich so as to give him the pleasure of taking them up, without any trouble, without even stretching out his hand. "What, does he suppose that I'm so weak that I can't stretch out my hand?" thinks Ivan Ilyich, and he forgets the trumps, and trumps his partner's cards, and plays his trump hand without making three tricks; and what's the most awful thing of all is that he sees how upset Mikhail Mikhaylovich is about it, while he doesn't care a bit, and it's awful for him to think why he doesn't care.

They all see that he's in pain, and say to him, "We can stop if you're tired. You go and lie down." Lie down? No, he's not in the least tired; they will play the rubber. All are gloomy and silent. Ivan Ilyich feels that it is he has brought this gloom upon them, and he cannot disperse it. They have supper, and the party breaks up, and Ivan Ilyich is left alone with the consciousness that his life is poisoned for him and poisons the life of others, and that this poison is not losing its force, but is continually penetrating more and more deeply into his whole existence.

And with the consciousness of this, and with the physical pain in addition, and the terror in addition to that, he must lie in his bed, often not able to sleep for pain the greater part of the night; and in the morning he must get up again, dress, go to the law court, speak, write, or, if he does not go out, stay at home for all the four-and-twenty hours of the day and night, of which each one is a torture. And he had to live thus on the edge of the precipice alone, without one man who would understand and feel for him.

V

In this way one month, then a second, passed by. Just before the New Year his brother-in-law arrived in the town on a visit to them. Ivan Ilyich was at the court when he arrived. Praskovya Fyodorovna had gone out shopping. Coming home and going into his study, he found there his brother-in-law, a healthy, florid man, engaged in unpacking his trunk. He raised his head, hearing Ivan Ilyich's step, and for a second stared at him without a word. That stare told Ivan Ilyich everything. His brother-in-law opened his mouth to utter an "Oh!" of surprise, but checked himself. That confirmed it all.

"What! have I changed?"

"Yes, there is a change."

And all Ivan Ilyich's efforts to draw him into talking of his appearance his brother-in-law met with obstinate silence. Praskovya Fyodorovna came in; the brother-in-law went to see her. Ivan Ilyich locked his door and began gazing at himself in the looking glass, first full face, then in profile. He took up his photograph, taken with his wife, and compared the portrait with what he saw in the looking glass. The change was immense. Then he bared his arm to the elbow, looked at it, pulled the sleeve down again, sat down on an ottoman and felt blacker than night.

"I mustn't, I mustn't," he said to himself, jumped up, went to the table, opened some official paper, tried to read it, but could not. He opened the door, went into the drawing room. The door into the drawing room was closed. He went up to it on tiptoe and listened.

"No, you're exaggerating," Praskovya Fyodorovna was saying.

"Exaggerating? You can't see it. Why, he's a dead man. Look at his eyes—there's no light in them. But what's wrong with him?"

"No one can tell. Nikolayev" (that was another doctor) "said something, but I don't know. Leshchetiski" (this was the celebrated doctor) "said the opposite."

Ivan Ilyich walked away, went to his own room, lay down, and fell to musing. "A kidney—a loose kidney." He remembered all the doctors had told him, how it had been detached, and how it was loose; and by an effort of imagination he tried to catch that kidney and to stop it, to strengthen it. So little was needed, he fancied. "No, I'll go again to Pyotr Ivanovich" (this was the friend who had a friend, a doctor). He rang, ordered the horse to be put in, and got ready to go out.

"Where are you off to, *Jean?*" asked his wife with a peculiarly melancholy and exceptionally kind expression.

This exceptionally kind expression exasperated him. He looked darkly at her.

"I want to see Pyotr Ivanovich."

He went to the friend who had a friend a doctor. And with him to the doctor's. He found him in, and had a long conversation with him.

Reviewing the anatomical and physiological details of what, according to the doctor's view, was taking place within him, he understood it all. It was just one thing—a little thing wrong with the intestinal appendix. It might all come right. Only strengthen one sluggish organ, and decrease the undue activity of another, and absorption would take place, and all would be set right. He was a little late for dinner. He ate his dinner, talked cheerfully, but it was a long while before he could go to his own room to work. At last he went to his study, and at once sat down to work. He read his legal documents and did his work, but the consciousness never left him of having a matter of importance very near to his heart which he had put off, but would look into later. When he had finished his work, he remembered that the matter near his heart was thinking about the intestinal appendix. But he did not give himself up to it; he went into the drawing room to tea. There were visitors; and there was talking, playing on the piano, and singing; there was the young examining magistrate, the desirable match for the daughter. Ivan Ilyich spent the evening, as Praskovya Fyodorovna observed, in better spirits than any of them; but he never forgot for an instant that he had the important matter of the intestinal appendix put off for consideration later. At eleven o'clock he said good night and went to his own room. He had slept alone since his illness in a little room adjoining his study. He went in, undressed, and took up a novel of Zola, but did not read it; he fell to thinking. And in his imagination the desired recovery of the intestinal appendix had taken place. There had been absorption, rejection, reestablishment of the regular action.

"Why, it's all simply that," he said to himself. "One only wants to assist nature." He remembered the medicine, got up, took it, lay down on his back, watching for the medicine to act beneficially and overcome the pain. "It's only to take it regularly and avoid injurious influences; why, already I feel rather better, much better." He began to feel his side; it was not painful to the touch. "Yes, I don't feel it—really, much better already." He put out the candle and lay on his side. "The appendix is getting better, absorption." Suddenly he felt the familiar, old, dull, gnawing ache, persistent, quiet, in earnest. In his mouth the same familiar loathsome taste. His heart sank, and his brain felt dim, misty. "My God, my God!" he said, "again, again, and it will never cease." And suddenly the whole thing rose before him in quite a different aspect. "Intestinal appendix! kidney!" he said to himself. "It's not a question of the appendix, not a question of the kidney, but of life and . . . death. Yes, life has been and now it's going, going away, and I cannot stop it. Yes. Why deceive myself? Isn't it obvious to every one, except me, that I'm dying, and it's only a question of weeks, of days—at once perhaps. There was light, and now there is darkness. I was here, and now I'm going! Where?" A cold chill ran over him, his breath stopped. He heard nothing but the throbbing of his heart.

"I shall be no more, then what will there be? There'll be nothing. Where then shall I be when I'm no more? Can this be dying? No; I don't want to!" He jumped up, tried to light the candle; and fumbling with trembling hands, he dropped the candle and the candlestick on the floor and fell back again on the pillow. "Why trouble? it doesn't matter," he said to himself, staring with open eyes into the darkness. "Death. Yes, death. And they—all of them—don't understand, and don't want to understand, and feel no pity. They are playing. (He caught through the closed doors the faraway cadence of a voice and the accompaniment.) They don't care, but they will die too. Fools! Me sooner and them later; but it will be the same for them. And they are merry. The beasts!" Anger stifled him. And he was agonizingly, insufferably miserable. "It cannot be that all men always have been doomed to this awful horror!" He raised himself.

"There is something wrong in it; I must be calm, I must think it all over from the beginning." And then he began to consider. "Yes, the beginning of my illness. I knocked my side, and I was just the same, that day and the days after; it ached a little, then more, then doctors, then depression, misery, and again doctors; and I've gone on getting closer and closer to the abyss. Strength growing less. Nearer and nearer. And here I am, wasting away, no light in my eyes. I think of how to cure the appendix, but this is death. Can it be death?" Again a horror came over him; gasping for breath, he bent over, began feeling for the matches, and knocked his elbow against the bedside table. It was in his way and hurt him; he felt furious with it, in his anger knocked against it more violently, and upset it. And in despair, breathless, he fell back on his spine waiting for death to come that instant.

The visitors were leaving at that time. Praskovya Fyodorovna was seeing them out. She heard something fall, and came in.

"What is it?"

"Nothing. I dropped something by accident."

She went out, brought a candle. He was lying, breathing hard and fast, like a man who has run a mile, and staring with fixed eyes at her.

"What is it, *Jean?*"

"No—othing, I say. I dropped something."—"Why speak? She won't understand," he thought.

She certainly did not understand. She picked up the candle, lighted it for him, and went out hastily. She had to say good-by to a departing guest. When she came back, he was lying in the same position on his back, looking upwards.

"How are you—worse?"

"Yes."

She shook her head, sat down.

"Do you know what, *Jean?* I wonder if we hadn't better send for Leshchetiski to see you here?"

This meant calling in the celebrated doctor, regardless of expense. He smiled malignantly, and said no. She sat a moment longer, went up to him, and kissed him on the forehead.

He hated her with all the force of his soul when she was kissing him, and had to make an effort not to push her away.

"Good night. Please God, you'll sleep."

"Yes."

VI

Ivan Ilyich saw that he was dying, and was in continual despair.

At the bottom of his heart Ivan Ilyich knew that he was dying; but so far from growing used to this idea, he simply did not grasp it—he was utterly unable to grasp it.

The example of the syllogism that he had learned in Kiseveter's logic —Caius is a man, men are mortal, therefore Caius is mortal—had seemed to him all his life correct only as regards Caius, but not at all as regards himself. In that case it was a question of Caius, a man, an abstract man, and it was perfectly true, but he was not Caius, and was not an abstract man; he had always been a creature quite, quite different from all others; he had been little Vanya with a mamma and papa, and Mitya and Volodya, with playthings and a coachman and a nurse; afterwards with Katenka, with all the joys and griefs and ecstasies of childhood, boyhood, and youth. What did Caius know of the smell of the leathern ball Vanya had been so fond of? Had Caius kissed his mother's hand like that? Caius had not heard the silk rustle of his mother's skirts. He had not made a riot at school over the pudding. Had Caius been in love like that? Could Caius preside over the sittings of the court?

And Caius certainly was mortal, and it was right for him to die; but for me, little Vanya, Ivan Ilyich, with all my feelings and ideas—for me it's a different matter. And it cannot be that I ought to die. That would be too awful.

That was his feeling.

"If I had to die like Caius, I should have known it was so, some inner voice would have told me so. But there was nothing of the sort in me. And I and all my friends, we felt that it was not at all the same as with

Caius. And now here it is!" he said to himself. "It can't be! It can't be, but it is! How is it? How's one to understand it?" And he could not conceive it, and tried to drive away this idea as false, incorrect, and morbid, and to supplant it by other, correct, healthy ideas. But this idea, not as an idea merely, but as it were an actual fact, came back again and stood confronting him.

And to replace this thought he called up other thoughts, one after another, in the hope of finding support in them. He tried to get back into former trains of thought, which in old days had screened off the thought of death. But, strange to say, all that had in old days covered up, obliterated the sense of death, could not now produce the same effect. Latterly, Ivan Ilyich spent the greater part of his time in these efforts to restore his old trains of thought which had shut off death. At one time he would say to himself, "I'll put myself into my official work; why, I used to live in it." And he would go to the law courts, banishing every doubt. He would enter into conversation with his colleagues, and would sit carelessly, as his old habit was, scanning the crowd below dreamily, and with both his wasted hands he would lean on the arms of the oak armchair just as he always did; and bending over to a colleague, pass the papers to him and whisper to him, then suddenly dropping his eyes and sitting up straight, he would pronounce the familiar words that opened the proceedings. But suddenly in the middle, the pain in his side, utterly regardless of the stage he had reached in his conduct of the case, began its work. It riveted Ivan Ilyich's attention. He drove away the thought of it, but it still did its work, and then *It* came and stood confronting him and looked at him, and he felt turned to stone, and the light died away in his eyes, and he began to ask himself again, "Can it be that *It* is the only truth?" And his colleagues and his subordinates saw with surprise and distress that he, the brilliant, subtle judge, was losing the thread of his speech, was making blunders. He shook himself, tried to regain his self-control, and got somehow to the end of the sitting, and went home with the painful sense that his judicial labors could not as of old hide from him what he wanted to hide; that he could not by means of his official work escape from *It*. And the worst of it was that *It* drew him to itself not for him to do anything in particular, but simply for him to look at *It* straight in the face, to look at *It* and, doing nothing, suffer unspeakably.

And to save himself from this, Ivan Ilyich sought amusements, other screens, and these screens he found, and for a little while they did seem to save him; but soon again they were not so much broken down as let the light through, as though *It* pierced through everything, and there was nothing that could shut *It* off.

Sometimes during those days he would go into the drawing room he had furnished, that drawing room where he had fallen, for which—how bitterly ludicrous it was for him to think of it!—for the decoration of which he had sacrificed his life, for he knew that it was that bruise that had started his illness. He went in and saw that the polished table had been scratched by something. He looked for the cause, and found it in the bronze clasps of the album, which had been twisted on one side. He took up the album, a costly one, which he had himself arranged with loving care, and was vexed at the carelessness of his daughter and her friends. Here a page was torn, here the photographs had been shifted out of their places. He carefully put it to rights again and bent the clasp back.

Then the idea occurred to him to move all this *établissement* of the albums to another corner where the flowers stood. He called the footman; or his daughter or his wife came to help him. They did not agree with him, contradicted him; he argued, got angry. But all that was very well, since he did not think of *It; It* was not in sight.

But then his wife would say, as he moved something himself, "Do let the servants do it, you'll hurt yourself again," and all at once *It* peeped through the screen; he caught a glimpse of *It.* He caught a glimpse of *It,* but still he hoped *It* would hide itself. Involuntarily though, he kept watch on his side; there it is just the same still, aching still, and now he cannot forget it, and *It* is staring openly at him from behind the flowers. What's the use of it all?

"And it's the fact that here, at that curtain, as if it had been storming a fort, I lost my life. Is it possible? How awful and how silly! It cannot be! It cannot be, and it is."

He went into his own room, lay down, and was again alone with *It.* Face to face with *It,* and nothing to be done with *It.* Nothing but to look at *It* and shiver.

VII

How it came to pass during the third month of Ivan Ilyich's illness, it would be impossible to say, for it happened little by little, imperceptibly, but it had come to pass that his wife and his daughter and his son and their servants and their acquaintances, and the doctors, and, most of all, he himself—all were aware that all interest in him for other people consisted now in the question how soon he would leave his place empty, free the living from the constraint of his presence, and be set free himself from his sufferings.

He slept less and less; they gave him opium, and began to inject morphine. But this did not relieve him. The dull pain he experienced in the half asleep condition at first only relieved him as a change, but then it became as bad, or even more agonizing, than the open pain. He had special things to eat prepared for him according to the doctor's prescriptions; but these dishes became more and more distasteful, more and more revolting to him.

Special arrangements, too, had to be made for his other physical needs, and this was a continual misery to him. Misery from the uncleanliness, the unseemliness, and the stench, from the feeling of another person having to assist in it.

But just from this most unpleasant side of his illness there came comfort to Ivan Ilyich. There always came into his room on these occasions to clear up for him the peasant who waited on table, Gerasim.

Gerasim was a clean, fresh, young peasant, who had grown stout and hearty on the good fare in town. Always cheerful and bright. At first the sight of this lad, always cleanly dressed in the Russian style, engaged in this revolting task, embarrassed Ivan Ilyich.

One day, getting up from the night stool, too weak to replace his clothes, he dropped on to a soft low chair and looked with horror at his bare, powerless thighs, with the muscles so sharply standing out on them.

Then there came in with light, strong steps Gerasim, in his thick boots, diffusing a pleasant smell of tar from his boots, and bringing in the freshness of the winter air. Wearing a clean hempen apron, and a clean cotton shirt, with his sleeves tucked up on his strong, bare young arms, without looking at Ivan Ilyich, obviously trying to check the radiant happiness in his face so as not to hurt the sick man, he went up to the night stool.

"Gerasim," said Ivan Ilyich faintly.

Gerasim started, clearly afraid that he had done something amiss, and with a rapid movement turned towards the sick man his fresh, good-natured, simple young face, just beginning to be downy with the first growth of beard.

"Yes, your honor."

"I'm afraid this is very disagreeable for you. You must excuse me. I can't help it."

"Why, upon my word, sir!" And Gerasim's eyes beamed, and he showed his white young teeth in a smile. "What's a little trouble? It's a case of illness with you, sir."

And with his deft, strong arms he performed his habitual task, and went out, stepping lightly. And five minutes later, treading just as lightly, he came back.

Ivan Ilyich was still sitting in the same way in the armchair.

"Gerasim," he said, when the latter had replaced the night stool all sweet and clean, "please help me; come here." Gerasim went up to him. "Lift me up. It's difficult for me alone, and I've sent Dimitri away."

Gerasim went up to him; as lightly as he stepped he put his strong arms round him, deftly and gently lifted and supported him, with the other hand pulled up his trousers, and would have set him down again. But Ivan Ilyich, asked him to carry him to the sofa. Gerasim, without effort, carefully not squeezing him, led him, almost carrying him, to the sofa, and settled him there.

"Thank you; how neatly and well . . . you do everything."

Gerasim smiled again, and would have gone away. But Ivan Ilyich felt his presence such a comfort that he was reluctant to let him go.

"Oh, move that chair near me, please. No, that one, under my legs. I feel easier when my legs are higher."

Gerasim picked up the chair, and without letting it knock, set it gently down on the ground just at the right place, and lifted Ivan Ilyich's legs on to it. It seemed to Ivan Ilyich that he was easier just at the moment when Gerasim lifted his legs higher.

"I'm better when my legs are higher," said Ivan Ilyich. "Put that cushion under me."

Gerasim did so. Again he lifted his legs to put the cushion under them. Again it seemed to Ivan Ilyich that he was easier at that moment when Gerasim held his legs raised. When he laid them down again, he felt worse.

"Gerasim," he said to him, "are you busy just now?"

"Not at all, sir," said Gerasim, who had learned among the town-bred servants how to speak to gentlefolks.

"What have you left to do?"

"Why, what I have to do? I've done everything, there's only the wood to chop for tomorrow."

"Then hold my legs up like that—can you?"

"To be sure, I can." Gerasim lifted the legs up. And it seemed to Ivan Ilyich that in that position he did not feel the pain at all.

"But how about the wood?"

"Don't you trouble about that, sir. We shall have time enough."

Ivan Ilyich made Gerasim sit and hold his legs, and began to talk to him. And, strange to say, he fancied he felt better while Gerasim had hold of his legs.

From that time forward Ivan Ilyich would sometimes call Gerasim, and get him to hold his legs on his shoulders, and he liked talking with him. Gerasim did this easily, readily, simply, and with a good nature that touched Ivan Ilyich. Health, strength, and heartiness in all other people were offensive to Ivan Ilyich; but the strength and heartiness of Gerasim did not mortify him, but soothed him.

Ivan Ilyich's great misery was due to the deception that for some reason or other every one kept up with him—that he was simply ill, and not dying, and that he need only keep quiet and follow the doctor's orders, and then some great change for the better would be the result. He knew that whatever they might do, there would be no result except more agonizing sufferings and death. And he was made miserable by this lie, made miserable at their refusing to acknowledge what they all knew and he knew, by their persisting in lying over him about his awful position, and in forcing him too to take part in this lie. Lying, lying, this lying carried on over him on the eve of his death, and destined to bring that terrible, solemn act of his death down to the level of all their visits, curtains, sturgeons for dinner . . . was a horrible agony for Ivan Ilyich. And, strange to say, many times when they had been going through the regular performance over him, he had been within a hair's-breadth of screaming at them: "Cease your lying! You know, and I know, that I'm dying; so do, at least, give over lying!" But he had never had the spirit to do this. The terrible, awful act of his dying was, he saw, by all those about him, brought down to the level of a casual, unpleasant, and to some extent indecorous, incident (somewhat as they would behave with a person who should enter a drawing room smelling unpleasant). It was brought down to this level by that very decorum to which he had been enslaved all his life. He saw that no one felt for him, because no one would even grasp his position. Gerasim was the only person who recognized the position, and felt sorry for him. And that was why Ivan Ilyich was only at ease with Gerasim. He felt comforted when Gerasim sometimes supported his legs for whole nights at a stretch, and would not go away to bed, saying, "Don't you worry yourself, Ivan Ilyich, I'll get sleep enough yet," or when suddenly dropping into the familiar peasant forms of speech, he added: "If thou weren't sick, but as 'tis, 'twould be strange if I didn't wait on thee." Gerasim alone did not lie; everything showed clearly that he alone understood what it meant, and saw no necessity to disguise it, and simply felt sorry for his sick, wasting master. He even said this once straight out, when Ivan Ilyich was sending him away.

"We shall all die. So what's a little trouble?" he said, meaning by this to express that he did not complain of the trouble just because he was taking this trouble for a dying man, and he hoped that for him too some one would be willing to take the same trouble when his time came.

Apart from this deception, or in consequence of it, what made the greatest misery for Ivan Ilyich was that no one felt for him as he would have liked them to feel for him. At certain moments, after prolonged suffering, Ivan Ilyich, ashamed as he would have been to own it, longed more than anything for some one to feel sorry for him, as for a sick child. He longed to be petted, kissed, and wept over, as children are petted and comforted. He knew that he was an important member of the law courts, that he had a beard turning grey, and that therefore it was impossible. But still he longed for it. And in his relations with Gerasim there was something approaching to that. And that was why being with Gerasim was a comfort to him. Ivan Ilyich longs to weep, longs to be petted and wept over, and then there comes in a colleague, Shebek; and instead of weeping and being petted, Ivan Ilyich puts on his serious, severe, earnest face, and from mere inertia gives his views on the effect of the last decision in the Court of Appeal, and obstinately insists upon them. This falsity around him and within him did more than anything to poison Ivan Ilyich's last days.

VIII

It was morning. All that made it morning for Ivan Ilyich was that Gerasim had gone away, and Pyotr the footman had come in; he had put out the candles, opened one of the curtains, and begun surreptitiously setting the room to rights. Whether it were morning or evening, Friday or Sunday, it all made no difference; it was always just the same thing. Gnawing, agonizing pain never ceasing for an instant; the hopeless sense of life always ebbing away, but still not yet gone; always swooping down on him that fearful, hated death, which was the only reality, and always the same falsity. What were days, or weeks, or hours of the day to him?

"Will you have tea, sir?"

"He wants things done in their regular order. In the morning the family should have tea," he thought, and only said—

"No."

"Would you care to move on to the sofa?"

"He wants to make the room tidy, and I'm in his way. I'm uncleanness, disorder," he thought, and only said—

"No, leave me alone."

The servant still moved busily about his work. Ivan Ilyich stretched out his hand. Pyotr went up to offer his services.

"What can I get out?"

"My watch."

Pyotr got out the watch, which lay just under his hand, and gave it to him.

"Half-past eight. Are they up?"

"Not yet, sir. Vladimir Ivanovich" (that was his son) "has gone to the high school, and Praskovya Fyodorovna gave orders that she was to be waked if you asked for her. Shall I send word?"

"No, no need. Should I try some tea?" he thought. "Yes, tea . . . bring it."

Pyotr was on his way out. Ivan Ilyich felt frightened of being left alone. "How keep him? Oh, the medicine. Pyotr, give me my medicine. Oh well, may be, medicine may still be some good." He took the spoon, drank it. "No, it does no good. It's all rubbish, deception," he decided, as soon as he tasted the familiar, mawkish, hopeless taste. "No, I can't believe it now. But the pain, why this pain; if it would only cease for a minute." And he groaned. Pyotr turned round. "No, go on. Bring the tea."

Pyotr went away. Ivan Ilyich, left alone, moaned, not so much from the pain, awful as it was, as from misery. Always the same thing again and again, all these endless days and nights. If it would only be quicker. Quicker to what? Death, darkness. No, no. Anything better than death!

When Pyotr came in with the tea on a tray, Ivan Ilyich stared for some time absent-mindedly at him, not grasping who he was and what he wanted. Pyotr was disconcerted by this stare. And when he showed he was disconcerted, Ivan Ilyich came to himself.

"Oh yes," he said, "tea, good, set it down. Only help me to wash and put on a clean shirt."

And Ivan Ilyich began his washing. He washed his hands slowly, and then his face, cleaned his teeth, combed his hair, and looked in the looking glass. He felt frightened at what he saw, especially at the way his hair clung limply to his pale forehead. When his shirt was being changed, he knew he would be still more terrified if he glanced at his body, and he avoided looking at himself. But at last it was all over. He put on his dressing gown, covered himself with a rug, and sat in the armchair to drink his tea. For one moment he felt refreshed; but as soon as he began to drink the tea, again there was the same taste, the same pain. He forced himself to finish it, and lay down, stretched out his legs. He lay down and dismissed Pyotr.

Always the same. A gleam of hope flashes for a moment, then again the sea of despair roars about him again, and always pain, always pain, always heartache, and always the same thing. Alone it is awfully dreary; he longs to call some one, but he knows beforehand that with others present it will be worse. "Morphine again—only to forget again. I'll tell him, the doctor, that he must think of something else. It can't go on; it can't go on like this."

One hour, two hours pass like this. Then there is a ring at the front door. The doctor, perhaps. Yes, it is the doctor, fresh, hearty, fat, and cheerful, wearing that expression that seems to say, "You there are in a panic about something, but we'll soon set things right for you." The doctor is aware that this expression is hardly fitting here, but he has put it on once and for all, and can't take it off, like a man who has put on a frock coat to pay a round of calls.

In a hearty, reassuring manner the doctor rubs his hands.

"I'm cold. It's a sharp frost. Just let me warm myself," he says with an expression, as though it's only a matter of waiting a little till he's warm, and as soon as he's warm he'll set everything to rights.

"Well, now, how are you?"

Ivan Ilyich feels that the doctor would like to say, "How's the little trouble?" but that he feels that he can't talk like that, and says, "How did you pass the night?"

Ivan Ilyich looks at the doctor with an expression that asks—

"Is it possible you're never ashamed of lying?"

But the doctor does not care to understand this look.

And Ivan Ilyich says—

"It's always just as awful. The pain never leaves me, never ceases. If only there were something!"

"Ah, you're all like that, all sick people say that. Come, now I do believe I'm thawed; even Praskovya Fyodorovna, who's so particular, could find no fault with my temperature. Well, now I can say good morning." And the doctor shakes hands.

And dropping his former levity, the doctor, with a serious face, proceeds to examine the patient, feeling his pulse, to take his temperature, and then the tappings and soundings begin.

Ivan Ilyich knows positively and indubitably that it's all nonsense and empty deception; but when the doctor, kneeling down, stretches over him, putting his ear first higher, then lower, and goes through various gymnastic evolutions over him with a serious face, Ivan Ilyich is affected by this, as he used sometimes to be affected by the speeches of the lawyers in court, though he was perfectly well aware that they were telling lies all the while and why they were telling lies.

The doctor, kneeling on the sofa, was still sounding him, when there was the rustle of Praskovya Fyodorovna's silk dress in the doorway, and she was heard scolding Pyotr for not having let her know that the doctor had come.

She comes in, kisses her husband, and at once begins to explain that she has been up a long while, and that it was only through a misunderstanding that she was not there when the doctor came.

Ivan Ilyich looks at her, scans her all over, and sets down against her whiteness and plumpness, and the cleanness of her hands and neck, and the glossiness of her hair, and the gleam full of life in her eyes. With all the force of his soul he hates her. And when she touches him it makes him suffer from the thrill of hatred he feels for her.

Her attitude to him and his illness is still the same. Just as the doctor had taken up a certain line with the patient which he was not now able to drop, so she too had taken up a line with him—that he was not doing something he ought to do, and was himself to blame, and she was lovingly reproaching him for his neglect, and she could not now get out of this attitude.

"Why, you know, he won't listen to me; he doesn't take his medicine at the right times. And what's worse still, he insists on lying in a position that surely must be bad for him—with his legs in the air."

She described how he made Gerasim hold his legs up.

The doctor smiled with kindly condescension that said, "Oh well, it can't be helped, these sick people do take up such foolish fancies; but we must forgive them."

When the examination was over, the doctor looked at his watch, and then Praskovya Fyodorovna informed Ivan Ilyich that it must, of course, be as he liked, but she had sent today for a celebrated doctor, and that he would examine him, and have a consultation with Mikhail Danilovich (that was the name of their regular doctor).

"Don't oppose it now, please. This I'm doing entirely for my own sake," she said ironically, meaning it to be understood that she was doing it all for his sake, and was only saying this to give him no right to refuse her request. He lay silent, knitting his brows. He felt that he was hemmed in by such a tangle of falsity that it was hard to disentangle anything from it.

Everything she did for him was entirely for her own sake, and she told him she was doing for her own sake what she actually was doing for her own sake as something so incredible that he would take it as meaning the opposite.

At half-past eleven the celebrated doctor came. Again came the sounding, and then grave conversation in his presence and in the other room about the kidney and the appendix, and questions and answers, with such an air of significance, that again, instead of the real question of life and death, which was now the only one that confronted him, the question that came uppermost was of the kidney and the appendix, which were doing something not as they ought to do, and were for that reason being attacked by Mikhail Danilovich and the celebrated doctor, and forced to mend their ways.

The celebrated doctor took leave of him with a serious, but not a hopeless face. And to the timid question that Ivan Ilyich addressed to him while he lifted his eyes, shining with terror and hope, up towards him, Was there a chance of recovery? he answered that he could not answer for it, but that there was a chance. The look of hope with which Ivan Ilyich watched the doctor out was so piteous that, seeing it, Praskovya Fyodorovna positively burst into tears, as she went out of the door to hand the celebrated doctor his fee in the next room.

The gleam of hope kindled by the doctor's assurance did not last long.

Again the same room, the same pictures, the curtains, the wallpaper, the medicine-bottles, and ever the same, his aching suffering body. And Ivan Ilyich began to moan; they gave him injections, and he sank into oblivion. When he waked up it was getting dark; they brought him his dinner. He forced himself to eat some broth; and again everything the same, and again the coming night.

After dinner at seven o'clock, Praskovya Fyodorovna came into his room, dressed as though to go to a *soirée,* with her full bosom laced in tight, and traces of powder on her face. She had in the morning mentioned to him that they were going to the theatre. Sarah Bernhardt was visiting the town, and they had a box, which he had insisted on their taking. By now he had forgotten about it, and her smart attire was an offence to him. But he concealed this feeling when he recollected that he had himself insisted on their taking a box and going, because it was an aesthetic pleasure, beneficial and instructive for the children.

Praskovya Fyodorovna came in satisfied with herself, but yet with something of a guilty air. She sat down, asked how he was, as he saw, simply for the sake of asking, and not for the sake of learning anything, knowing indeed that there was nothing to learn, and began telling him how absolutely necessary it was; how she would not have gone for anything, but the box had been taken, and Ellen, their daughter, and Petrishchev (the examining lawyer, the daughter's suitor) were going, and that it was out of the question to let them go alone. But that she would have liked much better to stay with him. If only he would be sure to follow the doctor's prescription while she was away.

"Oh, and Fyodor Dmitryevich" (the suitor) "would like to come in. May he? And Liza?"

"Yes, let them come in."

The daughter came in, in full dress, her fresh young body bare, while his body made him suffer so. But she made a show of it; she was strong, healthy, obviously in love, and impatient of the illness, suffering, and death that hindered her happiness.

Fyodor Dmitryevich came in too in evening dress, his hair curled *à la Capoul,* with his long sinewy neck tightly fenced round by a white collar, with his vast expanse of white chest and strong thighs displayed in narrow black trousers, with one white glove in his hand and a crush opera hat.

Behind him crept in unnoticed the little high school boy in his new uniform, poor fellow, in gloves, and with that awful blue ring under his eyes that Ivan Ilyich knew the meaning of.

He always felt sorry for his son. And pitiable indeed was his scared face of sympathetic suffering. Except Gerasim, Ivan Ilyich fancied that Volodya was the only one that understood and was sorry.

They all sat down; again they asked how he was. A silence followed. Liza asked her mother about the opera glass. An altercation ensued between the mother and daughter as to who had taken it, and where it had been put. It turned into an unpleasant squabble.

Fyodor Dmitryevich asked Ivan Ilyich whether he had seen Sarah Bernhardt? Ivan Ilyich could not at first catch the question that was asked him, but then he said, "No, have you seen her before?"

"Yes, in *Adrienne Lecouvreur*."

Praskovya Fyodorovna observed that she was particularly good in that part. The daughter made some reply. A conversation sprang up about the art and naturalness of her acting, that conversation that is continually repeated and always the same.

In the middle of the conversation Fyodor Dmitryevich glanced at Ivan Ilyich and relapsed into silence. The others looked at him and became mute, too. Ivan Ilyich was staring with glittering eyes straight before him, obviously furious with them. This had to be set right, but it could not anyhow be set right. This silence had somehow to be broken. No one would venture on breaking it, and all began to feel alarmed that the decorous deception was somehow breaking down, and the facts would be exposed to all. Liza was the first to pluck up courage. She broke the silence. She tried to cover up what they were all feeling, but inadvertently she gave it utterance.

"*If we are going,* though, it's time to start," she said, glancing at her watch, a gift from her father; and with a scarcely perceptible meaning smile to the young man, referring to something only known to themselves, she got up with a rustle of her skirts.

They all got up, said good-by, and went away. When they were gone, Ivan Ilyich fancied he was easier; there was no falsity—that had gone away with them, but the pain remained. That continual pain, that continual terror, made nothing harder, nothing easier. It was always worse.

Again came minute after minute, hour after hour, still the same and still no end, and ever more terrible the inevitable end.

"Yes, send Gerasim," he said in answer to Pyotr's question.

IX

Late at night his wife came back. She came in on tiptoe, but he heard her, opened his eyes, and made haste to close them again. She wanted to send away Gerasim and sit up with him herself instead. He opened his eyes and said, "No, go away."

"Are you in great pain?"

"Always the same."

"Take some opium."

He agreed, and drank it. She went away.

Till three o'clock he slept a miserable sleep. It seemed to him that he and his pain were being thrust somewhere into a narrow, deep, black sack, and they kept pushing him further and further in, and still could not thrust him to the bottom. And this operation was awful to him, and was accompanied with agony. And he was afraid, and yet wanted to fall into it, and struggled and yet tried to get into it. And all of a sudden he slipped and fell and woke up. Gerasim, still the same, is sitting at the foot of the bed half dozing peacefully, patient. And he is lying with his wasted legs clad in stockings, raised on Gerasim's shoulders, the same candle burning in the alcove, and the same interminable pain.

"Go away, Gerasim," he whispered.

"It's all right, sir. I'll stay a bit longer."

"No, go away."

He took his legs down, lay sideways on his arm, and he felt very sorry for himself. He only waited till Gerasim had gone away into the next room; he could restrain himself no longer, and cried like a child. He cried at his own helplessness, at his awful loneliness, at the cruelty of people, at the cruelty of God, at the absence of God.

"Why hast Thou done all this? What brought me to this? Why, why torture me so horribly?"

He did not expect an answer, and wept indeed that there was and could be no answer. The pain grew more acute again, but he did not stir, did not call.

He said to himself, "Come, more then; come, strike me! But what for? What have I done to Thee? what for?"

Then he was still, ceased weeping, held his breath, and was all attention; he listened, as it were, not to a voice uttering sounds, but to the voice of his soul, to the current of thoughts that rose up within him.

"What is it you want?" was the first clear idea able to be put into words that he grasped.

"What? Not to suffer, to live," he answered.

And again he was utterly plunged into attention so intense that even the pain did not distract him.

"To live? Live how?" the voice of his soul was asking.

"Why, live as I used to live before—happily and pleasantly."

"As you used to live before—happily and pleasantly?" queried the voice. And he began going over in his imagination the best moments of his pleasant life. But strange to say, all these best moments of his pleasant life seemed now not at all what they had seemed then. All—except the first memories of childhood—there, in his childhood there had been something really pleasant in which one could have lived if it had come back. But the creature who had this pleasant experience was no more; it was like a memory of some one else.

As soon as he reached the beginning of what had resulted in him as he was now, Ivan Ilyich, all that had seemed joys to him then now melted away before his eyes and were transformed into something trivial, and often disgusting.

And the further he went from childhood, the nearer to the actual present, the more worthless and uncertain were the joys. It began with life at the school of jurisprudence. Then there had still been something genuinely good; then there had been gaiety; then there had been friendship; then there had been hopes. But in the higher classes these good moments were already becoming rarer. Later on, during the first period of his official life, at the governor's, good moments appeared; but it was all mixed, and less and less of it was good. And further on even less was good, and the further he went the less good there was.

His marriage . . . as gratuitous as the disillusion of it and the smell of his wife's breath and the sensuality, the hypocrisy! And that deadly official life, and anxiety about money, and so for one year, and two, and ten, and twenty, and always the same thing. And the further he went, the more deadly it became. "As though I had been going steadily downhill, imagining that I was going uphill. So it was in fact. In public opinion I was going uphill, and steadily as I got up it life was ebbing away from me. . . . And now the work's done, there's only to die.

"But what is this? What for? It cannot be! It cannot be that life has been so senseless, so loathsome? And if it really was so loathsome and senseless, then why die, and die in agony? There's something wrong.

"Can it be I have not lived as one ought?" suddenly came into his head. "But how not so, when I've done everything as it should be done?" he said, and at once dismissed this only solution of all the enigma of life and death as something utterly out of the question.

"What do you want now? To live? Live how? Live as you live at the courts when the usher booms out: 'The Judge is coming!' . . . The judge is coming, the judge is coming," he repeated to himself. "Here he is, the judge! But I'm not to blame!" he shrieked in fury. "What's it for?" And he left off crying, and turning with his face to the wall, fell to pondering always on the same question, "What for, why all this horror?"

But however much he pondered, he could not find an answer. And whenever the idea struck him, as it often did, that it all came of his never having lived as he ought, he thought of all the correctness of his life and dismissed the strange idea.

X

Another fortnight had passed. Ivan Ilyich could not now get up from the sofa. He did not like lying in bed, and lay on the sofa. And lying almost all the time facing the wall, in loneliness he suffered all the inexplicable agonies, and in loneliness pondered always that inexplicable question, "What is it? Can it be true that it's death?" And an inner voice answered, "Yes, it is true." "Why these agonies?" and a voice answered, "For no reason." Beyond and besides this there was nothing.

From the very beginning of his illness, ever since Ivan Ilyich first went to the doctor's, his life had been split up into two contradictory moods, which were continually alternating—one was despair and the anticipation of an uncomprehended and awful death; the other was hope and an absorbed watching over the actual condition of his body. First there was nothing confronting him but a kidney or intestine which had temporarily declined to perform their duties, then there was nothing but unknown awful death, which there was no escaping.

These two moods had alternated from the very beginning of the illness; but the further the illness progressed, the more doubtful and fantastic became the conception of the kidney, and the more real the sense of approaching death.

He had but to reflect on what he had been three months before and what he was now, to reflect how steadily he had been going downhill, for every possibility of hope to be shattered.

Of late, in the loneliness in which he found himself, lying with his face to the back of the sofa, a loneliness in the middle of a populous town and of his numerous acquaintances and his family, a loneliness than which none more complete could be found anywhere—not at the bottom of the sea, not deep down in the earth;—of late in this fearful loneliness Ivan Ilyich had lived only in imagination in the past. One by one the pictures of his past rose up before him. It always began from what was nearest in time and went back to the most remote, to childhood, and rested there. If Ivan Ilyich thought of the stewed prunes that had been offered him for dinner that day, his mind went back to the damp, wrinkled French plum of his childhood, of its peculiar taste and the flow of saliva when the stone was sucked; and along with this memory of a taste there rose up a whole series of memories of that period—his nurse, his brother, his playthings. "I mustn't . . . it's too painful," Ivan Ilyich said to himself, and he brought himself back to the present. The button on the back of the sofa and the creases in the morocco. "Morocco's dear, and doesn't wear well; there was a quarrel over it. But the morocco was different, and different too the quarrel when we tore father's portfolio and were punished, and mamma bought us the tarts." And again his mind rested on his childhood, and again it was painful, and he tried to drive it away and think of something else.

And again at that point, together with that chain of associations, quite another chain of memories came into his heart, of how his illness had grown up and become more acute. It was the same there, the further back the more life there had been. There had been both more that was good in life and more of life itself. After the two began to melt into one. "Just as the pain goes on getting worse and worse, so has my whole life gone on getting worse and worse," he thought. One light spot was there at the back, at the beginning of life, and then it kept getting blacker and blacker, and going faster and faster. "In inverse ratio to the square of the distance from death," thought Ivan Ilyich. And the image of a stone falling downwards with increasing velocity sank into his soul. Life, a series of increasing sufferings, falls more and more swiftly to the end, the most fearful sufferings. "I am falling." He shuddered, shifted himself, would have resisted, but he knew beforehand that he could not resist; and again, with eyes weary with gazing at it, but unable not to gaze at what was before him, he stared at the back of the sofa and waited, waited expecting that fearful fall and shock and dissolution. "Resistance is impossible," he said to himself. "But if one could at least comprehend what it's for? Even that's impossible. It could be explained if one were to say that I hadn't lived as I ought. But that can't be alleged," he said to himself, thinking of all the regularity, correctness, and propriety of his life. "That really can't be admitted," he said to himself, his lips smiling ironically as though some one could see his smile and be deceived by it. "No explanation! Agony, death. . . . What for?"

XI

So passed a fortnight. During that fortnight an event occurred that had been desired by Ivan Ilyich and his wife. Petrishchev made a formal proposal. This took place in the evening. Next day Praskovya Fyodorovna went in to her husband, resolving in her mind how to inform him of Fyodor Dmitryevich's proposal, but that night there had been a change for the worse in Ivan Ilyich. Praskovya Fyodorovna found him on the same sofa, but in a different position. He was lying on his face, groaning, and staring straight before him with a fixed gaze.

She began talking of remedies. He turned his stare on her. She did not finish what she had begun saying; such hatred of her in particular was expressed in that stare.

"For Christ's sake, let me die in peace," he said.

She would have gone away, but at that moment the daughter came in and went up to say good morning to him. He looked at his daughter just as at his wife, and to her inquiries how he was, he told her drily that they would soon all be rid of him. Both were silent, sat a little while, and went out.

"How are we to blame?" said Liza to her mother. "As though we had done it! I'm sorry for papa, but why punish us?"

At the usual hour the doctor came. Ivan Ilyich answered, "Yes, no," never taking his exasperated stare from him, and towards the end he said, "Why, you know that you can do nothing, so let me be."

"We can relieve your suffering," said the doctor.

"Even that you can't do; let me be."

The doctor went into the drawing room and told Praskovya Fyodorovna that it was very serious, and that the only resource left them was opium to relieve his sufferings, which must be terrible. The doctor said his physical sufferings were terrible, and that was true; but even more terrible than his physical sufferings were his mental sufferings, and in that lay his chief misery.

His moral sufferings were due to the fact that during that night, as he looked at the sleepy, good-natured, broad-cheeked face of Gerasim, the thought had suddenly come into his head, "What if in reality all my life, my conscious life, has been not the right thing?" The thought struck him that what he had regarded before as an utter impossibility, that he had spent his life not as he ought, might be the truth. It struck him that those scarcely detected impulses of struggle within him against what was considered good by persons of higher position, scarcely detected impulses which he had dismissed, that they might be the real thing, and everything else might be not the right thing. And his official work, and his ordering of his daily life and of his family, and these social and official interests,— all that might be not the right thing. He tried to defend it all to himself. And suddenly he felt all the weakness of what he was defending. And it was useless to defend it.

"But if it's so," he said to himself, "and I am leaving life with the consciousness that I have lost all that was given me, and there's no correcting it, then what?" He lay on his back and began going over his whole life entirely anew. When he saw the footman in the morning, then his wife, then his daughter, then the doctor, every movement they made, every word they uttered, confirmed for him the terrible truth that had been revealed to him in the night. In them he saw himself, saw all in which he had lived, and saw distinctly that it was all not the right thing; it was horrible, vast deception that concealed both life and death. This consciousness intensified his physical agonies, multiplied them tenfold. He groaned and tossed from side to side and pulled at the covering over him. It seemed to him that it was stifling him and weighing him down. And for that he hated them.

They gave him a big dose of opium; he sank into unconsciousness; but at dinner time the same thing began again. He drove them all away, and tossed from side to side.

His wife came to him and said, "*Jean*, darling, do this for my sake" (for my sake?). "It can't do harm, and it often does good. Why, it's nothing. And often in health people——"

He opened his eyes wide.

"What? Take the sacrament? What for? No. Besides . . ."

She began to cry.

"Yes, my dear. I'll send for our priest, he's so nice."

"All right, very well," he said.

When the priest came and confessed him he was softened, felt as it were a relief from his doubts, and consequently from his sufferings, and there came a moment of hope. He began once more thinking of the intestinal appendix and the possibility of curing it. He took the sacrament with tears in his eyes.

When they laid him down again after the sacrament for a minute, he felt comfortable, and again the hope of life sprang up. He began to think about the operation which had been suggested to him. "To live, I want to live," he said to himself. His wife came in to congratulate him; she uttered the customary words and added—

"It's quite true, isn't it, that you're better?"

Without looking at her, he said, "Yes."

Her dress, her figure, the expression of her face, the tone of her voice,—all told him the same: "Not the right thing. All that in which you lived and are living is lying, deceit, hiding life and death away from you." And as soon as he had formed that thought, hatred sprang up in him, and with that hatred agonizing physical sufferings, and with these sufferings the sense of inevitable, approaching ruin. Something new was happening; there were screwing and shooting pains, and a tightness in his breathing.

The expression of his face as he uttered that "Yes" was terrible. After uttering that "Yes," looking her straight in the face, he turned on to his face, with a rapidity extraordinary in his weakness, and shrieked—

"Go away, go away, let me be!"

XII

From that moment there began the scream that never ceased for three days, and was so awful that through two closed doors one could not hear it without horror. At the moment when he answered his wife he grasped that he had fallen, that there was no return, that the end had come, quite the end, while doubt was still as unsolved, still remained doubt.

"Oo! Oo—o! Oo!" he screamed in varying intonations. He had begun screaming, "I don't want to!" and so had gone on screaming on the same vowel sound—oo!

All those three days, during which time did not exist for him, he was struggling in that black sack into which he was being thrust by an unseen resistless force. He struggled as the man condemned to death struggles in the hands of the executioner, knowing that he cannot save himself. And every moment he felt that in spite of all his efforts to struggle against it, he was getting nearer and nearer to what terrified him. He felt that his agony was due both to his being thrust into this black hole and still more to his not being able to get right into it. What hindered him from getting into it was the claim that his life had been good. That justification of his life held him fast and would not let him get forward, and it caused him more agony than all.

All at once some force struck him in the chest, in the side, and stifled his breathing more than ever; he rolled forward into the hole, and there at the end there was some sort of light. It had happened with him, as it had sometimes happened to him in a railway carriage, when he had thought he was going forward while he was going back, and all of a sudden recognized his real direction.

"Yes, it has all been not the right thing," he said to himself, "but that's no matter." He could, he could do the right thing. "What is the right thing?" he asked himself, and suddenly he became quiet.

This was at the end of the third day, two hours before his death. At that very moment the schoolboy had stealthily crept into his father's room and gone up to his bedside. The dying man was screaming and waving his arms. His hand fell on the schoolboy's head. The boy snatched it, pressed it to his lips, and burst into tears.

At that very moment Ivan Ilyich had rolled into the hole, and caught sight of the light, and it was revealed to him that his life had not been what it ought to have been, but that that could still be set right. He asked himself, "What is the right thing?"—and became quiet, listening. Then he felt some one was kissing his hand. He opened his eyes and glanced at his son. He felt sorry for him. His wife went up to him. He glanced at her. She was gazing at him with open mouth, the tears unwiped streaming over her nose and cheeks, a look of despair on her face. He felt sorry for her.

"Yes, I'm making them miserable," he thought. "They're sorry, but it will be better for them when I die." He would have said this, but had not the strength to utter it. "Besides, why speak, I must act," he thought. With a glance to his wife he pointed to his son and said—

"Take away . . . sorry for him. . . . And you too . . ." He tried to say "forgive," but said "forgo" . . . and too weak to correct himself, shook his hand, knowing that He would understand Whose understanding mattered.

And all at once it became clear to him that what had tortured him and would not leave him was suddenly dropping away all at once on both sides and on ten sides and on all sides. He was sorry for them, must act so that they might not suffer. Set them free and be free himself of those agonies. "How right and how simple!" he thought. "And the pain?" he asked himself. "Where's it gone? Eh, where are you, pain?"

He began to watch for it.

"Yes, here it is. Well, what of it, let the pain be.

"And death. Where is it?"

He looked for his old accustomed terror of death, and did not find it. "Where is it? What death?" There was no terror, because death was not either.

In the place of death there was light.

"So this is it!" he suddenly exclaimed aloud.

"What joy!"

To him all this passed in a single instant, and the meaning of that instant suffered no change after. For those present his agony lasted another two hours. There was a rattle in his throat, a twitching in his wasted body. Then the rattle and the gasping came at longer and longer intervals.

"It is over!" some one said over him.

He caught those words and repeated them in his soul.

"Death is over," he said to himself. "It's no more."

He drew in a breath, stopped midway in the breath, stretched and died.

QUESTIONS AND TOPICS

1. Does marriage necessarily lead to a life of caution and conformity? Are many husbands and wives as alienated from each other as Ivan Ilyich and Praskovya Fyodorovna?
2. What does Ivan discover during his illness? At the time of death?
3. Would you describe Ivan as a typical, middle-class person? Do you know many people like him? Are they happy with their lives? Should they be?
4. What better kind of life might Ivan have lived? Is this kind of life really possible, or is man destined to live the life of Ivan Ilyich?
5. Is Ivan's life shaped by forces outside of him? Describe these forces. What about the forces within Ivan?

Fyodor Dostoevsky

THE DREAM
OF A
RIDICULOUS MAN

*When he was a young man, Fyodor
Dostoevsky, 1821–1881, turned from
radicalism to the Russian Orthodox
church. This conversion signified a
profound change in his philosophy.
In rejecting socialism, Dostoevsky
denied that man could perfect himself and consequently create utopia
on earth. In accepting Orthodoxy,
Dostoevsky accepted the doctrine
that man is innately sinful and can
only be redeemed through suffering,
compassion, and faith in God.*

I

I am a ridiculous person. Now they call me a madman. That would be
a promotion if it were not that I remain as ridiculous in their eyes as
before. But now I do not resent it, they are all dear to me now, even when
they laugh at me—and, indeed, it is just then that they are particularly
dear to me. I could join in their laughter—not exactly at myself, but
through affection for them, if I did not feel so sad as I look at them. Sad
because they do not know the truth and I do know it. Oh, how hard it is
to be the only one who knows the truth! But they won't understand that.
No, they won't understand it.

In old days I used to be miserable at seeming ridiculous. Not seeming,
but being. I have always been ridiculous, and I have known it, perhaps,
from the hour I was born. Perhaps from the time I was seven years old
I knew I was ridiculous. Afterwards I went to school, studied at the university, and, do you know, the more I learned, the more thoroughly I
understood that I was ridiculous. So that it seemed in the end as though

all the sciences I studied at the university existed only to prove and make evident to me as I went more deeply into them that I was ridiculous. It was the same with life as it was with science. With every year the same consciousness of the ridiculous figure I cut in every relation grew and strengthened. Everyone always laughed at me. But not one of them knew or guessed that if there were one man on earth who knew better than anybody else that I was absurd, it was myself, and what I resented most of all was that they did not know that. But that was my own fault; I was so proud that nothing would have ever induced me to tell it to anyone. This pride grew in me with the years; and if it had happened that I allowed myself to confess to anyone that I was ridiculous, I believe that I should have blown out my brains the same evening. Oh, how I suffered in my early youth from the fear that I might give way and confess it to my schoolfellows. But since I grew to manhood, I have for some unknown reason become calmer, though I realised my awful characteristic more fully every year. I say 'unknown', for to this day I cannot tell why it was. Perhaps it was owing to the terrible misery that was growing in my soul through something which was of more consequence than anything else about me: that something was the conviction that had come upon me that *nothing in the world mattered*. I had long had an inkling of it, but the full realisation came last year almost suddenly. I suddenly felt that it was all the same to me whether the world existed or whether there had never been anything at all: I began to feel with all my being that there was *nothing existing*. At first I fancied that many things had existed in the past, but afterwards I guessed that there never had been anything in the past either, but that it had only seemed so for some reason. Little by little I guessed that there would be nothing in the future either. Then I left off being angry with people and almost ceased to notice them. Indeed this showed itself even in the pettiest trifles: I used, for instance, to knock against people in the street. And not so much from being lost in thought: what had I to think about? I had almost given up thinking by that time; nothing mattered to me. If at least I had solved my problems! Oh, I had not settled one of them, and how many they were! But I gave up caring about anything, and all the problems disappeared.

And it was after that that I found out the truth. I learnt the truth last November—on the third of November, to be precise—and I remember every instant since. It was a gloomy evening, one of the gloomiest possible evenings. I was going home at about eleven o'clock, and I remember that

I thought that the evening could not be gloomier. Even physically. Rain had been falling all day, and it had been a cold, gloomy, almost menacing rain, with, I remember, an unmistakable spite against mankind. Suddenly between ten and eleven it had stopped, and was followed by a horrible dampness, colder and damper than the rain, and a sort of steam was rising from everything, from every stone in the street, and from every by-lane if one looked down it as far as one could. A thought suddenly occurred to me, that if all the street lamps had been put out it would have been less cheerless, that the gas made one's heart sadder because it lighted it all up. I had had scarcely any dinner that day, and had been spending the evening with an engineer, and two other friends had been there also. I sat silent—I fancy I bored them. They talked of something rousing and suddenly they got excited over it. But they did not really care, I could see that, and only made a show of being excited. I suddenly said as much to them. "My friends," I said, "you really do not care one way or the other." They were not offended, but they all laughed at me. That was because I spoke without any note of reproach, simply because it did not matter to me. They saw it did not, and it amused them.

As I was thinking about the gas lamps in the street I looked up at the sky. The sky was horribly dark, but one could distinctly see tattered clouds, and between them fathomless black patches. Suddenly I noticed in one of these patches a star, and began watching it intently. That was because that star gave me an idea: I decided to kill myself that night. I had firmly determined to do so two months before, and poor as I was, I bought a splendid revolver that very day, and loaded it. But two months had passed and it was still lying in my drawer; I was so utterly indifferent that I wanted to seize a moment when I would not be so indifferent—why, I don't know. And so for two months every night that I came home I thought I would shoot myself. I kept waiting for the right moment. And so now this star gave me a thought. I made up my mind that it should certainly be that night. And why the star gave me the thought I don't know.

And just as I was looking at the sky, this little girl took me by the elbow. The street was empty, and there was scarcely anyone to be seen. A cabman was sleeping in the distance in his cab. It was a child of eight with a kerchief on her head, wearing nothing but a wretched little dress all soaked with rain, but I noticed particularly her wet broken shoes and I recall them now. They caught my eye particularly. She suddenly pulled me by the elbow and called me. She was not weeping, but was spasmodically crying out some words which she could not utter properly, because she was shivering and shuddering all over. She was in terror about something, and kept crying, "Mammy, mammy!" I turned facing her, I did not say a word and went on; but she ran, pulling at me, and there was that note in her voice which in frightened children means despair. I know that sound. Though she did not articulate the words, I understood that her mother was dying, or that something of the sort was happening to them, and that she had run out to call someone, to find something to help her mother. I did not go with her; on the contrary, I had an impulse to drive her away. I told her first to go to a policeman. But clasping her hands, she ran beside me sobbing and gasping, and would not leave me. Then I stamped my foot, and shouted at her. She called out "Sir! sir! . . ." but suddenly abandoned me and rushed headlong across the road. Some other passer-by appeared there, and she evidently flew from me to him.

I mounted up to my fifth storey. I have a room in a flat where there are other lodgers. My room is small and poor, with a garret window in the shape of a semicircle. I have a sofa covered with American leather, a table with books on it, two chairs and a comfortable arm-chair, as old as old can be, but of the good old-fashioned shape. I sat down, lighted the candle, and began thinking. In the room next to mine, through the partition wall, a perfect Bedlam was going on. It had been going on for the last three days. A retired captain lived there, and he had half a dozen visitors, gentlemen of doubtful reputation, drinking vodka and playing *stoss* with old cards. The night before there had been a fight, and I know that two of them had been for a long time engaged in dragging each other about by the hair. The landlady wanted to complain, but she was in abject terror of the captain. There was only one other lodger in the flat, a thin little regimental lady, on a visit to Petersburg, with three little children who had been taken ill since they came into the lodgings. Both she and her children were in mortal fear of the captain, and lay trembling and crossing themselves all night, and the youngest child had a sort of fit from fright. That captain, I know for a fact, sometimes stops people in the Nevsky Prospect and begs. They won't take him into the service, but strange to say (that's why I am telling this), all this month that the captain has been here his behaviour has caused me no annoyance. I have, of course, tried to avoid his acquaintance from the very beginning, and he, too, was bored with me from the first; but I never care how much they shout the other side of the partition nor how many of them there are in there: I sit up all night and forget them so completely that I do not even hear them. I stay awake till daybreak, and have been going on like that for the last year. I sit up all night in my arm-chair at the table, doing nothing. I only read by day. I sit—don't even think; ideas of a sort wander through my mind and I let them come and go as they will. A whole candle is burnt every night. I sat down quietly at the table, took out the revolver and put it down before me. When I had put it down I asked myself, I remember, "Is that so?" and answered with complete conviction, "It is." That is, I shall shoot myself. I knew that I should shoot myself that night for certain, but how much longer I should go on sitting at the table I did not know. And no doubt I should have shot myself if it had not been for that little girl.

II

You see, though nothing mattered to me, I could feel pain, for instance. If anyone had struck me it would have hurt me. It was the same morally: if anything very pathetic happened, I should have felt pity just as I used to do in old days when there were things in life that did matter to me. I had felt pity that evening. I should have certainly helped a child. Why, then, had I not helped the little girl? Because of an idea that occurred to me at the time: when she was calling and pulling at me, a question suddenly arose before me and I could not settle it. The question was an idle one, but I was vexed. I was vexed at the reflection that if I were going to make an end of myself that night, nothing in life ought to have mattered to me. Why was it that all at once I did not feel that nothing mattered and was sorry for the little girl? I remember that I was very sorry for her, so much so that I felt a strange pang, quite incongruous in my position. Really I do not know better how to convey my fleeting sensation at the moment, but the sensation persisted at home when I was sitting at the table, and I was very much irritated as I had not been for a long time past. One reflection followed another. I saw clearly that so long as I was still a human being and not nothingness, I was alive and so could suffer, be angry and feel shame at my actions. So be it. But if I am going to kill myself, in two hours, say, what is the little girl to me and what have I to do with shame or with anything else in the world? I shall turn into nothing, absolutely nothing. And can it really be true that the consciousness that I shall *completely* cease to exist immediately and so everything else will cease to exist, does not in the least affect my feeling of pity for the child nor the feeling of shame after a contemptible action? I stamped and shouted at the unhappy child as though to say—not only I feel no pity, but even if I behave inhumanly and contemptibly, I am free to, for in another two hours everything will be extinguished. Do you believe that that was why I shouted that? I am almost convinced of it now. It seemed clear to me that life and the world somehow depended upon me now. I may almost say that the world now seemed created for me alone: if I shot myself the world would cease to be at least for me. I say nothing of its being likely that nothing will exist for anyone when I am gone, and that as soon as my consciousness is extinguished the whole world will vanish too and become void like a phantom, as a mere appurtenance of my consciousness, for possibly all this world and all these people are only me myself. I remember that as I sat and reflected, I turned all these new questions that swarmed one after another quite the other way, and thought of something quite new. For instance, a strange reflection suddenly occurred to me, that if I had lived before on the moon or on Mars and there had committed the most disgraceful and dishonourable action and had there been put to such shame and ignominy as one can only conceive and realise in dreams, in nightmares, and if, finding myself afterwards on earth, I were able to retain the memory of what I had done on the other planet and at the same time knew that I should never, under any circumstances, return there, then looking from the earth to the moon—*should I care or not?* Should I feel shame for that action or not? These were idle and superfluous questions for the revolver was already lying before me, and I knew in every fibre of my being that *it* would happen for certain, but they excited me and I raged. I could not die now without having first settled something. In short, the child had saved me, for I put off my pistol shot for the sake of these questions. Meanwhile the clamour had begun to subside in the captain's room: they had finished their game, were settling down to sleep, and meanwhile were grumbling and languidly winding up their quarrels. At that point I suddenly fell asleep in my chair at the table—a thing which had never happened to me before. I dropped asleep quite unawares.

Dreams, as we all know, are very queer things: some parts are presented with appalling vividness, with details worked up with the elaborate finish of jewellery, while others one gallops through, as it were, without noticing them at all, as, for instance, through space and time. Dreams seem to be spurred on not by reason but by desire, not by the head but by the heart, and yet what complicated tricks my reason has played sometimes in dreams, what utterly incomprehensible things happen to it! My brother died five years ago, for instance. I sometimes dream of him; he takes part in my affairs, we are very much interested, and yet all through my dream I quite know and remember that my brother is dead and buried. How is it that I am not surprised that, though he is dead, he is here beside me and working with me? Why is it that my reason fully accepts it? But enough. I will begin about my dream. Yes, I dreamed a dream, my dream of the third of November. They tease me now, telling me it was only a dream. But does it matter whether it was a dream or reality, if the dream made known to me the truth? If once one has recognised the truth and seen it, you know that it is the truth and that there is no other and there cannot be, whether you are asleep or awake. Let it be a dream, so be it, but that real life of which you make so much I had meant to extinguish by suicide, and my dream, my dream—oh, it revealed to me a different life, renewed, grand and full of power!

Listen.

III

I have mentioned that I dropped asleep unawares and even seemed to be still reflecting on the same subjects. I suddenly dreamt that I picked up the revolver and aimed it straight at my heart—my heart, and not my head; and I had determined beforehand to fire at my head, at my right temple. After aiming at my chest I waited a second or two, and suddenly my candle, my table, and the wall in front of me began moving and heaving. I made haste to pull the trigger.

In dreams you sometimes fall from a height, or are stabbed, or beaten, but you never feel pain unless, perhaps, you really bruise yourself against the bedstead, then you feel pain and almost always wake up from it. It was the same in my dream. I did not feel any pain, but it seemed as though with my shot everything within me was shaken and everything was suddenly dimmed, and it grew horribly black around me. I seemed to be blinded and benumbed, and I was lying on something hard, stretched on my back; I saw nothing, and could not make the slightest movement. People were walking and shouting around me, the captain bawled, the landlady shrieked—and suddenly another break and I was being carried in a closed coffin. And I felt how the coffin was shaking and reflected upon it, and for the first time the idea struck me that I was dead, utterly dead, I knew it and had no doubt of it, I could neither see nor move and yet I was feeling and reflecting. But I was soon reconciled to the position, and as one usually does in a dream, accepted the facts without disputing them.

And now I was buried in the earth. They all went away, I was left alone, utterly alone. I did not move. Whenever before I had imagined being buried the one sensation I associated with the grave was that of damp and cold. So now I felt that I was very cold, especially the tips of my toes, but I felt nothing else.

I lay still, strange to say I expected nothing, accepting without dispute that a dead man had nothing to expect. But it was damp. I don't know how long a time passed—whether an hour, or several days, or many days. But all at once a drop of water fell on my closed left eye, making its way through a coffin lid; it was followed a minute later by a second, then a minute later by a third—and so on, regularly every minute. There was a sudden glow of profound indignation in my heart, and I suddenly felt in it a pang of physical pain. "That's my wound," I thought; "that's the bullet. . . ." And drop after drop every minute kept falling on my closed eyelid. And all at once, not with my voice, but with my whole being, I called upon the power that was responsible for all that was happening to me:

"Whoever you may be, if you exist, and if anything more rational than what is happening here is possible, suffer it to be here now. But if you are revenging yourself upon me for my senseless suicide by the hideousness and absurdity of this subsequent existence, then let me tell you that no torture could ever equal the contempt which I shall go on dumbly feeling, though my martyrdom may last a million years!"

I made this appeal and held my peace. There was a full minute of unbroken silence and again another drop fell, but I knew with infinite unshakable certainty that everything would change immediately. And behold my grave suddenly was rent asunder, that is, I don't know whether it was opened or dug up, but I was caught up by some dark and unknown being and we found ourselves in space. I suddenly regained my sight. It was the dead of night, and never, never had there been such darkness. We were flying through space far away from the earth. I did not question the being who was taking me; I was proud and waited. I assured myself that I was not afraid, and was thrilled with ecstasy at the thought that I was not afraid. I do not know how long we were flying, I cannot imagine;

it happened as it always does in dreams when you skip over space and time, and the laws of thought and existence, and only pause upon the points for which the heart yearns. I remember that I suddenly saw in the darkness a star. "Is that Sirius?" I asked impulsively, though I had not meant to ask any questions.

"No, that is the star you saw between the clouds when you were coming home," the being who was carrying me replied.

I knew that it had something like a human face. Strange to say, I did not like that being, in fact I felt an intense aversion for it. I had expected complete non-existence, and that was why I had put a bullet through my heart. And here I was in the hands of a creature not human, of course, but yet living, existing. "And so there is life beyond the grave," I thought with the strange frivolity one has in dreams. But in its inmost depth my heart remained unchanged. "And if I have got to exist again," I thought, "and live once more under the control of some irresistible power, I won't be vanquished and humiliated."

"You know that I am afraid of you and despise me for that," I said suddenly to my companion, unable to refrain from the humiliating question which implied a confession, and feeling my humiliation stab my heart as with a pin. He did not answer my question, but all at once I felt that he was not even despising me, but was laughing at me and had no compassion for me, and that our journey had an unknown and mysterious object that concerned me only. Fear was growing in my heart. Something was mutely and painfully communicated to me from my silent companion, and permeated my whole being. We were flying through dark, unknown space. I had for some time lost sight of the constellations familiar to my eyes. I knew that there were stars in the heavenly spaces the light of which took thousands or millions of years to reach the earth. Perhaps we were already flying through those spaces. I expected something with a terrible anguish that tortured my heart. And suddenly I was thrilled by a familiar feeling that stirred me to the depths: I suddenly caught sight of our sun! I knew that it could not be *our* sun, that gave life to *our* earth, and that we were an infinite distance from our sun, but for some reason I knew in my whole being that it was a sun exactly like ours, a duplicate of it. A sweet, thrilling feeling resounded with ecstasy in my heart: the kindred power of the same light which had given me light stirred an echo in my heart and awakened it, and I had a sensation of life, the old life of the past for the first time since I had been in the grave.

"But if that is the sun, if that is exactly the same as our sun," I cried, "where is the earth?"

And my companion pointed to a star twinkling in the distance with an emerald light. We were flying straight towards it.

"And are such repetitions possible in the universe? Can that be the law of Nature? . . . And if that is an earth there, can it be just the same earth as ours . . . just the same, as poor, as unhappy, but precious and beloved for ever, arousing in the most ungrateful of her children the same poignant love for her that we feel for our earth?" I cried out, shaken by irresistible, ecstatic love for the old familiar earth which I had left. The image of the poor child whom I had repulsed flashed through my mind.

"You shall see it all," answered my companion, and there was a note of sorrow in his voice.

But we were rapidly approaching the planet. It was growing before my eyes; I could already distinguish the ocean, the outline of Europe; and suddenly a feeling of a great and holy jealousy glowed in my heart.

"How can it be repeated and what for? I love and can love only that earth which I have left, stained with my blood, when, in my ingratitude, I quenched my life with a bullet in my heart. But I have never, never ceased to love that earth, and perhaps on the very night I parted from it I loved it more than ever. Is there suffering upon this new earth? On our earth we can only love with suffering and through suffering. We cannot love otherwise, and we know of no other sort of love. I want suffering in order to love. I long, I thirst, this very instant, to kiss with tears the earth that I have left, and I don't want, I won't accept life on any other!"

But my companion had already left me. I suddenly, quite without noticing how, found myself on this other earth, in the bright light of a sunny day, fair as paradise. I believe I was standing on one of the islands that make up on our globe the Greek archipelago, or on the coast of the mainland facing that archipelago. Oh, everything was exactly as it is with us, only everything seemed to have a festive radiance, the splendour of some great, holy triumph attained at last. The caressing sea, green as emerald, splashed softly upon the shore and kissed it with manifest, almost conscious love. The tall, lovely trees stood in all the glory of their blossom, and their innumerable leaves greeted me, I am certain, with their soft, caressing rustle and seemed to articulate words of love. The grass glowed with bright and fragrant flowers. Birds were flying in flocks in the air, and perched fearlessly on my shoulders and arms and joyfully struck me with their darling, fluttering wings. And at last I saw and knew the people of this happy land. They came to me of themselves, they surrounded me, kissed me. The children of the sun, the children of their sun—oh, how beautiful they were! Never had I seen on our own earth such beauty in mankind. Only perhaps in our children, in their earliest years, one might find, some remote faint reflection of this beauty. The eyes of these happy people shone with a clear brightness. Their faces were radiant with the light of reason and fullness of a serenity that comes of perfect understanding, but those faces were gay; in their words and voices there was a note of childlike joy. Oh, from the first moment, from the first glance at them, I understood it all! It was the earth untarnished by the Fall; on it lived people who had not sinned. They lived just in such a paradise as that in which, according to all the legends of mankind, our first parents lived before they sinned; the only difference was that all this earth was the same paradise. These people, laughing joyfully, thronged round me and caressed me; they took me home with them, and each of them tried to reassure me. Oh, they asked me no questions, but they seemed, I fancied, to know everything without asking, and they wanted to make haste and smoothe away the signs of suffering from my face.

IV

And do you know what? Well, granted that it was only a dream, yet the sensation of the love of those innocent and beautiful people has remained with me for ever, and I feel as though their love is still flowing out to me from over there. I have seen them myself, have known them and been convinced; I loved them, I suffered for them afterwards. Oh, I understood at once even at the time that in many things I could not understand them at all; as an up-to-date Russian progressive and contemptible Petersburger, it struck me as inexplicable that, knowing so much, they had, for instance, no science like ours. But I soon realised that their knowledge was gained and fostered by intuitions different from those of us on earth, and that their aspirations, too, were quite different. They desired nothing and were at peace; they did not aspire to knowledge of life as we aspire to understand it, because their lives were full. But their knowledge was higher and deeper than ours; for our science seeks to explain what life is, aspires to understand it in order to teach others how to live, while they without science knew how to live; and that I understood, but I could not understand their knowledge. They showed me their trees, and I could not understand the intense love with which they looked at them; it was as though they were talking with creatures like themselves. And perhaps I shall not be mistaken if I say that they conversed with them. Yes, they had found their language, and I am convinced that the trees understood them. They looked at all Nature like that—at the animals who lived in peace with them and did not attack them, but loved them, conquered by their love. They pointed to the stars and told me something about them which I could not understand, but I am convinced that they were somehow in touch with the stars, not only in thought, but by some living channel. Oh, these people did not persist in trying to make me understand them, they loved me without that, but I knew that they would never understand me, and so I hardly spoke to them about our earth. I only kissed in their presence the earth on which they lived and mutely worshipped them themselves. And they saw that and let me worship them without being abashed at my adoration, for they themselves loved much. They were not unhappy on my account when at times I kissed their feet with tears, joyfully conscious of the love with which they would respond to mine. At times I asked myself with wonder how it was they were able never to offend a creature like me, and never once to arouse a feeling of jealousy or envy in me? Often I wondered how it could be that, boastful and untruthful as I was, I never talked to them of what I knew—of which, of course, they had no notion—that I was never tempted to do so by a desire to astonish or even to benefit them.

They were as gay and sportive as children. They wandered about their lovely woods and copses, they sang their lovely songs; their fare was light— the fruits of their trees, the honey from their woods, and the milk of the animals who loved them. The work they did for food and raiment was brief and not laborious. They loved and begot children, but I never noticed in them the impulse of that *cruel* sensuality which overcomes almost every man on this earth, all and each, and is the source of almost every sin of mankind on earth. They rejoiced at the arrival of children as new beings to share their happiness. There was no quarrelling, no jealousy among them, and they did not even know what the words meant. Their children were the children of all, for they all made up one family. There was scarcely any illness among them, though there was death; but their old people died peacefully, as though falling asleep, giving blessings and smiles to those who surrounded them to take their last farewell with bright and lovely smiles. I never saw grief or tears on those occasions, but only love, which reached the point of ecstasy, but a calm ecstasy, made perfect and contemplative. One might think that they were still in contact with the departed after death, and that their earthly union was not cut short by death. They scarcely understood me when I questioned them about immortality, but evidently they were so convinced of it without reasoning that it was not for them a question at all. They had no temples, but they had a real living and uninterrupted sense of oneness with the whole of the universe; they had no creed, but they had a certain knowledge that when their earthly joy had reached the limits of earthly nature, then there would come for them, for the living and for the dead, a still greater fullness of contact with the whole of the universe. They looked forward to that moment with joy, but without haste, not pining for it, but seeming to have a foretaste of it in their hearts, of which they talked to one another.

In the evening before going to sleep they liked singing in musical and harmonious chorus. In those songs they expressed all the sensations that the parting day had given them, sang its glories and took leave of it. They sang the praises of nature, of the sea, of the woods. They liked making songs about one another, and praised each other like children; they were the simplest songs, but they sprang from their hearts and went to one's heart. And not only in their songs but in all their lives they seemed to do nothing but admire one another. It was like being in love with each other, but an all-embracing, universal feeling.

Some of their songs, solemn and rapturous, I scarcely understood at all. Though I understood the words I could never fathom their full significance. It remained, as it were, beyond the grasp of my mind, yet my heart unconsciously absorbed it more and more. I often told them that I had had a presentiment of it long before, that this joy and glory had come to me on our earth in the form of a yearning melancholy that at times approached insufferable sorrow; that I had had a foreknowledge of them all and of their glory in the dreams of my heart and the visions of my mind; that often on our earth I could not look at the setting sun without tears . . . that in my hatred for the men of our earth there was always a yearning anguish: why could I not hate them without loving them? why could I not help forgiving them? and in my love for them there was a yearning grief: why could I not love them without hating them? They listened to me, and I saw they could not conceive what I was saying, but I did not regret that I had spoken to them of it: I knew that they understood the intensity of my yearning anguish over those whom I had left. But when they looked at me with their sweet eyes full of love, when I felt that in their presence my heart, too, became as innocent and just as theirs, the feeling of the fullness of life took my breath away, and I worshipped them in silence.

Oh, everyone laughs in my face now, and assures me that one cannot dream of such details as I am telling now, that I only dreamed or felt one sensation that arose in my heart in delirium and made up the details myself when I woke up. And when I told them that perhaps it really was so, my God, how they shouted with laughter in my face, and what mirth I caused! Oh, yes, of course I was overcome by the mere sensation of my dream, and that was all that was preserved in my cruelly wounded heart; but the actual forms and images of my dream, that is, the very ones I really saw at the very time of my dream, were filled with such harmony, were so lovely and enchanting and were so actual, that on awakening I was, of course, incapable of clothing them in our poor language, so that they were bound to become blurred in my mind; and so perhaps I really was forced afterwards to make up the details, and so of course to distort them in my passionate desire to convey some at least of them as quickly as I could. But on the other hand, how can I help believing that it was all true? It was perhaps a thousand times brighter, happier and more joyful than I describe it. Granted that I dreamed it, yet it must have been real. You know, I will tell you a secret: perhaps it was not a dream at all! For then something happened so awful, something so horribly true, that it could not have been imagined in a dream. My heart may have originated the dream, but would my heart alone have been capable of originating the awful event which happened to me afterwards? How could I alone have invented it or imagined it in my dream? Could my petty heart and my fickle, trivial mind have risen to such a revelation of truth? Oh, judge for yourselves: hitherto I have concealed it, but now I will tell the truth. The fact is that I . . . corrupted them all!

V

Yes, yes, it ended in my corrupting them all! How it could come to pass I do not know, but I remember it clearly. The dream embraced thousands of years and left in me only a sense of the whole. I only know that I was the cause of their sin and downfall. Like a vile trichina, like a germ of the plague infecting whole kingdoms, so I contaminated all this earth, so happy and sinless before my coming. They learnt to lie, grew fond of lying, and discovered the charm of falsehood. Oh, at first perhaps it began innocently, with a jest, coquetry, with amorous play, perhaps indeed with a germ, but that germ of falsity made its way into their hearts and pleased them. Then sensuality was soon begotten, sensuality begot jealousy, jealousy—cruelty. . . . Oh, I don't know, I don't remember; but soon, very soon the first blood was shed. They marvelled and were horrified, and began to be split up and divided. They formed into unions, but it was against one another. Reproaches, upbraidings followed. They came to know shame, and shame brought them to virtue. The conception of honour sprang up, and every union began waving its flags. They began torturing animals, and the animals withdrew from them into the forests and became hostile to them. They began to struggle for separation, for isolation, for individuality, for mine and thine. They began to talk in different languages. They became acquainted with sorrow and loved sorrow; they thirsted for suffering, and said that truth could only be attained through suffering. Then science appeared. As they became wicked they began talking of brotherhood and humanitarianism, and understood those ideas. As they became criminal, they invented justice and drew up whole legal codes in order to observe it, and to ensure their being kept, set up a guillotine. They hardly remembered what they had lost, in fact refused to believe that they had ever been happy and innocent. They even laughed at the possibility of this happiness in the past, and called it a dream. They could not even imagine it in definite form and shape, but, strange and wonderful to relate, though they lost all faith in their past happiness and called it a legend, they so longed to be happy and innocent once more that they succumbed to this desire like children, made an idol of it, set up temples and worshipped their own idea, their own desire; though at the same time they fully believed that it was unattainable and could not be realised, yet they bowed down to it and adored it with tears! Nevertheless, if it could have happened that they had returned to the innocent and happy condition which they had lost, and if someone had shown it to them again and had asked them whether they wanted to go back to it, they would certainly have refused. They answered me:

"We may be deceitful, wicked and unjust, we *know* it and weep over it, we grieve over it; we torment and punish ourselves more perhaps than than that merciful Judge Who will judge us and whose Name we know not. But we have science, and by means of it we shall find the truth and we shall arrive at it consciously. Knowledge is higher than feeling, the consciousness of life is higher than life. Science will give us wisdom, wisdom will reveal the laws, and the knowledge of the laws of happiness is higher than happiness."

That is what they said, and after saying such things everyone began to love himself better than anyone else, and indeed they could not do otherwise. All became so jealous of the rights of their own personality that they did their very utmost to curtail and destroy them in others, and made that the chief thing in their lives. Slavery followed, even voluntary slavery; the weak eagerly submitted to the strong, on condition that the latter aided them to subdue the still weaker. Then there were saints who came to these people, weeping, and talked to them of their pride, of their loss of harmony and due proportion, of their loss of shame. They were laughed at or pelted with stones. Holy blood was shed on the threshold of the temples. Then there arose men who began to think how to bring all people together again, so that everybody, while still loving himself best of all, might not interfere with others, and all might live together in something like a harmonious society. Regular wars sprang up over this idea. All the combatants at the same time firmly believed that science, wisdom and the instinct of self-preservation would force men at last to unite into a harmonious and rational society; and so, meanwhile, to hasten matters, 'the wise' endeavoured to exterminate as rapidly as possible all who were 'not wise' and did not understand their idea, that the latter might not hinder its triumph. But the instinct of self-preservation grew rapidly weaker; there arose men, haughty and sensual, who demanded all or nothing. In order to obtain everything they resorted to crime, and if they did not succeed—to suicide. There arose religions with a cult of non-existence and self-destruction for the sake of the everlasting peace of annihilation. At last these people grew weary of their meaningless toil, and signs of suffering came into their faces, and then they proclaimed that suffering was a beauty, for in suffering alone was there meaning. They glorified suffering in their songs. I moved about among them, wringing my hands and weeping over them, but I loved them perhaps more than in old days when there was no suffering in their faces and when they were innocent and so lovely. I loved the earth they had polluted even more than when it had been a paradise, if only because sorrow had come to it. Alas! I always loved sorrow and tribulation, but only for myself, for myself; but I wept over them, pitying them. I stretched out my hands to them in despair, blaming, cursing and despising myself. I told them that all this was my doing, mine alone; that it was I had brought them corruption, contamination and falsity. I besought them to crucify me, I taught them how to make a cross. I could not kill myself, I had not the strength, but I wanted to suffer at their hands. I yearned for suffering, I longed that my blood should be drained to the last drop in these agonies. But they only laughed at me, and began at last to look upon me as crazy. They justified me, they declared that they had only got what they wanted themselves, and that all that now was could not have been otherwise. At last they declared to me that I was becoming dangerous and that they should lock me up in a madhouse if I did not hold my tongue. Then such grief took possession of my soul that my heart was wrung, and I felt as though I were dying; and then . . . then I awoke.

It was morning, that is, it was not yet daylight, but about six o'clock. I woke up in the same arm-chair; my candle had burnt out; everyone was asleep in the captain's room, and there was a stillness all round, rare in our flat. First of all I leapt up in great amazement: nothing like this had ever happened to me before, not even in the most trivial detail; I had never, for instance, fallen asleep like this in my arm-chair. While I was standing and coming to myself I suddenly caught sight of my revolver lying loaded, ready—but instantly I thrust it away! Oh, now, life, life! I lifted up my hands and called upon eternal truth, not with words, but with tears; ecstasy, immeasurable ecstasy flooded my soul. Yes, life and spreading the good tidings! Oh, I at that moment resolved to spread the tidings, and resolved it, of course, for my whole life. I go to spread the tidings, I want to spread the tidings—of what? Of the truth, for I have seen it, have seen it with my own eyes, have seen it in all its glory.

And since then I have been preaching! Moreover I love all those who laugh at me more than any of the rest. Why that is so I do not know and cannot explain, but so be it. I am told that I am vague and confused, and if I am vague and confused now, what shall I be later on? It is true indeed: I am vague and confused, and perhaps as time goes on I shall be more so. And of course I shall make many blunders before I find out how to preach, that is, find out what words to say, what things to do, for it is a very difficult task. I see all that as clear as daylight, but, listen, who does not make mistakes? And yet, you know, all are making for the same goal, all are striving in the same direction anyway, from the sage to the lowest robber, only by different roads. It is an old truth, but this is what is new: I cannot go far wrong. For I have seen the truth; I have seen and I know that people can be beautiful and happy without losing the power of living on earth. I will not and cannot believe that evil is the normal condition of mankind. And it is just this faith of mine that they laugh at. But how can I help believing it? I have seen the truth—it is not as though I had invented it with my mind, I have seen it, seen it, and *the living image* of it has filled my soul for ever. I have seen it in such full perfection that I cannot believe that it is impossible for people to have it. And so how can I go wrong? I shall make some slips no doubt, and shall perhaps talk in second-hand language, but not for long: the living image of what I saw will always be with me and will always correct and guide me. Oh, I am full of courage and freshness, and I will go on and on if it were for a thousand years! Do you know, at first I meant to conceal the fact that I corrupted them, but that was a mistake—that was my first mistake! But truth whispered to me that I was *lying,* and preserved me and corrected me. But how establish paradise—I don't know, because I do not know how to put it into words. After my dream I lost command of words. All the chief words, anyway, the most necessary ones. But never mind, I shall go and I shall keep talking, I won't leave off, for anyway I have seen it with my own eyes, though I cannot describe what I saw. But the scoffers do not understand that. It was a dream, they say, delirium, hallucination. Oh! As though that meant so much! And they are so proud! A dream! What is a dream? And is not our life a dream? I will say more. Suppose that this paradise will never come to pass (that I understand), yet I shall go on preaching it. And yet how simple it is: in one day, *in one hour* everything could be arranged at once! The chief thing is to love others like yourself, that's the great thing, and that's everything; nothing else is wanted—you will find out at once how to arrange it all. And yet it's an old truth which has been told and retold a billion times—but it has not formed part of our lives! The consciousness of life is higher than life, the knowledge of the laws of happiness is higher than happiness—that is what one must contend against. And I shall. If only everyone wants it, it can all be arranged at once.

And I tracked out that little girl . . . and I shall go on and on!

QUESTIONS AND TOPICS

1. What is the significance of the narrator's experience with the little girl? What impact does the dream have on his feelings for her?
2. Compare the paradise that the narrator sees in his dream to the Garden of Eden. Does the destruction of the narrator's paradise tell us something about Dostoevsky's views on the possibility of achieving Utopia?
3. Are there people in our world such as those who inhabit the first part of the narrator's dream? Are they doomed to the same fate?
4. The narrator discovers that he must contend against the belief that "The consciousness of life is higher than life, the knowledge of the laws of happiness is higher than happiness. . . ." What does he mean?
5. Describe the narrator. Have you met such people in real life? Who sees them as ridiculous, and why? Are they ridiculous in some sense?
6. Are all of man's limitations inevitable? Is the narrator ridiculous in his hope for mankind?